INTERMEDIATE ACCOUNTING

Volume 1

Ppd rent 8,400
    Cash   8,400

Rent exp. 2800
    Ppd rent 2800

Periodic   Perpetual

Purchases   Cash
    Cash   Sales Rev

Cash   CGS
    Sales Rev   Inv.

  71
 8400   350
 2800   24)8400   350
 3600   72   8
            120   2800

HARCOURT BRACE JOVANOVICH COLLEGE OUTLINE SERIES

INTERMEDIATE ACCOUNTING

Volume 1

Mary Ann Emery, CPA

Department of Economics
St. Olaf College

Books for Professionals
Harcourt Brace Jovanovich, Publishers
San Diego   New York   London

Printed in the United States of America

Library of Congress Cataloging in Publication Data

Emery, Mary Ann
    Intermediate accounting

    (Harcourt Brace Jovanovich college outline series)
(Books for professionals)
    Includes index.
    1. Accounting.   I. Title.   II. Series.   III. Series:
Books for professionals.
HF5635.E536   1985   657'.044   85-7647
ISBN 0-15-601502-1 (v.1)

First edition

A   B   C   D   E

PREFACE

The purpose of this book is to present the first half of a full year course in intermediate accounting theory in the clear, concise format of an outline. The remaining topics generally covered in an intermediate accounting sequence are presented in the companion text INTERMEDIATE ACCOUNTING VOLUME II. Although comprehensive enough to be used by itself for independent study, this outline is specifically designed to be used as a supplement to college courses and textbooks on the subject. Notice, for example, the *Textbook Correlation Table* that begins on the inside of the front cover. This table shows how the pages of this outline correspond by topic to the pages of 5 leading textbooks on intermediate accounting theory currently in use at major colleges and universities. So, even though the sequence of topics in this outline may differ from your text, you can easily locate the material you want by consulting the table.

Intermediate accounting courses typically look closely at the items on the balance sheet and income statement. Questions of valuation, and revenue and expense recognition are examined in more complex transactions than those discussed in introductory courses. The student must often differentiate between the results of using several acceptable accounting methods. Statements from official standard setting bodies such as the Financial Accounting Standards Board (FASB) are studied in detail. This book provides numerous straightforward examples and problems to illustrate various accounting standards and concepts. The book also contains a complete discussion of financial statements and basic accounting procedure to assist those who may need to review these topics.

Regular features at the end of each chapter are specially designed to supplement your textbook and course work in intermediate accounting:

• RAISE YOUR GRADES. This feature consists of a checkmarked list of open-ended thought questions to help you assimilate the material you have just studied. By inviting you to compare concepts, interpret ideas, explain concepts, and examine the whys and wherefores of chapter material, these questions help to prepare you for class discussions, quizzes, and tests.

• SUMMARY. This feature consists of a brief restatement of the main ideas in each chapter, including definitions of key terms. Because it is presented in the efficient form of a numbered list, you can use it to refresh your memory quickly before an exam.

• RAPID REVIEW. Like the summary, this feature is designed to provide you with a quick review of the principles presented in the body of each chapter. Consisting primarily of short problems, multiple-choice, and short-answer questions, it allows you to test your retention and reinforce your learning at the same time. Should you have trouble answering any of these questions, you can locate and review the relevant sections of the outline by following the cross references provided.

• SOLVED PROBLEMS. Each chapter of this outline concludes with a set of problems and their step-by-step solutions. Undoubtedly the most valuable feature of the outline, these problems allow you to apply your knowledge of intermediate accounting to the solution of both numerical and essay type questions. Along with the four examinations, they also give you ample exposure to the kinds of questions that you are likely to encounter on a typical college exam. To make the most of these problems, try writing your own solutions first. Then compare your answers to the detailed solutions provided in the book.

Of course, there are other features of this outline that you will find very helpful. One is the format itself, which serves both as a clear guide to important ideas and as a convenient structure upon which to organize your knowledge. A second is the step-by-step approach to applying various accounting methods. The text lists these steps and illustrates them with straightforward examples. You should be able to solve complex problems by carefully following the steps described in the text.

CONTENTS

1 OBJECTIVES AND QUALITIES OF FINANCIAL REPORTING

THIS CHAPTER IS ABOUT

☑ **Sources of Authoritative Accounting Standards**
☑ **Objectives of Financial Reporting**
☑ **Qualities of Useful Financial Information**
☑ **Threshold for Recognition and Pervasive Constraint**

1-1. Sources of Authoritative Accounting Standards

By definition, accountants record, classify, summarize, and interpret in terms of money the results of the operations of a business. In completing these tasks, accountants follow a set of standards called **generally accepted accounting principles** (GAAP). The term "generally accepted" indicates that these standards have the substantial support and the general acceptance of the members of the accounting profession. Certified public accountants, after completing an audit, are required to indicate whether the company followed generally accepted accounting principles in preparing the reports.

A. The Financial Accounting Standards Board (FASB) is the body currently responsible for setting accounting standards.

To assist accountants in applying these standards, the FASB issues *Statements of Financial Accounting Standards* (SFASs) plus interpretations and technical bulletins. Before the FASB, this responsibility was held by two other committees: the Accounting Principles Board, which issued the *APB Opinions* (APBs) and the *APB Statements*; and before it, the Committee on Accounting Procedure, which issued the *Accounting Research Bulletins* (ARBs). Today's generally accepted accounting principles are the work of all of these bodies; they are derived either from SFASs issued by the FASB or from APBS and ARBs that have not been set aside by the FASB.

EXAMPLE 1-1: Jo Smith, accountant, is auditing the books of Shifty Corporation. She has discovered that the firm lists all research and development costs as an asset. The asset is then written off as an expense over a 50-year period. This practice seems strange to Jo, so she decides to do some research. Jo first checks to see if the FASB has issued a statement on research and development costs. Then she checks to see if there are any relevant APB Opinions and Accounting Research Bulletins that have not been set aside by the FASB. The results of her research will tell her if the company's practice conforms to generally accepted accounting principles (GAAP).

1-2. Objectives of Financial Reporting

In 1976, the FASB began a project to establish a conceptual framework for financial accounting. As a result, in November 1978, the FASB issued the first in a series of *Statements of Financial Accounting Concepts* (SFAC No. 1). Its purpose was to establish concepts to be used in setting future standards and to assist in accounting for situations not specifically covered by the standards or to which several methods may apply. SFAC No. 1 defined the following five objectives of financial reporting.

A. **OBJECTIVE NO. 1: Provide information that is useful to present and potential investors or creditors in making investment or credit decisions.**

Investors and creditors need financial information in order to make investment and credit decisions. External users have no control over the types of reports provided by the investee, nor over the accounting procedures used to prepare those reports. By FASB standards, this information should be understandable to those investors and creditors or to anyone else who has a reasonable knowledge of business and is willing to study the information with reasonable diligence.

B. **OBJECTIVE NO. 2: Provide information that will allow present and potential investors and creditors to judge the amounts, timing, and uncertainty of the cash flows they expect to receive.**

Creditors require information to estimate the likelihood that the company will be able to pay interest and to repay its debt on time. Investors need information to judge the company's ability to pay dividends and/or to redeem securities. Ability to pay creditors and investors depends on the company's cash position now and in the future. Financial reporting should provide this information.

C. **OBJECTIVE NO. 3: Provide information about both cash and noncash resources.**

Present and potential investors need information not only about a company's cash flow, but also about its economic resources (assets), the claims to those resources (liabilities), the owner's claim to the company's resources (owner's equity), and the changes occurring to each of these items. Changes in assets, liabilities, and owner's equity are mainly due to the company's earning activities. Measurement of earnings is therefore an important objective of financial reporting.

D. **OBJECTIVE NO. 4: Report earnings accurately.**

Under FASB standards, earnings should generally be recognized in the accounting period in which the company performs the service or delivers the goods ("accrual basis" accounting) rather than in the period in which the cash payment is made or received ("cash basis" accounting).

1. *Accrual versus cash basis accounting.* Accrual basis accounting measures the result of business activities in the period when those activities take place. Profits are recognized at the time when the company earns the right to receive payment. Profit in this case is the difference between the value of services rendered (or goods delivered) to customers and the cost of resources used up in providing those services (or goods). Cash basis accounting, on the other hand, measures profits only when the cash payment is made or received. Profit in this case is the difference between cash receipts and cash payments.
2. *Why accrual basis accounting is preferred.* The FASB believes that accrual basis accounting is better than cash basis accounting for measuring changes in assets, liabilities, and owner's equity. It is also judged to be better at providing accurate information about future cash receipts and payments. Most accountants agree with both contentions and consider the accrual method to be the better measure of a company's efforts and accomplishments from year to year. For example, if the company delivers the same amount of goods at the same cost for two years, its efforts and accomplishments during those two years would be identical, and so—under the accrual method—would be its reported earnings. Under cash basis accounting, however, even though the company's actual efforts in the two years were identical, if it received or paid out more cash in one year than in the other, its reported earnings for the two years would be different. Cash basis accounting is thus open to considerable manipulation by companies; for example, a company can increase its reported profits by postponing paying bills until a later period.

EXAMPLE 1-2: Short'n'Sweet Company began operations on January 1, 19x1. The firm delivered goods with a selling price of $20,000 in 19x1 and again in 19x2. Those goods cost the firm $10,000 in each year. The firm incurred other costs of $5,000 in each year. Customers paid the firm $15,000 in 19x1 and the balance for all goods delivered at the end of 19x2. Short'n'Sweet paid its suppliers $8,000 in 19x1 and the balance owed at the end of 19x2. All other costs were paid in cash in the year in which they were incurred. Compute the profit for each year using the accrual basis and the cash basis. Note that the total profit made during the two-year period is the same under both methods. However, the timing of profit recognition is different.

ACCRUAL BASIS

	19x1	19x2	Total
Value of goods delivered	20,000	20,000	40,000
Cost of goods delivered	(10,000)	(10,000)	(20,000)
Other costs incurred	(5,000)	(5,000)	(10,000)
Profit accrual basis	5,000	5,000	10,000

CASH BASIS

	19x1	19x2	Total
Cash received	15,000	25,000	40,000
Cash disbursed—goods	(8,000)	(12,000)	(20,000)
Cash disbursed—other costs	(5,000)	(5,000)	(10,000)
Profit cash basis	2,000	8,000	10,000

E. OBJECTIVE NO. 5: Financial reporting should be complete and timely.

On at least a yearly basis, a firm should prepare an income statement, a statement of retained earnings, a balance sheet, and a statement of changes in financial position. (Most firms also supply quarterly information to their stockholders.) The **income statement** provides information on the earnings of the firm over a period of time. The **statement of retained earnings** explains the change in the owner's equity over the same period of time. The **balance sheet** provides information on the assets, debts or liabilities, and owner's equity. The **statement of changes in financial position** tells how the firm obtains and uses its funds. These statements are discussed in greater detail in subsequent chapters.

Financial reporting should provide information on how management has discharged its responsibility for the care of the firm's resources. The accountant is not limited to presenting the traditional financial statements. Good financial reporting often requires additional explanatory notes and interpretations.

EXAMPLE 1-3: In 19x6, sales and profits of the WESA ("We Sell to Anyone") Company were higher than ever before. However, collections from customers had fallen off drastically, and since the firm had no cash, it stopped paying its creditors. When it came time to send the annual report to the stockholders, the chief executive officer decided not to include a statement of changes in financial position. He claimed that the stockholders could get all the information they needed from the income statement (which reported the record earnings), the statement of retained earnings (which showed the record increase in owner's equity), and the balance sheet (which showed a large increase in the company's assets).

In reality, however, this claim is not true. A statement of changes in financial position would highlight the sources and uses of funds in a manner not presented in the other statements. The company is required to prepare *all four* financial statements annually.

1-3. Qualities of Useful Financial Information

SFAC No. 2 lists the qualities that financial information must have in order to be useful for decision making. Exhibit 1-1, which is taken from SFAC No. 2, is a pictorial representation of those qualities and of how they relate to each other.

EXHIBIT 1-1: A Hierarchy of Accounting Qualities

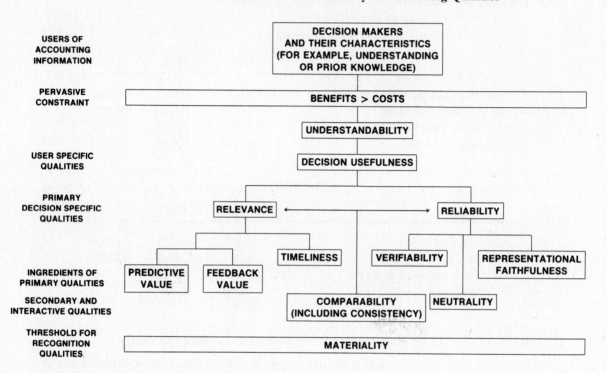

The major qualities listed in SFAC No. 2 and shown in Exhibit 1-1 are as follows:

A. To be useful, information must be *relevant*.

Relevant financial information has the following characteristics:

1. *Timeliness.* Information is timely and therefore relevant if it can affect a decision that is not yet made.
2. *Predictive and feedback value.* Information has predictive value if it can improve the user's ability to predict the future. Information has feedback value if it confirms or corrects earlier expectations.

B. To be useful, information must be *reliable*.

Reliable financial information has the following characteristics:

1. *Verifiability.* Information is considered reliable if it can be verified. A second person viewing a set of transactions should be able to duplicate the measurements made by the first person.
2. *Representational faithfulness.* Financial information must measure what it claims to measure.
3. *Neutrality.* Financial information must not favor any one point of view.

Note: Reliability and relevance can sometimes be at odds with each other. For some decisions the most relevant measure of an asset's value is its current market value or selling price. However, that value is often merely a personal opinion, and an opinion tends to be difficult to verify and is thus unreliable. Consequently, accountants tend to value assets at cost rather than at estimated current market value; the cost is easily verified and is therefore more reliable.

C. To be useful, information must have *comparability* and be prepared with *consistency* in accounting methods.

The usefulness of accounting information is increased if it can be compared with similar information from other companies. Therefore, one aim of generally accepted accounting principles is to reduce the number of allowable accounting methods. With fewer methods to choose from, firms are more likely to use the same ones. Results are also easier to compare if the same accounting methods are applied from one year to the next.

EXAMPLE 1-5: Each year, Laidback Corporation sends out its financial reports whenever its accountant returns from her year-end vacation in Florida. In some years the reports are not sent until nine months after the fiscal year has ended. When the reports are prepared, the accountant chooses accounting methods that maximize the reported profits. The firm even uses different accounting methods from year to year.

By these practices, the firm is violating the standards for providing relevant, consistent, and reliable financial information. First, the information is often not relevant because it is not available on a timely basis. It loses its predictive and feedback value. Late statements arrive after crucial investment decisions have already been made. Second, inconsistencies in accounting methods make it difficult to compare statements from one year with those of the next year, or with statements from other companies. Users of the information have no way to be certain what accounting methods will be used in the next report. Third, the information is not reliable because instead of presenting a neutral version of the company's activities, it presents a version that is intended to make the company look good.

1-4. Threshold for Recognition and Pervasive Constraint

In the hierarchy of accounting qualities depicted in Exhibit 1-1, the accountant is cautioned to operate between two boundaries: the threshold for recognition (materiality) and the pervasive constraint (benefits > costs). The **threshold for recognition** is the boundary between information that is **material**, or important enough to affect decision making, and information that is not material, usually because it is too detailed to make a difference. The **pervasive constraint** is the boundary between information whose benefits outweigh the cost of obtaining it (benefits > costs) and information for which the reverse is true. Under FASB guidelines, the information that accountants provide should fall between these two boundaries.

RAISE YOUR GRADES

Can you explain...?

☑ what body currently establishes GAAP
☑ the primary objective of financial reporting
☑ why cash flow information is important to creditors and investors
☑ how accrual basis accounting differs from cash basis accounting
☑ which method of accounting for earnings is generally required by the FASB
☑ which financial statements must be prepared on a regular basis
☑ what qualities financial information must have in order to be relevant
☑ what qualities financial information must have in order to be reliable
☑ how materiality and the benefits > costs constraint help determine what accounting information should be provided

SUMMARY

1. The Financial Accounting Standards Board (FASB) is the body currently responsible for setting generally accepted accounting principles (GAAP).
2. Financial reports should provide information that is useful to investors, creditors, and other external users of financial statements.
3. The accountant should regularly prepare a balance sheet, an income statement, a statement of retained earnings, and a statement of changes in financial position. All four should be prepared at least once a year.
4. To meet FASB standards, earnings should generally be measured on the accrual basis rather than on a cash basis.
5. Financial information should be relevant to the decisions that investors and creditors make. To be relevant, the information must be timely and have predictive and feedback value.
6. Financial information should be reliable. Reliable information has the qualities of verifiability, representational faithfulness, and neutrality.
7. Financial information is more useful when it can be compared to similar information provided by other firms and when the same accounting methods are used consistently from year to year.
8. Generally, the accountant should supply any information that is material, or important enough to affect decision making. However, the accountant need not supply information for which the cost of getting it outweighs the benefits of having it.

RAPID REVIEW

1. What do the following abbreviations stand for?
   (a) FASB
   (b) GAAP
   (c) SFAS
   (d) SFAC
2. The primary objective of financial reporting is to provide information for
   (a) internal managers
   (b) present and potential investors and creditors
   (c) the government for tax purposes
   (d) the firm's competitors
3. On what basis of accounting does the FASB generally require accountants to compute earnings?
4. What financial reports must a firm prepare on a regular basis?
5. What are the primary qualities that financial reporting must have to be useful for decision making?
   (a) timeliness and recognizability
   (b) neutrality and materiality
   (c) feedback value and understandability
   (d) relevance and reliability
6. A primary ingredient of relevance is
   (a) verifiability
   (b) neutrality
   (c) timeliness
   (d) representational faithfulness
7. A primary ingredient of reliability is
   (a) predictive value
   (b) feedback value
   (c) timeliness
   (d) verifiability

8. What is the definition of representational faithfulness?

9. Which of the following qualities of useful financial information can sometimes be at odds with each other?
   (*a*) relevance and timeliness
   (*b*) relevance and reliability
   (*c*) neutrality and feedback value
   (*d*) comparability and neutrality

10. When is an item considered to be material in accounting?

Answers:

1. (a) Financial Accounting Standards Board   (b) generally accepted accounting principles   (c) Statement of Financial Accounting Standards   (d) Statement of Financial Accounting Concepts [Sections 1-1 and 1-2]
2. (b) [Section 1-2A]
3. accrual basis [Section 1-2D]
4. income statement, statement of retained earnings, balance sheet, and statement of changes in financial position [Section 1-2E]
5. (d) [Exhibit 1-1]
6. (c) [Exhibit 1-1 and Section 1-3A]
7. (d) [Exhibit 1-1 and Section 1-3B]
8. Information has representational faithfulness if it measures what it claims to measure.
9. (b) [Section 1-3B]
10. An item is considered material in accounting if it is important enough to affect financial decision making. [Section 1-4]

SOLVED PROBLEMS

PROBLEM 1-1: Why is it necessary to have a conceptual framework for accounting?

Answer: Standards have been established that define acceptable methods of accounting for most common business situations. As times change, however, new situations arise for which standards have not yet been established. In many of these cases more than one accounting method would be allowed. The accountant needs a framework to help in deciding which of several accounting methods is most appropriate.   **[Section 1-2]**

PROBLEM 1-2: The FASB has determined that the primary objective of financial reporting is to provide information that is useful to investors and creditors. To be useful, that information must be understandable. To whom must it be understandable? Must it be clear to anyone who can read, or just to someone who holds a Ph.D. in business administration?

Answer: Under FASB rules, the information must be understandable to anyone who has a reasonable knowledge of business. The information need not be made so clear that even totally uninformed people can understand it, but neither should it be presented on a level that requires an advanced degree.   **[Section 1-2A]**

PROBLEM 1-3: What kinds of information do creditors and investors need? How do the four regularly prepared financial statements meet this need for information?

Answer: Creditors and investors need information on the amounts, timing, and uncertainty of cash flows that the firm expects to receive. They need information about the firm's assets, liabilities. and owner's equity and about the changes occurring in each of those items. The firm's earnings are the chief factor affecting changes in assets, liabilities, and equity. Earnings generate cash flow now and in the future. The income statement measures earnings over a period of time. The statement of retained earnings explains changes in the owner's equity. The balance sheet reports the amount of assets, liabilities, and owner's equity at a given time. The statement of changes in financial position highlights the sources and uses of the company's funds, providing further information on current cash flows.   **[Sections 1-2B, 1-2C, and 1-2E]**

PROBLEM 1-4: During June, the Happy Corporation rendered its customers services for which it charged $40,000. During that same month, Happy's customers paid the firm a total of $35,000 in cash, including a $5,000 payment for services rendered during May. The cost of providing the services rendered during June was $32,000. The firm paid its employees and suppliers a total of $33,500 during June, including $3,500 that was owed at the beginning of the month for services and supplies used in May. What are the reported earnings for June if the firm uses accrual basis accounting?

Answer: Under accrual basis accounting, profit is the difference between the value of services rendered and the cost of rendering the services.

$$\begin{array}{ll} \$40,000 & \text{(value of services rendered)} \\ -\ \underline{32,000} & \text{(cost of services rendered)} \\ \$\ 8,000 & \text{(profit)} \end{array}$$ **[Section 1-2D]**

PROBLEM 1-5: Based on the information in Problem 1-4, compute the Happy Corporation's profit for June using cash basis accounting.

Answer: Under cash basis accounting, profit equals cash receipts minus cash payments.

$$\begin{array}{ll} \$35,000 & \text{(cash receipts)} \\ -\ \underline{33,500} & \text{(cash payments)} \\ \$\ 1,500 & \text{(profit)} \end{array}$$ **[Section 1-2D]**

PROBLEM 1-6: Based on your answers to Problems 1-4 and 1-5, which accounting method better measures the results of Happy Corporation's efforts during June?

Answer: Most accountants would say that accrual basis accounting provides the better measure. Accrual basis accounting measures the value and cost of services performed during the month. The profits shown by this method indicate the future cash flow generated by these activities. Cash basis accounting measures only the difference between cash received and cash paid during the month, with no regard to the actual accomplishments and efforts made during that period. This method fails to distinguish the value of services rendered in May from the value of services rendered in June because cash was received and paid during June for both months.   **[Section 1-2D]**

PROBLEM 1-7: The need to provide reliable information limits the variety of allowable accounting methods. Explain why in each of the following situations the accounting method employed is considered unreliable and thus should not be used. In your explanations, consider the ingredients of reliability as illustrated in Exhibit 1-1.

(*a*) On January 1, 19x8, Speculators, Inc., purchased a parcel of land for $48,000. By year end, the accountant estimates that the land will sell for $60,000. Consequently, on the financial statements that accountant increases the value of the land to $60,000 and recognizes a profit of $12,000.

(*b*) Optimism Corporation's top salesperson is confident that he can sell Skeptic Company merchandise worth $1,000,000. The sale will increase Optimism's reported profits by 125 percent. Optimism's accountant recognizes the probable sale on the salesperson's word and reports the increased profits on the financial statements.

(*c*) Fairweather Company has discovered that by changing its method of accounting for inventory, it can increase its reported profits by $25,000. The company switches methods and does not mention this change in its financial reports.

Answer:

(*a*) Increasing the value of the land based only on the accountant's estimate results in a balance sheet entry that can not be verified, since two accountants might value the land differently. Because the information can not be verified, it is not reliable. Furthermore, the $12,000 profit recognized, which would appear on the income statement, misrepresents actual profits since none can be realized until the land is sold. Information that does not measure what it claims to measure lacks representational faithfulness and is therefore unreliable.

(*b*) The profit figure reported by Optimism Corporation does not measure the value of goods delivered to customers as it claims; therefore it lacks representational faithfulness. It represents only hopes, which are biased and not verifiable.

(*c*) Since the change in accounting methods was made in order to make the company look good, not only is it inconsistent, but also it lacks neutrality and it does not faithfully represent the profits of the firm. Because the change was not reported, it leads users to believe that the report was prepared using the same methods as before.

[Exhibit 1-1 and Sections 1-3B and 1-3C]

PROBLEM 1-8: During 19x1, Micro Corporation reported cash sales of $100,000. It also reported the sale of $250,000 in merchandise to customers on credit. Micro Corporation received $225,000 from its customers, of which $50,000 was in payment of credit sales made in 19x0. The company accumulated expenses of $75,000 during the year. Cash payments of $65,000 were made, of which $10,000 was to pay off expenses from 19x0. What would be the profits on a cash basis accounting system?

Answers:

Sales	$225,000	(amount of cash received)
Expenses	65,000	(amount of cash paid)
Profit	$160,000	(cash received − cash paid)

[Section 1-2D]

PROBLEM 1-9: Using the information in Problem 1-8, what would the profit be on an accrual basis?

Answer:

Sales	$350,000
Expenses	75,000
Profits	$275,000

[Section 1-2D]

PROBLEM 1-10: During 19x1, Inter Corporation reported cash sales of $50,000. It also reported the sale of $300,000 in merchandise to its customers on credit. Inter Corporation received $60,000 from its customers. The company incurred expenses of $75,000 during the year. Cash payments of $65,000 were made, of which $10,000 was to pay off debts from 19x1. What would be the profits on a cash basis accounting system?

Answer:

Sales	$ 60,000	(amount of cash received)
Expenses	65,000	(amount of cash paid)
Loss	$ (5,000)	(cash received − cash paid)

[Section 1-2D]

PROBLEM 1-11: Using the information in Problem 1-10, what would be the profit on an accrual basis?

Answer:

Sales	$350,000
Expenses	75,000
Profits	$275,000

[Section 1-2D]

PROBLEM 1-12: Review the information in Problems 1-8 through 1-11. Explain why two companies could have the same net income under one method of accounting and two different profits under another?

Answer: The total sales (cash plus credit) for both companies was the same. Therefore under the accrual system the two companies reported the same amount of revenue. The expenses incurred were also the same, thus the companies would report the same profit. However, under the cash method, profits are based on cash flow. Even though sales, expenses, and cash payments were the same for both companies, cash receipts differed by $165,000. Therefore, the profits differed by the same amount.   **[Section 1-2D]**

2 BASIC DEFINITIONS, ASSUMPTIONS, AND PRINCIPLES

THIS CHAPTER IS ABOUT

☑ **Definitions of Basic Accounting Terms**
☑ **Fundamental Underlying Assumptions**
☑ **Basic Principles**

2-1. Definitions of Basic Accounting Terms

FASB Statement of Financial Accounting Concepts (SFAC) No. 3 defines a group of terms that are fundamental to the understanding of financial reporting. These definitions are reviewed in the sections that follow. Study these sections carefully; the definitions are essential for understanding the rest of this volume.

A. *Assets* **are economic resources obtained or controlled by the firm for future benefit.**

The value of assets can be measured in terms of money based on the past transaction or event by which they were obtained.

1. *Essential qualities of an asset.* To be classified as an asset, a resource must have these three qualities:
   • It must have a chance of providing future benefit for the firm.
   • The firm must have control of it.
   • The transaction by which it was obtained must have already occurred so that an objective value can be measured.
2. *Resources that are not assets.* Many items are mistakenly described as assets by nonaccountants. For example, a firm may benefit from its owner's friendly personality. However, "friendly personality of owner" cannot be listed as an asset. It was neither obtained through a transaction nor does the firm control it.

EXAMPLE 2-1: On January 1, 19x1, Production, Inc., purchased a machine, paying $500 in cash upon its delivery. The machine is expected to have a useful life of three years. Can the machine be classified as an asset?

The answer is that the machine is definitely an asset. It is likely to provide three years of service to the firm, the firm has control of it, and the transaction through which the machine was obtained and valued has already taken place.

EXAMPLE 2-2: Production, Inc., invests $1,000 in the training of two machine operators. These employees are expected to operate the machine acquired in Example 2-1. Can this training cost be classified as an asset?

The answer is that the amount spent for the employees' training is not an asset. Although the company expects to receive future benefit from the training and the transaction for obtaining it has already taken place, the firm does not have control over the employees. The employees may choose to leave at any time, taking their training with them.

EXAMPLE 2-3: XYZ Corporation sells merchandise worth $300 to Example Company, which promises to pay for the merchandise within 90 days. XYZ Corporation has a legal right to receive Example's future payment (an account receivable), which is classified as an asset since the firm has control over it and the transaction by which it was obtained has already taken place.

B. *Liabilities* **are legal obligations to provide economic benefits to some other entity at a future time.**

The benefits in question may involve the transfer of tangible items such as cash or merchandise, or they may involve the performance of a service.

1. *Essential qualities of a liability.* To be classified as a liability, an obligation must have these two qualities:
   • It must be a legal obligation.
   • It must be the result of a transaction that has already occurred, so that an objective value can be measured.

EXAMPLE 2-4: On January 1, 19x1, Production, Inc., takes delivery of a machine costing $1,000 and agrees to pay for it in full on June 30, 19x1. The machine is expected to have a useful life of three years.

In this situation, Production, Inc., will recognize an asset, the machine (the firm has control over it, expects to receive future benefits from it, and has obtained it through a transaction that has already taken place). The firm will also recognize a liability, the amount owed to the seller on June 30, 19x1 (a transaction that has already occurred has legally bound the firm to pay $1,000 to the seller).

EXAMPLE 2-5: Pay First, Inc., accepts payment from one if its customers, in advance of delivery, for merchandise worth $600. By doing so, Pay First incurs a liability. The firm has the obligation to deliver merchandise worth $600 to the customer. If Pay First can not make the delivery, it must refund the customer's payment.

EXAMPLE 2-6: Wait-Ever Corporation has ordered supplies worth $200, but the supplies have not yet been delivered. Wait-Ever will be obligated to pay the $200 once the delivery takes place, but until that time it will not have incurred a liability. Only when delivery takes place will the transaction be complete; then the firm will be legally bound to pay for the supplies or return them.

C. *Equity* **is the owner's interest in the firm and equals the value of assets minus liabilities.**

1. *Increases in equity.* When assets increase (decrease) by a greater (lesser) amount than liabilities, equity increases. Equity also increases when the owner invests additional assets directly into the firm.

EXAMPLE 2-7: Prosperous Company sells merchandise that originally cost $900 to a customer for $1,000. What effect will this transaction have on Prosperous Company's owners' equity? This profit-earning transaction only affects two asset accounts. The asset account Cash is increased by $1,000 and the asset account Merchandise Inventory is decreased by $900; Using the formula for owner's equity, the total effect is figured as follows:

ASSETS		– LIABILITIES	=	OWNER'S EQUITY
$1,000	increase in Cash	– $0	=	$1,000
–$ 900	decrease in Merchandise Inventory			–$900
or				
$ 100		– $0	=	$100

In this case, Prosperous Company's owners' equity increased by $100.

EXAMPLE 2-8: Golden Touch, Inc., sells a parcel of land that originally cost $10,000 to ABC Corporation for $12,000. The sales agreement requires ABC to pay Golden Touch $3,000 in cash and to assume (take over the payments on) a $9,000 mortgage on the property. What effect will this transaction have on Golden Touch's owners' equity?

Using the formula for owners' equity, the total effect is figured as follows:

ASSETS	–	LIABILITIES	=	OWNERS' EQUITY
$ 3,000 increase in cash	–	–$9,000 decrease in mortgage debt	=	$12,000
–$10,000 decrease in land				–$10,000
or				
–$ 7,000	–	(–$9,000)	=	$2,000

In this case, Golden Touch's owners' equity is increased by $2,000.

2. *Reductions in equity.* When assets decrease by a greater amount than liabilities, equity is reduced.
3. *Transactions that do not affect equity.* Equity is not affected by transactions that involve only assets or only liabilities and where there is no net change in those accounts, or by transactions involving equal increases or decreases in assets and liabilities. For example, when a firm collects an account receivable, only asset accounts are involved. The asset account Cash is increased by the amount of the receivable and the asset account Accounts Receivable is decreased by exactly the same amount. Thus, there is no net change in assets, and given that equity equals assets minus liabilities, there is also no net change in equity. Similarly, when a firm pays off a debt, the asset account Cash is decreased by the amount of the debt, and the liability account Accounts Payable is likewise decreased by that same amount. Again, there is no net change in equity.

EXAMPLE 2-9: ABC Corporation purchased the land described in Example 2-8. How does the purchase affect ABC's owners' equity?

The transaction increases ABC's land assets by $12,000 and decreases its cash by $3,000. Its liabilities are increased by $9,000 due to its assumption of the mortgage. With both assets and liabilities increasing by $9,000, ABC's owners' equity is not changed.

D. *Revenue* is the increase in assets and/or decrease in liabilities due to delivery of goods or rendering of service.

According to SFAC No. 3, "revenues are inflows or other enhancements of assets of an entity, or settlements of its liabilities (or a combination of both), during a period from delivering or producing goods, rendering services, or other activities that constitute the entity's ongoing, major or central operations."

1. *A company typically earns revenue by delivering goods or rendering services.* The amount of revenue earned equals the expected or actual cash received and/or the amount of any liability assumed by the customer. It is important to remember that it is the act of *delivering* goods or *rendering* services that gives rise to the earning of revenue. Earning revenue is thus different from receiving cash. Cash payment may be received before or after delivery. Remember, however, that when cash is received in advance, the firm has incurred a liability: the obligation to deliver goods, services, or a refund. Revenue is not earned until the goods are delivered or the services are rendered.

EXAMPLE 2-10: On December 15, 19x1, XYZ Corporation delivered merchandise with a selling price of $500 to a customer. The customer, however, did not pay for the merchandise until January 20, 19x2. Was revenue earned, and if so, when?

XYZ Corporation earned $500 in revenue in the year 19x1, the year when the merchandise was delivered.

2. *Not all increases in assets are the result of earning revenue.* For example, if a firm borrows $10,000 from its bank, that $10,000 will not be considered revenue. The cash asset has increased, but so have the firm's liabilities. The firm has not delivered goods or services, so it has not earned revenue.

E. *Expenses* **are the decreases in assets and/or increases in liabilities that result when goods or services are used up to produce revenue.**

It is the *using up* of goods or services that gives rise to an expense. Incurring an expense is thus different from disbursing cash. A firm may use up a good or service in one period but make the corresponding cash payment in an earlier or later period.

EXAMPLE 2-11: On December 15, 19x1, XYZ Corporation acquired merchandise inventory at a cost of $750. On June 30, 19x2, the firm paid for the merchandise. On January 5, 19x3, the merchandise was finally sold to a customer for $1,000. Did the firm incur an expense, and if so, in what year?

The firm incurred an expense of $750 in 19x3 when the revenue was earned by selling goods to customers and the resource used up. Prior to January 5, 19x3, these two requirements for incurring an expense had not yet been met. In 19x1, when the merchandise was acquired, an asset (Merchandise Inventory) and a liability (Accounts Payable) were obtained. In 19x2, when the merchandise was paid for, an asset (Cash) and a liability (Accounts Payable) were decreased. Only in 19x3 was the resource used up to earn revenue. At that point the expense was incurred.

F. *Gains (losses)* **are defined as increases (decreases) in owner's equity due to transactions outside a firm's normal business activities.**

The FASB separates the results of a company's routine activities from the results of unusual or peripheral activities. Revenue and expenses are associated with routine activities; gains and losses with the nonroutine. For example, the sale of inventory to customers is a routine activity that involves revenue and expenses. However, the sale of used equipment is nonroutine for most businesses and would involve a gain or a loss.

EXAMPLE 2-12: XYZ Corporation owns 500 shares of Whizbang Corporation stock. Playing the stock market is not XYZ's major line of business. The 500 shares were originally purchased for $15,000. After five years, XYZ sells the shares for $95,000. The $80,000 difference between the selling price and the carrying value (purchase cost) would be reported as a gain.

G. *Comprehensive income* **is defined as the change in equity caused by all non-owner sources.**

Comprehensive income is a new concept that goes beyond the traditional definition of net income. It includes all revenue earned, expenses incurred, and gains and losses recognized during the accounting period. Comprehensive income also includes prior period adjustments and other items which will be discussed in later chapters. It does not include additional investments or withdrawals by the owner.

2-2. Fundamental Underlying Assumptions

Several fundamental assumptions underlie the accounting process. Many accounting practices make sense only if you are aware of these assumptions.

A. Accountants make a *unit of measure* assumption.

Accountants assume that the dollar is a reasonable and constant unit of measure. An accountant will add a dollar spent in 1975 to a dollar spent today without adjusting for the difference in purchasing power between the two dollars (*difference in purchasing power* means the difference between what the 1975 dollar bought and what today's dollar buys due to rising prices). The accountant assumes that this difference can be ignored.

In a period of *inflation* (continuous and significant rises in prices), this may not be a valid assumption. Because of concern about its validity, accountants have made an effort to supply additional information showing the effects of inflation on financial statements. Even so, basic accounting procedures make no adjustments for the changes in purchasing power of dollars from one year to the next.

B. Accountants make a *continuity* assumption.

Accountants assume that they are accounting for a going concern (i.e., that the firm will continue in operation forever). If the accountant assumed instead that the firm was going out of business, different information would have to be supplied to the user.

C. Accountants make a *periodicity* assumption.

Accountants assume that they can measure the results of a firm's activities for a certain period of time. Of course, the only period for which a firm's net income can be perfectly measured is the period between the first and last day of operations. That is, only when all the firm's assets have been sold and all its liabilities have been settled can one determine the true amount of owner's equity and whether or not the firm has made a profit over its operating life. Owners/creditors need information on a regular and timely basis in order to make decisions about future business activities. The accountant therefore assumes that it is possible to make periodic estimates of net income. It is important to remember that the figures the accountant reports are only objective estimates.

D. Accountants make a *separate entity* assumption.

Accountants assume that the activities of one entity can be separated from those of another. In other words, the activities of ABC Company can be separated from those of XYZ Corporation even though the two firms' claims to customers' assets may overlap.

2-3. Basic Principles

Accountants follow a set of basic principles that are even broader in scope than the generally accepted accounting principles (GAAP) mentioned in Chapter 1. The FASB keeps the following principles in mind as its sets standards for the profession.

A. The *objectivity principle* requires that accountants use information and measurements that are objective (facts) rather than subjective (personal opinions).

Because information from past transactions can be verified, accountants use it to value assets, establish the amount of liabilities, and measure revenue and expenses. Consequently, two accountants looking at the same set of transactions should, in most circumstances, prepare the same set of reports using identical accounting methods. Accountants are and should be reluctant to make guesses about the current value of assets. They should not report gains until those gains have actually been realized. Whenever an estimate is made, the basis for making the estimate and the amount of the estimate must be reported.

B. The *historical cost principle* dictates that assets be valued at what was originally paid for them.

Assets are valued at their historical or original cost, not at what the accountant guesses they are worth on the reporting date. Historical cost measurements can be verified and are generally the objective amounts that can be reported.

C. The *revenue recognition principle* dictates that revenue is to be recognized in the accounting period when goods are delivered or services are rendered.

The revenue recognition principle is an important part of the accrual system of accounting (see Chapter 1). The accounting profession believes that accurate measurement of the results of operations generally requires that revenue be credited to a firm when the firm has the right to be paid. This is usually when goods have been delivered or services have been rendered.

D. The *matching principle* requires that expenses be recognized in the accounting period in which goods and services are used up to produce revenue.

The matching principle is the second important part of the accrual system. Expenses are recognized when goods and services are used up, not when the firm pays for those goods and services.

E. The *full disclosure principle* requires the accountant to include in the financial statements all information that may affect the user's understanding of company activities.

The full disclosure principle emphasizes the importance of footnotes in financial statements. The accountant is required, for example, to disclose the accounting methods used to compute the numbers that appear in the statements. Any change in accounting methods by the firm must be reported, and the effect of that change must be disclosed. Information about any other significant transactions must also be included.

E. The *consistency principle* requires that firms use the same accounting methods from period to period.

Using the same accounting methods helps in comparing reports and statements prepared at different times. This does not mean that a firm can never change accounting methods. However, if a change is made, it must be proved that the change is an improvement over the previous method.

G. The *exception* or *modifying principle* allows the accountant to use some discretion in the application of other principles.

There are exceptional situations where application of the preceding principles would be inappropriate. The common reasons for making exceptions to those principles are immateriality, industry practice, and conservatism.

1. *Exceptions for immateriality.* Sometimes following a given principle would be costly, while making an exception would *be immaterial to* (not materially affect) the results. For example, the matching principle would dictate that the cost of a pencil be expensed as the pencil is used up. To fully comply with the matching principle, the accountant would have to figure out what part of each pencil was used up during the accounting period. Such computations would be time-consuming and expensive, and the result would not be materially different from expensing the pencils as they are requisitioned from the stockroom.
2. *Exceptions for industry practice.* Some industries have developed accounting practices that differ from the basic principles. The exception principle allows these industries to continue using their traditional accounting practices so long as they provide reasonable results. Many of the differences involve when revenue is recognized. Several such unique industry practices will be discussed in later chapters.
3. *Exceptions for conservatism.* Accountants tend to be conservative. They are careful not to overvalue assets. Sometimes the accountant can objectively prove that even the historical value overstates the asset's current value. In such cases the

accountant will reduce the asset's value to its current value and recognize a loss. This will happen even though no sale has taken place. Conservatism will not allow gains to be recognized until a sale or some other transaction has taken place.

RAISE YOUR GRADES

Can you explain...?

☑ what assets are and how they are valued
☑ what equity is and what kinds of transactions can change it
☑ what revenue is and in what accounting period it is recognized
☑ what an expense is and in what accounting period it is recognized
☑ why the unit of measure assumption may be unrealistic during inflation
☑ how the objectivity and historical cost principles are related
☑ why the full disclosure principle makes footnotes a required part of financial statements

SUMMARY

1. Assets are economic resources that are likely to provide future benefits to a firm. Assets must be obtained or controlled by the firm. Their value must be established by a past transaction.
2. Liabilities are current legal obligations of the firm to provide payments, goods, or services. The amount of the obligation must be determined through a transaction that has already occurred.
3. Equity is the difference between assets and liabilities. Equity represents the owner's financial interest in the firm.
4. Revenue is the increase in assets and/or decrease in liabilities due to normal business operations.
5. Expenses are the decreases in assets and/or increases in liabilities that result when goods or services are used up to produce revenue.
6. Gains (losses) are increases (decreases) in owner's equity due to transactions outside a firm's normal business activities.
7. Comprehensive income is the change in equity caused by all non-owner sources.
8. Accountants assume that the dollar is a reasonable unit of measure, that the firm is a going concern, that it is possible to periodically measure the net income of a firm, and that the firm's activities can be completely separated from those of other firms.
9. The objectivity principle requires that accountants use information and measurements that are objective (facts) rather than subjective (opinions) in preparing financial reports.
10. The historical cost principle dictates that assets be valued at the original purchase price.
11. Under the accrual system, revenue is recognized in the accounting period when goods are delivered or services are rendered, not when cash is received.
12. The matching principle requires that expenses be recognized in the accounting period in which goods and services are used up to produce revenue.
13. The full disclosure principle requires that the accountant report all information relevant to the user's understanding of the firm's activities.
14. The consistency principle requires that firms use the same accounting methods from period to period.
15. Exceptions are made to accounting principles for reasons of immateriality, industry practice, and conservatism.

RAPID REVIEW

1. Which of the following is NOT an *essential* characteristic of an asset?
   (a) The item is paid for.
   (b) The item has a chance of providing future benefits to the firm.
   (c) The firm has control over the use of the item.
   (d) The item's value is established by a past transaction.

2. Which of the following situations creates a liability for the XYZ Company?
   (a) XYZ signs a letter of intent to purchase goods worth $500 from the ABC Company. The goods will be delivered in six months.
   (b) Jones invests $500 in XYZ Company, expecting to earn a profit on his investment as an owner.
   (c) Jane Smith pays XYZ Company in advance for coal to be delivered throughout the winter.
   (d) All of the above situations create liabilities.

3. What must have taken place before a firm can recognize revenue?

4. What must have taken place before a firm can recognize an expense?

5. Which of the following accounting principles restrains an accountant from raising the value of land on a firm's books when that accountant believes that the land's value has gone up?
   (a) historical cost principle
   (b) matching principle
   (c) exception principle
   (d) full disclosure principle

6. On February 1, a customer orders a custom stereo, paying $500 of the $2,000 selling price when placing the order. On February 15, the stereo arrives in the store and, on February 17, it is delivered to the customer. On March 5 the customer pays the $1,500 balance. On which date or dates should revenue be recognized and for what amount(s)?
   (a) $500 on February 1 and $1,500 on February 15
   (b) $500 on February 1 and $1,500 on February 17
   (c) $2,000 on March 5
   (d) $2,000 on February 17

7. XYZ Corporation paid $650 for 16 widgets that it expected to sell to its customers. At the end of 19x1, all 16 widgets remained unsold. The firm's accountant figured that by the year's end the value of the widgets had dropped to $420 and changed the value of the widgets to that amount on the books. The accountant is justified in doing this by the
   (a) unit of measure assumption
   (b) continuity assumption
   (c) matching principle
   (d) exception principle

8. What is the definition of *comprehensive income*?

9. Which of the following transactions increases equity?
   (a) purchase of inventory worth $300 on account
   (b) delivery of goods costing $100 to a customer who pays $125 for them
   (c) collection of $50 from a customer on account
   (d) payment of $120 to a creditor on account

10. On January 1, 19x4, XYZ Corporation acquired 100 widgets at a cost of $2 each. During 19x4, the firm sold 75 of the widgets. The remaining stock was sold in 19x5. What expense amount should be recognized in 19x4 and 19x5, respectively?
    (a) $200 in 19x4; $0 in 19x5
    (b) $0 in 19x4; $200 in 19x5
    (c) $150 in 19x4; $50 in 19x5
    (d) $50 in 19x4; $150 in 19x5

Answers:

1. (a) [Section 2-1A]
2. (c) [Section 2-1B]
3. Goods must have been delivered or services must have been rendered. [Sections 2-1D and 2-3C]
4. Goods or services must have been used up to produce revenue. [Section 2-1E and 2-3D]
5. (a) [Section 2-3B]
6. (d) [Sections 2-1D and 2-3C]
7. (d) [Section 2-3G]
8. Comprehensive income is the change in equity caused by all non-owner sources. [Section 2-1G]
9. (b) [Section 2-1C]
10. (c) [Sections 2-1E and 2-3D]

SOLVED PROBLEMS

PROBLEM 2-1: In 1960, QRS Company purchased a parcel of land at a cost of $10,000. For this current year, the land is valued for tax purposes at $35,000. However, a friend of the president of the company has suggested that the true current value of the land is $40,000. Furthermore, assuming that $1 in 1960 bought three times as much as $1 today, one might say that the original cost of the land in current dollars was $30,000. Which of these values should be shown for the land in the company books? What principles and assumptions would the accountant use to justify using that value and rejecting the others?

Answer: The value shown for the land in the company books should be $10,000, the amount originally paid. The accountant will justify this value by citing the

- *historical cost principle*: assets must be valued at their original cost.
- *objectivity principle:* only measures that can be verified (facts) should be used.
- *unit of measure assumption*: the dollar is a reasonable unit of measure, and dollar amounts can be used without considering changes in purchasing power.
- *exception principle*: even though conservatism allows for losses to be recognized when no transaction has taken place, gains may never be recognized until a sale is made.

[Sections 2-2 and 2-3]

PROBLEM 2-2: For each of the following expenditures, would the result be an expense, an asset, or a combination of the two *as of the end of 19x1*? What would be the amount(s)?

(a) JKL, Inc., purchases inventory worth $2,000 during 19x1. All but $500 of the inventory is sold to customers by 12/31/x1.
(b) Wages totaling $30,000 are paid to JKL's sales staff during 19x1 for work done in January through December, 19x1.
(c) JKL acquires a truck for making deliveries to customers. The purchase is made on 12/31/x1 for $8,000. The truck is expected to have a useful life of three years.
(d) JKL engages in an advertising campaign costing $3,000 during 19x1. It is hoped that the company image will be improved and that sales in 19x1 and 19x2 will be greater because of it.
(e) JKL buys an insurance policy on 12/1/x1 at a cost of $2,400. The policy will provide coverage for a 24-month period beginning 1/1/x2.

Answer:

(a) The full $2,000 of inventory is initially recorded as an asset. The inventory will provide future benefit when it is sold, the company has title to it, and the transaction through which it was obtained has already taken place. By the end of 19x1, $1,500 of the inventory will be recognized as an expense because it will have been used up to produce sales revenue. The remaining $500 will still be reported on the books as an asset.

(b) The full $30,000 expenditure will be recognized as an expense in 19x1. The firm has used the services of the sales staff to earn revenue.

(c) Upon acquisition in 19x1, the $8,000 cost of the truck is recorded as an asset. The firm expects to receive future benefits from it and has gained possession of the truck through a transaction that has already taken place.

(d) The full $3,000 will be recognized as an expense in 19x1. Advertising expenditures are not recognized as an asset. Even though the firm expects future benefits, the amount of those benefits can not be figured objectively.

(e) The full $2,400 will be recorded as an asset in 19x1. None of the insurance services are used up in 19x1 since the coverage doesn't begin until 19x2. The prepayment to the insurance company buys an asset. The firm has the right to insurance benefits, access to those benefits is limited to the firm, and the transaction giving the firm those rights has already taken place.   **[Sections 2-1A, 2-1E, and 2-3D]**

PROBLEM 2-3: For each of the following, what amount of revenue, if any, should be recognized, and in what year should it be recognized?

(a) On 12/20/x1, a firm delivers merchandise worth $500 to a customer. The customer pays for the merchandise on 1/15/x2.

(b) On 12/15/x1, Whatsit Company borrows $500 from the Good Deal State Bank.

(c) On 12/20/x1, a customer pays Whosis Company $2,500 in advance for merchandise. On 12/22/x1, Whosis delivers the first portion of the merchandise, worth $1,000. On 1/6/x2, Whosis delivers the remainder of the merchandise.

(d) On 6/30/x1, SLY Accountants enters into a contract to provide accounting services to Zippy Corporation upon request. SLY receives $300 from Zippy in advance. No services are performed in 19x1 or 19x2.

Answer:

(a) Revenue totaling $500 would be recognized upon delivery of the merchandise in 19x1.

(b) Goods have not been delivered nor services rendered, so no revenue is recognized. In this case, assets and liabilities have been increased by equal amounts.

(c) Whosis Company will recognize $1,000 in revenue upon delivery of the merchandise in 19x1 and $1,500 in revenue upon delivery of the merchandise in 19x2.

(d) Revenue is not recognized in either year since no services have been rendered.
                                                                  [Sections 2-1D and 2-3C]

PROBLEM 2-4: Which of the following transactions cause(s) a change in the amount of owner's equity? What is the amount of each change?

(a) Example Company sells goods costing $750 in a close-out sale for $700 in cash.

(b) On 1/1/x1, the owner invests an additional $1,500 in the Ringer Company. During the year, the firm earns net income totaling $25,000. At the end of the year, the owner withdraws $5,000 in cash.

(c) At the start of the year, Marie owes Typical Company $1,500. During the year, she pays $500 of that amount.

(d) On 1/16/x1, the Excel Company pays its suppliers the $4,000 that it owes them.

Answer:

(a) The goods are sold at a loss of $50 (the selling price less the cost). The asset account Cash will be increased by $700, but the asset account Merchandise Inventory will be decreased by $750, so the net change in assets will be a decrease of $50. Nothing in this transaction affects liabilities; therefore, the net change in owner's equity is also a decrease of $50.

(*b*) Additional investments by the owner and net income (profits) both increase owner's equity; withdrawals decrease equity. The change in equity is calculated as follows: $1,500 + $25,000 − $5,000 = $21,500.

(*c*) There is no change in owner's equity as a result of this transaction. The payment increases Cash (an asset) by $500 and decreases Accounts Receivable (also an asset) by the same amount. The total amount of assets remains the same.

(*d*) The payment decreases Cash (an asset) by $4,000 and likewise decreases Accounts Payable (a liability) by the same amount. Consequently, this transaction does not affect owner's equity.   **[Section 2-1C]**

PROBLEM 2-5: For each of the following cases, discuss the basic assumption or principle that has been violated by the accounting procedure described.

(*a*) ABC Corporation is involved in a major lawsuit. If the outcome is unfavorable, the firm will face a substantial loss. The firm's lawyers are unable to predict the outcome of the case. Since it is uncertain how the case will turn out, the firm's accountant decides not to mention the suit in the financial reports.

(*b*) CDE Company has a policy of recording all purchases of supplies as an expense at the time of purchase, even though the supplies may not be used in that accounting period. The value of the unused supplies represents a large portion of the firm's assets and varies greatly from period to period.

(*c*) THE Magazine Company sells one-, two- and three-year subscriptions. The firm recognizes revenue as soon as the customer pays for the subscription.

(*d*) Lucky Land Company purchased some land in the middle of the desert for $20,000. Water has just been discovered on the property, increasing its market value to $50,000. The president of the company insists that the company books should be changed to recognize this increase in value.

Answer:

(*a*) The full disclosure principle requires the accountant to include in the financial statements any facts that may affect the user's understanding of the firm's activities. If an unfavorable verdict would cause a major loss, this fact should be reported in a footnote.   **[Section 2-3E]**

(*b*) The matching principle requires that expenses be recognized in the accounting period in which the goods or services are used up to produce revenue. The only exception is if the amount of the expense is not significant. This is not the case here.
                                                        [Section 2-3D]

(*c*) THE Magazine Company should recognize revenue only when the goods are delivered (accrual basis), not when cash is received (cash basis) THE Magazine Company has violated the revenue recognition principle.   **[Section 2-3C]**

(*d*) If the Lucky Land Company changes its books as its president insists, it would be violating the historical cost principle and the objectivity principle. Accountants should use measurements that are based on facts, such as the land's original cost, not on personal opinions.   **[Sections 2-3A and 2-3B]**

The following information pertains to Problems 2-6 through 2-12. For each of the following transactions, tell what type of account increases or decreases and the amount of the increase or decrease.

PROBLEM 2-6: MCA Corporation sold merchandise for $2,000,000 cash. What effect did this have on revenue and assets.

Answer: The sale of merchandise is a normal business activity. The company has increased its revenue and therefore its equity. Since the sales were for cash, the asset, Cash, was also increased. In each case the amount of increase was $2,000,000.
                                                        [Section 2-1]

PROBLEM 2-7: The cost of the merchandise sold by MCA Corporation in Problem 2-6 was $1,400,000.

Answer: The cost incurred during normal business operations is an expense. Expenses were therefore increased by $1,400,000. Expenses decrease equity, therefore, equity was decreased by the same amount, $1,400,000. Inventory is an asset of the company. The inventory account has been decreased by the amount of merchandise sold, $1,400,000.

[Section 2-1]

PROBLEM 2-8: MCA Corporation bought a new delivery truck for $20,000 cash.

Answer: The company plans to receive future benefit from the truck. It has control over its use due to a transaction that has already taken place. The truck is an asset (Equipment). The asset, Equipment, is increased by $20,000 while the asset, Cash, is decreased by the same amount. **[Section 2-1]**

PROBLEM 2-9: MCA bought another truck a few months later. This time the company paid only $5,000 down and promised to pay the other $15,000 within a year.

Answer: Again, the equipment account would be increased by $20,000. This time, however, the cash account will only be decreased by $5,000. The remaining $15,000 represents an increase in liabilities. MCA, due to a past transaction, has the legal obligation to pay $15,000 at some future date in exchange for the truck. **[Section 2-1]**

PROBLEM 2-10: MCA Corporation paid the $15,000 owed in Problem 2-9.

Answer: The liability has now been paid off (reduced to $0). At the same time the asset cash was also reduced by $15,000. **[Section 2-1]**

PROBLEM 2-11: MCA Corporation purchased a parcel of land as an investment for $8,000. This year the company decided to sell the land for $12,000 cash.

Answer: The asset Land is decreased by $8,000. The asset Cash is not only increased by $8,000 to cover the cost of the land but it is increased an additional $4,000. This additional $4,000 is profit which is an increase to equity. Since the profit was made outside normal business operations, it is called a gain. **[Section 2-1]**

PROBLEM 2-12: MCA Corporation ordered $30,000 in merchandise, $5,000 in supplies, and $14,000 in new equipment from a supplier, all of which the company wants delivered within two months.

Answer: None of the company accounts are affected. Even though MCA expects to receive future benefit from each of these items, it will not have control or access to them for another two months. An order has simply been placed, a deal has not actually occurred. The transaction will not be recognized until the supplier acknowledges the order by delivering the goods to MCA Corporation. **[Section 2-1]**

3 THE ACCOUNTING PROCEDURE: RECORDING DAILY TRANSACTIONS

THIS CHAPTER IS ABOUT

- ☑ **Reviewing Basic Accounting Procedure**
- ☑ **Accounts, Debits, and Credits**
- ☑ **Journalizing Daily Transactions**
- ☑ **Posting Journal Entries to the Accounts**
- ☑ **The Trial Balance**

3-1. Reviewing Basic Accounting Procedure

In the standard basic accounting procedure, the accountant handles daily transactions on a routine basis; then at the end of each accounting period, the accountant prepares the financial statements. These statements summarize the effects of all of the firm's transactions during that period.

A. Reviewing basic terms.

Here is a list of important terms that should be familiar to every student of basic accounting. These terms will be discussed in more detail later in this chapter and in the chapters that follow.

- **adjusting entries**: journal entries made to bring the ledger accounts up to date
- **closing entries**: journal entries used to prepare temporary capital accounts for the next accounting period
- **credit**: an entry made to the right side of an account
- **debit**: an entry made to the left side of an account
- **entry**: any item recorded in a journal or ledger
- **journal**: the record in which information about transactions is first recorded according to the date the transaction took place; also known as the *book of original entry*
- **ledger**: a group of accounts
- **posting**: transferring information from a journal to an account
- **reversing entries**: entries made at the beginning of an accounting period to reverse adjusting entries from the previous period
- **T account**: a form used to quickly sort and summarize changes or events concerning a particular item
- **trial balance**: a proof of the equality of debits and credits in the ledger

B. Reviewing basic steps.

The basic accounting procedure consists of four major parts, each of which involves several specific steps. The four major parts are (1) recording daily transactions, (2) adjusting the accounts, (3) preparing the financial statements, and (4) closing the accounts. (A fifth major part, the reversing process, is optional.) The full basic accounting procedure is outlined in Exhibit 3-1. All of these steps should be familiar to any student of basic accounting. This chapter and Chapters 4 and 5 will review them briefly; if at the end of Chapter 5 you are still uncertain about any step in the basic accounting procedure, you should refer to a principles of accounting textbook.

EXHIBIT 3-1: The Basic Accounting Procedure

I. Record Daily Transactions

    A. Analyze the daily transactions
    B. Journalize the daily transactions
    C. Post journal entries to the accounts
    D. Find the balances in the accounts
    E. Prepare a trial balance

II. Adjust the Accounts

    A. Identify accounts that must be adjusted
    B. Journalize adjusting entries
    C. Post adjusting entries to the accounts
    D. Find the balance in the accounts
    E. Prepare the adjusted trial balance

III. Prepare the Financial Statements

    A. Income statement
    B. Statement of retained earnings (owner's equity)
    C. Balance sheet
    D. Statement of changes in financial position

IV. Close the Accounts

    A. Journalize closing entries
    B. Post closing entries to the accounts
    C. Balance and rule the accounts
    D. Prepare a post-closing trial balance

V. The Reversing Process (optional)

    A. Identify adjusting entries to be reversed
    B. Journalize reversing entries
    C. Post reversing entries to the accounts

3-2. Accounts, Debits, and Credits

An **account** is a record of all the financial changes and events involving a particular item. Each account has a title, indicating the particular type of item that it covers. Transactions are recorded and summarized in the accounts.

A. A firm will keep at least one account for each item on the income statement and balance sheet.

A firm will keep at least one account for each item on the income statement and balance sheet. Information involving each account is first recorded on a daily basis in the journal, then transferred periodically to accounts in a general ledger. At the end of each accounting period, the balances in the ledger accounts are used to prepare the financial statements.

1. *Subsidiary accounts.* Besides the general ledger accounts, firms may also keep subsidiary (supporting) accounts when it is necessary to keep very detailed records. These accounts are kept in subsidiary ledgers. For example, a firm will have an Accounts Receivable account in the general ledger to keep track of the *total* amount owed to the firm by customers, and it may also keep a subsidiary account in a subsidiary ledger for each customer in order to record *individual* amounts owed to the firm. The sum of the subsidiary accounts must equal the balance in the Accounts Receivable account in the general ledger.

B. Transactions are recorded in accounts as debits and credits.

Even the simplest representation of an account has a column on the left for recording debits and a column on the right for recording credits. Increases and decreases resulting from transactions are recorded as debits or credits depending on the type of account, according to the rules for debiting and crediting accounts (see Section 3-2C, below).

1. *The T account.* The simplest representation of an account is the T account, which is named for its T-shaped layout. Accountants use T accounts to quickly sort and summarize transaction information involving individual items. Exhibit 3-2 shows the format of a T account.

EXHIBIT 3-2: Format of a T account

Title	
Left side	Right side
(*Debit*)	(*Credit*)

C. The rules for debiting and crediting accounts come from the basic accounting equation.

The **basic accounting equation** is

$$\text{ASSETS} \quad = \quad \text{LIABILITIES} \quad + \quad \text{OWNER'S EQUITY}$$

The logic of debiting and crediting is tied to this equation. In general, an increase in any particular type of account is recorded on the left (debit) side or the right (credit) side depending on whether the affected account type appears on the left or right side of the basic accounting equation. A decrease, on the other hand, is recorded on the side opposite to increases. Here are the specific rules for each type of account.

1. *Assets.* Increases in an asset account are recorded on the left (debit) side since assets appear on the left side of the basic accounting equation. Decreases are therefore recorded on the right (credit) side.
2. *Liabilities and Owner's Equity.* Increases in these types of accounts are recorded on the right (credit) side since these account types appear on the right side of the basic accounting equation. Decreases are therefore recorded on the left (debit) side.
3. *Revenue and expenses.* Revenue increases owner's equity; therefore, an increase in a revenue account is recorded on the right (credit) side since equity appears on that side in the basic accounting equation. Decreases in a revenue account are recorded on the left (debit) side. Expenses decrease owner's equity; thus an increase in an expense account is recorded on the left (debit) side while a decrease is recorded on the right (credit) side.
4. *Gains and Losses.* Gains increase owner's equity and thus an increase in this account is recorded on the right (credit) side. Losses decrease owner's equity and thus an increase in this account is recorded on the left (debit) side.

Exhibit 3-3 summarizes the rules for debiting and crediting the different types of accounts.

EXHIBIT 3-3: Debit and Credit Rules

Asset		Liability		Equity	
Dr	Cr	Dr	Cr	Dr	Cr
(+)	(−)	(−)	(+)	(−)	(+)

Expense		Revenue	
Dr	Cr	Dr	Cr
(+)	(−)	(−)	(+)

Loss		Gain	
Dr	Cr	Dr	Cr
(+)	(−)	(−)	(+)

Legend: "(+)" represents the side for recording increases (which is also the normal balance side); see Section 3-4C. "(−)" represents the side for recording decreases.

D. The double-entry bookkeeping system requires that each transaction be recorded in at least two accounts.

The logic of the double-entry bookkeeping system is also tied to the basic accounting equation. Every time a transaction is recorded, equality must be maintained on both sides of the equation; thus there must be at least one debit entry and at least one credit entry, and the total amounts debited and credited must be equal. Double-entry bookkeeping is used throughout the basic accounting procedure, starting when daily transactions are first recorded in the journal.

3-3. Journalizing Daily Transactions

Daily transactions are first recorded in generally chronological order in the firm's journal. For this reason, the journal is often called the **book of original entry**. A distinctive feature of the journal—and one that differentiates it from other types of accounting records—is that because of the way transactions are entered, all the information about each particular transaction appears together in one place.

A. Daily transactions produce source documents.

Each of a firm's transactions produces *source documents*, such as suppliers' invoices, cancelled checks, check stubs, credit sales slips, or cash register tapes. These documents provide the information upon which the journal entries are based.

B. The accountant analyzes the documents to make the proper journal entries.

The accountant must analyze the source documents in order to determine which accounts have been affected and what amounts are involved. The accountant must also determine whether to record those amounts (increases and decreases) as debits or credits, depending on the types of accounts involved. Then the transaction is recorded in the journal.

C. Journal entries follow a standard format.

The standard format for a simple journal entry is as follows:

Date	Title of account to be debited	Amount	
	Title of account to be credited.		Amount
	Explanation if necessary to		
	clarify entry		

Note that the entry lists all the accounts affected by the transaction. Note too that the amount debited is recorded in a lefthand column, the amount credited is recorded in a righthand column, and at least two accounts are involved as required in double-entry bookkeeping. Remember that for each transaction, the total amounts debited and credited must be equal.

EXAMPLE 3-1. XYZ Corporation began the month of June with the following balances in its accounts:

Cash.	$ 4,000	Accounts Payable	$ 5,400
Accounts Receivable	15,950	Unearned Revenue	200
Allowance for Uncollectable		Wages Payable	400
Accounts	350	Notes Payable	20,000
Inventory.	24,200	Common Stock.	5,000
Prepaid insurance	75	Retained Earnings	20,175
Equipment.	12,000		
Accumulated Depreciation .	4,700		

During June, the firm entered into the following transactions:

(*a*) Purchased inventory worth $30,000 on credit
(*b*) Paid $28,300 on account to suppliers
(*c*) Acquired an additional three-year insurance policy for $3,600
(*d*) Received $13,200 from customers for cash sales
(*e*) Sold merchandise worth $41,000 to credit customers
(*f*) Received $47,400 from customers on account
(*g*) Purchased additional equipment for $6,000
(*h*) Borrowed $5,000 from the bank, signing a five-year, 10% note
(*i*) Paid employees $2,300 in wages
(*j*) Received $500 in payments from customers in advance of delivery of goods
(*k*) Paid a $600 utility bill for the month of June.

The journal entries for these transactions are as follows (the letter of the transaction is substituted for the date):

JOURNAL

DATE	ACCOUNTS	DEBIT	CREDIT
(a)	Purchases	30,000	
	Accounts Payable		30,000
	Purchased inventory on credit.		
(b)	Accounts Payable	28,300	
	Cash		28,300
	Paid $28,300 on account.		
(c)	Prepaid Insurance	3,600	
	Cash		3,600
	Paid for insurance in advance.		
(d)	Cash	13,200	
	Sales		13,200
	Sales made for cash.		
(e)	Accounts Receivable	41,000	
	Sales		41,000
	Sales made on credit.		
(f)	Cash	47,400	
	Accounts Receivable		47,400
	Received on account.		
(g)	Equipment	6,000	
	Cash		6,000
	Purchased equipment.		

JOURNAL

DATE	ACCOUNTS	DEBIT	CREDIT
(h)	Cash	5,000	
	Notes Payable		5,000
	Signed 5 year, 10% note.		
(i)	Wages Payable	400	
	Wage Expense	1,900	
	Cash		2,300
	Paid employee wages.		
(j)	Cash	500	
	Unearned Revenue		500
	Received $500 in advance from customer.		
(k)	Utilities Expense	600	
	Cash		600
	Paid utilities for June.		

Some of these entries require additional explanation.

In entry (a), the purchase of inventory was debited to a Purchases account rather than directly to the Inventory account. This indicates that the firm is using a periodic inventory system, in which no attempt is made to update the Merchandise Inventory account as goods are acquired or sold. Instead, acquisitions of inventory are debited to the Purchases account, and the firm does not know exactly what is in inventory until a physical count is made at the end of the period. This system has the advantage of relatively light bookkeeping, but it also has the disadvantages of not providing up-to-date information on the contents of inventory and not indicating when to reorder.

In entry (c), the firm pays for the insurance policy in advance of use. Since the expense of purchasing the policy can not be recognized until the insurance is used, the debit entry is made to the asset account Prepaid Insurance, not to an expense account.

In entry (i), the wages paid to employees first cover $400 that was owed as of the beginning of the month for work done in May. The remainder of the cash paid was for work done in June and is properly included as an expense for the month of June.

In entry (j), the payments received in advance are recorded as a liability in the Unearned Revenue account. They cannot be recorded as sales revenue because goods have not yet been delivered.

3-4. Posting Journal Entries to the Accounts

A. The information in the journal entries is periodically posted to accounts.

The debits and credits in the journal entries are periodically **posted** (transferred) to corresponding account listings in the general ledger, where they accumulate until the end of the accounting period. In this way, the information that, in the journal, is organized *by transaction* is reorganized in the ledger *by account*. For example, in the journal, Accounts Receivable debits and credits might be scattered among numerous separate transaction entries, but after posting to the ledger, they are all collected in a single Accounts Receivable account.

B. The balance in each account is computed at the end of each period.

At the end of each accounting period, the accountant computes a (temporary) ending balance for each account in the ledger. The accountant uses these balances to prepare the financial statements. The ending balance is always equal to the beginning balance plus the sum of entries that increase the balance, minus the sum of entries that decrease the balance. In other words,

Ending Balance = Beginning Balance + Increases − Decreases

In Example 3-1, Accounts Payable began the month with a $5,400 credit balance.

During the month, two entries were made in the account: the balance was increased by the $30,000 purchase of goods on credit, and it was decreased by the $28,300 payment on account. On June 30, the ending balance in Accounts Payable was therefore $7,100 ($5,400 + $30,000 − $28,300).

C. Accounts normally have balances on the side where increases are recorded.

Accounts normally have positive ending balances. In other words, the combination of the beginning balance and the increases normally exceeds the decreases. By logic, then, each type of account normally balances on the side where increases are recorded. For example, asset accounts have balances on the debit side, liability and equity accounts have balances on the credit side, and so on.

EXAMPLE 3-2: Based on the information in Example 3-1, here are T accounts for the XYZ Corporation. The journal information from Example 3-1 has been posted to the accounts, and for each account, a (temporary) ending balance has been computed.

Cash

Bal.	4,000	(b)	28,300
(d)	13,200	(c)	3,600
(f)	47,400	(g)	6,000
(h)	5,000	(i)	2,300
(j)	500	(k)	600
Bal.			
29,300			

Accounts Receivable

Bal.	15,950	(f)	47,400
(e)	41,000		
Bal.			
9,550			

Allowance for Uncollectible Accounts

		Bal.	350

Inventory

Bal.	24,200		

Prepaid Insurance

Bal.	75	
(c)	3,600	
Bal.		
3,675		

Equipment

Bal.	12,000	
(g)	6,000	
Bal.		
18,000		

Accumulated Depreciation

		Bal.	4,700

Accounts Payable

(b)	28,300	Bal.	5,400
		(a)	30,000
		Bal.	
		7,100	

Unearned Revenue

		Bal.	200
		(j)	500
		Bal.	
		700	

Wages Payable

(i)	400	Bal.	400

Notes Payable

		Bal.	20,000
		(h)	5,000
		Bal.	
		25,000	

Common Stock

		Bal.	5,000

Retained Earnings

		Bal.	20,175

Purchases

(a)	30,000	

	Sales				Wage Expense	
	(d)	13,200		(i)	1,900	
	(e)	41,000				
		Bal.				
		54,200				

	Utilities Expense	
(k)	600	

3-5. The Trial Balance

The trial balance is a listing of all accounts and their temporary balances. In the trial balance, the debit balances are summed and compared to the sum of the credit balances. If the two sums are equal, the books are in balance. If the two sums are not equal, a mistake has been made in the process of recording daily transactions.

The trial balance provides a minimal check on the process of recording daily transactions. It helps the accountant detect the kinds of errors that result in unequal debits and credits. However, many errors do not produce unequal debits and credits, and these will not show up in the trial balance. These errors include

- equal debits and credits recorded in the wrong accounts
- equal but wrong debit and credit amounts
- entire transactions omitted or recorded more than once

EXAMPLE 3-3: Based on the journal entries in Example 3-1 and the postings and ending balances in Example 3-2, here is a trial balance for the XYZ Corporation.

XYZ Corporation
Trial Balance
June 30, 19x1

	Debit	Credit
Cash	$29,300	
Accounts Receivable.	9,550	
Allowance for Uncollectible Accounts.		$ 350
Inventory	24,200	
Prepaid Insurance.	3,675	
Equipment	18,000	
Accumulated Depreciation.		4,700
Accounts Payable		7,100
Unearned Revenue		700
Wages Payable.		—
Notes Payable		25,000
Common Stock		5,000
Retained Earnings		20,175
Purchases	30,000	
Sales		54,200
Wage Expense	1,900	
Utilities Expense.	600	
	$117,225	$117,225

EXAMPLE 3-4: Accuracy Corporation's accountant made a journal entry to record the receipt of $1,500 from a customer for payment on account. In the entry, she debited Cash for $1,500, but by mistake she credited Sales for that amount when she should have credited Accounts Receivable. This error will not cause unequal totals in the trial balance since the debit and credit, even though one is entered to the wrong account, are equal. The error will only be found when the customer receives another bill for the $1,500 already paid.

EXAMPLE 3-5: Accuracy Corporation's accountant paid a utility bill of $400, but when she entered the transaction in the journal, she mistakenly entered $40 instead of $400 for the debit to Utilities Expense and for the credit to Cash. This error will not show up in the trial balance since the amounts recorded, though wrong, were equal. The error will only be discovered when the firm tries to balance its bank account. The bank statement and cancelled check will show $400, but the books will show $40 (a $360 difference).

EXAMPLE 3-6: Accuracy Corporation's accountant was computing the ending balances in the accounts prior to preparing the trial balance. The Cash account showed the following:

	Cash	
Bal.	1,675	44
	500	178
	180	199
	62	680

Based on these figures, the correct cash balance is $1,316. However, the accountant made a mistake in computation and listed the balance as $866. This is the kind of error that will show up in the trial balance since each cash entry has a corresponding entry in another account, and thus an incorrect Cash balance will result in unequal overall debit and credit totals.

RAISE YOUR GRADES

Can you explain . . . ?

☑ the steps in the basic accounting procedure
☑ the meaning of the terms *debit* and *credit*
☑ the essential parts of a T account
☑ how the rules for debiting and crediting accounts relate to the basic accounting equation
☑ why an increase in a revenue account is recorded as a credit
☑ why an increase in an expense account is recorded as a debit
☑ why each transaction must be recorded in at least two accounts
☑ how to compute the ending balance in an account
☑ why a trial balance is only a minimal check of accuracy

SUMMARY

1. The basic accounting procedure consists of four major parts: recording daily transactions, adjusting the accounts, preparing the financial statements, and closing the accounts.
2. An account is a record of all the financial changes and events involving a particular item.
3. A firm will keep at least one account for each item on the balance sheet and income statement.
4. Increases and decreases resulting from transactions are recorded as debits or credits depending on the type of account.
5. The basic accounting equation (assets = liabilities + owner's equity) is the foundation of the rules for debiting and crediting accounts.
6. Increases in an asset account are recorded on the left (debit) side. Decreases are recorded on the right (credit) side.
7. Increases in liability and owner's equity accounts are recorded on the right (credit) side. Decreases are recorded on the left (debit) side.
8. The rules for recording increases and decreases in revenue, expense, gain, and loss accounts are determined by how those items affect owner's equity.

9. Increases in a revenue account are recorded on the right (credit) side. Decreases are recorded on the left (debit) side. Increases in expense accounts are recorded on the left (debit) side. Decreases are recorded on the right (credit) side.
10. Gains are recorded on the right (credit) side. Losses are recorded on the left (debit) side.
11. The double-entry bookkeeping system requires that each transaction be recorded in at least two accounts.
12. Daily transactions are first recorded in generally chronological order in the firm's journal.
13. Journal entries are based on transaction source documents, which the accountant analyzes in order to determine which accounts have been affected and what amounts are involved. The accountant must also determine whether to record the amounts as debits or credits.
14. The information in the journal entries is periodically posted to the ledger accounts.
15. The balance in each ledger account is computed at the end of each accounting period.
16. The ending balance in an account equals its beginning balance plus the sum of the entries that increase the balance, minus the sum of the entries that decrease the balance.
17. The trial balance is a listing of all accounts and their balances. If the sum of the debit balances equals the sum of the credit balances, the books are in balance.
18. The trial balance helps the accountant detect the kinds of accounting errors that result in unequal debits and credits. It will not help detect errors that involve equal debits and credits recorded in the wrong accounts, equal but wrong debit and credit amounts, and omitted or duplicated transactions.

RAPID REVIEW

1. What is the correct order of the following steps in the recording of daily transactions?
   (a) post journal entries to accounts
   (b) analyze daily transactions
   (c) prepare a trial balance
   (d) journalize daily transactions
   (e) find the balances in the accounts

2. For each of the following types of accounts, is the balance normally on the debit side or the credit side?
   (a) asset
   (b) revenue
   (c) owner's equity
   (d) gain
   (e) liability
   (f) loss
   (g) expense

3. What would be the firm's journal entries to record each of the following events?
   (a) Firm sells merchandise with a selling price of $600 on credit.
   (b) Customer pays the firm $320 of the amount owed in (a).

4. If the firm in Question 3 had a prior Account Receivable balance of $2,346, what would be the new balance after the transactions in Question 3?

5. What would be the journal entry to record the receipt of $500 from a customer in advance of delivery of merchandise?

6. When the journal entry from Question 5 is posted to the accounts, how will the balances in the two affected accounts be changed?

7. What would be the journal entry to record the delivery of the merchandise mentioned in Question 5?

8. When the journal entry from Question 7 is posted to the accounts, how will the balances in the two affected accounts be changed?

9. Which of the following errors would cause unequal totals in the trial balance?
   (a) The firm records $100 cash received from a customer in advance of delivery of goods as a debit of $100 to Cash and a credit of $100 to Sales.
   (b) The firm fails to enter the cost of the utilities used during the month as an expense and fails to recognize the $200 owed to the utility company.
   (c) The $400 paid to the bank in interest for the month is recorded as a debit of $400 to Cash and a credit of $400 to Notes Payable.
   (d) All of these errors will cause unequal trial balance totals.
   (e) None of these errors will cause unequal trial balance totals.

10. What would be the correct journal entries for the transactions described in Question 9?

Answers:

1. b, d, a, e, c [Exhibit 3-1]
2. (a) debit   (b) credit   (c) credit   (d) credit   (e) credit   (f) debit   (g) debit
   [Section 3-4C]
3. (a) Accounts Receivable | 600 |
      Sales | | 600

   (b) Cash | 320 |
      Accounts Receivable | | 320
      [Section 3-3C]
4. $2,626 debit balance [Sections 3-4B and 3-4C]
5. Cash | 500 |
      Unearned Revenue | | 500
      [Section 3-3C]
6. The Cash balance will be increased by $500, and the Unearned Revenue balance will also be increased by $500. [Sections 3-4A and 3-4B]
7. Unearned Revenue | 500 |
      Sales | | 500
      [Section 3-3C]
8. The Unearned Revenue balance will be decreased by $500, and the Sales balance will be increased by $500. [Sections 3-4A and 3-4B]
9. e [Section 3-5]
10. Cash . . . . | 100 |
      Unearned Revenue . . . . | | 100

   Utilities Expense. . . . . | 200 |
      Accounts Payable . . . . | | 200

   Interest Expense. . . . . | 400 |
      Cash . . . . | | 400

   [Sections 3-3B and 3-3C]

SOLVED PROBLEMS

PROBLEM 3-1: Happy Company acquired inventory from Serious, Inc. Serious sent invoices to Happy when the goods were shipped from Serious's warehouse. Happy did not pay for the goods until 30 days after they arrived and were checked by Happy's receiving department. You are auditing Happy's books. You wish to ascertain that the amounts paid to Serious were correct and that the receipt of the inventory and the payment of the bills have been properly entered in the journal. What source documents would you look for to verify these transactions?

Answer: You would want to compare the information on Serious's invoices with the receiving reports prepared by Happy's warehouse staff to be sure that all goods paid for were in fact received in acceptable condition. You would also match invoices to Happy's cancelled checks to be sure that the proper amount was paid and to be certain that no bills were paid more than once.   **[Section 3-3A]**

Problems 3-2 through 3-4 are based on the following information.

Hitechie Corporation began the month of June with the following balances in its account:

Cash	$ 7,150	
Accounts Receivable	10,220	
Inventory	18,480	
Notes Receivable	2,000	
Accounts Payable		$ 6,610
Wages Payable		1,210
Interest Payable		50
Notes Payable		5,000
Unearned Revenue		780
Common Stock		4,000
Retained Earnings		20,200
	$37,850	$37,850

During June, the firm entered into the following transactions:

(a) Sold merchandise with a selling price of $14,500 on credit.
(b) Sold merchandise with a selling price of $7,800 for cash.
(c) Purchased additional inventory worth $3,500 on credit.
(d) Delivered merchandise worth $600 to a customer who had paid for the merchandise in advance.
(e) Paid $4,050 to a supplier on account.
(f) Paid employees $3,840 in wages.
(g) Paid $1,200 to the Amnity Insurance Company for special insurance coverage. The policy takes effect in July.
(h) Paid $500 in rent for June.
(i) Paid employees $2,200 in wages.
(j) Owed employees an additional $1,900 for work done during June; this money will be paid in July.
(k) Paid $150 in interest on a note payable.
(l) Paid $1,000 of the principal amount owed under the note payable.
(m) Received $12,200 from customers on account.

PROBLEM 3-2: Journalize each of Hitechie's transactions in proper journal entry form. You may assume that the company uses a periodic inventory system. No explanations are needed.

Answer:

(a)	Accounts Receivable	14,500	
	Sales		14,500
(b)	Cash	7,800	
	Sales		7,800
(c)	Purchases	3,500	
	Accounts Payable		3,500
(d)	Unearned Revenue	600	
	Sales		600

(e)	Accounts Payable.	4,050	
	Cash		4,050
(f)	Wages Payable.	1,210	
	Wage Expense	2,630	
	Cash		3,840
(g)	Prepaid Insurance	1,200	
	Cash		1,200
(h)	Rent Expense.	500	
	Cash		500
(i)	Wage Expense	2,200	
	Cash		2,200
(j)	Wage Expense	1,900	
	Wages Payable.		1,900
(k)	Interest Payable	50	
	Interest Expense.	100	
	Cash		150
(l)	Notes Payable	1,000	
	Cash		1,000
(m)	Cash	12,200	
	Accounts Receivable		12,200

[Section 3-3C]

PROBLEM 3-3: Set up T accounts for each account mentioned in Problem 3-2. Find the beginning balance for each account in the introduction to this set of problems, then enter it in the account. Post the journal entries from Problem 3-2 to the accounts. Compute the ending balance in each account.

Answer:

Cash

Bal.	7,150	(e)	4,050
(b)	7,800	(f)	3,840
(m)	12,200	(g)	1,200
		(h)	500
		(i)	2,200
		(k)	150
		(l)	1,000
Bal.			
14,210			

Accounts Receivable

Bal.	10,220	(m)	12,200
(a)	14,500		
Bal.			
12,520			

Inventory

| Bal. | 18,480 | | |

Prepaid Insurance

| (g) | 1,200 | | |

Notes Receivable

| Bal. | 2,000 | | |

Accounts Payable

(e)	4,050	Bal.	6,610
		(c)	3,500
		Bal.	
		6,060	

Unearned Revenue

(d)	600	Bal.	780
		Bal.	
		180	

Wages Payable

(f)	1,210	Bal.	1,210
		(j)	1,900
		Bal.	
		1,900	

Interest Payable			
(k)	50	Bal.	50

Notes Payable			
(l)	1,000	Bal.	5,000
		Bal.	*Bal.*
			4,000

Common Stock		
	Bal.	4,000

Retained Earnings		
	Bal.	20,200

Sales		
	(a)	14,500
	(b)	7,800
	(d)	600
	Bal.	
	22,900	

Purchases	
(c)	3,500

Wage Expense	
(f)	2,630
(i)	2,200
(j)	1,900
Bal.	
6,730	

Interest Expense	
(k)	100

Rent Expense	
(h)	500

[Section 3-4]

PROBLEM 3-4: Based on the T accounts in Problem 3-4, prepare a trial balance for Hitechie Corporation.

Answer:

Hitechie Corporation
Trial Balance
June 30, 19x1

Cash	$14,210	
Accounts Receivable	12,520	
Inventory	18,480	
Prepaid Insurance	1,200	
Notes Receivable	2,000	
Accounts Payable		$ 6,060
Unearned Revenue		180
Wages Payable		1,900
Interest Payable		0
Notes Payable		4,000
Common Stock		4,000
Retained Earnings		20,200
Sales		22,900
Purchases	3,500	
Wage Expense	6,730	
Interest Expense	100	
Rent Expense	500	
	$59,240	$59,240

[Section 3-5]

Problems 3-5 through 3-9 are based on the following information.

Jones Company began the month of January with the following account balances: Cash, $1,500; Accounts Receivable, $3,700; Supplies, $600; Equipment, $2,000; Accumulated Depreciation, $800; Accounts Payable, $2,600; Wages Payable, $400; Jones, Capital, $4,000. During January, the firm entered into the following transactions:

(a) Purchased $50 of supplies on credit.
(b) Sold merchandise with a selling price of $5,000 on credit.
(c) Collected $6,200 from customers on their accounts.
(d) Purchased additional equipment for $450 in cash.
(e) Paid employees $1,800 in wages.
(f) Paid $2,150 of the amounts owed to suppliers.
(g) Paid $250 in rent for January.
(h) Jones withdrew $700 in cash from the business.

Based on this information, the firm's bookkeeper prepared the following ledger accounts:

Cash					Accounts Receivable			
Bal.	1,500	(d)	450		Bal.	3,500	(c)	6,200
(c)	6,200	(e)	1,800		(b)	5,000	(f)	2,150
Bal.		(g)	250		Bal.			
5,450		(h)	700		150			

Supplies			Equipment	
Bal.	600		Bal.	2,000
(a)	50			
(d)	450			
Bal.				
1,100				

Accumulated Depreciation			Accounts Payable			
	Bal.	800	(a)	50	Bal.	2,600
			(f)	2,150		
			Bal.			
			400			

Wages Payable			Jones, Capital		
Bal.	400			Bal.	4,000

Sales			Expenses		
	(b)	5,000	(e)	1,800	
			(g)	250	
			(h)	700	
			Bal.		
			1,750		

[Section 3-4]

PROBLEM 3-5: Using the bookkeeper's ledger accounts, prepare a trial balance for Jones Company to find out if the bookkeeper has made any errors.

Answer: Here is the trial balance based on the bookkeeper's ledger accounts.

Jones Company
Trial Balance
January 31, 19x1

Cash	$ 5,450	
Accounts Receivable.	150	
Supplies.	1,100	
Equipment	2,000	
Accumulated Depreciation.		$ 800
Accounts Payable	400	
Wages Payable.	400	
Jones, Capital.		4,000
Sales		5,000
Expenses	1,750	
	11,250	9,800

Since this trial balance shows a wide disparity between the total debits and the total credits, the bookkeeper must have made errors in preparing the ledger accounts.

[Section 3-5]

PROBLEM 3-6: Recheck the bookkeeper's ledger accounts and identify all of the errors made in accounting for the firm's transactions.

Answer: The bookkeeper has made nine errors as follows:

1. The beginning Accounts Receivable balance was $3,700 not $3,500.
2. Wages Payable should have a beginning $400 credit balance rather than a $400 debit balance.
3. For transaction (a), $50 should have been credited, not debited, to Accounts Payable.
4. For transaction (d), $450 should have been debited to the Equipment account instead of to the Supplies account.
5. For transaction (e), $400 of the $1,800 paid to employees was undoubtedly intended to cover the $400 in Wages Payable owed at the beginning of the accounting period. Thus, only $1,400 of the amount paid was for work done in January. Therefore, the correct entries should have been a $400 debit to Wages Payable and a $1,400 debit to Expenses.
6. For transaction (f), the $2,150 payment should have been credited to Cash instead of to Accounts Receivable.
7. For transaction (h), Jones' $700 should have been debited to the Jones, Capital account rather than to Expenses. An owner's withdrawal is a direct reduction in the owner's investment in the business; it is not an expense.
8. The Accounts Payable account should have an ending credit balance of $500, not a debit balance of $400.
9. The ending balance in Expenses should be $2,750, given the amounts the bookkeeper debited to the account.   **[Sections 3-3 and 3-4]**

PROBLEM 3-7: Which of the errors identified in Problem 3-6 would not contribute to the unequal totals in the trial balance and would therefore not be detected?

Answer: Errors 4, 5, 6, and 7 do not involve unequal debits and credits. They would not cause unequal totals in the trial balance, and therefore they would not be detected by that procedure.   **[Section 3-5]**

PROBLEM 3-8: Based on the information in Problem 3-5 through 3-7, prepare a complete set of corrected ledger accounts for Jones Company for January 19x1.

Answer:

Cash					Accounts Receivable			
Bal.	1,500	(d)	450		Bal.	3,700	(c)	6,200
(c)	6,200	(e)	1,800		(b)	5,000		
		(f)	2,150		*Bal.*			
		(g)	250		*2,500*			
		(h)	700					
Bal.								
2,350								

Supplies				Equipment			
Bal.	600			Bal.	2,000		
(a)	50			(d)	450		
Bal.				*Bal.*			
650				*2,450*			

Accumulated Depreciation				Accounts Payable			
		Bal.	800	(f)	2,150	Bal.	2,600
						(a)	50
						Bal.	
						500	

Wages Payable				Jones, Capital			
(e)	400	Bal.	400	(h)	700	Bal.	4,000
						Bal.	
						3,300	

Sales				Expenses			
		(b)	5,000	(e)	1.400		
				(g)	250		
				Bal.			
				1,650			

[Sections 3-3 and 3-4]

PROBLEM 3-9: Based on the corrected ledger accounts in Problem 3-8, prepare a corrected trial balance for Jones Company for January 19x1.

Jones Company
Trial Balance
January 31, 19x1

Cash	$2,350	
Accounts Receivable.	2,500	
Supplies.	650	
Equipment	2,450	
Accumulated Depreciation.		$ 800
Accounts Payable		500
Wages Payable.		0
Jones, Capital.		3,300
Sales		5,000
Expenses	1,650	
	9,600	9,600

[Section 3-5]

PROBLEM 3-10: At the end of 19x1, the accountant for Fortra Corporation reported the following balances for the company's accounts.

Cash	$ 45,800
Accounts Payable	22,000
Buildings	250,000
Inventory	60,700
Mortgage Payable	175,000
Wages Payable	15,500
Accounts Receivable	34,000
Capital Stock	100,000
Retained Earnings	78,000

Set up T accounts and post these amounts to the proper side of the ledger accounts.

Answer:

Cash		Accounts Receivable		Inventory	
45,800		34,000		60,700	

Buildings		Accounts Payable		Wages Payable	
250,000			22,000		15,500

Mortgage Payable		Capital Stock		Retained Earnings	
	175,000		100,000		78,000

[Section 3-4]

PROBLEM 3-11: Prepare a trial balance for Fortra Corporation in Problem 3-10.

Answer:

Fortra Corporation
Trial Balance
December 31, 19x1

Cash	$ 45,800	
Accounts Receivable	34,000	
Inventory	60,700	
Buildings	250,000	
Accounts Payable		$ 22,000
Wages Payable		15,500
Mortgage Payable		175,000
Capital Stock		100,000
Retained Earnings		78,000
	390,500	390,500

[Section 3-5]

PROBLEM 3-12: Suppose that the $45,800 balance in the cash account in Problem 3-10 had been posted as $45,000. Would this error be discovered in the trial balance in Problem 3-11?

Answer: Yes. The total debits would have been $389,700 and the total credits would have been $390,500. The variance would have clued the accountant to recheck the computations in the trial balance and then to recheck the postings to the ledger accounts.

[Section 3-5]

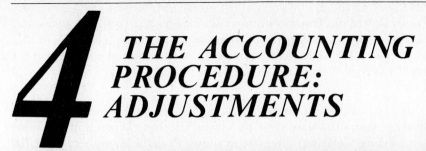

4 THE ACCOUNTING PROCEDURE: ADJUSTMENTS

THIS CHAPTER IS ABOUT

☑ **The Purpose and Process of Adjustment**
☑ **Situations Commonly Requiring Adjustments**
☑ **Consequences of Omitting Adjustments**

4-1. The Purpose and Process of Adjustment

A. The purpose of adjustment.

In many common business situations, cash received in one accounting period actually represents revenue earned in another period, or cash paid (or owed) in one accounting period is actually an expense of another period. When this happens, the ending balances in accounts will not accurately reflect the results of operations unless they are **adjusted** (or corrected) through the use of special adjusting entries. Unless these entries are made when needed, the accountant's financial statements will not be accurate.

B. The adjustment process.

In the adjustment process, the accountant prepares the appropriate adjusting entries and follows the standard basic accounting procedure. The process has five steps:

1. *Identify which account balances need correcting* and determine whether those balances should be increased or decreased.
2. *Prepare and journalize adjusting entries* in order to correct the inaccurate balances.
3. *Post the adjusting entries to the accounts.*
4. *Find the adjusted balances in the accounts* by figuring in the adjusting entries.
5. *Prepare an adjusted trial balance* to check the equality of the debits and credits in the adjusted account balances.

4-2. Situations Commonly Requiring Adjustments

Adjustments are required when (1) an expense must be allocated to two or more accounting periods, (2) revenue must be allocated to two or more accounting periods, (3) an expense would not otherwise be recognized in the proper accounting period, (4) revenue would not otherwise be recognized in the proper accounting period, or (5) specific adjusting entries are required under certain commonly used accounting methods.

A. Adjustments are required to allocate an expense to two or more accounting periods.

A firm may acquire an asset but not use it up during a single accounting period. Since the expenses relating to any asset can only be recorded when the asset is used, the accountant determines the "portion" of the asset used during each accounting period until the asset is used up. The accountant then assigns a corresponding portion of the cost to each period by preparing an adjusting entry. A common example of this situation is the purchase of buildings or equipment. In each period the accountant records a portion of the cost of these assets as "depreciation."

EXAMPLE 4-1: On 7/1/x1, Cautious Company paid $2,700 for an 18-month insurance policy (an asset). Coverage started on the date of purchase. The firm's accountant recorded the transaction by increasing (debiting) the asset account, Prepaid Insurance, by $2,700 and by decreasing (crediting) the Cash account by $2,700. No entry was made to Insurance Expense, which at that time had a balance of $0.

By 12/31/x1, the firm has used up six months' worth of coverage. This fact must be reflected in the accounts with an adjusting entry for a corresponding portion of the total policy expense. Since the monthly cost of the policy is $150 ($2,700 ÷ 18), the expense for six months is $150 × 6 = $900. The adjusting entry will record this expense as an increase in the Insurance Expense account, and it will also reduce the balance in the Prepaid Insurance account by the same amount since that portion of the asset has been used up. The adjusting entry in the journal is therefore

| 12/31/x1 | Insurance Expense . . . . | 900 | |
| | Prepaid Insurance . . . . | | 900 |

After posting, the corresponding T accounts would appear as follows:

Insurance Expense				Prepaid Insurance			
1/1/x1 Balance	0			1/1/x1 Balance	0		
12/31/x1				7/1/x1	2,700	12/31/x1	
Adjusting	900					Adjusting	900
12/31/x1				12/31/x1			
Balance	900			Balance	1,800		

At the end of 19x2, Cautious will have used up the remaining twelve months' worth of coverage. Its accountant will then make another adjusting entry for the remaining portion of the total policy expense ($150 × 12 = $1,800). Like the first portion, this amount will be recorded as an increase in the Insurance Expense account and as a decrease in the Prepaid Insurance account (which will then have a debit balance of $0).

Now suppose the accountant debited Insurance Expense, in error, on 7/1/x1, the day the insurance policy described in Example 4-1 was acquired. What adjusting entry should be made on 12/31/x1?

The account balances on 12/31/x1 prior to adjustment indicate that the firm has used up $2,700 of insurance services because Insurance Expense has a balance of $2,700. The unadjusted account balances further indicate that there is no Prepaid Insurance because the balance in the Prepaid Insurance account is $0. These balances are not correct. We know that the firm used up six months of insurance services at a cost of $150 per month. Insurance Expense for 19x1 should be $900 which is $1,800 less than the unadjusted balance in the account. The Prepaid Insurance account should have a balance equal to 12 months of insurance services with a value of $1,800. The balance in Prepaid Insurance must be increased by $1,800 from $0 to $1,800. The entry that will correct the balances is shown below.

| Prepaid Insurance . . . . | 1,800 | |
| Insurance Expense . . . . | | 1,800 |

The T accounts are shown below.

Insurance Expense		
1/1/x1 Balance 0		
7/1/x1 2,700		
	12/31/x1 (Adjusting)	1,800
12/31/x1 Balance 900		

Prepaid Insurance		
1/1/x1 Balance 0		
12/31/x1 (Adjusting) 1,800		
12/31/x1 Balance 1,800		

Note, the adjusting entry required to correct the account balances is related to the entry made when the insurance policy was acquired. Be sure you understand the logic of the adjusting procedure. You cannot memorize adjustments.

Adjustments at the end of 19x2 will charge the last 12 months of the insurance policy's cost to 19x2. The adjusting entry will reduce the balance in the Prepaid Insurance account to $0. After adjustments are made in 19x2, $900 of the cost of the policy will have been allocated to 19x1, the year in which 6 months of service was used and $1,800 will be an expense of 19x2 when 12 months of service was used.

B. Adjustments are required to allocate revenue to two or more accounting periods.

A firm may sell a good or service but not actually deliver all of the amount sold in a single accounting period. Since the sales revenue can only be recorded when delivery is made, the accountant calculates the portion that is delivered in each accounting period and then recognizes a corresponding amount of the total selling price as revenue in each period by using an adjusting entry. Two common examples of this situation are the sale of long-term services, such as insurance coverage or legal services, and the sale of goods that are delivered periodically over a long term, such as newspapers or magazines.

EXAMPLE 4-2: We Print Anything, Inc. ("WPA"), publishes a monthly magazine to which it sells three-year subscriptions for $72. On 8/15/x1, a customer sent a check for a subscription. WPA's accountant recorded the cash receipt by increasing (debiting) the Cash account by $72 and by increasing (crediting) the liability account, Unearned Revenue, by $72. No entry was made to Earned Revenue, which at that time had a balance of $0. The customer's first magazine was sent on 9/1/x1.

By 12/31/x1, WPA has delivered four month's worth of magazines. This fact must be reflected in the accounts with an adjusting entry for a corresponding portion of the total subscription revenue earned. Since the subscription price of each magazine is $2 ($72 ÷ 36), the four months' revenue is $8 ($2 × 4). The adjusting entry will record this revenue as an increase in the Earned Revenue account, and it will also reduce the balance in the Unearned Revenue account by the same amount since that portion of the liability has been paid off through delivery of the magazines. The adjusting entry in the journal is therefore

12/31/x1	Unearned Revenue	8	
	Earned Revenue		8

After posting, the corresponding T accounts would appear as follows:

Earned Revenue		
	1/1/x1 Bal.	0
	12/31/x1 Adj.	8
	12/31/x1 Bal.	8

Unearned Revenue		
12/31/x1 Adj. 8	1/1/x1 Bal.	0
	8/15/x1	72
	12/31/x1 Bal.	64

At the end of 19x2, WPA will have delivered another twelve magazines. Its accountant will then make another adjusting entry for the corresponding portion of the total price ($2 × 12 = $24). Like the first portion, this amount will be recorded as an increase in Earned Revenue and as a decrease in Unearned Revenue. In 19x3, WPA will deliver another twelve magazines and record another $24 of revenue earned. In 19x4, WPA will deliver the final eight magazines and record the final $16 of revenue earned. Through this series of adjusting entries, the initial $72 advance payment is allocated to the periods in which it is actually earned.

Now assume that the accountant records in error, the receipt of the advance payment from Joe Doe described in the preceding example by debiting Cash and crediting Earned Revenue for $72. Prepare the adjusting entry required on 12/31/x1.

The accounts now indicate that the firm has earned $72 of revenue during 19x1 and that it owes no service to Joe Doe. We can conclude this because the unadjusted balance in the Earned Revenue account is $72 and the unadjusted balance in the Unearned Revenue account is $0. The firm has really earned only $8 of the amount received and it still owes Joe Doe $64 worth of magazines as of 12/31/x1. The adjusting entry must reduce the balance in the Earned Revenue account by $64 from its unadjusted balance of $72 to the correct balance of $8. The entry must increase the balance in the Unearned Revenue account from $0 to $64. The required adjusting entry is:

Earned Revenue..........................	64	
Unearned Revenue....................		64

Earned Revenue			Unearned Revenue		
	1/1/x1 Balance	0		1/1/x1 Balance	0
	8/15/x1	72		12/31/x1	
12/31/x1				(Adjusting)	64
(Adjusting) 64					
	12/31/x1 Balance	8		12/31/x1 Balance	64

At the end of 19x2, the firm will adjust the books to recognize that $24 of revenue that was previously unearned has been earned due to the delivery of 12 magazines in 19x2. In 19x3 the company will deliver another 12 magazines and recognize $24 of revenue as earned. During 19x3 the company will deliver the final 8 magazines under the subscription and will recognize the last $16 of the advance payment as earned revenue. The series of adjusting entries allocates the $72 advance payment to the years in which it is earned.

C. Adjustments are required to record expenses that would not otherwise be recognized in the proper accounting period.

Sometimes a firm incurs an expense during a given period but there is no transaction to create a source document for the accountant. This is the case, for example, when interest expense, utilities expense, or wage expense is incurred during a given accounting period but not actually paid until a later period. Events such as these create no source documents because the bank sends no bill at all for the interest, the utility company may bill in the next accounting period, and wages owed are often not paid until the next accounting period. In cases like these, since expenses must be recorded when the goods or services are used up, the accountant calculates the amount actually incurred in the given period and records it as an adjusting entry for the period. In this way, the accounts for each period show all the expenses incurred during that period, regardless of whether bills have actually been received for them.

EXAMPLE 4-3: Endmonth Corporation pays its employees each Friday. Its monthly accounting period ends on June 30, a Tuesday. Consequently, the wages it owes for

Monday, June 29, and for Tuesday, June 30, are an expense of the June accounting period but will not be paid until the following Friday, in the July accounting period. Endmonth must adjust the accounts at the end of June to include the wages owed at the end of the month. The adjusting entry will increase (debit) the Wage Expense account by the amount owed, and it will also increase (credit) the liability account, Wages Payable, by the same amount. Assuming that the wages owed for those two days total $2,000, the adjusting entry in the journal would be as follows:

| 6/30/x1 | Wage Expense . . . . | 2,000 | |
| | Wages Payable . . . . | | 2,000 |

EXAMPLE 4-4: On 8/1/x1, Debtor Corporation borrowed $10,000 by signing a note in which it agreed to repay the full sum plus 12% interest one year later, on 7/31/x2.

December 31, 19x1, is the end of Debtor's yearly accounting period. By that time the firm has had the use of the $10,000 for five months, or 5/12 of the term of the loan. It has therefore incurred 5/12 of the total interest expense, even though this amount will not be paid in cash until the note comes due on 7/31/x2. This portion of the interest expense incurred in 19x1 must be recorded in the 19x1 accounts by using an adjusting entry. The actual dollar amount of this portion of the interest expense is computed as follows:

Principal (amount borrowed)	×	Interest Rate	×	Length of Time	=	Interest
P	×	r	×	t	=	i
$10,000	×	.12	×	5/12	=	$500

The portion of the total interest expense incurred in 19x1 is $500. In the adjusting entry, this amount will be recorded as an increase (debit) in the Interest Expense account and also as an increase (credit) in the liability account, Interest Payable. The adjusting entry will appear as follows:

| 12/31/x1 | Interest Expense . . . . | 500 | |
| | Interest Payable . . . . | | 500 |

Once this entry is included, Debtor's income statement for 19x1 will show $500 in interest expense for that year. The balance sheet will show a liability of $10,000 (the loan principal) plus $500 of interest owed.

EXAMPLE 4-5: Consider again the situation described in Example 4-4. When the $10,000 note is paid off on 7/31/x2, further entries will be needed to complete the transaction and to properly allocate the remaining portion of the interest expense.

When the note is paid off, the amount remitted to the bank will be $11,200 (the $10,000 originally borrowed plus the entire interest payment of $1,200). However, of that total interest payment, $500 has already been allocated as an expense in 19x1. Only the remaining $700 is an interest expense incurred in 19x2. Therefore, the entry to record payment of the debt will show the following: (1) a decrease (debit) of $10,000 in the liability account, Notes Payable; (2) a decrease (debit) of $500 in the liability account, Interest Payable (since the payment in full of the interest has eliminated the $500 credited to that account in 19x1); (3) an increase (debit) of $700 in the Interest Expense account (reflecting the portion of the total interest expense incurred in 19x2); and (4) a decrease (credit) of $11,200 in the Cash account (reflecting the actual cash payment). The entry would appear as follows:

7/31/x2	Notes Payable	10,000	
	Interest Payable	500	
	Interest Expense.	700	
	Cash.		11,200

D. Adjustments are required to record revenue that would not otherwise be recognized in the proper accounting period.

Sometimes a firm will earn revenue during a given period but there is no transaction to create a source document for the accountant. This happens most commonly when a firm lends out money for a term that covers more than one accounting period. When this happens, the firm earns a portion of the interest in each accounting period for the term of the loan even though there may be no actual payment until the end of that term. In a case like this, since revenue must be recorded in the period when it is actually earned, the accountant calculates the amount actually earned in each period and records it as an adjusting entry for that period. In this way, the accounts for each period show all the revenue earned during that period, regardless of whether payment has actually been received.

EXAMPLE 4-6: Consider again the situation described in Examples 4-4 and 4-5, but this time from the point of view of the bank that made the loan. By 12/31/x1, the bank has earned 5/12 of the total interest revenue on its loan to Debtor Corporation, even though no payment will be made until the loan comes due on 7/31/x2. The portion of the interest revenue earned in 19x1 must be recorded in the 19x1 accounts by using an adjusting entry. As we have seen, this portion amounts to $500. In the adjusting entry in the bank's books, this amount will be recorded as an increase (debit) in the asset account, Interest Receivable, and as an increase (credit) in the Interest Revenue account. The adjusting entry would appear as follows:

12/31/x1	Interest Receivable	500	
	Interest Revenue		500

On 7/31/x2, when the loan is repaid, the corresponding entry will allocate the remaining $700 of interest revenue to 19x2. The entry to record payment of the debt will show the following: (1) an increase (debit) of $11,200 to Cash (representing the full amount of cash received); (2) a decrease (credit) of $10,000 to Notes Receivable (signifying the repayment of the entire principal); (3) a decrease (credit) of $500 to Interest Receivable (signifying that the payment has eliminated in full the $500 remaining in the interest account from 19x1); and (4) an increase (credit) of $700 to Interest Revenue (representing the portion of the total interest revenue earned in 19x2). The entry would appear as follows:

7/31/x2	Cash	11,200	
	Notes Receivable		10,000
	Interest Receivable		500
	Interest Revenue		700

E. Specific adjusting entries are required under certain accounting methods.

1. *The allowance method of accounting for bad debts.* This method requires an adjusting entry at the end of each accounting period to record the bad debt expense associated with the credit sales made during the period. The entry debits Bad Debt Expense and credits Allowance for Uncollectable Accounts. The latter account is a **contra**, or negative, asset account, meaning that on the balance sheet its balance is deducted from the balance in the asset account Accounts Receivable. A discussion of how to calculate bad debt expense will be presented in Chapter 14.
2. *The periodic inventory system.* This system is a way of updating the Inventory and Cost of Goods Sold balances by making adjusting entries at the end of each period instead of separate entries each time merchandise is sold. Under this system, all purchases of inventory are debited to a Purchases account instead of to Inventory. Then when merchandise is sold, no entries are made to record the reduction in Inventory or the increase in Cost of Goods Sold. Instead, at the end of each period, the ending balance in Inventory is established by a physical count. Then based on

this balance, the accountant computes the cost of goods sold for the whole period by using the following formula:

$$\frac{\text{Cost of}}{\text{Goods Sold}} = \frac{\text{Goods available for sale}}{\text{(Beginning Inventory + Purchases)}} - \frac{\text{Goods not sold}}{\text{(Ending Inventory)}}$$

Once the cost of goods sold for the whole period has been figured, the accountant makes adjusting entries to add the purchases to the Inventory account and then correct the Inventory balance by recording the cost of goods sold. The proper entries are as follows:

Inventory	XXX	
Purchases		XXX
To add purchases to Inventory.		
Cost of Goods Sold.	XXX	
Inventory		XXX
To record cost of goods sold and remove goods sold from the Inventory balance.		

The corresponding T accounts for Inventory and Cost of Goods Sold would appear as follows:

Inventory		
Bal. Beg. Inventory		
Adj. Purchases		
	Adj. Cost of Goods Sold	
Bal. End Inventory		

Cost of Goods Sold		
Bal. $0		
Adj. Cost of Goods Sold		
Bal. Cost of Goods Sold		

EXAMPLE 4-7: Periodic Company, which uses the periodic inventory system, began the 19x1 accounting period with a balance of $4,000 in Inventory. During 19x1, it acquired additional inventory worth $24,000, and this amount was debited to the Purchases account. It also sold inventory, but its accountant made no entries to record the reduction in Inventory or the increase in Cost of Goods Sold. At year end, a physical count indicated that inventory worth $4,500 remained in the warehouse. The accountant therefore computed the year's cost of goods sold as follows: $4,000 + $24,000 − $4,500 = $23,500. Then, to add the purchases to Inventory and to correct the Inventory balance by recording this cost of goods sold, the accountant made the following adjusting entries:

12/31/x1	Inventory	24,000	
	Purchases.		24,000
	To add purchases to Inventory.		
	Cost of Goods Sold	23,500	
	Inventory.		23,500
	To record cost of goods sold and remove goods sold from the Inventory balance.		

The corresponding T accounts would appear as follows:

Inventory		
1/1/x1 Bal. 4,000		
12/31/x1 Adj. 24,000		
	12/31/x1 Adj 23,500	
12/31/x1 Bal. 4,500		

Cost of Goods Sold		
1/1/x1 Bal. 0		
12/31/x1 Adj. 23,500		
12/31/x1 Bal. 23,500		

3. *Accounting for supplies.* A common method of accounting for supplies resembles the periodic inventory system in that the accountant updates the accounts with adjusting entries at the end of each period instead of making separate entries for every change. Under this system, all purchases of supplies are debited to Supplies Inventory. No entry is made to record the reduction in Supplies Inventory or the increase in Supplies Expense as each supply item is requisitioned for use. Instead, at the end of each period the ending balance in Supplies Inventory is established by a physical count. Then based on this balance, the accountant computes the cost of the supplies used as follows:

$$\text{Cost of Supplies Used} = \text{Beginning Balance} + \text{Purchases of Supplies} - \text{Ending Balance}$$

Once the cost of supplies used for the whole period has been figured, the accountant makes an adjusting entry to correct the Supplies Inventory balance by debiting the cost of supplies to Supplies Expense. The proper entry is as follows:

Supplies Expense......................	XXX	
Supplies Inventory....................		XXX

The corresponding T accounts for Supplies Inventory and Supplies Expense are as follows:

Supplies Inventory		Supplies Expense	
Bal. Beg. Supplies		Bal. Beg.	
Acquisition Supplies		Adj. Supplies Expense	
	Supplies Expense Adj.		
Bal. End. Supplies		Bal. End.	

4-3. Consequences of Omitting Adjustments

When an accountant fails to include the proper adjusting entries, the resulting financial statements will not accurately reflect the results of operations. Furthermore, since accounting is a continuous process, inaccuracies in one accounting period can produce further inaccuracies in the statements of subsequent periods.

EXAMPLE 4-8: On 7/1/x1, Buynow Corporation borrowed $100,000 by signing an 18-month note at 16% annual interest. The principal and all the interest are to be repaid when the note matures on 12/31/x2. By 12/31/x1, Buynow had incurred interest expense totaling $8,000 ($100,000 × .16 × 6/12). This sum should have been recorded in an adjusting entry as a debit to Interest Expense and as a credit to the liability account, Interest Payable; however, the accountant failed to make the entry.

The consequences for the financial statements are as follows:

1. On the 19x1 income statement, interest expense is understated by $8,000, and thus profits are overstated by the same amount. As a result, on the 19x1 balance sheet, retained earnings are also overstated by $8,000. In addition, since no entry was made to the liability account Interest Payable, liabilities on the balance sheet are understated by $8,000.
2. On 12/31/x2, the note matures and the principal and all the interest are paid in cash. Since no adjusting entry was made to allocate the first $8,000 of interest expense to 19x1, the entire interest amount ($100,000 × .16 × 18/12 = $24,000) is mistakenly allocated to 19x2 as a debit to Interest Expense (the correct interest expense for 19x2 would have been $100,00 × .16 × 12/12 = $16,000). Consequently, on the 19x2 income statement, interest expense is overstated by $8,000, and thus profits are understated by the same amount.

3. Fortunately, however, on the 19x2 balance sheet this understatement of 19x2 profits will cancel out the $8,000 overstatement of retained earnings left from 19x1, so that error will finally be eliminated. Also, the 19x2 balance sheet will show no liability remaining for principal or interest. This is correct because the payment made in 19x2 settles all obligations regarding the note.

Thus in this example, the errors resulting from an omitted adjusting entry are corrected on the balance sheet by the end of the second accounting period. Even so, however, great harm may well have been done because in the process, the firm produced two erroneous income statements and one erroneous balance sheet.

Exhibit 4-1 summarizes the entries described in this example and their effects on the financial statements.

EXHIBIT 4-1: Entries Described in Example 4-8 and Their Effects on the Financial Statements

Date	Entries With Proper Adjustments		Entries Without Proper Adjustments	
7/1/x1	Cash 100,000		Cash 100,000	
	Note Payable	100,000	Note Payable	100,000
12/31/x1	Interest Expense 8,000		No Entry	
	Interest Payable	8,000		
12/31/x2	Note Payable 100,000		Note Payable 100,000	
	Interest Payable 8,000		Interest Expense 24,000	
	Interest Expense 16,000		Cash	124,000
	Cash	124,000		

Errors In Financial Statements When Adjusting Entry Is Not Made:

Statement	19x1	19x2
Income Statement:		
Expenses	8,000 under	8,000 over
Profits	8,000 over	8,000 under
Balance Sheet:		
Retained Earnings	8,000 over	OK
Liabilities	8,000 under	OK

EXAMPLE 4.9: Consider again the situation described in Example 4-8. Assume this time that if the adjusting entry allocating $8,000 of interest expense to 19x1 has been made properly, the firm would have reported a net income of $50,000 each year in 19x1 and 19x2. However, since the entry was not made, the firm reported incorrect net incomes as follows:

	19x1	19x2	Total
Correct Net Income *With* Proper Adjustment .	50,000	50,000	100,000
Net Income Reported *Without* Proper Adjustment	58,000	42,000	100,000

These two sets of net income figures provide quite different pictures of the firm's performance. The total net income for the two-year period is the same, but while the correct figures show a pattern of stability, the incorrect ones give the appearance of a sharp decline. Also, the two sets of figures would result in very different tax statements being submitted to the government. This firm would pay higher taxes because of a higher reported income in 19x1 and lower taxes because of a lower income in 19x2.

RAISE YOUR GRADES

handwritten: $1, 20,000 \times 3/12 \times .12 =$

Can you explain...?

☑ the purpose of adjusting entries

☑ the five steps in the adjustment process

☑ why adjusting entries are needed when a firm acquires an asset for use during more than one accounting period

☑ why an entry to Unearned Revenue signals that an adjusting entry might be needed

☑ how failure to make an adjusting entry will affect the income statement and the balance sheet

☑ how some adjusting entry errors work themselves out over two accounting periods

SUMMARY

1. Adjustments are made to correct account balances so that they accurately reflect the results of operations during the accounting period.
2. The steps in the adjusting process are (1) identify which account balances need correcting, (2) prepare and journalize adjusting entries, (3) post the adjusting entries to the accounts, (4) find the adjusted balances in the accounts, and (5) prepare an adjusted trial balance.
3. Adjustments are required to allocate an expense to two or more accounting periods.
4. Adjustments are required to allocate revenue to two or more accounting periods.
5. Adjustments are required to record expenses that would not otherwise be recognized in the proper accounting period.
6. Adjustments are required to record revenue that would not otherwise be recognized in the proper accounting period.
7. Specific adjusting entries are required under certain accounting methods.
8. Failure to make a necessary adjusting entry in one year will cause the financial statements for that year to be incorrect. The financial statements in subsequent years may also be incorrect.

RAPID REVIEW

1. On 10/1/x1, XYZ Corporation borrows $20,000 to be repaid on 9/30/x2 at 12% interest. What adjusting entry must XYZ make on 12/31/x1 to recognize interest expense?
2. Based on the information in Question 1, what entry will XYZ Corporation make when the loan is repaid on 9/30/x2?
3. On 5/1/x1, CBA Corporation pays two years' rent in advance, for a total payment of $8,400. The accountant debits the Prepaid Rent account. What adjusting entry must CBA make on 12/31/x1 to allocate rent expense?
4. On 8/1/x1, TRS Corporation accepts payment in advance for 25 shmoos at $50 each. During 19x1, 10 shmoos are delivered and the proper adjusting entry is made on 12/31/x1. During 19x2, the remaining shmoos are delivered. What adjusting entry must TRS make on 12/31/x2 to allocate revenue?
5. On 3/1/x1, TUV Corporation lends $25,000 to ABC Corporation. The note is payable on 8/31/x3 plus 18% yearly interest. What adjusting entry must TUV Corporation make on 12/31/x1 to recognize interest revenue?
6. Based on the information in Question 5, what adjusting entry must TUV Corporation make on 12/31/x2 to recognize interest revenue?

7. Based on the information in Questions 5 and 6, what entry must TUV Corporation make on 8/31/x3 to record receipt of payment from ABC Company?

8. On 6/1/x1, JKL Company purchases a one-year insurance policy, paying the full $2,400 fee in advance. JKL's accountant debits that sum to Prepaid Insurance and credits Cash. No adjustment is made on 12/31/x1. What errors will appear on JKL's 19x1 income statement and balance sheet?

9. Based on the information in Question 8, what errors will appear on JKL's 19x2 income statement and balance sheet if the accountant recognizes the full cost of the policy as an expense in 19x2?

10. CDE Company uses the periodic inventory system. The firms begins the accounting period with inventory worth $400. During the period, it acquires inventory worth $1,600 and debits this amount to Purchases. It also sells inventory but makes no entries to record the reduction in Inventory or the increase in Cost of Goods sold. At the end of the period, a physical count reveals an ending Inventory balance of $220. What adjusting entries must CDE make to add the purchases to the Inventory account and to correct the Inventory balance by recording the cost of goods sold?

Answers:

1. Interest Expense ($20,000 × .12 × 3/12) . . . . . . | 600 |
   Interest Payable . . . . | | 600 |
   [Section 4-2C]

2. Notes Payable . . . . | 20,000 |
   Interest Payable . . . . | 600 |
   Interest Expense. . . . . | 1,800 |
   Cash . . . . | | 22,400 |
   [Section 4-2C]

3. Rent Expense ($350 × 8) . . . . | 2,800 |
   Prepaid Rent. . . . . | | 2,800 |
   [Section 4-2A]

4. Unearned Revenue ($50 × 15) . . . . | 750 |
   Earned Revenue . . . . | | 750 |
   [Section 4-2B]

5. Interest Receivable ($25,000 × .18 × 10/12) . . . | 3,750 |
   Interest Revenue. . . . . | | 3,750 |
   [Section 4-2D]

6. Interest Receivable ($25,000 × .18 × 1). . . . . . . | 4,500 |
   Interest Revenue. . . . . | | 4,500 |
   [Section 4-2D]

7. Cash . . . . | 36,250 |
   Notes Receivable . . . . | | 25,000 |
   Interest Receivable ($3,750 + $4,500). . . . . . . | | 8,250 |
   Interest Revenue ($25,000 × .18 × 8/12) . . . . | | 3,000 |
   [Section 4-20]

8. Expenses understated by ($200 × 7). . . . . | 1,400

   Profits overstated by . . . . | 1,400

   Retained Earnings overstated by . . . . | 1,400

   Assets overstated by . . . . | 1,400
   [Section 4-3]

9. Expenses overstated by . . . . | 1,400

   Profits understated by . . . . | 1,400

   Retained Earnings will be correct.

   Assets will be correct
   [Section 4-3]

10. Inventory	1,600	
Purchases		1,600
Cost of Goods Sold.	1,780	
Inventory		1,780

[Section 4-2E]

SOLVED PROBLEMS

PROBLEM 4-1: Every two weeks, XYZ Corporation pays its employees' wages. The last two days of the 19x1 accounting period, Monday and Tuesday, fall at the start of a two-week pay period, so the employees will not be paid for those days until the second week of the 19x2 accounting period.

(*a*) What adjusting entry must XYZ make in its 19x1 accounts to record the wage expense of $500 for those two days?

(*b*) What entry must XYZ make when it pays $3,600 of wages at the end of the first 19x2 pay period?

(*c*) If the adjusting entry is not made in the 19x1 accounts, what errors will appear in the 19x1 financial statements?

Answer:

(*a*) To record the wage expense incurred during the final two days of 19x1, XYZ must make the following adjusting entry in its 19x1 accounts:

| Wage Expense . . . . | 500 | |
| Wages Payable . . . . | | 500 |

(*b*) To record the payment of wages totaling $3,600 at the end of the first 19x2 pay period, XYZ must make the following entry:

Wages Payable.	500	
Wage Expense	3,100	
Cash		3,600

(*c*) If the adjusting entry is not made at the end of 19x1, the 19x1 and 19x2 financial statements will contain the following errors:

Income Statement:	19x1	19x2
Expenses	500 under	500 over
Profits	500 over	500 under
Balance Sheet:		
Retained Earnings.	500 over	OK
Liabilities (Wages Payable)	500 under	OK

[Sections 4-2C and 4-3]

PROBLEM 4-2: On 4/1/x1, Inhoc Company borrowed $400,000. Inhoc agreed to repay the loan at the end of ten years and to pay 10% annual interest. The interest is payable twice a year (semiannually) on 4/1 and 10/1 throughout the term of the loan. In 19x1 and 19x2,

Inhoc made its interest payments on schedule. What entries must Inhoc make in its 19x1 and 19x2 accounts to accurately record these business operations?

Answer:

4/1/x1	Cash	400,000	
	Notes Payable		400,000
	To record loan.		
10/1/x1	Interest Expense	20,000	
	Cash		20,000
	To record first interest payment ($400,000 × .10 × 6/12)		
12/31/x1	Interest Expense	10,000	
	Interest Payable		10,000
	Adjusting entry. ($400,000 × .10 × 3/12)		
4/1/x2	Interest Payable	10,000	
	Interest Expense	10,000	
	Cash		20,000
	To record second interest payment.		
10/1/x2	Interest Expense	20,000	
	Cash		20,000
	To record third interest payment.		
12/31/x2	Interest Expense	10,000	
	Interest Payable		10,000
	Adjusting entry.		

[Section 4-2C]

PROBLEM 4-3: Periodic Company uses the periodic inventory system. At the start of 19x1 the firm had merchandise inventory worth $14,800. During the year it purchased additional inventory for $58,200. At year end, however, a physical count showed only inventory worth $12,700 remaining in the warehouse. The firm's accountant had debited all inventory acquisitions to a Purchases account but had not updated the Inventory or Cost of Goods Sold balances as merchandise was sold.

(a) Calculate Periodic's cost of goods sold for 19x1.
(b) Prepare adjusting entries to add the purchases to the Inventory account and to correct the Inventory balance by recording the cost of goods sold.
(c) Prepare the Inventory T account to prove that the adjusting entries correct the balance in that account.

Answer:

(a) Periodic's cost of goods sold is calculated as follows:

Beginning Inventory	+	Purchases	−	Ending Inventory	=	Cost of Goods Sold
$14,800	+	$58,200	−	$12,700	=	$60,300

(b) The proper adjusting entries are follows:

Inventory	58,200	
Purchases		58,200
Cost of Goods Sold	60,300	
Inventory		60,300

(*c*) The Inventory T account is as follows:

Inventory

Bal. (Beg. Inv.) 14,800	Adj. (Cost of Goods Sold) 60,300
Adj. (Purchases) 58,200	
Bal. (End. Inv.) 12,700	

[Section 4-2E]

PROBLEM 4-4: On 1/1/x1, XYZ Company had a balance of $4,250 in its Supplies Inventory account. During the year, the firm acquired additional supplies worth $12,325. Whenever supplies were acquired, the accountant debited Supplies Inventory; however, when supplies were requisitioned from the storeroom for use, the acccountant made no entries to record the reduction in Supplies Inventory or the increase in Supplies Expense. At the end of the year, a physical count revealed supplies worth $6,190 left in the storeroom.

(*a*) Calculate the cost of the supplies used up during the year.

(*b*) Prepare the adjusting entry required on 12/31/x1 to account for the supplies used up.

(*c*) Prepare T accounts for Supplies Expense and Supplies Inventory to show that your adjusting entry produces the correct ending balances.

Answer:

(*a*) Calculate the cost of the supplies used up as follows:

Beginning Balance	+	Purchases	−	Ending Balance	=	Cost of Supplies Used
$4,250	+	$12,325	−	$6,190	=	$10,385

(*b*) The adjusting entry required on 12/31/x1 to account for the supplies used up is as follows:

12/31/x1	Supplies Expense.............	10,385	
	Supplies Inventory..........		10,385

(*c*) The T accounts for Supplies Expense and Supplies Inventory are as follows:

Supplies Expense

1/1/x1 (Bal.) 0	
12/31/x1 (Adj.) 10,385	
12/31/x1 (Bal.) 10,385	

Supplies Inventory

1/1/x1 (Bal.) 4,250	
(Supplies Acq.) 12,325	
	12/31/x1 (Adjusting) 10,385
12/31/x1 (Bal.) 6,190	

Note that the adjusting entry produces the correct ending balances of $10,385 in Supplies Expense (= cost of supplies used) and $6,190 in Supplies Inventory (= amount of supplies remaining at the end of the year).   [Section 4-2E]

PROBLEM 4-5: A firm's Prepaid Insurance account is represented as follows:

Prepaid Insurance

7/1/x1 Bal. 0	
7/1/x1 3,600	7/31/x1 Adj. 400
7/31/x1 Bal. 3,200	

(*a*) What does the debit of $3,600 on 7/1/x1 represent?

(*b*) How much insurance coverage did the firm use up during July?

(*c*) What does the ending debit balance of $3,200 represent?

Answer:

(*a*) The debit of $3,600 on 7/1/x1 must represent payment in advance for a long-term insurance policy. The accountant debits the Prepaid Insurance account by the full purchase price to record the increase in insurance coverage (an asset). No entry is made to record insurance expense, since on 7/1/x1 no coverage has yet been used up.

(*b*) The 7/31/x1 adjusting entry crediting $400 to Prepaid Insurance indicates that of the firm's total $3,600 insurance coverage, $400 was used up during July. This expense is recorded in the July accounts by the $400 decrease (credit) in Prepaid Insurance and by a $400 increase (debit) in the Insurance Expense account.

(*c*) The ending debit balance of $3,200 represents the portion of the firm's total insurance coverage that is not yet used up at the end of July. Since $400 was used up during the single month of July, we may assume that the policy will continue for another eight months ($3,200 ÷ $400 = 8). **[Section 4-2A]**

PROBLEM 4-6: In July 19x1 a firm made interest payments totaling $6,500 in cash. The firm's Interest Payable account for July was as follows:

Interest Payable

		7/1/x1 Bal.	1,200
7/15/x1	1,200		
		7/31/x1 Adj.	1,000
		7/31/x1 Bal.	1,000

(*a*) Show the journal entries affecting this account during July.

(*b*) What was the firm's total interest expense during July?

(*c*) What does the ending credit balance of $1,000 represent?

Answer:

(*a*) The T account indicates that on 7/15/x1 the entire $1,200 balance in Interest Payable was paid off. Since the total interest payments for the month were $6,500, and since the difference must result from the payment of interest expenses, the first journal entry must have been

7/15/x1	Interest Payable	1,200	
	Interest Expense	5,300	
	Cash		6,500

On 7/31/x1, there was an adjusting entry for another Interest Payable liability of $1,000, indicating that the firm had incurred, but not paid, another $1,000 in interest expenses. Thus the complete adjusting entry must have been

7/31/x1	Interest Expense	1,000	
	Interest Payable		1,000

(*b*) The firm's total interest expense for July was $5,300 + $1,000 = $6,300.

(*c*) The ending credit balance indicates interest expense incurred, but not paid, as of the end of July totaled $1,000. Most likely these expenses will be paid off when a cash interest payment is made in a future accounting period. **[Section 4-2C]**

PROBLEM 4-7: Faces Fraternity members are required to pay a nine months' room and board in advance. The total amount received on September 1 19x1 was $270,000. This amount was credited to the house's Unearned Residence Fees account. What would the adjusting entry be on June 30, if adjustments are made quarterly? (Quarters end 9/30, 12/31, 3/31, and 6/30).

Answer: The nine months ended on 5/31.

Residence Fees Earned	60,000	
Unearned Residence Fees		60,000
April–May income		

PROBLEM 4-8: On 10/1/x2, Hiudt Corporation borrowed $50,400 by signing a note in which it agreed to repay the full sum plus 14% interest one year later. December 31, 19x2, is the end of Hiudt Corporation's yearly accounting period. What will be the amount of interest expense incurred at that time? What will be the adjusting entry made?

Answer:

$$\text{interest} = \$50,400 \times .14 \times 3/12 = \$1,764$$

12/31/x1	Interest Expense.	1,764	
	Interest Payable		1,764
	To record 3 months'		
	interest expense.		

[Section 4-2C]

PROBLEM 4-9: Using the information in Problem 4-8, what will be the entry made on 9/30/x3 when the loan is paid off?

Answer: When the note is paid off, the amount remitted will be $57,456 (the $50,400 originally borrowed plus the entire interest payment of $7,056). However, of that total interest payment, $1,764 has already been allocated to an expense in 19x1. The entry to record the payment would be as follows:

9/30/x3	Notes Payable	50,400	
	Interest Payable	1,764	
	Interest Expense.	5,292	
	Cash		57,456

[Section 4-2C]

PROBLEM 4-10: Consider again the situation described in Problems 4-8 and 4-9, but this time from the point of view of the bank receiving the note from Hiudt Corporation. What would be the entry made by the bank on December 31, 19x2? What would be the entry made when the loan is paid off?

Answer:

Interest Receivable.	1,764	
Interest Revenue.		1,764
Cash	57,456	
Notes Receivable		50,400
Interest Receivable		1,764
Interest Revenue.		5,292

[Section 4-2D]

PROBLEM 4-11: Jackson Company uses a periodic inventory system. It began operations on January 1, 19x5 with a balance in its Inventory account of $81,000. During the year, it acquired an additional $267,000 in inventory. At the end of the year, a physical count indicated that inventory worth $78,000 remained in the warehouse. Compute the cost of goods sold.

Answer:

Cost of goods sold	=	**Beginning Inventory**	+	**Purchases**	−	**Ending Inventory**
	=	$81,000	+	$267,000	−	$78,000
	=	$270,000				

[Section 4-2E]

PROBLEM 4-12: Using the information in Problem 4-12, what would be the two adjusting entries to the Inventory account?

Answer:

12/31/x5	Inventory	267,000	
	Purchases		267,000
	To record the purchases.		
	Cost of Goods Sold	270,000	
	Inventory		270,000
	To record cost of goods sold.		

[Section 4-2E]

5 THE ACCOUNTING PROCEDURE: FINANCIAL STATEMENTS AND CLOSING

THIS CHAPTER IS ABOUT

☑ **Preparing the Financial Statements**
☑ **The Closing Procedure**
☑ **Optional Reversing Entries**
☑ **Using the Accounts to Find Missing Information**

5-1. Preparing the Financial Statements

Once the adjusting entries have been recorded and the adjusted trial balance has been prepared, the accountant prepares the financial statements.

A. The statements are prepared in a prescribed order.

The financial statements are prepared in a prescribed order, as follows:

1. **Income statement**. This statement shows the computation of the firm's net income.
2. **Statement of retained earnings** (or *statement of owner's equity*). This statement uses the net income figure from the income statement to explain the change in retained earnings (owner's equity)
3. **Balance sheet.** This statement is prepared based on the final retained earnings (owner's equity) balance on the statement of retained earnings (statement of owner's equity).
4. **Statement of changes in financial position**. This statement is prepared based on information from the income statement and the balance sheet. (*Note:* the statement of changes in financial position will not be covered in this chapter. Instead, a full discussion of this statement will be found in Chapters 9 and 10.)

EXAMPLE 5-1: Assume that L & G's accountant has correctly posted the adjusting entries to the accounts and found the adjusted account balance. Here is the firm's adjusted trial balance.

L & G Corporation
Adjusted Trial Balance
12/31/x1

Cash	$ 4,200	
Accounts Receivable.	18,500	
Inventory	32,000	
Prepaid Insurance.	2,300	
Plant, Property, Equipment	102,000	
Accumulated Depreciation		$ 41,000
Accounts Payable		6,500
Wages Payable.		4,100
Unearned Income		1,200
Notes Payable		61,100
Common Stock (1,000 shares)		20,000
Retained Earnings		20,100
Sales		99,000
Interest Revenue		3,700
Cost of Goods Sold	49,200	
Wage Expense	21,400	
Interest Expense	6,200	
Depreciation Expense	10,500	
Income Tax Expense	2,100	
Utilities Expense	6,300	
Dividends	2,000	
	$256,700	$256,700

Based on the preceding adjusted trial balance, L & G's 19x1 income statement would appear as follows:

L & G Corporation
Income Statement
For the Year Ended 12/31/x1

Revenue:		
Sales	$99,000	
Interest Revenue	3,700	
Total Revenue		$102,700
Expenses:		
Cost of Goods Sold	$49,200	
Wages	21,400	
Interest	6,200	
Depreciation Expense	10,500	
Utilities Expense	6,300	
Total Expenses		93,600
Net Income before Income Taxes		$ 9,100
Income Taxes		2,100
Net Income		$ 7,000
Earnings per Share		$ 7.00

Based on the adjusted trial balance and the income statement, here is L & G's 19x1 statement of retained earnings.

L & G Corporation
Statement of Retained Earnings
For Year Ended 12/31/x1

Retained Earnings 1/1/x1.	$20,100
Add: Net Income	7,000
	$27,100
Less: Dividends.	2,000
Retained Earnings 12/31/x1	$25,100

(*Note:* Dividends appear on the statement of retained earnings and not the income statement. Dividends are a distribution of profits, not an expense of the business.) Finally, based on the adjusted trial balance and on the final retained earnings balance on the statement of retained earnings, here is L & G's 19x1 balance sheet.

L & G Corporation
Balance Sheet
12/13/x1

Assets			Liabilities	
Cash.		$ 4,200	Accounts Payable	$ 6,500
Accounts Receivable		18,500	Wages Payable	4,100
Inventory.		32,000	Unearned Income	1,200
Prepaid Insurance . .		2,300	Notes Payable.	61,100
Plant, Property,			Total Liabilities	$ 72,900
Equip.	$102,000			
Less Accumulated			Stockholder's Equity	
Depreciation	41,000	61,000	Common Stock	20,000
			Retained Earnings.	25,100
			Total Liabilities and Stock-	
Total Assets		$118,000	holders' Equity.	$118,000

5-2. The Closing Procedure

After the income statement, statement of retained earnings, and balance sheet have been prepared, the accountant begins the closing procedure. The purpose of the closing procedure is to prepare the books for the next accounting period. The procedure consists of four steps: (1) journalize closing entries for certain types of accounts, (2) post the closing entries to those accounts, (3) balance and rule the accounts, and (4) prepare a post-closing trial balance.

A. Journalize closing entries for certain types of accounts.

The first step in the closing process is to record closing journal entries so that all temporary (non balance sheet) accounts are closed out. Since the balances in these accounts represent amounts for the current period only, the accounts must be cleared before amounts for the next accounting period are entered. To clear or **close out** an account means to make its balance equal zero. Thus the account is ready to record the next period's work. Temporary accounts include revenue, expense, gain, loss, and dividend accounts.

1. *All revenue accounts are closed out to Income Summary.* Revenue accounts have credit balances. To close out a revenue account, you must debit it for an amount

equal to the balance, then credit a corresponding amount to Income Summary, a temporary account opened at the end of each period to summarize all events affecting income. Note that since the revenue balances are credited to Income Summary, all credits in the Income Summary account represent revenue. All gain accounts will be closed out in a like manner.

2. *All expense accounts are closed out to Income Summary.* Expense accounts have debit balances. To close out an expense account, you must credit it for an amount equal to the balance, then debit a corresponding amount to Income Summary. Note that since the expense balances are debited to Income Summary, all debits in the Income Summary account represent expenses. All loss accounts will be closed out in a like manner.

3. *The Income Summary account is closed out to Retained Earnings.* When all the appropriate accounts have been closed out, the balance in Income Summary represents the net income for the period. If revenue and gains exceeds expenses and losses, Income Summary will have a credit balance equal to the net income. If the reverse is true, Income Summary will have a debit balance equal to the net loss. Income Summary is then closed out to Retained Earnings, thus increasing (decreasing) Retained Earning by the amount of the net income (loss) for the period.

4. *The Dividends account is closed out to Retained Earnings.* The Dividends account must also be closed out so that the dividends of several periods are not combined. This step follows the closing out of Income Summary. Since dividends reduce retained earnings, the Dividends account has a debit balance; thus to close it out, you must credit it for an amount equal to the balance. The corresponding debit is then made to Retained Earnings, reducing the balance in that account by the amount of the dividends declared during the period.

EXAMPLE 5-2: Based on the adjusted trial balance for the L & G Corporation shown in Example 5-1, here are the firm's closing entries.

(1) Sales.	99,000	
Interest Revenue	3,700	
Income Summary		102,700
To close revenue accounts		
to Income Summary.		
(2) Income Summary	95,700	
Cost of Goods Sold		49,200
Wage Expense		21,400
Interest Expense		6,200
Depreciation Expense		10,500
Utilities Expense		6,300
Income Tax Expense		2,100
To close expense accounts		
to Income Summary.		
(3) Income Summary	7,000	
Retained Earnings.		7,000
To close Income Summary		
to Retained Earnings.		
(4) Retained Earnings	2,000	
Dividends		2,000
To close dividends to		
Retained Earnings.		

B. Post the closing entries to the accounts.

After the closing entries are recorded in the journal, they are posted to the corresponding ledger accounts.

C. Balance and rule the accounts.

1. *Revenue, expense, gain, and loss accounts, Dividends, and Income Summary.* In all the revenue and gain accounts, the closing debit entry should equal the existing credit balance, so the new balance should be zero (if it is not, recheck your figures again.) In all the expense and loss accounts, the closing credit entry should equal the existing debit balance, so the new balance should be zero (if it is not, recheck your figures again). In the Dividends account, the closing credit entry should equal the existing debit balance, so the new balance should be zero. In the Income Summary account, the closing entry should equal the existing balance, so the new balance should be zero. Once each of these accounts has a zero balance, draw a double rule beneath both sides of the account. Each of these accounts will start the next accounting period with a zero balance.

2. *Retained Earnings.* The closing entries to retained earnings were a debit entry representing dividends and a credit entry representing net income. Once these entries are posted, the account balance is again computed. The balance is then written beneath the side having the smaller total (this can be either debits or credits). Next, both sides are again totaled; this time the totals should be equal (if they are not, recheck your figures). A double rule is then drawn beneath both sides. Finally, the balance is again recorded on the credit side, so that the account is ready for the next accounting period.

EXAMPLE 5-3: Based on the adjusted trial balance for the L & G Corporation shown in Example 5-1, here are the firm's ledger accounts. The closing entries from Example 5-2 have been posted to the firm's revenue, expense, Income Summary, and Retained Earnings accounts (each closing entry is identified with the numbers used in Example 5-2), and these accounts have been balanced and ruled.

Cash				Accounts Receivable		
Balance	4,200			Balance	18,500	

Inventory				Prepaid Insurance		
Balance	32,000			Balance	2,300	

Plant, Property, Equipment				Accumulated Depreciation		
Balance	102,000				Balance	41,000

Accounts Payable				Wages Payable		
	Balance	6,500			Balance	4,100

Unearned Revenue				Notes Payable		
	Balance	1,200			Balance	61,100

Common Stock				Retained Earnings			
	Balance	20,000	(4)	2,000			20,100
			Balance	25,100	(3)		7,000
					Balance		25,100

Sales				Interest Revenue		
(1)	99,000	99,000		(1)	3,700	3,700

Cost of Goods Sold		
49,200	(2)	49,200

Wage Expense		
21,400	(2)	21,400

Interest Expense		
6,200	(2)	6,200

Depreciation Expense		
10,500	(2)	10,500

Income Tax Expense		
2,100	(2)	2,100

Utilities Expense		
6,300	(2)	6,300

Dividends		
2,000	(4)	2,000

Income Summary			
(2)	95,700	(1)	102,700
(3)	7,000		

Note that the only accounts that continue to have balances after the closing process is complete are those accounts that appear on the balance sheet. All revenue, expense, gain, loss, and Dividend accounts have been closed out, and so has been the Income Summary account.

D. Prepare a post-closing trial balance.

The post-closing trial balance serves as a check on the closing process. The post-closing trial balance will detect errors that involve unequal debits and credits in the closing process.

EXAMPLE 5-4: Based on the ledger accounts for the L & G Corporation shown in Example 5-3, here is the firm's post-closing trial balance.

L & G Corporation
Post-Closing Trial Balance
12/31/x1

Cash	$ 4,200	
Accounts Receivable	18,500	
Inventory	32,000	
Prepaid Insurance	2,300	
Plant, Property, Equipment	102,000	
Accumulated Depreciation		$ 41,000
Accounts Payable		6,500
Wages Payable		4,100
Unearned Income		1,200
Notes Payable		61,100
Common Stock		20,000
Retained Earnings		25,100
	$159,000	$159,000

5-3. Optional Reversing Entries

Some firms begin each new accounting period by reversing certain kinds of adjusting entries that were made at the end of the preceding period. The reversing process is optional; it is done solely for the convenience of the bookkeeper, and it may only be used with specific types of adjusting entries.

A. The reversing entry turns the adjusting entry around and removes its effect from the books.

A reversing entry is simply the reverse of the related adjusting entry. For example, if there is an adjusting entry for an expense that is incurred in one period but not paid until the next, and if that entry debits an expense account and credits a liability account, the reversing entry in the next period will debit the liability account and credit the expense account for the same amounts. The reversing entry does not result from any transaction; it simply removes the effect of the adjusting entry in order to make the subsequent bookkeeping more convenient.

EXAMPLE 5-5. When the 19x1 accounting period ends, L & G Corporation owes its employees $450 in unpaid wages. The firm's accountant therefore makes an adjusting entry in the 19x1 books to reflect this expense. Then on January 10, 19x2, the firm pays its employees $1,750 in wages, which includes the $450 owed from 19x1. In this situation, a reversing entry may or may not be used, depending on the accountant's preference. Here is how the books would appear in each case.

Without reversing entry:

(Adjusting)

| 12/31/x1 | Wage Expense . . . . | 450 | |
| | Wages Payable . . . . | | 450 |

(Date of Payment)

1/10/x2	Wages Payable.	450	
	Wage Expense	1,300	
	Cash.		1,750

Note that without a reversing entry, when the wages are paid on January 10, 19x2, the accountant has to go back and figure how much of the cash disbursed is for wage expenses incurred in the current period and how much is for wage expenses from the preceding period. This step can be avoided by using a reversing entry.

With reversing entry:

(Adjusting)

| 12/31/x1 | Wage Expense . . . . | 450 | |
| | Wages Payable . . . . | | 450 |

(Reversing)

| 1/1/x2 | Wages Payable. . . . . | 450 | |
| | Wage Expense. . . . . | | 450 |

(Date of Payment)

| 1/10/x2 | Wage Expense . . . . | 1,750 | |
| | Cash. | | 1,750 |

This time the reversing entry eliminates the need to keep track of how much of the 1/10/x2 payment was allocated to each of the two accounting periods. When the adjusting entry is reversed on January 10, 19x2, the accountant can simply debit the entire cash wage payment to Wage Expense. Furthermore, when the accounts with the reversing entry and without it are later totaled, the results will be the same. In both cases, the $450 credit in

19x1 to Wages Payable is eliminated by the $450 debit to that account in 19x2 (even though on different dates) since no debt remains after payment of the wages; also in both cases, the overall wage expense for 19x2 as of January 10 is $1,300 (with the reversing entry this results when the credit of $450 to Wage Expense is subtracted from the debit of $1,750 to that same account).

B. Reversing entries may not be used with some kinds of adjusting entries.

It is very important to note that reversing entries may *not* be used with adjusting entries that (1) allocate prepaid items among several periods, or that (2) record unearned revenue that will be earned in later periods. Reversing entries may only be used with adjusting entries that recognize revenue receivable or expenses payable in the *next* accounting period. Typical accounts in which reversing entries are used are Interest Receivable, Wages Payable, Interest Payable and the like.

5-4. Using the Accounts to Find Missing Information

Since in double-entry bookkeeping everything is recorded in at least two places, you do not need a complete set of accounts to find out many facts about a firm's operations. Indeed, many times you can use the account balances to deduce information about other accounts that might be missing. This skill is a useful one to practice, since exercises of this type appear frequently on CPA examinations.

EXAMPLE 5-6: Easy Buy Corporation reported $1,500,000 in sales during 19x1. For Accounts Receivable, it reported an ending balance in 19x0 of $200,000 and an ending balance in 19x1 of $450,000. With only these figures, it should be possible to deduce how much the firm collected in cash from its customers in 19x1.

We know that the Accounts Receivable balance indicates the amount owed to the firm by its customers. We know too that all the firm's sales are debited to Accounts Receivable, while all cash received from customers is credited to Accounts Receivable. Therefore, based on the figures given, the firm's 19x1 Accounts Receivable account would have looked like this:

Accounts Receivable

1/1/x1			
(Balance)	200,000		
(Credit			
Sales)	1,500,000	x	(Cash Collections)
12/31/x1			
(Balance)	450,000		

Based on this ledger account, we can deduce the amount of cash collections as follows. The ending balance in an account always equals the beginning balance plus increases minus decreases. Therefore:

$$\$450,000 = \$200,000 + \$1,500,000 - X$$
$$X = \$200,000 + \$1,500,000 - \$450,000 = \$1,250,000$$

The firm collected only $1,250,000 in cash from its credit customers, even though its sales totaled $1,500,000. (Note that this answer is reasonable even if some of the sales were made for cash rather than on credit. In effect, this calculation treats cash sales as if they were credit sales that were instantly paid for; in other words, when a cash sale took place, Accounts Receivable was debited and then immediately credited for the amount of the cash received.)

EXAMPLE 5-7: On Merchandising Company's 19x1 income statement, Cost of Goods Sold totaled $400,000. The firm's merchandise Inventory account totaled $75,000 at the beginning of 19x1 and $130,000 at the end of the year. All merchandise is purchased on credit. Accounts Payable to suppliers of merchandise totaled $40,000 at the beginning of the year and $35,000 at the end of the year. With only these figures, it should be possible to deduce how much inventory the firm acquired during 19x1 and how much cash it spent for inventory.

The three ledger accounts involved would appear as follows (note that the missing figures for the amount of inventory acquired and for the amount of cash spent for inventory are represented by X and Y.

Cost of Goods Sold

1/1/x1 (Balance)	0		
	400,000		
12/31/x1 (Balance) Pre-Closing	400,000		

Inventory

1/1/x1 (Balance)	75,000		
Acquisitions	X	(Cost of Goods Sold)	400,000
12/31/x1 (Balance)	130,000		

Accounts Payable

		1/1/x1 (Balance)	40,000
		Acquisitions	X
Payments	Y		
		12/31/x1 (Balance)	35,000

First, to find out the amount of inventory acquired during 19x1, remember that in the Inventory account the given ending balance equals the given beginning balance plus acquisitions minus the given cost of goods sold. Therefore, you can calculate the amount of acquisitions as follows:

$$\$130,000 = \$ 75,000 + X - \$400,000$$
$$X = \$130,000 - \$75,000 + \$400,000 = \$455,000$$

Inventory acquisitions during 19x1 therefore totaled $455,000. This answer is logical since the balance in the Inventory account increased by $55,000 ($130,000 − $75,000) during the year, and $55,000 is the amount by which acquisitions ($455,000) exceeded the cost of goods sold ($400,000).

The total amount of cash spent for inventory is shown as a decrease (debit) in Accounts Payable. Since you have just found the total amount of acquisitions, and since the given ending balance in Accounts Payable equals the given beginning balance plus the increase and minus the decrease, you can now calculate the total amount of cash spent as follows:

$$\$35,000 = \$40,000 + \$455,000 - Y$$
$$Y = \$40,000 + \$455,000 - \$35,000 = \$460,000$$

The cash spent for inventory in 19x1 therefore totaled $460,000. This was $60,000 more than the $400,000 cost of goods sold, a difference that resulted from two factors: first, the firm's inventory acquisitions exceeded the cost of goods sold by $55,000, and second, its cash payments exceeded its acquisitions by $5,000, which reduced the Accounts Payable balance by that amount and indicated that the firm had paid off an additional $5,000 in outstanding bills beyond what it owed for its 19x1 purchases.

RAISE YOUR GRADES

Can you explain . . . ?

☑ why financial statements must be prepared in the prescribed order
☑ the purpose of the closing procedure
☑ how to close out revenue, expense, and dividend accounts
☑ how to balance and rule accounts
☑ what kinds of errors are detected in a post-closing trial balance
☑ what kinds of adjusting entries may be reversed
☑ what kinds of adjusting entries may not be reversed

SUMMARY

1. The financial statements are prepared from the adjusted account balances.
2. The financial statements are prepared in the following order: (1) income statement, (2) statement of retained earnings, (3) balance sheet, and (4) statement of changes in financial position.
3. The closing procedure prepares the books for the next accounting period.
4. Closing entries create zero balances in the temporary revenue, expense, gain, loss, Dividend, and Income Summary accounts. In the other types of accounts, the existing balances continue into the next accounting period.
5. The closing entries bring the balance in the Retained Earnings account up to date.
6. The closing entries are posted to the accounts. The accounts are then balanced and ruled.
7. A post-closing trial balance detects errors involving unequal debits and credits in the closing process.
8. Some firms use reversing entries with certain types of adjusting entries in order to simplify the bookkeeping in the next accounting period.
9. Reversing entries may only be used with adjusting entries for revenue receivable or expenses payable in the next accounting period.
10. Reversing entries may not be used with adjusting entries that allocate prepaid items among several periods or that record unearned revenue that will be earned in later periods.
11. Since in double-entry bookkeeping everything is recorded in at least two places, it is often possible to use the final account balances at the end of a period to deduce information about other accounts that may be missing.

RAPID REVIEW

1. What are the four financial statements that are prepared following the adjusted trial balance, and in what order are they prepared?
2. What types of accounts are closed out at the end of each accounting period?
3. If the Income Summary account has a debit balance, has the firm earned a net profit or a net loss on its operations?
4. Which of the following is likely to be an incorrect closing entry?
   (*a*) debit Dividends, credit Retained Earnings
   (*b*) debit Sales Revenue, credit Income Summary

(c) debit Income Summary, credit Rent Expense

(d) debit Income Summary, credit Retained Earnings

5. At the end of 19x1, XYZ Corporation owes $500 in interest and properly records this debt in an adjusting entry. If XYZ does not use reversing entries, what entry would it make on 3/1/x2 to record its first 19x2 interest payment, which totals $2,000?

6. Based on the information in Question 5, what entry would XYZ make on 3/1/x2, if the firm did use reversing entries?

7. Based on the information in Question 5 and 6, what would be XYZ Corporation's reversing entry in this situation?

8. With which of the following adjusting entries may a reversing entry be used?

(a) debit Insurance Expense, credit Prepaid Insurance

(b) debit Depreciation Expense, credit Accumulated Depreciation

(c) debit Unearned Rental Fees, credit Earned Rental Fees

(d) debit Interest Receivable, credit Interest Revenue

9. During 19x1, the balance in ABC Company's Prepaid Insurance account increased from $500 to $2,200. Insurance Expense on the firm's 19x1 income statement was $13,500. How much cash did ABC Company spend for insurance during 19x1?

10. During 19x1, XYZ Company spent $4,200 in cash for rent. The balance in the firm's Prepaid Rent account decreased from $1,400 to $1,100 during 19x1. What was XYZ's rent expense for 19x1?

Answers:

1. (1) income statement, (2) statement of retained earnings, (3) balance sheet, and (4) statement of changes in financial position [Section 5-1A]

2. revenue accounts, expense accounts, gain and loss accounts, the Dividends account, and the Income Summary account [Section 5-2A]

3. net loss [Section 5-2A]

4. (a) The correct entry would be: debit Retained Earnings, credit Dividends [Section 5-2A]

5. 3/1/x2

Interest Payable	500		
Interest Expense	1,500		
Cash			2,000

[Section 5-3A]

6. 3/1/x2

Interest Expense	2,000		
Cash			2,000

[Section 5-3A]

7. 1/1/x2

Interest Payable	500		
Interest Expense			500

[Section 5-3A]

8. (d) The other entries involve prepaid items allocated among several periods or unearned revenue that will be earned in later periods. [Section 5-3B]

9. $2,200 = $500 + X − $13,500; X = $15,200 [Section 5-4]

10. $1,100 = $1,400 + $4,200 − X; X = $4,500 [Section 5-4]

SOLVED PROBLEMS

PROBLEM 5-1: Based on the following adjusted trial balance for the Review Corporation, prepare the firm's income statement, statement of retained earnings, and balance sheet. The firm's books are closed once each year on December 31.

Review Corporation
Adjusted Trial Balance
12/31/x1

Cash	$ 5,700	
Accounts Receivable.	9,800	
Supplies Inventory	4,200	
Prepaid Rent	600	
Equipment	8,100	
Accumulated Depreciation.		$ 3,300
Accounts Payable.		6,600
Notes Payable		2,000
Unearned Fees.		400
Income Taxes Payable		200
Common Stock (1,000 shares)		5,000
Retained Earnings		2,200
Earned Fees.		30,800
Interest Revenue		100
Wage Expense	9,200	
Supplies Expense.	6,800	
Depreciation Expense.	800	
Interest Expense.	200	
Income Tax Expense.	4,200	
Dividends.	1,000	
	$50,600	$50,600

Answer:

Review Corporation
Income Statement
for Year Ended 12/31/x1

Revenue:		
Earned Fees	$30,800	
Interest Revenue.	100	
Total Revenue.		$30,900
Expenses:		
Wage Expense	$9,200	
Supplies Expense	6,800	
Depreciation Expense	800	
Interest Expense	200	
Total Expenses		$17,000
Net Income Before Income Taxes.		$13,900
Income Taxes.		4,200
Net Income.		9,700
Earnings per share		$ 9.70

Review Corporation
Statement of Retained Earnings
For Year Ended 12/31/x1

Retained Earnings 1/1/x1	$ 2,200
Add: Net Income	9,700
	$11,900
Deduct: Dividends	1,000
Retained Earnings 12/31/x1	$10,900

Review Corporation
Balance Sheet
12/31/x1

Assets			Liabilities		
Cash		$ 5,700	Accounts Payable		$ 6,600
Accounts Receivable		9,800	Notes Payable.		2,000
Supplies Inventory		4,200	Unearned Fees		400
Prepaid Rent		600	Income Tax Payable		200
Equipment	$8,100		Total Liabilities		$ 9,200
Less Accum. Depn.	3,300	4,800			
			Stockholders Equity		
			Common Stock		5,000
			Retained Earnings.		10,900
			Total Liabilities		
Total Assets		$25,100	& Stockholders Equity.		$25,100

[Section 5-1A]

PROBLEM 5-2: Based on the information in Problem 5-1, prepare the appropriate closing entries for the Review Corporation.

Answer:

Earned Fees.	30,800	
Interest Revenue	100	
Income Summary		30,900
Income Summary	21,200	
Wage Expense		9,200
Supplies Expense		6,800
Depreciation Expense		800
Interest Expense.		200
Income Tax Expense		4,200
Income Summary	9,700	
Retained Earnings.		9,700
Retained Earnings	1,000	
Dividends		1,000

[Section 5-2A]

PROBLEM 5-3: Summarized Company presented a 19x2 income statement that showed $40,200 in revenue earned, $44,600 in expenses incurred, and $3,600 in dividends paid. Prepare the firm's 19x2 closing entries.

Answer:

Revenue	40,200	
Income Summary		40,200
Income Summary	44,600	
Expenses		44,600
Retained Earnings	4,400	
Income Summary		4,400
Retained Earnings	3,600	
Dividends		3,600

[Section 5-2A]

PROBLEM 5-4: On 8/1/x1, Borrower Corporation borrowed $10,000 in cash from Helpful National Bank. To obtain the loan, Borrower signed a note promising to repay the principal plus 20% interest on 7/31/x2. Assuming that Borrower closes its books on 12/31/x1 and that it does *not* use reversing entries, prepare all of the firm's entries with regard to this loan.

Answer:

8/1/x1	Cash..........................	10,000	
	Notes Payable		10,000
12/31/x1	Interest Expense	833	
	Interest Payable.............		833
	Interest amount =		
	($10,000 × .20 × 5/12)		
	Income Summary.............	833	
	Interest Expense.............		833
7/31/x2	Notes Payable...............	10,000	
	Interest Payable..............	833	
	Interest Expense	1,167	
	Cash		12,000

[Section 5-3A]

PROBLEM 5-5: Based on the information in Problem 5-4, prepare all the entries with regard to the loan assuming that Borrower *does* use reversing entries.

Answer:

8/1/x1	Cash..........................	10,000	
	Notes Payable		10,000
12/31/x1	Interest Expense	833	
	Interest Payable.............		833
	Income Summary.............	833	
	Interest Expense.............		833
1/1/x2	Interest Payable..............	833	
	Interest Expense		833
	(Reversing entry)		
7/31/x2	Notes Payable...............	10,000	
	Interest Expense	2,000	
	Cash		12,000

[Section 5-3A]

PROBLEM 5-6: XYZ Corporation's income statement for the year ended 12/31/19x1 showed interest revenue of $4,800. Interest receivable on the corporation's 12/31/x0 balance sheet was $1,000. Interest receivable increased to $3,000 by the end of 19x1. Compute the amount of interest collected in cash during 19x1.

Answer: The amount of interest revenue that appears on the income statement represents interest earned by the firm. Not all of that interest was received in cash. We know this because the balance in the Interest Receivable account increased by $2,000. The amount of cash collected for interest equals the $4,800 of interest earned less the $2,000 increase in the Interest Receivable account. Cash collected for interest totaled $2,800.

[Section 5-4]

PROBLEM 5-7: XYZ Corporation's income statement for the year ended 12/31/19x1 showed wage expense of $10,000. The comparative balance sheet indicated that wages payable totaled $2,000 at the end of 19x0. This liability increased to $3,000 by the end of 19x1. How much cash was paid to the workers during 19x1?

Answer: Wage Expense on the income statement indicates the amount owed workers for work done during 19x1. The cash payments to workers differed from this amount. The firm owed its workers $2,000 at the beginning of the year and $3,000 at the end of the year. The increase in the wages payable liability indicates that the firm did not pay its workers for all of the work done in 19x1. The amount of cash paid will equal the wages earned by workers during 19x1, $10,000, less the increase in the wages payable liability, $1,000. Cash paid totaled $9,000. We could reproduce the likely entries as follows:

Wages Payable.	2,000	
Cash		2,000
Entry to record payment of amount owed at beginning of year.		
Wage Expense	10,000	
Cash		7,000
Wages Payable		3,000
Entry to record wage expense incurred during 19x1; the portion paid in cash and the portion still owed at year end.		

Total Cash Paid to Workers = $2,000 + $7,000 = $9,000 **[Section 5-4]**

PROBLEM 5-8: Rent Expense on XYZ Corporation's income statement for the year ended 12/31/x1 was $7,000. The comparative balance sheets indicated that the asset account, Prepaid Rent, totaled $3,500 on 12/31/x0 and $5,000 on 12/31/x1. How much cash did XYZ Corporation pay to landlords during 19x1?

Answer: The rent expense on the income statement tells us the value of rental services used up during 19x1. XYZ Corporation pays for rental services in advance of using them as indicated by the Prepaid Rent account. The increase in the balance in the Prepaid Rent account indicates that the firm paid cash to landlords that exceeded the amount of rental services used up. Some of the cash paid increased the Prepaid Rent asset account. The amount of cash paid to landlords equals the $7,000 value of rental services used up plus the $1,500 increase in the prepaid rent account. Total cash paid to landlords was $8,500.

[Section 5-4]

PROBLEM 5-9: Interest Expense on XYZ Corporation's 19x1 income statement totaled $4,000. At the beginning of 19x1, the firm had no interest payable, but by the end of the year it owed $1,600 in interest. How much cash did XYZ Corporation pay for interest during 19x1?

Answer: The interest expense that appears on XYZ Corporation's income statement indicates the amount of interest owed on funds borrowed during 19x1. The firm did not pay all of the interest owed in cash. We know this because the interest payable increased from $0 to $1,600. The cash paid would equal the interest expense of $4,000 less the $1,600 increase in the interest payable liability account. Total cash paid for interest during 19x1 was $2,400. **[Section 5-4]**

PROBLEM 5-10: Cost of goods sold on XYZ Corporation's 19x1 income statement totaled $82,000. The firm buys its merchandise on credit and during the year the balance in the Accounts Payable account increased from $6,000 to $8,800. The balance in the Merchandise Inventory account decreased from $20,000 to $18,400. How much cash did XYZ Corporation pay to its merchandise suppliers during 19x1?

Answer: This is a complex question because the firm is buying goods on credit, placing them in inventory, and then selling them. The cost of the goods becomes an expense only when they are sold. We are looking for the debit entry made in the Accounts Payable account. This will tell us the amount paid to the suppliers during 19x1. Set up the three T accounts to get the big picture.

Cost of Goods Sold

BAL	0	
CGS	82,000	

Inventory

BAL	20,000		
Cost of Goods Acquired(?)		CGS	82,000
BAL	18,400		

Accounts Payable

	BAL	6,000
	Cost of Goods Acquired(?)	
Amount Paid(?)		
	BAL	8,800

By careful analysis, we can fill in the question marks. The inventory balance decreased by $1,600 when the firm sold goods costing $82,000. The acquisitions did not keep up with the sales causing the inventory balance to decline. The cost of goods acquired must have been $80,400, the cost of goods sold less the $1,600 decrease in the inventory balance. We can now enter our computed value for the cost of goods acquired into Accounts Payable as a credit. The firm began the year owing suppliers $6,000. The firm acquired $80,400 of additional goods. The total amount owed during the year was $6,000 plus $80,400 or $86,400. Of this total, $8,800 is still owed to suppliers at year end. The amount paid must have been equal to the amount owed, $86,400, less the amount not paid by year end, $8,800. The cash paid to suppliers was $77,600. You can check this answer by putting the numbers into the T accounts above and determining whether the numbers properly explain the changes in the balances. **[Section 5-4]**

PROBLEM 5-11: Shown below is the adjusted trial balance for Evans Corporation.

Evans Corporation
Adjusted Trial Balance
December 31, 19x4

Cash	$ 23,600	
Notes Receivable	10,000	
Accounts Receivable	20,900	
Inventory	65,000	
Supplies	1,500	
Prepaid Insurance	1,600	
Land	20,000	
Building	140,000	
Accounts Payable		$ 23,000
Salaries Payable		1,150
Capital Stock		100,000
Retained Earnings		60,000
Sales		765,950
Cost of Goods Sold	590,000	
Advertising Expense	8,500	
Insurance Expense	2,000	
Supplies Expense	2,000	
Salaries Expense	23,000	
Income Tax Expense	42,000	
	$950,100	$950,100

Prepare the income statement for the year 19x4.

Answer:

Evans Corporation
Income Statement
For the Year Ended December 31, 19x4

Sales		$765,950
Expenses:		
Cost of Goods Sold	$590,000	
Advertising Expense	8,500	
Insurance Expense	2,000	
Supplies Expense	2,000	
Salaries Expense.	23,000	
Total Expenses		625,500
Net Income Before Taxes		$140,450
Income Tax Expense.		42,000
Net Income After Taxes		$ 98,450

[Section 5-1]

PROBLEM 5-12: Based on the information in Problem 5-11, prepare the statement of retained earnings.

Evans Corporation
Statement of Retained Earnings
For Year Ended December 31, 19x4

Retained Earnings 1/1/x4.	$ 60,000
Net Income	98,450
Retained Earnings 12/31/x4	$158,450

[Section 5-1]

EXAMINATION I (CHAPTERS 1 THROUGH 5)

I. Multiple Choice Questions

1. Relevant accounting information has the characteristics of
   (a) neutrality, predictive value, verifiability
   (b) predictive value, materiality, representational faithfulness
   (c) timeliness, predictive value, feedback value
   (d) reliability, neutrality, comparability
   (e) materiality, verifiability, neutrality

2. The use of historical cost rather than current market value for assets on the financial statements emphasizes quality of
   (a) materiality over cost/benefit
   (b) reliability over relevance
   (c) representational faithfulness over neutrality
   (d) timeliness over neutrality
   (e) predictive value over feedback value

3. The organization currently responsible for setting accounting standards is the
   (a) GAAP
   (b) APB
   (c) AICPA
   (d) SEC
   (e) FASB

Information for Questions 4 and 5 is given below.

At the end of its first quarter of operations, Salvatore Service Company had collected $300,000 from its customers and had accounts receivable of $92,000. During the quarter, the firm paid for and used the following:

	Paid For	Used
Supplies	$ 75,000	$ 68,000
Salaries of Employees	204,000	226,000
Rent	24,000	20,000
Insurance	10,000	2,500
Utilities	22,000	45,000

4. On the accrual basis, net income or net loss for the quarter would be
   (a) net income of $35,000
   (b) net loss of $35,000
   (c) net loss of $61,500
   (d) net income of $57,000
   (e) net income of $30,500

5. On the cash basis, net income or net loss for the quarter would be
   (a) net income of $35,000
   (b) net loss of $35,000
   (c) net loss of $61,500
   (d) net income of $57,000
   (e) net income of $30,000

Questions 6 and 7 relate to the information below.

Ready Retailer engaged in the following transactions with regard to a yacht:

May 25	Customer gives $12,000 down payment on a yacht
June 1	Ordered yacht, sent $10,000 payment along with order

June 30   Received yacht
July 5   Delivered yacht to customer
July 15   Paid balance owed to supplier of $80,000
August 10   Received final payment of $100,000 from customer

6. On what day(s) and in what amount(s) should Ready Retailer recognize revenue with regard to the yacht sold?
   (a) $112,000 on August 10
   (b) $112,000 on May 25
   (c) $112,000 on July 5
   (d) $10,000 on May 25 and $100,000 on August 10
   (e) $90,000 on July 15

7. On what day(s) and in what amount(s) should ready retailer recognize an expense for the cost of the yacht sold?
   (a) $10,000 on June 1 and $80,000 on July 15
   (b) $90,000 on June 1
   (c) $90,000 on June 30
   (d) $90,000 on July 5
   (e) $90,000 on August 10

historical cost

8. During 1910 Jones Company purchased a parcel of land for $3,000. The land is currently worth $100,000 according to at least one expert and $110,000 according to another. Assuming that a dollar in 1910 had the purchasing power of $20 today, the value that should be assigned to the land is
   (a) $3,000
   (b) $105,000
   (c) $110,000
   (d) $100,000
   (e) $60,000

9. Movinup Company entered into a contract to acquire a custom airplane. Movinup made a $50,000 down payment when the contract was signed and agreed to pay the $500,000 balance upon delivery of the plane next year. The company should recognize an asset on the day the contract was signed of
   (a) $0
   (b) $550,000
   (c) $50,000
   (d) $500,000
   (e) none of the above

10. On August 1, Sellingfast Corporation ordered $5,000 of merchandise; received a shipment of merchandise costing $2,300 on account; received $3,200 from customers on their accounts; received $200 from a customer as an advance payment for goods to be included in the next order to the supplier; paid supplier $900 for merchandise received last week; delivered goods with a selling price of $500 to a customer who had paid $50 in advance of the delivery. The transactions described would cause total liabilities to increase by
    (a) $7,500
    (b) $6,400
    (c) $1,400
    (d) $1,550
    (e) $3,350

11. Carefree Computer Company made the following errors in journalizing the transactions for the month of May. A $50 payment for supplies was debited into the Wage Expense account instead of into the Supplies account. A $500 check written for office equipment was recorded as a $500 debit to equipment and a $600 credit to Cash. A payment of $150 received on account from a customer was credited to the Sales account rather than to Accounts Receivable; $200 received from a customer was

recorded as a debit to Accounts Receivable of $200; and a credit to Cash of $20. The bookkeeper recorded the payment of a $40 account payable twice. The trial balance will show
- (a) debits exceeding credits by $80
- (b) credits exceeding debits by $80
- (c) debits exceeding credits by $130
- (d) debits exceeding credits by $170
- (e) none of the above

12. Debits
- (a) decrease the balance in a loss account
- (b) decrease the balance in a contra-asset account
- (c) increase the balance in a gain account
- (d) increase the balance in a revenue account
- (e) decrease the balance in an expense account

13. On July 1, 19x1, Smith Enterprises purchased a four-year insurance policy paying $4,800. The policy went into force on August 1, 19x1. The bookkeeper recorded the acquisition of the policy with a debit to Insurance Expense for $4,800 and a credit to Cash for the same amount. The adjusting entry on 12/31/x1 relating to the insurance policy would
- (a) debit Insurance Expense for $600
- (b) debit Prepaid Insurance for $600
- (c) debit Insurance Expense for $500
- (d) debit Prepaid Insurance for $4,300
- (e) credit Insurance Expense for $4,200

14. Mike's Service Station pays its workers on Fridays. The accounting period ended on Tuesday with Mike owing his workers $400. Mike made all of the proper adjustments at the end of the period and does not use reversing entries. The entry to record the payment of $750 to workers on the first Friday of the new accounting period would
- (a) debit Wage Expense for $400
- (b) debit Wage Expense for $750
- (c) debit Wages Payable for $350
- (d) credit Wages Payable for $400
- (e) debit Wage Expense for $350

15. Laura's Laundry Service began the month with $280 of supplies. During the month, Laura acquired $500 of additional supplies. At the end of the month, an inventory revealed that $150 of supplies remained. The entry to adjust the books would
- (a) debit Supplies Expense for $130, if the acquisition of supplies was initially recorded by debiting the Supplies Inventory account.
- (b) debit Supplies Expense for $630, if the acquisition of supplies was initially recorded by debiting the Supplies Inventory account.
- (c) credit Supplies Expense for $500, if the acquisition of supplies was initially recorded by debiting the Supplies Inventory account.
- (d) credit Supplies Inventory for $130, if the acquisition of supplies was initially recorded by debiting the Supplies Inventory account.
- (e) credit Supplies Inventory for $630, if the acquisition of the supplies was initially recorded by debiting the Supplies Expense account.

16. Bob's Barber Shop paid two years' rent in advance. The monthly rental was $300 and the check was written on October 1, 19x1, the beginning of the first month of the lease. The bookkeeper debited Prepaid Rent and credited Cash to record this payment. The adjustment required with regard to rent expense on 12/31/x3 would
- (a) debit Rent Expense for $900
- (b) debit Rent Expense for $3,600
- (c) credit Rent Expense for $2,700
- (d) credit Prepaid Rent for $900
- (e) credit Prepaid Rent for $2,700

17. On October 30, 19x1, Space Age Industries borrowed $150,000. The firm signed a one-year, 18% note. The adjustment required on December 31, 19x1 with regard to the note would
    (a) debit Interest Payable for $27,000
    (b) credit Interest Expense for $4,500
    (c) debit Interest Expense for $6,750
    (d) credit Interest Payable for $27,000
    (e) debit Interest Expense for $4,500

18. On July 1, 19x1, Marcus Corporation borrowed $5,000, signing a one-year, 10% note. At the end of 19x1, the firm's accountant failed to make an adjusting entry with regard to the note. As a result of this error
    (a) net income for 19x1 will be overstated by $500
    (b) net income for 19x2 will be understated by $500
    (c) net income for 19x1 will be understated by $250
    (d) net income for 19x2 will be overstated by $250
    (e) net income for 19x2 will be understated by $250

19. During 19x1, Jones and Company collected $1,200 in advance payments from customers. The bookkeeper credited the Sales account as the cash was received. The goods were delivered in 19x2. No adjusting entry was made at the end of 19x1 with regard to the advance payments. The failure to adjust the books would cause
    (a) liabilities to be understated by $1,200 on the 12/31/x2 balance sheet
    (b) owners equity to be understated by $1,200 on the 12/31/x1 balance sheet
    (c) assets to be overstated by $1,200 on the 12/31/x1 balance sheet
    (d) owners equity to be overstated by $1,200 on the 12/31/x1 balance sheet
    (e) have no effect on owners equity on the 12/31/x1 balance sheet

20. Identify the adjusting entry described below that can be reversed if the firm uses optional reversing entries.
    (a) an adjustment to record the using up of supplies
    (b) an adjustment to recognize interest expense on a note to be settled during the next accounting period
    (c) an adjustment to recognize depreciation
    (d) an adjustment to recognize the using up of prepaid insurance
    (e) an adjustment to recognize bad debt expense

21. Financial statements are prepared in the following order:
    (a) balance sheet, income statement, statement of owners' equity, and statement of changes in financial position
    (b) income statement, statement of owners' equity, balance sheet, statement of changes in financial position
    (c) income statement, statement of changes in financial position, statement of owners' equity, balance sheet
    (d) statement of owners' equity, income statement, balance sheet, statement of changes in financial position
    (e) balance sheet, statement of owners' equity, income statement, statement of changes in financial position

22. If the Income Summary account has a credit balance after closing out all revenue and expense accounts, we can say that
    (a) the firm showed a profit on its operations for the period
    (b) the firm showed a loss on its operations for the period
    (c) the firm may have had a profit, but we won't know until we close out the drawing or dividends account
    (d) the firm had a loss that will be increased after closing out the dividends or drawing account
    (e) none of the above

Questions 23 and 24 relate to the following information:

XYZ Corporation began the period with $400 of supplies and ended with $520 left in the supplies inventory. The firm began the accounting period owing its supplier $900. During the period, the firm paid $1,830 to suppliers and reduced the balance owed to suppliers to $320.

23. Supplies acquired by the firm during the period totaled
   (a) $1,250
   (b) $1,830
   (c) $120
   (d) $2,410
   (e) $1,950

24. Supplies Expense for the period totaled
   (a) $1,370
   (b) $120
   (c) $1,280
   (d) $580
   (e) $1,130

25. Easy Credit Association lent $1,000 to Shifty Jones on September 1, 19x1. The 12% loan is to be repaid on February 1, 19x2. Easy Credit Association closes its books on December 31, 19x1 and makes all of the proper adjusting entries. The entry to record the receipt of payment on February 1, 19x2 will
   (a) credit Interest Revenue for $60, if reversing entries are used
   (b) credit Interest Revenue for $10, if reversing entries are used
   (c) credit Interest Revenue for $50, if reversing entries are used
   (d) credit Interest Revenue for $50, if no reversing entries are made
   (e) credit Interest Revenue for $60, if no reversing entries are made

II. Problems

1. Prepare the income statement, statement of retained earnings and balance sheet from the following adjusted trial balance. The books are closed once a year.

Smart Merchant Corporation
Adjusted Trial Balance
12/31/x1

Cash	$ 2,180	
Accounts Receivable	7,480	
Accounts Payable		$ 2,700
Supplies Inventory	9,800	
Prepaid Rent	600	
Unearned Rent		250
Rent Expense	3,600	
Rent Revenue		2,180
Sales		35,940
Supplies Expense	13,020	
Plant Property and Equipment	40,700	
Depreciation Expense	1,720	
Accumulated Depreciation		12,880
Wage Expense	10,460	
Other Expenses	4,060	
Income Tax Expense	1,830	
Income Taxes Payable		650
Dividends	2,800	
Dividends Payable		1,400
Common Stock (1,000 shares)		5,000
Retained Earnings		37,250
	$98,250	$98,250

2. Analyze the effect that each of the following errors would have on the income statement and balance sheet. Use (O), if the amount would be overstated; (U), if the amount would be understated; or N, if the amount is not affected by the error.

Description	Revenue	Expenses	Assets	Liabilities	Equity
Failed to recognize accrued interest revenue at year-end	U	N	U	N	U
(a) Recorded payment on account as a cash sale					
(b) Failed to recognize depreciation for the year					
(c) Underestimated the amount of the year end supplies inventory					
(d) Failed to recognize wages owed at year end					
(e) Recorded investment by owner as a cash sale					

3. In reviewing the financial statements of the Butterfly Corporation, Etchem S. Pinafore, CPA, noticed that the income statement contained an unrealized gain on property of $35,000. Upon investigation, he discovered that the firm had increased the value of a parcel of land from its original cost of $10,000 to $45,000, its current estimated market value. The firm did not value other assets in this manner, nor had it increased the value of assets in previous years. No disclosure was made regarding this unusual accounting practice. In what ways does increasing the value of the land to its current market value violate the basic underlying principles of accounting?

ANSWERS TO EXAMINATION IV

Multiple Choice Questions

1. c	6. c	11. a	16. e	21. b
2. b	7. d	12. b	17. e	22. a
3. e	8. a	13. d	18. e	23. a
4. e	9. c	14. e	19. d	24. e
5. b	10. d	15. b	20. b	25. c

Problems

Problem 1: The financial statements for Smart Merchant Corporation are presented below.

Smart Merchant Corporation
Income Statement
For the Year Ended 12/31/x1

Sales		$35,940
Rent Revenue.		2,180
Total Revenue		$38,120
Less Expenses:		
Rent Expense	$ 3,600	
Supplies Expense	13,020	
Depreciation Expense	1,720	
Wage Expense	10,460	
Other Expenses.	4,060	
Total Expenses		$32,860
Net Income Before Taxes.		$ 5,260
Income Taxes.		1,830
Net Income.		$ 3,430

Smart Merchant Corporation
Statement of Retained Earnings
For the Year Ended 12/31/x1

Retained Earnings 1/1/x1.	$37,250
Add: Net Income	3,430
	$40,680
Deduct: Dividends.	2,800
Retained Earnings 12/31/x1	$37,880

Smart Merchant Corporation
Balance Sheet
12/31/x1

Assets			Liabilities		
Cash.		$ 2,180	Accounts Payable		$ 2,700
Accounts Receivable		7,480	Unearned Rent		250
Supplies Inventory.		9,800	Income Tax Payable		650
Prepaid Rent.		600			
PP&E at Cost	$40,700		Dividends Payable.		1,400
Less Accum. Depn.	12,880	27,820	Total Liabilities		$ 5,000
			Owners' Equity		
			Common Stock		5,000
			Retained Earnings.		37,880
			Total Liabilities and		
Total Assets		$47,880	Owner's Equity.		$47,880

PROBLEM 2:

Description	Revenue	Expenses	Assets	Liabilities	Equity
Failed to recognize accrued interest revenue at year-end	U	N	U	N	U
(a) Recorded payment on account as a cash sale	O	N	O	N	O
(b) Failed to recognize depreciation for the year	N	U	O	N	O
(c) Underestimated the amount of the year end supplies inventory	N	O	U	N	U
(d) Failed to recognize wages owed at year end	N	U	N	U	O
(e) Recorded investment by owner as a cash sale	O	N	N	N	N

PROBLEM 3: Increasing the value of the land to its current market value and recognizing a gain violates the following basic principles of accounting.

(*a*) Objectivity Principle: the accountant has substituted a subjective value (current market value) for an objective one (cost).

(*b*) Historical Cost Principle: assets are to be valued at their cost, not at what we think they could be sold for on the balance sheet date.

(*c*) Revenue Recognition Principle: revenue/gains are recognized when goods or property are sold, not when the firm assumes that the assets have increased in value.

(*d*) Full Disclosure Principle: the firm must disclose the accounting methods used and any unusual events that might influence the decisions of the reader of the statements.

(*e*) Consistency Principle: the firm has not consistently applied accounting methods period to period or even among assets during the current period.

(*f*) The firm cannot justify its departure from the basic principles by using the Exception Principle because the firm has not abandoned cost valuation to be conservative. It is using a non-conservative deviation from basic accounting principle.

6 THE INCOME STATEMENT: CONTINUING OPERATIONS

THIS CHAPTER IS ABOUT

☑ **The Purpose of the Income Statement**
☑ **Revenue**
☑ **Expenses**
☑ **Gains and Losses**
☑ **Alternative Measurements of Net Income**
☑ **Sections of the Income Statement**
☑ **Income Statement Formats—Continuing Operations Section**
☑ **Earnings Per Share**
☑ **What an Income Statement Tell You**
☑ **Income Statements of Non-corporate Businesses**

6-1. The Purpose of the Income Statement

The income statement shows the results of operations over a specified period of time called the **accounting period**.

A. The purpose of the income statement is illustrated by its basic equation.

The basic equation of the income statement is as follows:

Revenue Earned Over an Accounting Period	−	Expenses Incurred Over an Accounting Period	+	Gains Recognized During an Accounting Period	−	Losses Recognized During an Accounting Period	=	Net Income (Loss) Earned for the Accounting Period

B. Net Income must be reported on a timely basis.

Users of financial statements require timely information, if it is to be of relevance to their decisions. The accountant will therefore prepare an income statement at least once each year. Most firms also prepare quarterly statements for distribution to stockholders, and monthly statements for internal use.

1. Measuring revenue and expenses within arbitrary time periods is very difficult. The periodicity assumption suggests that it is possible to divide the activity of a firm into arbitrary time periods and measure the results of operations for those time periods.
2. We must follow specific rules and guidelines in deciding which revenues and expenses to include on the income statement for a particular period. Generally accepted accounting principles (GAAP) provide the direction needed to prepare periodic income statements.

3. The period of time covered by the income statement will be called the accounting period. The date in the title to the income statement should clearly define the period of time for which net income is being measured.

6-2. Revenue

Revenue is an increase in equity (increase in assets and/or decrease in liabilities) due to main activities of the firm. Revenue is recognized in the accounting period when the firm has delivered goods or performed services and has earned the right to be paid in cash or other assets. (Remember, the recognition of revenue does not necessarily mean that cash has been received.) Care must be taken in measuring the amount of revenue earned. The amount of revenue recognized is measured by the cash received on the date of the sale *or* the current value of assets or other consideration to be received in the future.

EXAMPLE 6-1: The XYZ Corporation delivered goods to ABC Company. The goods would normally have sold for $5,850. Rather than pay cash, the ABC Company forgave a $5,550 debt that XYZ Corporation owed to ABC Company. What amount of revenue should XYZ Corporation recognize at the point of the sale? XYZ Corporation received a cash-equivalent reduction of its liabilities of $5,550. This is the amount of revenue that should be recognized on the date of the sale.

A. Interest charges hidden in the selling price must be removed when revenue is recognized.

When the credit period is longer than one year, the selling price may include a hidden interest charge. The interest included in the selling price is not revenue that is earned at the time of the sale. It will be earned over the time period for which credit is extended. Any interest charge included in the selling price must be removed in measuring revenue earned on a sale.

EXAMPLE 6-2: The Paylater Corporation delivered $100,000 of goods to a credit customer. The customer agreed to pay $120,000 in 18 months from the date of delivery. How much revenue should Paylater Corporation recognize at the time of the sale?
   The corporation will recognize revenue of $100,000 at the time of the sale. The other $20,000 is an interest charge. The customer is in effect borrowing $100,000 for 18 months and paying $20,000 in interest to do so. We know this must be the case because the customer could have purchased the goods for $100,000 in cash. Paylater Corporation will recognize interest revenue over the 18 month period totaling $20,000. The interest revenue has not been earned at the date of sale. The interest is earned between the date of sale and the date of payment, and will be recognized as it is earned.

B. Revenue must be adjusted for sales returns and discounts.

Not all merchandise delivered to a customer will be in perfect condition. Some may be damaged in transit, some may have been imperfect when produced. Such merchandise will often be returned or the customer may keep the merchandise but pay a discounted price. The customer's account will be reduced and so will the net amount of revenue from the sale.

EXAMPLE 6-3: Davidson Company delivered goods with a selling price of $100,000 to HDV Company. Upon checking the merchandise, HDV Company found that $1,000 of the goods were the wrong model and another $2,000 of goods were slightly damaged. Davidson Company agreed to credit HDV Company's account for the goods not ordered upon their return and offered a 20% discount on the damaged goods. HDV accepted the discount.
   Davidson Company recognized $100,000 of sales revenue when the merchandise was delivered. The company would reduce the revenue earned from the sale by $1,000 for the goods returned and by $400 for the discount ($2,000 × 20%) given on the damaged

merchandise. The income statement would report net revenue of $98,600 ($100,000 − $1,000 − $400), the amount the company now has the right to collect.

C. The firm must recognize an expense for uncollectible accounts when it sells to its customers on credit.

When a firm extends credit to its customers it knows that some of the accounts will probably never be collected. The revenue reported on a credit sale must be reduced by the amount of estimated uncollectibles to avoid overstating the resulting profit. Some authors believe that the adjustment for bad debts should be made in a negative or contra revenue account. The typical adjustment is made by debiting the Bad Debt Expense account which appears as one of the firm's operating expenses on the income statement.

EXAMPLE 6-4: The Paylater Corporation delivered $100,000 of goods to its credit customers during March. Typically Paylater Corporation collects 98% of the amounts owed to it by its credit customers. What amount of revenue should the corporation recognize net of estimated bad debt expense for the month of March on its sales to credit customers?

Paylater Corporation will recognize $100,000 of sales during March because the goods have been delivered and the corporation has earned the right to receive payment. It will also recognize that 2% or $2,000 will probably not be collected. The income statement will show revenue net of estimated bad debt expense of $98,000 equal to the amount of cash the firm eventually expects to collect.

6-3. Expenses

Expenses are incurred as goods or services are used up in order to earn revenue. The amount of the expense is measured by the cost of the items used. The matching principle requires that an effort be made to match revenue with related expenses. This is not always possible. Some expense items cannot be directly related to specific revenue amounts. The corporate president's salary, the cost of office supplies, advertising costs, cannot be identified with a specific sale as can the cost of the goods sold. These goods and services are used up in the course of earning revenue as a part of general operations and must be recognized as an expense of the period. Other costs are arbitrarily recognized as expenses on a systematic basis. The cost of a piece of equipment which will be used for an extended time period is recognized as an expense over the equipment's useful life. Depreciation methods offer a systematic way of allocating the cost to the accounting periods in which the asset is used.

EXAMPLE 6-5: During the month of March, SDU Corporation sold $100,000 of merchandise to its customers. For every sale made, the respective salesperson received a 10% commission. This means that for every $1.00 of sales, the company incurred a $.10 commission expense. The commission expense for March was $10,000. This expense is directly matched to sales.

EXAMPLE 6-6: Big Sales Corporation owes its salespeople $1,200 at the beginning of March for commissions on sales made in February. During March, sales of $100,000 were made. The commission rate is 10% on all sales. During March, the corporation paid its salespeople $9,500 in cash for commissions. What is the commissions expense for March? What commissions were included in the $9,500 paid to the salespeople during March? How much was owed to the salespeople as of the end of March?

The March commissions expense should be equal to commissions owed for sales during March. We can match the commission expense to the related revenue. March sales were $100,000. The commission rate is 10%. Therefore, commissions expense for March is $10,000. The $9,500 paid to the salespeople first represents payment for the $1,200 owed them as of the beginning of the month for sales made in February. The remaining $8,300 paid must be for commissions on March sales. At the end of March, the company owes its salespeople $1,700. Of the $10,000 of commissions owed for March sales, $8,300 has been paid leaving a balance owed to the salespeople of $1,700.

EXAMPLE 6-7: During the month of March, SDUL Corporation used $500 in office supplies, paid the receptionist's salary of $2,000, and paid $200 for newspaper ads. Even though none of these costs can be directly associated with a particular sale, they were incurred in the course of earning revenue for March. Therefore, the $2,700 in expenses must be matched with the March revenue of $100,000.

EXAMPLE 6-8: On January 1, 19x1, CWL Corporation paid $5,000 for a new computer. The company estimates that the computer will be used for five years at which time it will be obsolete and have no salvage value. The company must charge off the $5,000 cost of the computer over its five year useful life in some systematic manner. If it chooses the straight-line depreciation method, it will charge $1,000 of depreciation expense in each of the five years of the computer's useful life.

6-4. Gains and Losses

The results of non-routine or peripheral activities are also included in net income. While the effects of routine activities are reported as revenue and expenses, the results of non-routine transactions are reported as gains or losses. The amount of the gain or loss equals the difference between the cash or other consideration received in the transaction and the cost of the special item or service sold. Gains and losses will generally appear in the main body of the income statement unless they are categorized as "extraordinary" or are incurred by a discontinued operation (See Chapter 7).

EXAMPLE 6-9: Retail Corporation made sales of $100,000 to its regular customers. In addition, the company sold 1,000 shares of High Flyer common stock for $10,000. Retail Corporation is not in the business of trading stock. The stock trade would be categorized as a peripheral activity. Retail paid $4,000 for the shares of stock five years ago.

Sales to customers would be reported on the income statement as revenue. The expenses of operating the retail store would be listed separately. The difference between the cash received for the stock and the stock's original cost would be shown as a gain on the sale of stock of $6,000.

6-5. Alternative Measurements of Net Income

As presented in the income statement equation, the entity's profit for an accounting period equals the amount remaining after expenses and losses have been deducted from revenue and gains for the period. If revenue and gains exceed expenses and losses, the entity operated at a profit. If the reverse is true, it operated at a loss.

A. Some theorists believe that net income should show only the results of current operations.

Some accountants believe that the income statement should show only the results of the firm's major ongoing activities. Gains and losses, particularly those that are extraordinary or related to discontinued operations would be excluded from the income statement and placed directly into retained earnings. The **current-operating** measurement of net income has been rejected by GAAP.

B. Some theorists believe that the income statement should explain all changes in retained earnings other than those caused by owner related transfers.

Some accountants believe that the income statement should summarize all changes in retained earnings other than those associated with dividend payments and certain stock transactions that occasionally affect retained earnings. The income statement would include revenue, expenses, all gains and losses, cumulative effects of accounting changes, and adjustments to retained earnings for errors made in prior periods. GAAP has also rejected this particular **all-inclusive** definition of net income.

C. Some theorists believe that the income statement should explain all changes in retained earnings other than those caused by owner related transfers and prior period adjustments.

Current computations of net income fall closest to this **modified all-inclusive** definition of net income. The income statement includes all revenue, expenses, gains, and losses, and the cumulative effect of accounting changes. It excludes adjustments made to retained earnings for prior period errors.

D. The FASB has established a new definition of comprehensive net income, but has not established guidelines for implementation of the new concept.

The FASB has established a new definition of net income called **comprehensive net income**. Comprehensive net income includes all changes in owners' equity from by non-owner sources. It is a broader definition than any of those previously described. Comprehensive net income includes all revenue, expenses, gains, and losses. It also includes the cumulative effect of changes in accounting principle, prior period adjustments, and changes in owners' equity due to unrealized losses on long-term marketable securities (covered in Chapter 19) and allowances set up by firms to account for certain foreign currency translation adjustments (discussed in advanced accounting courses). The FASB has not set up specific guidelines for implementation of this new concept. (SFAC No. 5)

E. The FASB has defined a subset of comprehensive income called earnings.

The FASB has established a subset of comprehensive net income called **earnings**. Earnings includes revenue, expenses, gains, and losses. It does not include cumulative effect of a change in accounting principle or other adjustments to owners' equity such as those related to long-term marketable equity securities. Earnings is a measure of performance for the period and excludes items that are associated with prior periods. (SFAC No. 5)

F. We will use the traditional modified all-inclusive definition of net income in this text.

We will use the traditional modified all-inclusive definition of net income in this text. You should be aware that the measurement of net income is in a transition phase. The FASB has established two new concepts of income measurement and will be providing guidelines for the implementation of these concepts. Exhibit 6-1 shows the relationship between the alternative measurements of net income.

EXHIBIT 6-1: Alternative Measurements of Net Income

	Compre-hensive Net Income	All-Inclusive Net Income	Modified All-Inclusive Net Income	Earnings	Current Operating Net Income
Income from Continuing Operations	Included	Included	Included	Included	Included
Discontinued Operations	Included	Included	Included	Included	Excluded
Extraordinary Item	Included	Included	Included	Included	Excluded

	Compre-hensive Net Income	All-Inclusive Net Income	Modified All-Inclusive Net Income	Earnings	Current Operating Net Income
Cumulative Effect of Chg. Acctg. Principle	Included	Included	Included	Excluded	Excluded
Prior Period Adjustment	Included	Included	Excluded	Excluded	Excluded
Other adjustments to Equity	Included	Excluded	Excluded	Excluded	Excluded

6-6. Sections of the Income Statement

An income statement is divided into five sections. The five sections are continuing operations, discontinued operations, extraordinary items, cumulative effect of a change in accounting principle, and earnings per share. It would be rare to find a company which used all of the sections on a single income statement.

The continuing operations section lists revenue and expenses resulting from the company's ongoing areas of business. It would include gains and losses that were not categorized as extraordinary or related to discontinued operations. All firms will report the results of continuing operations. This section is of great significance to those who use the income statement to predict future earnings because it contains information about the activities which are likely to recur in the future.

Discontinued operations, extraordinary items, and changes in accounting principle are not routine happenings. Financial analysts view the information in these sections as unique to the particular year and this information is given less weight in predicting future earnings. These more unusual sections of the income statement are discussed in the next chapter.

Earnings per share information must be reported on the face of the income statement, if the corporation's stock and/or bonds are traded on a public market. Earnings per share information is not required, if the stock and bonds of the company are privately held.

6-7. Income Statement Formats: Continuing Operations Section

The two commonly used income statement presentations are the multiple-step and single-step formats.

A. The multiple-step format separates operating revenue and expenses from financing activities.

In a multiple-step income statement, income from continuing operations is divided into sales, cost of goods sold, operating expenses, and other revenue, and other expenses. Net sales less cost of goods sold is reported as gross profit. The gross profit figure indicates the amount of the selling price that is left after the cost of items sold is deducted. Selling and administrative expenses are deducted from gross profit to compute operating income. The Other Revenue section accounts for financial revenue such as interest or rental income and gains on peripheral activities. The Other Expense section contains information about interest expense and losses on peripheral activities. Since peripheral activities are generally financial in nature, the multiple-step format separates production and sales from financing activities. This separation is reasonable because different people are generally responsible for each activity. Exhibit 6-2 presents the continuing operations section of Friendly Corporation's income statement using the multiple-step format.

EXHIBIT 6-2

Friendly Corporation
Income Statement
For the Year Ended 12/31/85

Sales		$1,500,000
Less Sales Discounts and Returns		63,000
Net Sales		$1,437,000
Less Cost of Goods Sold		842,000
Gross Profit		$ 595,000
Operating Expenses:		
Selling Expenses.	$85,000	
Administrative Expenses	92,000	
Total Operating Expenses		177,000
Operating Income.		$ 418,000
Other Income:		
Rental Income.	$10,000	
Gain on Sale of Stock	12,000	
Dividend Income	3,000	
Total Other Income		25,000
		$ 443,000
Other Expenses:		
Interest Expense		61,000
Net Income from Continuing Operations Before Taxes. . .		$ 382,000
Income Taxes.		153,000
Income From Continuing Operations		$ 229,000
Earnings per Share:		
Income From Continuing Operations.		$ 2.29

B. The single-step format does not separate operations from financing.

A single-step format does not separate operations from financing. Exhibit 6-3 presents the continuing operations section of Friendly Corporation's income statement in the alternative single-step format.

EXHIBIT 6-3

Friendly Corporation
Income Statement
For the Year Ended 12/31/x1

Revenue:		
Net Sales		$1,437,000
Other Revenue and Gains		25,000
Total Revenue		$1,462,000
Expenses:		
Cost of Goods Sold	$842,000	
Selling and Administrative.	177,000	
Interest Expense	61,000	
Total Expenses.		$1,080,000
Net Income From Continuing Operations before Taxes . .		$ 382,000
Income Taxes.		153,000
Net Income From Continuing Operations		$ 229,000
Earnings per Share:		
Income From Continuing Operations.		$ 2.29

6-8. Earnings Per Share

Stockholders not only want to know how much the company is earning, they want to know what the earnings on their individual investments are. The common way of determining this is to compute earnings per share (EPS). Companies whose stock or bonds are traded on public markets are required to present earnings per share information on the face of the Income Statement.

A. Earnings per share may be computed using a basic formula, if the firm has a simple capital structure.

The calculation of earnings per share is generally relatively simple. For most companies earnings per share is computed using the following formula:

$$\text{EPS} = \frac{\text{Net Income} - \text{Preferred Dividends (if any)}}{\text{Weighted Average Common Stock Shares Outstanding}}$$

Companies with "complex capital structures" will face a more difficult calculation. A complex capital structure includes securities which are not now common stock but which might become common stock. Convertible bonds, convertible preferred stock, stock options, and stock warrants are examples of securities which may be turned into common stock at some future date. Computation of earnings per share for firms with complex capital structures is covered in a later chapter.

EXAMPLE 6-10: Friendly Corporation in Exhibits 6-1 and 6-2 has 100,000 shares of stock outstanding throughout the year. It has no preferred stock and therefore no preferred dividends. The earnings per share from continuing operations is computed by dividing the $229,000 of net income from continuing operations by the 100,000 weighted-average number of common stock shares outstanding. Friendly Corporation earned net income from continuing operations of $2.29 per share of common stock.

B. Earnings per share should not be confused with dividends per share.

Earnings per share represent the ratio of earnings to the number of shares of stock. Earnings per share should not be confused with the dividends paid per share which are actual distributions to stockholders per share owned. Earnings may be distributed as dividends or they may be retained in the business.

EXAMPLE 6-11: JKL Corporation has 100,000 shares of stock outstanding throughout the year. During the past month, sales revenue totaled $580,000 and expenses were $360,000. The company declared dividends equal to $1.60 per share of outstanding stock.
From this information, we know that JKL Corporation earned a net income of $220,000 ($580,000 − $360,000). The earnings per share equaled $2.20 ($220,000/100,000). Dividends declared amounted to $160,000 ($1.60 × 100,000). The firm reinvested $60,000 ($220,000 − $160,000) of its reported profit in the business.

6-9. What an Income Statement Tells You

An income statement measures the results of activities over an accounting period.

A. An income statement shows the total revenue earned over an accounting period.

The revenue that appears on the income statement shows the value of goods delivered and/or services rendered during that time period. Revenue shown on the income statement does not tell you how much cash the company collected.

B. The income statement shows the total expenses incurred over an accounting period.

The expenses that appear on the income statement measure the value of resources used up to produce revenue. The total expense figure does not tell you how much cash the company spent.

C. The income statement shows the amount of net income earned over an accounting period.

The net income figure shows the difference between the value of the goods and services provided and the cost of the resources used up to supply those goods and services. It does not tell how much cash was added to the firm's bank account. Many people assume that when a company shows a profit it is able to pay dividends equal to the net income. This may or may not be the case. The net income figure does not attempt to measure cash receipts and disbursements. The net income figure does not tell you how much cash was generated during the accounting period. Cash flow information appears on another financial statement called a statement of changes in financial position which is discussed in a later chapter.

EXAMPLE 6-12: New Corporation began business on January 1, 1985. The shareholders invested $100,000 in cash in the business. During the first year of operations, the firm acquired a building, equipment, and inventory. Because the firm was new, suppliers refused to extend credit beyond 30 days. The firm borrowed heavily from the bank to get started. Business went well. Sales were greater than expected because the firm was willing to allow its customers more time to pay than its competitors allowed. By year end, the firm reported net income of $45,000. The board of directors met and decided to declare no dividends. Angry stockholders protested. What explanation could the President of the company make to the unhappy stockholders?

The President should explain that the profit figure overstates the amount of cash generated by operations for the year. Revenue earned has not been collected in cash because of the extension of credit to customers. Cash expenditures for the building, equipment, and inventories have exceeded the amounts reported as expenses. The company is currently "cash poor", but the future is bright. The company's profits have generated non-cash assets such as accounts receivable and inventories. Non-cash assets cannot easily be distributed to stockholders as dividends.

6-10. Income Statements of Non-corporate Businesses

In most respects, the income statements of corporate and non-corporate businesses are the same. Non-corporate businesses are not subject to corporation income taxes so their income statements do not include a deduction for corporation income taxes. All reported net income flows through to the owners and is included as income in computing the owner's personal taxable income. This is true even if the profits are not withdrawn from the company. Corporations pay income taxes on taxable profits. In addition, the stockholders pay personal income taxes on any dividends they receive from the corporation, but shareholders pay no personal income taxes on profits retained by the firm. Since non-corporate businesses do not issue shares of stock they do not compute earnings per share. In all other respects the income statements of corporate and non-corporate businesses are alike.

EXAMPLE 6-13: Gary Carnes is the sole owner of Carnes Company. He is also the sole stockholder of Paxton Corporation. During the past year, Carnes Company and Paxton Corporation earned $250,000 and $1,500,000 in net income, respectively. Gary withdrew $50,000 over the past year from Carnes Company and received $10,000 in dividends from Paxton Corporation. What amount of income will Gary report on his income tax return?

Gary would have reportable income of $260,000. Even though Gary only withdrew $50,000 of the $250,000 of Carnes Company's income, the full amount of the firm's earnings are reported as part of his personal income. He will report the $10,000 he received in dividends from Paxton Corporation. He would not report the portion of Paxton Corporation's income that was retained by the corporation.

RAISE YOUR GRADES

Can you explain...?

☑ the purpose of the income statement
☑ the basic equation of the income statement
☑ when revenue is recognized on the income statement
☑ what adjustments to selling price may be required in recognizing revenue
☑ when expenses are recognized on the income statement
☑ how gains and losses differ from revenue and expense
☑ why financial analysts concentrate their attention on the continuing operations section of the income statement
☑ the difference between a multiple-step and single-step format for the income statement
☑ why net income is not the same as net cash inflow
☑ what EPS is and how it is calculated for a company with a simple capital structure?
☑ what three things an income statement tells you
☑ how an income statement for a non-corporate business differs from a corporation's income statement
☑ how the net income of a non-corporate business is taxed

SUMMARY

1. The purpose of the income statement is to report the results of operations over a specified period of time.
2. The basic income statement equation is revenue and gains less expenses and losses equals net income or loss for the accounting period.
3. The income statement must be prepared on a timely basis.
4. Revenue is an increase in equity due to delivery of goods or rendering of service in the normal course of business.
5. Revenue is earned when goods are delivered or services are rendered. The concept of earning revenue is different from the concept of collecting cash.
6. The amount of revenue earned is measured by the cash received or the cash-equivalent value of other items received.
7. Revenue must be adjusted for returns, discounts, and amounts expected to be uncollectible.
8. Interest charges hidden in the selling price must be removed when recognizing revenue from a sale.
9. Expenses are incurred as goods or services are used up to produce revenue. The concept of incurring an expense is different from the concept of disbursing cash.
10. The matching principle requires that expenses be matched with their related revenue and recorded in the same accounting period the revenue is recognized.
11. Expenses not directly related to a specific sale are recognized in the accounting period in which they are incurred or on a systematic basis.
12. The results of transactions that are peripheral to a firm's main activities are reported as gains and losses.
13. If revenue and gains exceed expenses and losses, the firm has earned a profit. If the reverse is true, the firm has incurred a loss.
14. The currently used modified all-inclusive measurement of net income includes all gains and losses but excludes prior period adjustments.
15. The income statement is divided into five sections: continuing operations, dis-

continued operations, extraordinary items, cumulative effect of a change in accounting principle, and earnings per share.

16. The continuing operations section is most relevant for assessing the company's future prospects since it includes those activities that are expected to be ongoing in the future.

17. Earnings per share equals net income less preferred dividends (if any) divided by the weighted average number of shares outstanding.

18. Earnings per share does not necessarily represent the amount that can be paid as dividends per share.

19. The multiple-step income statement format separates operations from financing activities.

20. The single-step income statement format does not separate operations from financing activities.

21. The income statement does not explain cash flow. This information is presented in the statement of changes in financial position.

22. A non-corporate business will not have income tax expense or earnings per share figures on the income statement.

23. The profits from a non-corporate business flow through to its owners and are reported as a part of personal income even if the profits are not withdrawn by the owners.

RAPID REVIEW

1. The basic equation of the income statement is

2. Which of the following will involve revenue for the month of March?
   (a) $600 is collected on March 3 in payment for goods delivered on February 15.
   (b) $600 is paid by a customer on March 26 for goods to be delivered on April 5.
   (c) $600 of cash is invested in the firm by the owner on March 14.
   (d) $600 of goods are delivered on March 19, payment is to be received in May.

3. XYZ Corporation sold goods with a normal selling price of $500 to a customer. The customer promised to pay $580 in a single payment 18 months after the date of delivery. How much revenue should XYZ Corporation recognize at the date of delivery?

4. Easy Credit Company sold goods with a normal selling price of $50,000 to its credit customers during March. The firm has ascertained that 10% of its credit sales prove to be uncollectible. What is the amount of revenue earned net of bad debt expense?

5. XYZ Corporation acquired $5,000 of new inventory from its supplier during March. It paid $4,800 to that supplier in cash during the month. Goods costing $5,300 were delivered to the customers. What amount will appear as an expense on XYZ Corporation's income statement?

6. Nice Corporation made contributions to charity totaling $5,000 during 1985. The corporation feels that such contributions enhance the company's image in the community and that the firm might receive future benefits in 1986 and 1987 from the improvement in image. How much of the $5,000 expenditure should be included on the 1985 income statement as an expense and why?

7. XYZ Corporation paid in advance for a 36 month insurance policy at the rate of $200 per month. The policy came into force on 3/1/x1. How much insurance expense would appear on the income statement for the year 19x1 with regard to this policy?

8. A multiple-step format for an income statement separates the _____ activities from the _____ activities of the continuing operations of the company.

9. Which of the following dates is in an appropriate format for an income statement?
   (a) 1/1/x1 to 12/31/x1
   (b) For period ending 12/31/x1
   (c) 12/31/x1
   (d) For period beginning 1/1/x1

10. Define the term accounting period.

11. Which of the following would be included in the other expenses or other revenue section of a multiple-step income statement for a retail grocery store?
    (*a*) Spoilage Costs
    (*b*) Depreciation of Store Fixtures
    (*c*) Rental Expense
    (*d*) Interest Expense

12. Gains and losses are included in the calculation of net income even if they are extraordinary or related to a discontinued operation because we have traditionally used a (an) (all inclusive/current operating/modified all-inclusive) measurement of net income.

13. Determine whether the following would appear in the continuing operations section under a single-step format (SS), multiple-step (MS), both formats (B), or neither format (N).
    (*a*) Net sales
    (*b*) Gross profit
    (*c*) Gains that are not extraordinary
    (*d*) Extraordinary losses
    (*e*) Income taxes for a corporation
    (*f*) Operating income

14. Net income from continuing operations will be (greater/smaller/the same) when reported using the single-step format as compared to the multiple-step format.

Answers:

1. Revenue Earned − Expenses Incurred + Gains − Losses = Net Income earned during the accounting period [Section 6-1]
2. d [Section 6-2]
3. $500 [Section 6-2A]
4. $45,000 [Section 6-2C]
5. $5,300 [Section 6-3]
6. $5,000. This is a general expense of doing business and the amount will be expensed in the period incurred. [Section 6-3]
7. ($200)(10) = $2,000. This cost is systematically allocated. [Section 6-3]
8. production and sales (or operating); financing [Section 6-7A]
9. a. Date must define period for which profit is measured [Section 6-7A or 6-7B]
10. An accounting period is the time period covered by the income statement. [Section 6-1]
11. d [Section 6-7A]
12. Modified all-inclusive [Section 6-5]
13. (a) B   (c) B   (e) B
    (b) MS   (d) N   (f) MS [Section 6-7]
14. same [Section 6-7]

SOLVED PROBLEMS

PROBLEM 6-1: Acme Corporation was owed $10,400 by its customers as of the beginning of November. During November, the company collected $22,000 in cash from its customers. At the end of November, Acme Corporation's customers still owed the firm $14,200 on account. What were sales during the month of November?

Answer: You must determine the value of goods *delivered* during the month of November. This amount is not given in the problem, but you can determine it using the following reasoning. Customers made payments totaling $22,000. One can assume that $10,400 of the cash received was paid for goods delivered prior to November because customers owed that amount as of the beginning of the month. Of the $22,000 collected in cash then, $11,600 ($22,000 − $10,400) must have been paid for goods delivered during November. In addition, customers owed the firm $14,200 at the end of November. This amount must represent goods delivered during November for which the company has not received payment. The total value of goods delivered during November must be equal to $25,800, the value of the goods delivered for which payment was received plus the value of the goods delivered for which payment is expected in the future.   **[Section 6-2]**

PROBLEM 6-2: Apex Corporation began February with $4,900 of merchandise inventory. During the month, the company acquired $15,200 of additional merchandise. A count of the inventory indicated that at the end of the month $3,700 of inventory remained in the warehouse. What is the amount of cost of goods sold expense?

Answer: You must determine the cost of the goods that were delivered to customers during February. Cost of goods sold is an expense that can be directly matched with its related sales revenue. The firm began the month with $4,900 of inventory adding $15,200 to its stock during the month. The goods available for sale totaled $20,100, the sum of $4,900 and $15,200. By the end of the month, only $3,700 of the goods available for sale were left in the warehouse which suggests that $16,400 ($20,100 − $3,700) of goods were sold. You assume that any goods available for sale which are not left in the ending inventory have been sold.   **[Section 6-3]**

PROBLEM 6-3: Superior Corporation owed its merchandise supplier $7,800 at the beginning of June. During June, Superior Corporation paid $54,200 to its supplier but, at the end of the month, it still owed $4,400. How much merchandise was acquired by Superior Corporation during June? Will the number you compute to answer this problem appear as an expense on the income statement?

Answer: Of the $54,200 paid to the supplier, $7,800 must have settled the balance owed at the beginning of the month for merchandise that was delivered prior to June. Therefore, $46,400 ($54,200 − $7,800) of the cash expended must have been for merchandise acquired during June. In addition, the firm acquired $4,400 of goods that were not paid for during June because this amount is still owed to the merchandise supplier as of the end of June. Total goods acquired during June were $46,400 plus $4,400 equals $50,800. The expense for cost of goods sold measures the cost of the goods delivered to customers. This problem asked you to compute the cost of goods acquired by the company. The $50,800 does not represent an expense. You do not have enough information to compute the cost of goods sold expense.   **[Section 6-3]**

PROBLEM 6-4: In what part of the income statement will gains and losses which are not extraordinary or related to a discontinued operation appear, if the firm uses a multiple-step format and if the firm uses a single-step format?

Answer: Gains and losses which are not extraordinary or related to a discontinued operation will appear in the continuing operations section of the income statement. If the firm uses the multiple-step format the gains will be presented as Other Income; losses will appear as Other Expenses. If the firm uses the single-step format gains will be shown in the Revenue section and losses will appear in the Expense section.   **[Section 6-7]**

PROBLEM 6-5: Lantz Corporation shipped $3,000,000 in goods to credit customers during the past year. Of the goods shipped, $80,000 worth were returned because of damage. Due to strict credit standards, the corporation expects that only 1% of the accounts will prove to be uncollectible. What amount of revenue net of bad debt expense will Lantz recognize for the year?

Answer: To avoid overstating sales revenue and resulting profits, Lantz Corporation must reduce revenue by the value of the returned goods. The net sales totaled $2,920,000

($3,000,000 − $80,000). Bad debt expense equal to 1% of this amount must also be recognized. The bad debt expense will equal $29,200. The amount of revenue net of bad debt expense would therefore be $2,890,800 ($3,000,000 − $80,000 − $29,200). Note the importance of the order of calculation in this problem. Bad debt expense is computed on the basis of sales after reduction for returns. **[Section 6-2]**

PROBLEM 6-6: During the month of October, TLYC Corporation sold $185,650 in toys. Of this amount, $150,000 was collected in cash and the rest was still owed to the firm by its customers. The firm earned $150 in interest revenue from its overdue accounts receivable. The sales staff not only received salaries totaling $17,000, but they also received a 20% commission on each sale. Other operating expenses for the firm included $200 for utilities, $150 for advertising, $800 for rent, and $90,500, the actual cost of the toys sold. The firm owned store fixtures which cost $10,000 when purchased four years ago. These fixtures had a useful life of ten years with no estimated salvage value at the time they were purchased. The firm also incurred $700 of interest expense for the month. TLYC Corporation sold 100 shares of stock it was holding as an investment at a loss of $3,200. Prepare a single-step income statement for TLYC Corporation for the month of October, 19x1. You may omit the earnings per share section. The firm pays corporation income taxes equal to 40% of its net income before taxes and uses the straight-line method of depreciation.

Answer:

TLYC Corporation
Income Statement
For the Month Ended 10/31/x1

Revenue:		
Sales		$185,650
Interest Revenue		150
Total Revenue		$185,800
Expenses:		
Cost of Goods Sold	$90,500	
Commissions (.20 × $185,650)	37,130	
Salaries	17,000	
Utilities	200	
Advertising	150	
Rent	800	
Depreciation ($10,000/10)	1,000	
Interest Expense	700	
Loss on Sale of Stock	3,200	
Total Expenses		$150,680
Net Income Before Taxes		$ 35,120
Income Taxes		14,048
Net Income		$ 21,072

[Section 6-7B]

PROBLEM 6-7: Compute earnings per share, if TLYC Corporation described in Problem 6-6 had 10,000 shares of common stock outstanding throughout the year. The firm has no other securities outstanding.

Answer:

$$\text{EPS} = \frac{\text{Net Income}}{\text{Weighted Average \# Common Stock Shares Outstanding}}$$

$$= \frac{\$21,072}{10,000} = \$2.11 \text{ per share}$$

[Section 6-8]

PROBLEM 6-8: Prepare a multiple-step income statement for TLYC Corporation using the information given in Problems 6-6 above. You may omit the earnings per share section.

Answer:

TLYC Corporation
Income Statement
For the Month Ended 10/31/x1

Sales		$185,650
Less Cost of Goods Sold		90,500
Gross Profit		$ 95,150
Operating Expenses:		
Commissions	$37,130	
Salaries	17,000	
Utilities	200	
Advertising	150	
Rent	800	
Depreciation	1,000	
Total Operating Expenses		$ 56,280
Operating Income		$ 38,870
Other Income:		
Interest Income		150
		$ 39,020
Other Expenses:		
Loss on Sale of Stock	$ 3,200	
Interest Expense	700	
Total Other Expenses		3,900
Net Income Before Taxes		$ 35,120
Income Taxes		14,048
Net Income		$ 21,072

[Section 6-7A]

Problems 6-9, 6-10, and 6-11 refer to the information below:

Jones Company (not a corporation) began business on 1/1/x1 when Ms. Jones invested $10,000 in cash in the business. On 1/2/x1, the firm borrowed $5,000 from the bank. Interest of 10% per year is charged on the loan but will not be paid until the loan matures on 7/1/x2. The firm signed a two year lease for office space on 2/1/x1 paying the full amount in advance. One month's rent is $300. The company moved into the space rented as of 2/1/x1. Office equipment with a three year useful life and no salvage value was purchased for $3,600. Payment was made in cash on 2/1/x1 when the equipment was delivered to the new office. The company uses the straight-line depreciation method for office equipment.

Inventory costing $30,000 was acquired during the remainder of 19x1. The company paid its supplier $24,000 in cash. Sales totaling $45,000 were made to customers on credit. $32,000 was collected in cash from the customers, the balance was owed to Jones Company at the end of 19x1.

Jones Company paid the following in cash during the year: Wages $11,000; utilities $450; office supplies $300.

Unpaid bills in addition to the amount owed to the merchandise supplier were: to employees $500; to the power company $65; to office supplies company $200.

On 12/31/x1, an inventory count revealed that $7,000 of merchandise remained in the warehouse and $120 of office supplies were unused.

PROBLEM 6-9: Prepare a single-step income statement for Jones Company for the year ended 12/31/x1. Explain your computations. Jones Company is not subject to income taxes.

Answer:

Jones Company
Income Statement
For the Year Ended 12/31/x1

Sales		$45,000
Expenses:		
Cost of Goods Sold	$23,000	
Wages	11,500	
Rent	3,300	
Utilities	515	
Office Supplies	380	
Interest	500	
Depreciation	1,100	
Total Expenses		40,295
Net Income		$ 4,705

Computations:

(a) *Cost of goods sold.* The company acquired $30,000 of inventory. Of that amount, $7,000 was left in the warehouse as of year end. $23,000 ($30,000 − $7,000) of the inventory acquired must have been sold.

(b) *Wages.* The company paid $11,000 of wages in cash and owed $500 at the end of the year. It must have incurred wage expense of $11,500 ($11,000 + $500).

(c) *Rent.* Rent was $300 per month. The company used the space for 11 months so the rent expense for the year is $3,300 (11 × $300).

(d) *Utilities.* The company paid $450 to the utility company in cash and owed an additional $65. Utilities expense must have been $515 ($450 + $65).

(e) *Office Supplies.* The company acquired $300 of office supplies paying cash plus another $200 of office supplies on credit. At the end of the year, $120 of supplies were left. Office supplies used must be $380 ($300 + $200 − $120).

(f) *Interest.* The company borrowed $5,000 at 10% interest for the full year. Interest expense is $500 (.10 × 5,000 × 1).

(g) *Depreciation.* The company used its office equipment for 11 months. The equipment cost $3,600, has no salvage value, and is estimated to have a useful life of 3 years or 36 months. The depreciation expense per month is $100 per month $3,600/36 months. Depreciation for 11 months is $1,100 (11 × $100).   **[Sections 6-2, 6-3, 6-7A]**

PROBLEM 6-10: Ms. Jones notes that the net income of the firm is $4,705 but that the balance in the cash account is only $4,050. She wishes to withdraw the profits from the business, but cannot do so. Explain why net income does not measure the amount of cash available for withdrawal from the firm as of year end.

Answer: The revenue shown on an income statement measures the value of goods delivered, not the amount of cash collected from the customers. Only $32,000 was actually collected from the customers during 19x1. Customers still owed Jones Company $13,000. The expenses recognized on an income statement measure resources used up to produce revenue. Some expenses are paid for in advance of use, others are paid for after their use. The company paid $3,600 rent in advance, and has paid the supplier of merchandise $1,000 more than the amount listed as cost of goods sold expense. $3,600 was paid for equipment, but the equipment expenditure becomes an expense over the three year useful life of the equipment. The revenue recognition and matching principles are used to determine what items will appear on the income statement. The income statement does not measure cash receipts and cash disbursements.   **[Section 6-9]**

PROBLEM 6-11: Now assume that Jones Company is organized as a corporation — Jones Company, Incorporated. The corporation is subject to income taxes of 25% of income before taxes. There are 500 shares of stock outstanding during the entire year. Prepare an income statement for Jones Company, Incorporated including the earnings per share section.

Answer:

Jones Company, Incorporated
Income Statement
For the Year Ended 12/31/x1

Sales		$45,000
Less Expenses:		
Cost of Goods Sold	$23,000	
Wages	11,500	
Rent.	3,300	
Utilities.	515	
Office Supplies	380	
Interest.	500	
Depreciation	1,100	
Total Expenses.		$40,295
Net Income From Continuing Operations Before Taxes . .		$ 4,705
Income Taxes.		1,176
Net Income From Continuing Operations		$ 3,529
Earnings Per Share.		$ 7.06

[Section 6-7 and 6-8]

PROBLEM 6-12: J&B Corporation was owed $68,000 by its customers as of the beginning of May. During May, the company collected $81,000 in cash from its customers. At the end of May, J&B Corporation's customers still owed the firm $10,065 on account. What were sales during the month of May?

Answer: You must determine the value of goods *delivered* during the month of May. This amount is not given in the problem, but you can determine it using the following reasoning. Customers made payments totaling $81,000. One can assume that $68,000 of the cash received was paid for goods delivered prior to May because customers owed that amount as of the beginning of the month. Of the $81,000 collected in cash then, $13,000 ($81,000 − $68,000) must have been paid for goods delivered during May. In addition, customers owed the firm $10,065 at the end of November. This amount must represent goods delivered during May for which the company has not received payment. The total value of goods delivered during May must be equal to $23,065, the value of the goods delivered for which payment was received plus the value of the goods delivered for which payment is expected in the future. **[Section 6-2]**

7 INCOME STATEMENT (CONCLUDED) AND STATEMENT OF RETAINED EARNINGS

THIS CHAPTER IS ABOUT

- ☑ **An Income Statement Illustrating All Sections**
- ☑ **Discontinued Operations**
- ☑ **Extraordinary Items**
- ☑ **Cumulative Effect of a Change in Accounting Principle**
- ☑ **Reporting Earnings Per Share**
- ☑ **Statement of Retained Earnings**
- ☑ **Statement of Owners' Equity**
- ☑ **Combined and Condensed Statement**

7-1. Income Statement Illustrating All Sections

As mentioned in Chapter 6, the income statement may have five sections: continuing operations, discontinued operations, extraordinary items, cumulative effect of a change in accounting principle, and earnings per share. Exhibit 7-1, on the next page, is an example of an income statement which includes all five sections. All firms will report the results of continuing operations. Corporations whose stock or bonds are publicly traded will report EPS information. The other sections are used only under carefully defined circumstances to be discussed as the chapter progresses.

7-2. Discontinued Operations

If a firm plans to terminate operations of a *major segment* of the business, all activities concerning this segment must be reported in a special section of the income statement, Discontinued Operations. The information on the discontinued segment is reported separately from continuing operations so that the reader will exclude its net income (loss) in any calculations of the firm's expected future earnings.

A. The Discontinued Operations section is used only to disclose information concerning a *major* segment of the firm which will be terminating its operations.

Only major segments of a firm are included in the Discontinued Operations section of the income statement. For a segment to be classified as major it must

1. be an entire identifiable division of the firm
2. have its own assets, revenues, and expenses that can clearly be distinguished from the rest of the company.

The Discontinued Operations section is not used for disclosing the disposal of part or all of a product or service line, changes due to technological improvement, or a change in the location of operations.

EXAMPLE 7-1: Friendly Corporation went through a few structural changes during 19x5 since several areas of business had been progressively losing more and more money. As a result, the company first discontinued the F.C. 2000 series. The product was outdated.

Second, due to larger sales on the east coast and the increasing cost of shipment, the Heavy Division moved from California to New Jersey, Finally, Nasty Division, formerly the Nasty Company which Friendly Corporation took over ten years ago, was shut down completely and all its assets sold. Which of these activities will be reported in the Discontinued Operations section of the income statement?

An shown in Exhibit 7-1, only the termination of Nasty Division would be shown. The discontinuation of a product line, such as the F.C. 2000, does not qualify as a major segment of the firm. Moving Heavy Division from one location to another is not terminating its operations. Only Nasty Division is both a major business segment and one whose operations were terminated, not just relocated.

EXHIBIT 7-1: All-inclusive Income Statement

Friendly Corporation
Income Statement
For the Year Ended 12/31/x5

Revenue:		
Net Sales	$1,437,000	
Other Revenue	25,000	
Total Revenue		$1,462,000
Expenses:		
Cost of Goods Sold	$ 842,000	
Selling Expense	85,000	
Administrative Expense	92,000	
Interest Expense	61,000	
Total Expenses		1,080,000
Net Income From Continuing Operations before Taxes		$ 382,000
Income Taxes		153,000
Net Income From Continuing Operations		$ 229,000
Discontinued Operations:		
Income from Operations of Nasty Division (Net of $24,000 Tax)	$ 46,000	
Loss on Disposal of Nasty Division Including Provision for Loss of $30,000 on Operations during Phaseout Period (Net of $40,000 Tax Savings)	(60,000)	
Total Loss from Discontinued Operations		(14,000)
Income Before Extraordinary Items		$ 215,000
Extraordinary Item;		
Flood Loss (Net of $36,000 Tax Savings)		(54,000)
		$ 161,000
Cumulative Effect of Change in Accounting Principle:		
Cummulative Difference in Prior Years' Net Income Due to Change from Sum-of-Years' Digits to Straightline Depreciation (Net of $20,000 Income Tax)		30,000
Net Income		$ 191,000
Earnings Per Share: (100,000 shares outstanding)		
Net Income From Continuing Operations		$2.29
Discontinued Operations		(.14)
Income Before Extraordinary Item		$2.15
Extraordinary Item		(.54)
Cumulative Effect of Change in Accounting Principle		.30
Net Income		$1.91

B. The amounts shown in the Discontinued Operations section are based on the measurement date and the disposal date.

The **measurement date** is the date on which the company commits itself to a formal plan to dispose of the business segment. The **disposal date** is the date on which the assets are actually sold or abandoned. The period between these two dates is called the **phase-out period**.

1. *Prior to the measurement date.* The net income (loss) earned by the segment before the measurement date is reported on the income statement as the net income (loss) from operation of the segment.
2. *On the measurement date.* The net income (loss) for the phase-out period and the gain (loss) on the disposal of the assets are both estimated. If the total of these two estimates is a loss, it is recognized now and shown on the income statement as the loss on the disposal of the segment. If the total of the estimates is a gain, it cannot be recognized until the actual disposal takes place.
3. *On the disposal date.* Since the amounts computed on the measurement date are only estimates, more than likely an adjustment will have to be made to bring the actual and estimated amounts in line. The adjustment is made to the estimated loss recognized on the disposal date, if the measurement date and disposal dates fall into the same accounting period. The adjustment is reported as an additional gain (loss) on disposal of the segment, if the disposal occurs in a subsequent accounting period.

Since income taxes have already been computed on the income from continuing operations, the figures in the Discontinued Operations section must be computed net of their effect on taxes. The Discontinued Operations section of Exhibit 7-1 helps to illustrate these points.

EXAMPLE 7-2: On May 1, 19x5, XYZ Company committed itself to a plan to dispose of the assets of one its major segments, the CDE Division. It expected the sale of the assets to be complete on November 1, 19x5. During the first four months of 19x5, CDE had already lost $17,000 after taxes. On the measurement date, XYZ Company estimated that the division would lose an additional $40,000 after taxes and gain $10,000 on the sale of assets. On the actual disposal date, it was found that the gain on the sale of assets after taxes was only $8,000. The accountant turns the information over to you to interpret and report. How would you do it?

The measurement date is May 1, 19x5. The $17,000 loss that occurred before the measurement date should be reported as the loss from operation of the division. The estimated $40,000 loss during the phase-out period and the $10,000 gain on sale of the assets would be combined and recorded as the loss on the disposal of the division. Since the gain on the sale of the assets was not as much as expected, there would be an additional $2,000 *loss* recorded before the end of the accounting period.

The information would be disclosed on the income statement as follows:

Discontinued Operations:		
Loss from Operations of CDE Division.	$(17,000)	
Loss on Disposal of CDE Division Including Provision for Loss of $40,000 on Operations during Phase-out Period	(32,000)	
Total Loss from Discontinued Operations		$ 49,000

C. The sequence of activities in accounting for discontinued operations can be illustrated in a time line.

Exhibit 7-2 illustrates the accounting activities and reporting requirements for a company that decides to dispose of a major segment of its business.

EXHIBIT 7-2: Time Line for Discontinued Operations

1/1/x1	Measurement Date	Phase-out Period	Disposal Date *	12/31/x1

Income (Loss) on operations up to the measurement date is shown as Income (Loss) on Operation of (Discontinued Segment)

Estimated Gain (Loss) on Disposal is sum of:

1. Estimated profit (loss) on operations during phase-out period
2. Estimated profit (loss) on sale of assets

If 1 + 2 = loss, recognize loss on measurement date

If 1 + 2 = gain, do not recognize gain until disposal data

Actual Gain (Loss) on Disposal is sum of:

1. Actual profit (loss) on operation during phase-out period
2. Actual gain (loss) on sale of assets

Recognize actual gain

Adjust estimated loss so that total loss recognized equals actual loss.

* The disposal date may not fall in the same year as the measurement date as shown here.

EXAMPLE 7-3: Milktoast Corporation's board of directors voted unanimously to dispose of the firm's Zweiback Division. On March 31, 19x1, the corporation adopted a plan for the disposal, calling for the sale of all the division's assets. It is estimated that the sale of the assets will be completed by March 31, 19x2. During the first three months of 19x1, the Zweiback Division showed a net loss of $40,000. It is estimated that the firm will incur another $60,000 of operating losses between March 31, 19x1 and March 31, 19x2, and that the sale of the assets will involve an additional loss of $100,000. Milktoast will have to pay $75,000 in severance pay to the employees of the Zweiback Division who cannot be absorbed into the company's other divisions. The company's tax rate is 40%. How will Milktoast Corporation report the information about the Zweiback Division on its 19x1 income statement?

All information regarding Zweiback Division will appear in the Discontinued Operations section of the income statement. The loss incurred prior to the adoption of the disposal plan will appear as Loss from Operation of Zweiback Division (net the tax that would be saved). A $40,000 loss will provide a tax savings of $16,000 ($40,000 loss × .40 tax rate). Therefore, net loss from operations will be reported as $24,000 ($40,000 loss − $16,000 tax savings). Adding the estimated loss on operations between March 31, 19x1 and March 31, 19x2 of $60,000, the anticipated $100,000 loss on the sale of assets, and severance pay of $75,000 gives a loss on disposal of $235,000 before taxes. A $235,000 loss will result in a tax savings of $94,000. The net loss on disposal, therefore, is estimated to be $141,000 ($235,000 loss − $94,000 tax savings). The loss will be recognized on the measurement date and reported on the 19x1 income statement.

After all is done, the Discontinued Operations section will be presented as follows:

Discontinued Operations:
Loss from Operation of Zweiback Division. . . . . $(24,000)
Loss on Disposal of Zweiback Division including $60,000 loss on operations during the phase-out period (net of $94,000 tax savings) . . . . . . (141,000)

Total Loss from Discontinued Operations . . . . $(165,000)

Let's suppose the final accounting for the disposal indicates that the net loss from operations during the full phase-out period actually turned out to be $75,000. The loss on the sale of the assets was only $96,000, and the severance payments totaled $88,000. How will this information be presented on Milktoast Corporation's 19x2 income statement?

The actual loss on disposal of the Zweiback Division was $259,000 (the sum of the $75,000 operating loss, the $96,000 loss on the sale of assets, and the $88,000 of actual severance pay). The $259,000 loss yielded tax savings of $103,600, which is 40% of $259,000. The actual loss on disposal net of tax was therefore $155,400. The $141,000 recognized in 19x1 should be subtracted from this amount to get the loss to be recognized in 19x2 of $14,400. It would be recorded as follows:

Discontinued Operations:
Additional loss on disposal of Zweiback Division net of tax . . . . $(14,400)

7-3. Extraordinary Items

Extraordinary items are not to be confused with items classified as Other Revenue or Expenses. To be extraordinary, and event must be material in amount, unusual in nature, and nonrecurring. Many of the items that are classified as other revenue or other expenses have some but not all of these characteristics.

A. Extraordinary items are material to the decision-making process.

An item is material if specific knowledge of the item would make a difference in the judgments made by a reasonably informed user of the finanical statements. Determining whether an item is material is a subjective matter. An item that changes net income by 10% or more, or turns a net loss into a profit would generally be considered material. However, the are *no specific rules for deciding whether an item is material or not.*

B. Extraordinary items must generally be the result of highly abnormal events given the environment in which the firm operates.

An item must be unusual in nature to be classified as extraordinary. Determining whether an event is unusual requires that the firm's environment be taken into consideration. An event may be unusual to one company but not to another. A firm may not classify an item as extraordinary unless it is clearly outside that firm's normal course of business. This rule is intended to discourage firms from classifying all losses as extraordinary items leading the reader of the financial statement to disregard the loss in forecasting future earnings.

C. Extraordinary items relate to events that occur infrequently.

For an item to be extraordinary, the underlying circumstances must be ones that would not be expected to recur again in the foreseeable future considering the environment in which the firm operates. Once again the firm's unique situation must be considered.

D. Even though a event may be material, unusual, and nonrecurring, it may still be excluded from extraordinary treatment.

Some events may not be classified as extraordinary even though they meet all the requirements unless they are the direct result of a major casualty, expropriation, or prohibition under a newly enacted law. The APB lists six events in Opinion No. 30 that are generally excluded from extraordinary treatment.

1. Write-downs in the values of receivables, inventories, equipment leased to others, deferred research and development costs, or other intangible assets.
2. Gains or losses from the exchange or translation of foreign currencies, including those relating to major devaluations and revaluations.
3. Gains or losses on disposal of a segment of business.
4. Other gains or losses from the sale or abandonment of property, plant, or equipment used in the business.
5. Effects of a strike, including those against competitors and major suppliers.
6. Adjustments for accruals on long-term contracts.

(*Source:* "*Reporting the Results of Operations,*" *Opinions of the Accounting Principles Board No. 30, New York: AICPA 1973, para. 23.*)

Items in this list may be considered extraordinary only if they occur as the direct result of a major casualty (such as a volcanic eruption), expropriation (a government takeover of property), or as the result of prohibition or a change in the law which makes previously legal activities illegal (a patent on alcoholic beverages becomes worthless because a law prohibiting the sale of alcohol is passed).

EXAMPLE 7-4: XYZ Company owned a division located in Jamocha. The government of Jamocha enacted a law which required that 80% of any firm operating within its borders be locally owned. In response to the new law, XYZ Company adopted a plan to divest itself of the division. The firm sold 100% of its ownership of the division at a loss of $100,000 after taxes. How will the firm report the $100,000 loss?

Two treatments of this event seem possible. The sale might be presented in the Discontinued Operations section or it might be shown as an extraordinary item. The underlying event which created the loss was a change in the law which forced the firm to sell at least 80% of its ownership. Generally, a loss on the sale of stock would not be given extraordinary item status. Since this loss, however, is the result of a law prohibiting majority ownership by foreigners, it can be considered extraordinary.

The firm is also disposing of a major segment of the firm. As such, the loss might be presented in the Discontinued Operations section. One might argue that the circumstances surrounding the disposal suggest that this would not be appropriate. The firm did not dispose of the division because it was not making a profit or because it received an offer that was too good to refuse. The decision was based on a government action. The circumstances seem to weigh heavily toward reporting the sale as an extraordinary item.

E. The FASB has decreed that three items which *do not* meet all the requirements of an extraordinary item must be treated as such.

The various standard setting boards have defined the following three events as extraordinary even though they do not meet all the requirements:

1. gains or losses on early extinguishment of a debt
2. tax benefits of a loss carryforward
3. profit or loss on the disposal of a significant part of the assets acquired in a business combination under certain circumstances.

EXAMPLE 7-5: Monopolist, Inc. found that its inventory had lost 60% of its value when a competitor entered the market during 19x1. The president of the company argued that the write-down of the inventory value should be reported as an extraordinary item because it resulted from an unusual and nonrecurring event. The event was unusual because the firm had not had a viable competitor in the entire 105 years of its existence. The event was nonrecurring because the firm fully intended to eliminate or absorb the competitor within the next year. Do you agree with the president?

Write-downs of inventory are specifically excluded from extraordinary treatment unless they occur as a direct result of a major casualty, expropriation, or new prohibition in the law. The rules prevent Monopolist, Inc. from suggesting that the losses incurred in 19x1 should be discounted as unlikely to happen again.

EXAMPLE 7-6: Borrower Corporation was able to buy back $1,000,000 of its outstanding bonds at a discount, paying only $780,000. This gain on early extinguishment of debt resulted in increased taxes of $66,000. How should the event be reported on Borrower Corporation's income statement?

The gain should be reported as extraordinary even though early retirement of a debt is neither unusual nor is it nonrecurring. The FASB has decreed that gains and losses on early extinguishment of a debt be treated as an extraordinary item. The amount of the gain would equal $154,000 ($1,000,000 face value − $780,000 discounted price − $66,000 increase in taxes).

7-4. Cumulative Effect of a Change in Accounting Principle

A change in accounting principles not only effects the current accounting period. It also changes amounts reported in past accounting periods. The cumulative effect of a change in accounting methods is therefore reflected in a special section of the income statement.

A. A change in accounting principles effects the information reported in past accounting periods.

Most changes in accounting methods require a computation of what retained earnings would have been if the firm had used the newly adopted method since the inception of the company. Therefore, the Retained Earnings and asset balances must be adjusted. The adjustment required in Retained Earnings is reported on the income statement as Cumulative Effect of Change in Accounting Principle. The cumulative effect of the change in accounting principle is reported net of related tax effects.

EXAMPLE 7-7: Friendly Corporation has changed from sum-of-years' digits method to the straight line method of depreciation. If Friendly Corporation had used the straight-line method from the inception of the company's operations, it would have reported $50,000 of additional net income before taxes because depreciation deductions would have been less. If the firm had reported $50,000 of additional income, its income tax expense would have also increased by $20,000. How would Friendly Corporation report this information?

Friendly Corporation would have to correct the balance in its accumulated depreciation account and its deferred tax liability account at the time the cumulative effect of the change in accounting principle is recognized. The net effect of all changes would then be reported on the income statement. Since income would have been $50,000 higher and expenses would have been $20,000 higher, the net effect would be an increase of $30,000 in retained earnings. Therefore, the information would be reported as shown in Exhibit 7-1 in the section, Cumulative Effect of Change in Accounting Principle.

B. Changes in accounting principle should only happen occasionally.

One of the basic qualities desired in financial reporting is consistency. Frequent changes in accounting methods can eliminate the quality of consistency, if carried to an extreme. Changes in accounting principles should be made only if the newly adopted method more fairly presents the results of operations.

C. A change in accounting principles must not be made to enhance the image of the company.

The neutrality of reporting financial information is placed in question, if changes are made in accounting principle simply to make the company's financial status look better. Auditors are required to mention any changes in accounting principles in their reports and to indicate whether or not they concur with the change. Reporting the effects of such changes in a separate section of the income statement highlights the changes for readers.

7-5. Reporting Earnings Per Share

Earnings per share figures must be presented for the following amounts:

1. Income from Continuing Operations
2. Income before Extraordinary Items
3. Cumulative Effect of a Change in Accounting Principle
4. Net Income

Most companies also present earnings per share figures for discontinued operations and extraordinary items. Friendly Corporation, in Exhibit 7-1, computed its earnings per share by dividing its income figures by 100,000 shares of common stock outstanding.

7-6. Statement of Retained Earnings

The purpose of the statement of retained earnings is to explain the change in retained earnings over an accounting period.

A. The purpose of the statement of retained earnings is illustrated in its basic equation.

The basic equation for the statement of retained earnings is as follows

STATEMENT OF RETAINED EARNINGS EQUATION

$$\begin{array}{l}\text{Retained Earnings} \\ \text{(end of period)}\end{array} = \begin{array}{l}\text{Retained Earnings} \\ \text{(beg. of period)}\end{array} +(-) \begin{array}{l}\text{Prior Period} \\ \text{Adjustments}\end{array} +(-) \begin{array}{l}\text{Net} \\ \text{Income} \\ \text{(loss)}\end{array} - \text{Dividends}$$

Retained earnings are increased by profits and decreased by losses and dividend payments to stockholders. Sometimes adjustments will have to be made to the beginning balance of retained earnings to correct errors made in calculating prior periods' net income. The statement of retained earnings provides a link between beginning and ending balances in the retained earnings. The number that appears as the ending balance on the statement of retained earnings is the same amount that will appear on the balance sheet.

B. The statement of retained earnings has a very simple format.

The format of the statement of retained earnings is a simple vertical restatement of its basic equation with the respective amounts included. The heading lists the name of the firm, the name of the statement, and the period of time covered.

EXAMPLE 7-8: Friendly Corporation began the year with a balance of $42,000 in retained earnings. An error in the calculation of depreciation expense for 19x0 was discovered. If depreciation had been correctly computed the net income reported would have been $6,000 lower after taxes. During 19x5, the company earned $191,000 in net income and declared dividends totaling $120,000. Prepare the statement of retained earnings.

Exhibit 7-3 shows how the statement of retained earnings would appear.

EXHIBIT 7-3: Statement of Retained Earnings

Friendly Corporation
Statement of Retained Earnings
For the Year Ended 12/31/x5

Retained Earnings 1/1/x5	$ 42,000
Less Prior Period Adjustment — Error in Calculation of Depreciation 19x4 .	6,000
Adjusted Retained Earnings 1/1/x5.	$ 36,000
Add Net Income.	191,000
	$227,000
Less Dividends	120,000
Retained Earnings 12/31/x5	$107,000

7-7. Statement of Owners' Equity

The statement of owners' equity is similar to the statement of retained earnings. The only difference is that the statement of owners' equity is prepared for a noncorporate business. The equity accounts of such businesses do not separate direct investment from retained earnings. The owner's total financial contribution is reported in the capital account. The purpose of the statement of owners' equity is therefore to explain the change in the owner's capital account over an accounting period.

A. The purpose of the statement of owners' equity is illustrated in its basic equation.

The equation for the statement of owners' equity is as follows:

**STATEMENT OF OWNERS'
EQUITY EQUATION**

Capital (End of period)	=	Capital (Beg. of period)	+(−)	Prior Period Adjustments	+	Additional Investments	+(−)	Net Income (Loss)	− Withdrawals

The only real difference between this equation and that of the statement of retained earnings is that this equation includes investments made by the owner during the period.

B. The statement of owners' equity has a very simple format.

Just as the statement of retained earnings, the statement of owners' equity is a simple vertical restatement of its equation with the respective amounts included.

EXAMPLE 7-9: Keith Jackson owns Jackson Company. At the beginning of 19x1, the balance in his capital account was $45,000. During the year, Mr. Jackson invested an additional $2,500. The firm earned a net income of $22,000. Jackson made withdrawals totaling $20,500. Prepare his statement of owners' equity.

Exhibit 7-4 shows how the statement of owners' equity would appear.

EXHIBIT 7-4: Statement of Owners' Equity

Jackson Company
Statement of Owners' Equity
For the Year Ended 12/31/x1

Jackson, Capital 1/1/x1	$45,000
Add: Investments	2,500
Net Income	22,000
	$69,500
Deduct Withdrawals	20,500
Jackson, Capital 12/31/x1	$49,000

7-8. Combined and Condensed Statements

Many members of the profession present the statement of retained earnings as part of the income statement. The primary reason for combining the statements is to bring these closely related groups of information together in one place for the user's convenience. Other members of the profession feel that the statements should be as condensed as possible, presenting only the most important figures and using supplements and footnotes to show any other information.

RAISE YOUR GRADES

Can you explain...?

☑ what information appears in the Discontinued Operations section of the income statement

☑ what information appears in the Extraordinary Items section of the income statement

☑ what the amount listed as the cumulative effect of a change in accounting principles measures

☑ the equation for the statement of retained earnings

☑ the equation for the statement of owners' equity

☑ what is meant by a combined statement

SUMMARY

1. Information concerning the activities of a major segment of a firm whose operations are being terminated are disclosed in the Discontinued Operations section of the income statement.
2. For a division to be considered a major segment of the firm it must be completely identifiable and have its own assets, revenues, and expenses separate from the firm's.
3. The measurement date is the date on which the firm commits itself to a formal plan to dispose of a major business segment.
4. The disposal date is the date on which the assets of the major business segment are actually sold.
5. The phase-out period is the time between the measurement date and the disposal date.
6. Income earned by the discontinued segment prior to the measurement date is reported as its Income from Operations in the discontinued operations section of the income statement.
7. Income earned by the discontinued segment during the phase-out period plus any gain or loss on the sale or abandonment of its assets are totaled and reported as a gain or loss on the disposal of the segment.
8. For an item to be considered extraordinary, it must be material in amount, unusual in nature, and nonrecurring.
9. Even though some events may meet all the requirements of an extraordinary item, they may be excluded from such treatment unless they are the result of a major casualty, expropriation, or prohibition under a newly enacted law.
10. The FASB has decreed that gains (losses) on early extinguishment of a debt, tax benefits of a loss carryforward, and gains (losses) on the disposal of a significant part of the assets acquired in a business combination under certain circumstances can be given extraordinary treatment.
11. Changes in accounting principles should only happen occasionally and then only if it can be proved that the newly adopted method more fairly reports the results of operations.
12. Accounting principles may not be changed merely to enhance the company's financial image.
13. The cumulative difference in prior years' net income due to a change in accounting methods net of taxes is reported in a separate section of the income statement following extraordinary items.
14. The purpose of the statement of retained earnings is to explain the total change in the balance of retained earnings over a period of time.
15. The purpose of the statement of owners' equity is to explain the change in the balance of owners' equity over a period of time.

RAPID REVIEW

1. List the sections of the income statement in the order in which they would appear on the income statement.
2. Which of the following terminations would be reported in the Discontinued Operations section of the income statement?
   (*a*) Termination of a donut line by a cake manufacturer.
   (*b*) Termination of plant's operations in Hoboken. The firm moved these operations to South Dakota.
   (*c*) Termination of the fast food restaurant division by a manufacturer of toys.
   (*d*) Termination of an outdated steel plant by a steel manufacturer.
   (*e*) All of the above would qualify.

Questions 3-8 refer to the information below.

On April 1, 19x1, Shifty Corporation adopted a plan to dispose of the assets of the Straightforward Division, a clearly identifiable division of the firm. The assets were expected to be sold by June 1, 19x1. During 19x1, prior to the adoption of the plan, the

Straightforward Division reported a net loss of $5,000 after taxes. The accountant estimates that Straightforward will suffer a loss of $15,000 after taxes from operations during the phase-out period and lose $17,000 after taxes on the sale of the assets.

3. The measurement date is _____?

4. The "Loss from Operations of Straightforward Division" reported on the 19x1 income statement will be _____.

5. The "Loss on Disposal of Straightforward Division" reported on the 19x1 income statement will be _____.

6. The year in which the loss of the disposal of Straightforward Division will be recognized is _____.

7. The Total from Discontinued Operations reported on the 19x1 income statement will be _____.

8. The Earnings per Share from Discontinued Operations reported on the 19x1 income statement will be _____, if the firm has 5,000 common shares outstanding throughout the year.

Questions 9-11 refer to the information below.

On January 1, 19x1, Lucky Corporation adopted a plan to dispose of the assets of Ducky division. The assets are expected to be sold by May 31, 19x2. On January 1, 19x1, the firm estimates that the Ducky Division will earn a net profit of $40,000 during the phase-out period. The assets will be sold at a net loss of $62,000. The firm's tax rate is 40%.

9. What amount will be reported as the "Income from Operations of Ducky Division" on the 19x1 income statement?

10. What gain or loss from the disposal will appear on the 19x1 income statement?

11. What additional gain or loss from disposal will appear on the 19x2 income statement, if the sale of assets actually results in the loss of $68,000 rather than $62,000?

12. Which of the following item(s) would be given extraordinary treatment? (All losses may be assumed to be material in amount.)
    (a) The eruption of Mount St. Rushmore causes $50,000 damage to a firm's headquarters building.
    (b) A sudden improvement in technology makes much of the firm's inventory obsolete and less valuable.
    (c) The firm loses $1,000,000 when its employees go on strike.
    (d) The firm loses $1,000,000 when anti-firm demonstrators organize a boycott of the firm's products.
    (e) The government of Chihuahua expropriates the firm's property.
    (f) Frost destroys a banana crop in South America. The temperatures experienced were the coldest in the past 150 years.

13. Earnings per share figures must be presented for four income figures if all sections of the income statement are included. List the income amounts for which earnings per share must be computed and reported.

14. What is the equation for the statement of retained earnings?

15. Joe Jones had a balance of $40,000 in his capital account at the beginning of the year. He made no additional investments in the firm during the year. The firm earned net income of $26,000. By year-end, the balance of his capital account was $50,000. How much did Joe withdraw from the business during the year?

Answers:

1. Continuing Operations; Discontinued Operations; Extraordinary Items; Cumulative Effect of a Change in Accounting Principle; Earnings Per Share. [Section 7-1]
2. (c) [Section 7-2A]
3. April 1, 19x1 [Section 7-2B]
4. $5,000 [Section 7-2B]

5. $32,000 [Section 7-2B]
6. 19x1 [Section 7-2B]
7. $37,000 loss [Section 7-2B]
8. $7.40 loss [Section 7-5]
9. $0 [Section 7-2B]
10. 13,200 loss. Hint: don't forget to include related tax effects. [Section 7-2B]
11. $3,600 loss [Section 7-2B]
12. (a), (e), and (f) [Section 7-3]
13. Income from Continuing Operations; Income before Extraordinary Items; Cumulative Effect of a Change in Accounting Principle; Net Income [Section 7-5]
14. Retained Earnings (end) = Retained Earnings (beg.) +(−) Prior Adjustments + Net Income − Dividends [Section 7-6]
15. $16,000 Section [7-7]

SOLVED PROBLEMS

PROBLEM 7-1: McGowan Manufacturers decided to terminate operations in its small amusement park in Missouri. With the money from the sale of the park the firm planned to pay off some long-term debts early for an additional gain. Meanwhile, word was received that conflict had broken out on Mathis Islands, where the company has a plant, and all of the firm's property was taken over by the government and operations were discontinued. How would each of these three events be handled on the income statement?

Answer: The termination of the park operations would be listed in the Discontinued Operations section. Since amusement service is much different than manufacturing, the operations must be entirely identifiable and have separate assets, revenue, and expenses from those of the firm. The pay-off of long-term debts would qualify for extraordinary status by decree of the FASB. Even though the firm discontinued operations on Mathis Islands, the termination was due to expropriation. Therefore, this item would be treated as extraordinary rather than be included in the Discontinued Operations section of the income statement. **[Section 7-2 and 7-3]**

PROBLEM 7-2: On July 1, 19x1, Albatross Corporation adopted a plan to dispose of one of its major segments, Ostrich Division. The plan called for operating the division through March 31, 19x2, when all the assets would be sold. During the first six months of the year, Ostrich Division reported a net profit of $25,000 before taxes. The firm estimates that the division will report an additional profit of $36,000 before taxes during the phase-out period; however, the assets will be sold at a loss of $150,000 before taxes. In addition, the Albatross Corporation will pay early retirement bonuses totaling $50,000 to the division's executives who cannot be used elsewhere in the company. Assuming that the tax rate is 40%, present the Discontinued Operations section of the income statement for 19x1.

Answer:

Discontinued Operations:	
Net Income From Operation of Ostrich	
Division (Net of $10,000 Income Tax)	$ 15,000
(Loss) on Disposal of Ostrich Division	
Including Provision for Net Income of $36,000 on Operations During the	
Phase-out Period (Net of $65,600 of Tax Savings)	(98,400)
Total From Discontinued Operations	$(83,400)

The net income earned by the division before the measurement date, July 31, 19x1, is presented as Net Income from Operation of Ostrich Division and is shown net of taxes. The amount of tax is $10,000 ($25,000 × 40%). The amount shown as the Loss on Disposal of Ostrich Division is the sum of the profit the firm expects the division to earn during the phase-out period, $36,000, minus the loss it expects to incur on the sale of the assets, $150,000, and the early retirement expenditure, $50,000. The total estimated loss of $164,000 is reported net of its tax savings of $65,600 ($164,000 × 40%).   **[Section 7-2]**

PROBLEM 7-3: On December 31, 19x1, Movin On Corporation decided to adopt a formal plan to dispose of one of its major segments, the Slow-n-Steady Division. The sale of assets is expected to be complete by June 30, 19x2. For the year 19x1 the division reported a profit of $50,000 before taxes. The division expects to earn an additional $30,000 during the first six months of 19x2 before taxes. Its assets are expected to be sold at a profit of $100,000, again, before taxes. Assuming that the tax rate is 40%, how will this information appear on Movin On's 19x1 income statement?

Answer:

Discontinued Operations:

Net Income From Operation of Slow-n-Steady Division (Net of $20,000 of Income Taxes)	$30,000
Total From Discontinued Operations.	$30,000

The firm is estimating a net gain on both the operations and sale of the division. The gain on the sale will not be recognized until the sale is complete. Therefore, in 19x1, only the net income from the operation of the division will be reported.

In Problems 7-4 through 7-8, determine whether the event should be reported on the income statement in the Continuing Operations section, Discontinued Operations section, Extraordinary Items section, or the Cumulative Effect of a Change in Accounting Principle section. Explain your answer.

PROBLEM 7-4: The firm is forced to write-down the value of its accounts receivables due to a major slow-down in the economy. The firm blames government policy for the recession.

Answer: The write-down will appear in the Continuing Operations section of the income statement. Extraordinary item status cannot be given to a write-down of receivables unless the write-down is the direct result of a major casualty, expropriation, or prohibition in a newly enacted law. Write-downs of accounts receivables are neither unusual nor infrequent.   **[Section 7-3D]**

PROBLEM 7-5: A firm decides to change its method for costing inventory. This change causes retained earnings to increase by $500,000. The firm feels strongly that the change more fairly reflects operations.

Answer: The effect on retained earnings will be presented net of taxes in the Cumulative Effect of a Change in Accounting Principle section. The firm is changing accounting methods for a good reason. It must therefore revalue its assets and liabilities to adjust the account balances to what they would have been had the FIFO method been used since the company's inception.   **[Section 7-4]**

PROBLEM 7-6: Toys, Inc. decides to stop producing Cooters, one of its major lines of toys. The abandonment of the Cooter product line is a material event.

Answer: The loss will appear in the Continuing Operations section of the income statement. The Discontinued Operations section is not the proper place to present this loss since it is the disposal of a product line not a division with its own assets, revenues, and expenses.   **[Section 7-2A]**

PROBLEM 7-7: The firm decides to stop producing toys. It sells its toy division to a competitor at a profit.

Answer: The gain on sale of the division will appear in the discontinued operations section of the income statement. The firm is selling what appears to be a major division of the company.   **[Section 7-2A]**

Problem 7-8: Which of the following would be classified as extraordinary items? Defend your classification in each case. You may assume that the amounts involved are material.

(*a*) $500,000 of bonds payable are settled with a cash payment of $525,000.
(*b*) War breaks out in the Recuta. The firm's property in that country is totally destroyed.
(*c*) The firm has major investments in France. A major devaluation of French currency occurs creating a large loss to the firm.
(*d*) The firm is involved in a major long-term contract with a purchaser. The purchaser unexpectedly declares bankruptcy causing a major loss to the firm.

Answer:

(*a*) The loss on early extinguishment of the bonds will be presented as an extraordinary item. The FASB has decreed that material gains or losses on early extinguishment of debt be treated as extraordinary items.   **[Section 7-3E]**
(*b*) The loss will be treated as an extraordinary item. Firms would not be expected to invest in areas where war is a common hazzard. Being caught in a war zone should be unusual and should not occur frequently.   **[Section 7-3D]**
(*c*) Loss or gain due to devaluation or revaluation of foreign currencies is specifically excluded from extraordinary item treatment.   **[Section 7-3D]**
(*d*) Write-downs of receivables, even major ones, are excluded from extraordinary item classification unless they are the result of a major casualty, expropriation, or a newly enacted prohibition in the law. This write-down will not receive extraordinary item treatment.   **[Section 7-3D]**

PROBLEM 7-9: Compute the missing amount in each of the following independent cases.

	a	b	c
Retained Earnings 1/1/x1	10,000	6,000	?
Prior Period Adjustments	(3,000)	0	2,000
Net Income	15,000	?	15,000
Dividends	?	1,000	20,000
Retained Earnings 12/31/x1	9,000	3,000	5,000

Answer: Answering this question requires finding the missing parts of the equation for the statement of retained earnings. The equation for the statement of retained earnings is:

Retained	Retained	+ Prior	Net
Earnings =	Earnings (−)	Period +	Income − Dividends
(End)	(Beg.)	Adj.	

(*a*) 9,000 = 10,000 − 3,000 + 15,000 − X
   X = 10,000 − 3,000 + 15,000 − 9,000 = 13,000
Dividends declared are equal to $13,000
(*b*) 3,000 = 6,000 + 0 + X − 1,000
   −X = 6,000 + 0 − 1,000 − 3,000
   −X = 2,000 therefore X = −2,000
The company suffered a net loss of $2,000
(*c*) 5,000 = X + 2,000 + 15,000 − 20,000
   −X = 2,000 + 15,000 − 20,000 − 5,000
   −X = −8,000 therefore X = 8,000
The firm began the period with $8,000 in retained earnings.   **[Section 7-6]**

PROBLEM 7-10: Listed below are the revenues and expenses for Brown Corporation as of December 31, 19x5. In addition, Brown discontinued a major segment of its business the Bear Division. The income before adoption of a disposal plan was $60,000. The loss on disposal of the division was $100,000, including a loss of $30,000 on operations during the phase-out period. A fire destroyed a section of the corporation's warehouse. Damages totaled $90,000. The company also changed from sum-of-years' digits to straight-line depreciation. The effect was an increase in reported income of $50,000.

Net Sales	$2,500,000
Other Revenue	125,000
Cost of Goods Sold	792,000
Selling Expense	35,000
Administrative Expense	42,000
Interest Expense	11,000
Total Expenses	880,000
Income Taxes	698,000

Prepare an all-inclusive income statement for Bear Corporation. Assume the firm's tax rate is 40%. There were 100,000 shares of stock outstanding throughout the year.

Answer:

Brown Corporation
Income Statement
For the Year Ended 12/31/x5

Revenue:		
Net Sales	$2,500,000	
Other Revenue	125,000	
Total Revenue		$2,625,000
Expenses:		
Cost of Goods Sold	$ 792,000	
Selling Expense	35,000	
Administrative Expense	42,000	
Interest Expense	11,000	
Total Expenses		880,000
Net Income From Continuing Operations Before Taxes		$1,745,000
Income Taxes		698,000
Net Income From Continuing Operations		$1,047,000
Discontinued Operations:		
Income from Operations of Bear Division (Net of $24,000 Tax)	$ 36,000	
Loss on Disposal of Bear Division $100,000 Including Loss of 30,000 on Operations during Phase-Out Period (Net of $40,000 Tax Savings)	(60,000)	
Total Loss from Discontinued Operations		(24,000)
Income Before Extraordinary Items		$1,023,000
Extraordinary Item;		
Fire Loss (Net of $36,000 Tax Savings)		(54,000)
		$ 969,000
Cumulative Effect of Change in Accounting Principle:		
Cumulative Difference in Prior Year's Net Income Due to Change from Sum-of-Years' Digits to Straight-line Depreciation (Net of $20,000 Income Tax)		30,000
Net Income		$ 999,000
Earnings Per Share: (100,000 shares outstanding)		
Net Income After Taxes		$10.47
Discontinued Operations		(.24)
Income Before Extraordinary Item		$10.23
Extraordinary Item		(.54)
Income Before Cumulative Effect of Change in Accounting Principle		$ 9.69
Cumulative Effect of Change in Accounting Principle		.30
Net Income		$ 9.99

[Section 7-1 through Sections 7-5]

PROBLEM 7-11: Brown Corporation, Problem 7-10, had a balance in its retained earnings account of $85,000 at the beginning of 19x5. During the year, it was discovered that depreciation expense for 19x2 was computed to be $5,000 higher than it was. The company also paid $500,000 in dividends. Prepare the statement of retained earnings for Brown Corporation.

Answer:

Brown Corporation
Statement of Retained Earnings
For the Year Ended 12/31/x5

Retained Earnings 1/1/x5	$ 85,000
Prior Period Adjustment-Error in 19x2 depreciation	5,000
Adjusted Retained Earnings 1/1/x5	$ 90,000
Add Net Income	999,000
	$1,089,000
Less Dividends	500,000
Retained Earnings 12/31/x5	$ 589,000

[Section 7-6]

PROBLEM 7-12: David Lantz Company earned $65,000 during the year 19x6. On March 1, Mr. Lantz invested an additional $2,000 in the company. His salary was taken out as a withdrawal of $20,000. Prepare the capital statement for the David Lantz Company, if the balance in the capital account was $50,000 at the beginning of the year.

Answer:

David Lantz Company
Statement of Owner's Equity
For the Year Ended 12/31/x6

Lantz, Capital 1/1/x6	$ 50,000
Add: Investments	2,000
Net Income	65,000
	$117,000
Deduct Withdrawals	20,000
Lantz, Capital 12/31/x6	$ 97,000

[Section 7-7]

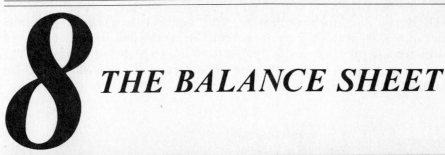

8 THE BALANCE SHEET

THIS CHAPTER IS ABOUT

☑ **The Purpose of the Balance Sheet**
☑ **The Balance Sheet Format**
☑ **Assets**
☑ **Liabilities**
☑ **Owners' Equity**
☑ **Working Capital**
☑ **Net Assets**
☑ **Common Misconceptions about the Balance Sheet**
☑ **Financing Ratios**

8-1. The Purpose of the Balance Sheet

The purpose of the balance sheet, simply stated, is to show the balance between what is owned (assets) and what is owed, either to creditors (liabilities) or the owners (equity). This is illustrated in the balance sheet equation. (*Note:* the balance sheet equation is the same as the basic accounting equation.)

BALANCE SHEET EQUATION   **Assets = Liabilities + Owners' Equity**

The balance sheet reports a firm's financial position at one particular point in time. It is as if the accountant took a snapshot and froze the financial picture for an instant. For this reason, the balance sheet is also known as the **statement of financial position**.

8-2. The Balance Sheet Format

Exhibit 8-1, on the next page, shows the balance sheet format used by XYZ Corporation. This is known as the **account form** of balance sheet because the arrangement of the information is similar to that of a T account. Notice that assets are listed on the left side of the form and liabilities and owners' equity are listed on the right side of the form just as they appear with respect to the equal sign in the balance sheet equation. Exhibit 8-2 shows the same balance sheet in report form. The **report form** of balance sheet simply lists all items in a vertical arrangement.

8-3. Assets

Assets are defined as economic resources which are controlled by a firm, have reasonable probability of producing future benefits, and whose values have been established by a transaction that has already taken place. The future benefit may be the right to receive cash or the right to exclusive use of an item for a specified period of time (competitive advantage). Note that the definition does not suggest that the item must really be owned to be claimed as an asset. The firm must simply have control or access.

EXHIBIT 8-1: Balance Sheet—Account Form

XYZ Corporation
Balance Sheet
December 31, 19x1

ASSETS

Current Assets:	
Cash	$ 50,000
Marketable Securities	4,800
Accounts Receivable (net of $5,000 allowance for uncollectibles)	115,000
Notes Receivable	6,000
Inventories	85,000
Supplies	8,500
Prepaid Insurance	1,200
Total Current Assets	$270,500
Long-term Investments:	
Common Stock—ABC Company (at cost)	$ 12,000
Plant, Property, and Equipment:	
Land	$ 55,000
Building (net of $32,000 accumulated depreciation)	118,000
Equipment (net of $85,000 accumulated depreciation)	80,000
Total Plant, Property, and Equipment	$253,000
Intangible Assets:	
Patent	$ 38,000
Total Assets	$573,500

LIABILITIES

Current Liabilities:	
Notes Payable	$ 70,000
Accounts Payable	85,000
Income Taxes Payable	10,000
Wages Payable	6,200
Unearned Revenue (advances from customers)	800
Total Current Liabilities	$172,000
Long-term Liabilities:	
Bonds Payable	$100,000
Deferred Income Taxes	50,000
Total Long-term Liabilities	$150,000
Total Liabilities	$322,000

STOCKHOLDERS' EQUITY

Paid-in Capital:	
Common Stock($10 par value)	$100,000
Capital Contributed in Excess of Par Value	44,000
Total Paid-in Capital	$144,000
Retained Earnings	107,500
Total Stockholders' Equity	$251,500
Total Liabilities and Stockholders' Equity	$573,500

EXHIBIT 8-2: Balance Sheet—Report Form

XYZ Corporation
Balance Sheet
December 31, 19x1

ASSETS

Current Assets
Cash.	$ 50,000	
Marketable Securities	4,800	
Accounts Receivable (net of $5,000 Allowance for uncollectible accounts)	115,000	
Notes Receivable.	6,000	
Inventories	85,000	
Supplies	8,500	
Prepaid Insurance	1,200	
Total Current Assets.		$270,500

Long-term Investments:
Common Stock—ABC Company (at cost)		12,000

Plant, Property, and Equipment:
Land.	$ 55,000	
Building (net $32,000 accumulated depreciation)	118,000	
Equipment (net $85,000 accumulated depreciation)	80,000	
Total Plant, Property, and Equipment.		253,000

Intangible Assets:
Patent.		38,000
Total Assets		$573,500

LIABILITIES

Current Liabilities:
Notes Payable.	$ 70,000	
Accounts Payable	85,000	
Income Taxes Payable.	10,000	
Wages Payable	6,200	
Unearned Revenue (Advances from Customers)	800	
Total Current Liabilities		$172,000

Long-term Liabilities:
Bonds Payable	$100,000	
Deferred Income Taxes	50,000	
Total Long-term Liabilities		150,000
Total Liabilities		$322,000

STOCKHOLDERS' EQUITY

Paid-In Capital:
Common Stock ($10 par value)	$100,000	
Capital Contributed in Excess of Par Value	44,000	
Total Paid-in Capital.		$144,000
Retained Earnings.		107,500
Total Stockholders' Equity.		$251,500
Total Liabilities and Stockholders' Equity.		$573,500

A. Assets are classified on the balance sheet as either current or non-current.

Current assets are those which are expected to be turned into cash or used up within one year or an operating cycle, *whichever is longer*. The **operating cycle** is the average length of time required to convert raw materials into a finished product, sell that product to a customer, and receive payment. **Non-current assets** are those which are not expected to be turned into cash or used up in the near future. Non-current assets are also referred to a **long-term assets**.

EXAMPLE 8-1: REW Manufacturing Company has an operating cycle of 18 months. Most customers give the company a two-year note payable for the merchandise. The accountant classifies all notes payable as long-term until their due date is a year or less away. Is the accountant correct?

No. Even though 18 months does not seem like a short term, it is for this company. Only those items due in more than 18 months should be classified as non-current or long-term.

B. Proper classification of assets as current and non-current is very important.

It is assumed that the current assets will be used to meet the current debts or liabilities. Therefore, if a company is to stay in business, current assets must be greater than current liabilities. Financial analysts and creditors pay close attention to what items are classified as current and non-current. This enables them to assess the firm's ability to pay back debts as they fall due. Because some firms try to overstate current assets and understate current liabilities to appear less risky, the FASB has established guidelines for determining what assets and liabilities can be classified as long-term.

C. Assets are generally valued on the balance sheet in relation to their original cost (historical-cost principle).

The historical-cost principle dictates that assets be valued on the balance sheet at what the company paid for them, not at the amount for which they could be sold.

1. *Cash.* Cash is the sum of cash on hand plus cash in the bank. Some portion of cash may be restricted as to its use. In such cases, the restricted portion of cash should be reported separately with the nature of the restrictions fully disclosed.
2. *Marketable Securities.* Both short- and long-term investments in marketable securities where the firm does not influence the investee, are valued at cost unless the current market value has fallen to an amount less than cost. If current market value is less than cost, the market value of securities is placed on the balance sheet. This type of valuation is referred to as **lower of cost or market value**. This variation from the historical-cost principle is justified by the exception principle allowing for conservatism in valuing assets.
3. *Accounts Receivable.* Accounts receivable are amounts owed to a firm by its customers. Based on its own past experience or the experience of similar businesses, a firm knows that not all credit accounts will be collected. In order to be conservative in reporting Accounts Receivable, a firm must therefore allow for estimated uncollectible accounts on the balance sheet.
4. *Notes Receivable.* Notes receivable are amounts owed to a firm under a more formal arrangement than an account receivable. The firm receives a signed note from the creditor acknowledging the amount owed and the conditions under which the amount will be repaid. Notes receivable are also valued net of estimated uncollectible amounts.
5. *Inventories.* Inventories include finished goods for resale, raw materials to be used in production, and/or goods in the process of production. Inventories may be valued at cost or at lower of cost or market. If lower of cost or market is chosen, the accountant will compare the original cost of the inventory to its replacement cost (called market). The value that appears on the balance sheet will be the lower of the two numbers.

EXAMPLE 8-2: At the end of 19x1, Speedy Calc, Inc. has 10 micro-computers in its inventory. The firm originally paid $1,500 for each of the computers. Due to the incredibly quick advancements in the computer industry these computers are outdated and only have a value on the market of $1,000 each. The micro-computers would then be valued at $1,000 each using lower of cost or market valuation on the balance sheet. Their value in the company books would remain unchanged at $1,500 each.

6. *Supplies*. Supplies are goods held for internal use, such as paper, forms, pencils. These items are valued at cost.
7. *Prepaid Insurance*. Prepaid Insurance is insurance coverage paid in advance. It is a type of account receivable, only the firm expects to receive services over a period time rather than cash. As time passes, the amount of service remaining decreases and likewise the value of the account. The value of this account is the cost of the services paid for but not yet received.
8. *Land*. Land is valued at cost. Land usually increases in market value. The accountant may not report this higher value on the balance sheet. Reporting the higher value would violate the historical-cost principle and would not concur with conservative reporting.
9. *Buildings and Equipment*. Buildings and equipment will eventually wear out with use or become outdated because of technological advancements. The accountant must recognize that the benefits to be received from these assets will decrease with time, leaving the asset with little or no value to the firm. Each year the value assigned to buildings and equipment is systematically reduced so the value assigned to the asset at its time of disposal equals its estimated scrap (or salvage) value. This systematic reduction in value is called **depreciation**. Buildings and equipment are reported at cost less the estimate of the depreciation accumulated up to the balance sheet date.

EXAMPLE 8-3: On January 1, 19x1, Transit Corporation purchases a truck at a cost of $10,000. The truck will be used for three years at which time the company estimates that it will be sold for $1,000. The company computes depreciation using the straight-line method as formulized below.

STRAIGHT-LINE DEPRECIATION FORMULA

$$\frac{\text{Depreciation for each}}{\text{accounting period}} = \frac{\text{cost} - \text{salvage value}}{\text{number of accounting periods item to be used}}$$

What value should be reported on the balance sheets for each of the three years the truck is in use?

The depreciation for each year would equal the $10,000 cost less $1,000 salvage value, the difference then being divided by 3, the number of accounting periods in the truck's useful life. The annual depreciation is therefore $3,000.

	19x1	19x2	19x3
Cost or Reported Value at the beginning of the year	$10,000	$7,000	$4,000
Less depreciation	3,000	3,000	3,000
Reported value at the end of the year	$ 7,000	$4,000	$1,000

(It is important to remember here that the value shown does not represent what the asset could be sold for.)

10. *Intangible Assets*. Intangible assets have no physical substance. Often there is considerable uncertainty as to the amount of future benefit to be expected. For example, a patent gives the holder the right to exclusive use of a product or process for a certain period of time. Its real value to the holder is the competitive advantage and additional profits that can be made because of this exclusive use. Establishing a real value for intangible assets would require a subjective estimate of future profits. Such subjective measures are rarely allowed in accounting. Intangible assets are therefore valued at cost including legal expenses associated

with acquiring and defending them. The value of a patent does include the cost of research and development of the respective product or process. Research and development costs are expensed because at the time such costs are incurred there is no guarantee that they will lead to a valuable discovery.

8-4. Liabilities

Liabilities are debts owed by a firm. A liability is a legal obligation to pay a debt by delivering goods or cash or rendering services at some future date. A liability is the result of a transaction which has taken place and therefore represents a future payment that the firm expects to make.

A. Liabilities are classified on the balance sheet as current or non-current.

Current liabilities are debts which must be settled within one year or the operating cycle, whichever is the longer period. The current liability section of Exhibit 8-2 shows several different types of current liabilities. The titles given to the accounts often indicate to whom the debt is owed. Accounts and notes payable are usually owed to general creditors and suppliers. Taxes payable are owed to a governmental unit. Wages payable are owed to the firm's employees. Unearned revenue includes amounts owed to the firm's customers which will be settled by delivering goods or services and not cash. Non-current or long-term debts are debts which are not expected to be settled in the near future. Some debts are paid off on an installment basis. That portion of the debt due within one year or the operating cycle, whichever is longer, should be classified as a current liability; the remainder should be classified as non-current.

B. A liability may be classified as a deferred credit.

Some debts are extremely long term in nature. The company probably does not expect to settle these debts until it goes out of business. Such debts are classified as deferred credits. There is considerable controversy over whether deferred credits should even be listed as liabilities since the probability of them being settled is so low. Deferred income taxes often fall into this category. Note that in Exhibit 8-1, income taxes appear as a liability in two categories. The amount of deferred income taxes in the long-term liability sections arises because of certain legal differences between the amount of income reported to the government for tax purposes and the amount reported to the stockholders. More than likely, the balance in the account will not be paid in the foreseeable future.

C. Liabilities are generally valued on the balance sheet at the amount currently owed.

The amount that is currently payable or the value of goods (services) that must be rendered to settle a debt will determine the amount of the liability reported on the balance sheet. The rule may sound straight-forward, but the application of the rule is very complex.

EXAMPLE 8-4: On January 1, 19x0, TCB Corporation borrowed $150,000 from Nice National Bank. The terms of the loan specify that TCB Corporation is to pay 10% interest on the unpaid balance on January 1 each year. One-third of the principal amount is to be repaid 1/1/x3, 1/1/x6, and 1/1/x9. What is the liability shown on TCB's balance sheet on 12/31/x0? How will the liability be classified?

The total amount owed by TCB Corporation as of the end of 19x0 is $165,000. This is made up of the $150,000 principal and $15,000 interest for the year (10% of the unpaid balance, $150,000). The $15,000 interest will be classified as a current liability since it must be paid by 1/1/x1. The remaining $150,000 will be classified as long-term because TCB Corporation is not obligated to pay any of this amount until 19x3 and later.

EXAMPLE 8-5: How will the liability for the loan described in Example 8-4 appear on the balance sheet for 19x5?

The total amount owed as of 12/31/x5 is $110,000. This is comprised of $100,000 principal and $10,000 in interest for the year. $60,000 will classified as current because the company is obligated to pay $50,000 of the principal and the $10,000 interest on 1/1/x6. The remaining $50,000 will be classified as long-term since it is not due until 19x9.

8-5. Owners' Equity

The amount of the owners' financial interest in a firm is called **owners' equity**. Owners' equity may be increased by the owners investing new assets or by income earned and reinvested in the firm (retained earnings). The format of the owners' equity section of the balance sheet will vary depending on whether the firm is a corporation, partnership, or single (sole) proprietorship. For partnerships and sole proprietorships, direct investments by owners and profits are combined with the owners' equity from previous periods. One equity (capital) amount is shown for each owner. On the other hand, direct investment by owners of a corporation is made by purchasing shares of stock. This is reported separately from retained earnings from previous periods. No individual capital accounts are shown for each owner. The direct investment made by the group is reported in a part of the Equity section of the balance sheet called Paid-in Capital as the par value of the stock and as any amount in excess of par value. Par value is an arbitrary value placed on a stock certificate.

EXAMPLE 8-6: Tom Foley and Glenn Lindsay are partners in T & G Pharmacy. All profits and losses are shared equally. At the beginning of 19x2, the balance in each capital account was $45,000. During 19x2, the pharmacy made a profit of $40,000. In addition, Tom invested additional assets worth $2,200. How would the Owners' Equity section of the balance sheet appear on 12/31/x2?

The $40,000 profit for the year would be divided equally among the two owners and added to their previous capital balances. Tom would also have his additional investment of $2,200 added to his balance. Therefore, the owners' equity section would appear as follows:

Owners' Equity

Tom Foley, Capital.	$ 67,200
Glenn Lindsay, Capital.	65,000
Total Owners' Equity	$132,200

EXAMPLE 8-7: Since the inception of XYZ Corporation, stockholders have purchased 10,000 shares of stock which had a par value of $10 per share. The 10,000 shares of stock were purchased for a total of $144,000. Retained earnings thus far totaled $107,500. How would the Owners' Equity section of the balance sheet for the corporation appear?

The par value of the stock is $100,000 (10,000 shares @ $10). The remaining $44,000 paid is recorded as Capital Contributed in Excess of Par Value. Retained Earnings is reported separately from these two amounts. Exhibits 8-1 and 8-2 illustrates this information as it would be shown on XYZ Corporation's balance sheet.

8-6. Working Capital

Working capital is defined as current assets minus current liabilities. A firm needs a positive amount of working capital if it is to meet its debts as they fall due. However, a large amount in working capital is not necessarily a good idea. Current assets tend to be low-return assets. Holding cash provides flexibility for the firm's management, but the return earned on the cash balances is very low compared to what could be earned if the money were invested in other assets. Inventory is required to meet customer needs, but goods sitting in the warehouse yield a low return. A firm wants to have enough working capital to maintain its day-to-day operations, but it does not want to tie up more funds than necessary in low-return current assets.

EXAMPLE 8-8: On a given day, the return being paid on certificates of deposit may vary from $8\frac{1}{2}\%$ on 3-month certificates to $12\frac{1}{4}\%$ on 48-month certificates. A firm can increase its returns by investing in longer-term certificates but it loses some of its flexibility to make investments in the meantime. Likewise, funds invested in long-term assets generally yield higher rates of return than do funds invested in current assets. The higher yield is obtained at the cost of reduced flexibility and perhaps greater risk of loss.

8-7. Net Assets

Net assets are total assets minus total liabilities. The definition is the same as the definition given by the FASB for equity.

8-8. Common Misconceptions about the Balance Sheet

Most people have misconceptions about the balance sheet and read more into it than they should.

A. The balance sheet does not tell you the current value of the assets held by the company.

On the balance sheet, assets are valued at cost not at their current market value (unless it is lower). The figure does not represent what the assets could be sold for on the balance sheet date.

B. Owners' equity does not measure the amount of cash that would be left if the assets of the business were sold and the liabilities settled.

Since assets are not valued at current market value, equity does not reflect what would actually be left over if the assets were sold and all the liabilities were settled. Keep in mind that a company is assumed to be a going concern. The objective of reports is not to measure the probable results, if the company were to go out of business.

C. Owners' equity does not tell how much a buyer should be willing to pay for the company.

The current worth of a business depends on many things such as the value of the assets being purchased and the future profits the buyer might make from the business. The balance sheet does not show either of these amounts. Estimates of future earnings are left to the buyer.

8-9. Financing Ratios

A balance sheet is a statement of *financing*. It tells what a company paid for its assets and who financed them. For example, in Exhibit 8-2, the assets of the firm cost $573,500. Creditors financed $322,000 and $251,500 was financed by the owners. Users of the balance sheet often compute several ratios from the information on the balance sheet to learn more about the company's financial stability.

A. The *debt ratio* indicates the percentage of assets financed by creditors.

Creditors prefer that the ratio of liabilities to assets be rather low. A low ratio would mean that even in bad times the company would still be able to cover its debts. This is of course extremely important to individuals or companies extending credit. The formula for debt ratio is as follows

DEBT RATIO $$\text{debt ratio} = \frac{\text{total liabilities}}{\text{total assets}} \times 100$$

Multiplying the fraction by 100 converts it to a percentage.

B. The *equity ratio* indicates the percentage of assets financed by the owners.

Since all assets are either financed by creditors or the owners, the equity ratio must be the flip-side of the debt ratio. The total of the two ratios must equal 100%. Creditors therefore prefer high equity ratios for the same reason that they prefer a low debt ratio. The formula for computing the equity ratio is as follows

EQUITY RATIO $$\text{equity ratio} = \frac{\text{total equity}}{\text{total assets}} \times 100$$

EXAMPLE 8-9: XYZ Corporation, in Exhibit 8-2, is seeking a loan from Watson Lending Corporation. In reviewing XYZ Corporation's financial statements, the loan officer computes the firm's debt and equity ratios based on the information shown on its balance sheet. The loan officer computes a debt ratio of 56.15% and an equity ratio of 53.85%. Do you agree with the loan officer's computations?

From the information given in Exhibit 8-2, you know that total assets equal $573,500, total liabilities equal $322,000, and total equity equals $251,500. Using the formulas, you should find

$$\text{debt ratio} = \frac{\text{total liabilities}}{\text{total assets}} \times 100 = \frac{\$322,000}{\$573,500} \times 100 = 56.15\%$$

$$\text{equity ratio} = \frac{\text{total equity}}{\text{total assets}} \times 100 = \frac{\$251,500}{\$573,500} \times 100 = 43.85\%$$

The loan office computed the debt ratio correctly. However, the equity ratio is incorrect. The loan officer should have been alerted by the fact that the sum of the ratios computed was 110% not 100%.

C. The *current ratio* shows the number of times current assets exceed current liabilities.

The relationship between current assets and current liabilities is of special interest to creditors and investors because it is an indication of the firm's ability to pay its current debts as they fall due. The computation of working capital (current assets minus current liabilities) is one way to investigate this relationship. The current ratio is another. The current ratio is calculated as follows:

CURRENT RATIO $$\text{Current Ratio} = \frac{\text{Current Assets}}{\text{Current Liabilities}}$$

Creditors would probably like this ratio to be in the range of 2:1 for assurance that the firm would not default on its current liabilities.

D. The *quick* or *acid-test* ratio is a more stringent test of a company's ability to pay its current debts as they fall due.

Some current assets are less liquid than others. A **liquid (or quick) asset** is an asset that can be turned into cash at close to its balance sheet amount in a short period of time.

1. *Cash.* Cash is clearly the most liquid of assets.
2. *Marketable Securities.* Marketable securities can be quickly sold. Since they are valued at lower of cost or market on the balance sheet, the amount of cash obtained should be approximately equal to the balance sheet value.

3. *Accounts Receivable/Current Notes Receivable*. Accounts and current notes receivable are generally short-term credit. An estimate of uncollectible accounts has already been deducted in figuring the balance sheet value. Therefore the amount of cash collected should be close to the balance sheet value.

4. *Inventories*. Inventories must be sold to customers. Quick sales of an entire inventory would usually require substantial discounts from the balance sheet value. They are therefore not considered very liquid.

5. *Prepaid Items*. Prepaid items usually provide some future benefit such as a utility or service. These items may not be capable of being sold. They are therefore not considered very liquid.

The quick ratio compares only the highly liquid current assets to current liabilities; quick assets being cash, marketable securities, accounts receivable, and current notes receivable.

QUICK RATIO
or
ACID-TEST RATIO

$$\text{Quick Ratio} = \frac{\text{Quick Current Assets}}{\text{Current Liabilities}}$$

Creditors would like a quick ratio in excess of 1:1.

EXAMPLE 8-10: Based on the information in Exhibit 8-2, what are the current ratio and quick ratios for XYZ Corporation?

Total current assets for XYZ Corporation equal $270,500. Total current liabilities equal $172,000.

$$\text{current ratio} = \frac{\text{current assets}}{\text{current liabilities}} = \frac{\$270,500}{\$172,000} = 1.57:1 \text{ or } 1.57$$

Quick assets equal cash, marketable securities, accounts receivable, and notes receivable. The total amount of these assets equals $175,800 ($50,000 + $4,800 + $115,000 + $6,000).

$$\text{quick ratio} = \frac{\text{quick current assets}}{\text{current liabilities}} = \frac{\$175,800}{\$172,000} = 1.02:1 \text{ or } 1.02$$

E. Owners of a firm usually seek to achieve slightly different ratios than creditors prefer.

To achieve the ratios that creditors prefer, a firm would often have to choose a less profitable, albeit safer, system of operations.

1. *Debt and Equity Ratios*. Owners want to take advantage of borrowed funds if the funds can be invested in projects that yield a greater return than the interest rate for borrowing. This might lead you to think that owners would always prefer a high debt ratio. This is not the case. Interest must be paid in both the good times and the bad. Large interest payments could be a significant burden during hard times. Owners therefore want to borrow money within a safe limit. The safe debt ratio will be lower for businesses that fluctuate with the business cycle, so that the debt would not be too much to handle during periods of recession.

    Owners must also consider creditors evaluations. If a creditor judges the firm's structure to be too heavily debt financed (financed by creditors) and therefore a greater risk, credit may be refused or extended only at a higher rate.

2. *Current Ratio and Quick Ratio*. Owners are reluctant to overinvest in low return current assets, especially quick assets. Owners want to see some degree of safety but are unwilling to sustain a ratio as high as two. The trend toward lower current ratios became apparent when rates of return on real assets like plant and equipment increased dramatically with the acceleration of inflation in the early 1970's. The current and quick ratios should be in excess of 1:1. How much greater is a matter of debate.

RAISE YOUR GRADES

Can you explain . . . ?

☑ the purpose of the balance sheet
☑ what are the two balance sheet formats
☑ the difference between current and non-current assets
☑ what lower of cost or market means
☑ the definition of working capital
☑ the definition of net assets
☑ how to compute the debt, equity, currrent, and quick ratios
☑ why creditors prefer high equity and current ratios

SUMMARY

1. The purpose of the balance sheet is to show the balance between assets and liabilities and equity.
2. The balance sheet equation is assets equal liabilities plus owners' equity.
3. The balance sheet is also known as the statement of financial position.
4. The account form of balance sheet has a two column format similar to that of a T account.
5. The report form of balance sheet lists all items in a vertical arrangement.
6. Assets and liabilities are classified on the balance sheet as either current or noncurrent.
7. A current asset is an asset which is expected to be turned into cash or used up within one year or an operating cycle, whichever is longer.
8. An operating cycle is the average length of time required to convert raw materials into a finished product, sell that product to a customer, and receive payment.
9. Non-current assets are also known as long-term assets.
10. Current assets must be greater than current liabilities for a company to stay in business.
11. Some assets are valued at lower of cost or market. This variation from the historical-cost principle is justified by the exception principle allowing conservatism in valuing assets.
12. Straight-line depreciation is computed as (cost − salvage value) ÷ number of accounting periods the item is to be used.
13. Salvage value is the estimated value of an asset at its time of disposal.
14. Intangible assets have no physical substance.
15. Deferred credits are liabilities that the company probably does not expect to settle until it goes out of business.
16. Working capital is defined as current assets minus current liabilities.
17. Net assets are total assets minus total liabilities.
18. The balance sheet does not tell you the current value of the assets held by the company.
19. Owners' equity does not tell you the amount of cash that would be left if all the assets were sold and all liabilities settled nor does it tell how much a buyer should be willing to pay for the company.
20. Debt ratio = (total liabilities ÷ total assets) × 100
21. Equity ratio = (total equity ÷ total assets) × 100
22. Current ratio = current assets ÷ current liabilities

23. Liquid assets are assets that can be turned into cash at close to their balance sheet amount in a short period of time.
24. Quick or acid-test ratio = quick current assets divided by current liabilities.

RAPID REVIEW

1. The equation for the balance sheet is _____.
2. The formula for working capital is _____.
3. The formula for the current ratio is _____.
4. Quick current assets include _____, _____, _____, and
   _____.

5. Which of the following balance sheet dates is appropriate?
   (a) For the Year 19x5
   (b) 1/1/x5 to 12/31/x5
   (c) December 31, 19x5
   (d) For the Year Ending 12/31/x5
6. What does the debt ratio tell you?
7. How are current marketable securities valued on the balance sheet?
8. ABC Company requires six months from the time raw materials are acquired to produce the widgets it sells. It takes another four months on the average to find a buyer for the widgets and three months to collect from customers. What is the time period for classifying assets and liabilities as current? Why?
9. Which of the following is part of owners' equity but not paid-in capital?
   (a) retained earnings
   (b) common stock
   (c) deferred credits
   (d) capital contributed in excess of par value
10. Which of the following statements about owners' equity is true?
    (a) It is the amount the company should be sold for.
    (b) It is what the owners would have if all the assets were sold and all the liabilities were settled.
    (c) It is the owners' financial interest in the company.
    (d) None of the above.

Answers:

1. Assets = Liabilities + Owners' Equity [Section 8-1]
2. Working Capital = Current Assets − Current Liabilities [Section 8-6]
3. Current Ratio = (Current Assets ÷ Current Liabilities) [Section 8-9C]
4. Cash, Marketable Securities, Accounts Receivable, and Current Notes Receivable [Section 8-9D]
5. c [Section 8-1]
6. The debt ratio indicates the percentage of total assets financed by creditors. [Section 8-9A]
7. Lower of cost or market [Section 8-3C]
8. 13 months. Current assets (liabilities) are expected to be turned into cash (paid) within one year or the operating cycle whichever is *longer*. The operating cycle in this case is longer by one month. [Section 8-3A]
9. a [Section 8-5]
10. c [Section 8-5]

SOLVED PROBLEMS

PROBLEM 8-1: HJB Corporation has an operating cycle of ten months. The accountant prepared the following balance sheet. Find the misclassified information and prepare a corrected statement.

HJB Corporation
Balance Sheet
December 31, 19x5

ASSETS

Current Assets:

Cash	$ 40,000	
Accounts Receivable (net $6,000 allowance for uncollectibles	90,000	
Inventory	67,000	
Supplies	3,150	
Total Current Assets		$200,150

Long-term Investments:

Note Receivable (due 12/31/x9)	$ 12,000	
Common Stock — DeMille Company	10,500	
Note Receivable (due 12/15/x6)	3,350	
Patent	25,000	
Total Long-term Investments		50,850

Plant, Property, and Equipment:

Land	$ 80,000	
Building (net $53,000 accum. depreciation)	216,000	
Equipment (net $24,000 accum. depreciation	59,000	
Total Plant, Property, and Equipment	355,000	
Total Assets		$606,000

LIABILITIES

Current Liabilities:

Accounts Payable	$ 65,000	
Notes Payable (due 11/30/x6)	26,000	
Wages Payable	9,600	
Bonds Payable (due 3/21/x6)	12,500	
Total Current Liabilities		$113,100

Long-term Liabilities:

Deferred Income Taxes	30,800	
Total Liabilities		$143,900

STOCKHOLDERS' EQUITY

Paid-In Capital:

Common Stock ($25 par value)	$250,000	
Retained Earnings	202,100	
Capital Contributed in Excess of Par Value	10,000	
Total Stockholders' Equity		$462,100
Total Liabilities and Stockholders' Equity		$606,000

Answer:

HJB Corporation
Balance Sheet
December 31, 19x5

ASSETS

Current Assets:

Cash	$ 40,000	
Accounts Receivable (net $6,000 allow.).	90,000	
Inventory	67,000	
Supplies.	3,150	
Note Receivable (due 12/15/x6)	3,350	
Total Current Assets.		$203,500

Long-term Investments:

Notes Receivable (due 12/31/x9)	$ 12,000	
DeMille Company Common Stock. . . .	10,500	
Total Long-term Investments.		22,500

Plant, Property, and Equipment:

Land.	$ 80,000	
Building (net $53,000 accum. depreciation).	216,000	
Equipment (net $24,000 accum. depreciation).	59,000	
Total Plant, Property, and Equipment.		355,000

Intangible Assets:

Patent.	25,000	
Total Assets		$606,000

LIABILITIES

Current Liabilities:

Accounts Payable	$ 65,000	
Notes Payable (due 11/30/x6).	26,000	
Wages Payable	9,600	
Bonds Payable (due 3/21/x6)	12,500	
Total Current Liabilities		$113,100

Long-term Liabilities:

Deferred Income Taxes	30,800	
Total Liabilities		$143,900

STOCKHOLDERS' EQUITY

Paid-In Capital:

Common Stock ($25 par value)	$250,000	
Capital Contributed in Excess of Par Value	10,000	
Total Paid-In Capital.		260,000
Retained Earnings		$202,100
Total Stockholders' Equity.		$462,100
Total Liabilities and Stockholders' Equity		$606,000

The note receivable, due 12/15/x6 was incorrectly classified as a long-term asset. Since it is due within one year or the operating cycle, whichever is longer (in this case the year is longer), it should be classified as current. The patent should have been listed as an intangible asset, since it has no physical substance. The liabilities section was correct. Retained Earnings should not be reported under Paid-In Capital but as a separate item in the Owners' Equity section.

[Sections 8-2, 8-3, 8-4, and 8-5]

PROBLEM 8-2: Royal Company has the following assets listed on its books. What would be the amount of total assets shown on the balance sheet?

(a) Cash on hand — $65,000
(b) Marketable securities — cost $36,000; market value of $34,500.
(c) Accounts Receivable — $45,000; allowance for uncollectible accounts totals $450.
(d) Inventories—book value of $133,000; market value of $135,000; to be valued at lower of cost or market
(e) Supplies — cost — $8,400

Answer: Marketable securities should be valued at lower of cost or market. Therefore, the marketable securities would be valued at $34,500. Accounts receivable would be valued at $45,000 less the $450 allowance. Subtracting this amount from the total balance in accounts receivable gives a net balance sheet value of $44,550. Inventory is valued at cost because the market value exceeds the cost. Supplies are valued at cost. The total assets would be computed as follows

Cash on Hand	$ 65,000
Marketable Securities	34,500
Accounts Receivable	44,550
Inventories	133,000
Supplies	8,400
Total	$285,450

[Section 8-3]

PROBLEM 8-2: Royal Company has the following assets listed on its books. What

Equipment	Cost	Salvage Value	To be Used	Date Purchased
a	$5,000	$500	50 months	1/1/x2
b	$1,400	$200	5 years	4/1/x2
c	$4,000	$40	10 years	5/1/x2

Compute the monthly depreciation using the straight-line method for each and show their net value on 12/31/x2.

Answer:

$$\text{depreciation} = \frac{\text{cost} - \text{salvage value}}{\text{number of months to be used}}$$

$$\text{Equipment a} = \frac{\$5,000 - \$500}{50} = \$90$$

$$\text{Equipment b} = \frac{\$1,400 - \$200}{60} = \$20$$

$$\text{Equipment c} = \frac{\$4,000 - \$40}{120} = \$33$$

After 12 months, Equipment a would have depreciated $1,080 ($90 × 12) leaving

a net value of $3,920 ($5,000 − $1,080).

After 9 months, Equipment b would have depreciated $180 ($20 × 9) leaving a net

value of $1,220 ($1,400 − $180).

After 8 months, Equipment c would have depreciated $264 ($33 × 8) leaving a net

value of $3,736 ($4,000 − $264).

[Section 8-3]

PROBLEM 8-4: XYZ Corporation borrows $400,000 on 1/1/x1, signing a note agreeing to repay $100,000 on 1/1/x3, 1/1/x5, 1/1/x7, and 1/1/x9. XYZ Corporation also agrees to pay 5% interest on the amount of principal still owed each January 1.

(a) How will XYZ Corporation's liability for the note appear on its 12/31/x1 balance sheet?
(b) How will the liability appear on XYZ Corporation's 12/31/x3 balance sheet?
(c) How will the liability appear on XYZ Corporation's 12/31/x6 balance sheet?

Answer:

(a) On 12/31/x1, XYZ Corporation has a total liability under the note of $420,000 composed of the $400,000 principal plus $20,000 of interest owed for 19x1. The interest is calculated as 5% of the unpaid principal of $400,000. The $20,000 of interest must be paid during the next year and will appear as a current liability, Interest Payable. The $400,000 principal will appear as a noncurrent liability, Long-term Notes Payable.

(b) On 12/31/x3, XYZ Corporation has a total liability of $315,000 under the note composed of $300,000 of unpaid principal and $15,000 of interest owed for the year 19x3. The interest represents 5% of the unpaid principal of $300,000. The interest will be listed in the current liabilities section as Interest Payable. The $300,000 principal will be listed as a noncurrent liability, Long-term Notes Payable.

(c) On 12/31/x6, XYZ Corporation has a total liability under the note of $210,000 composed once again of $200,000 of unpaid principal plus $10,000 of interest owed for 19x6. The $10,000 of interest will be listed as a current liability, Interest Payable. The $100,000 portion of the principal that must be paid on 1/1/x7 will also be included as a current liability. The title of the account might be Current Portion of Long-term Notes Payable. The remaining $100,000 of principal will be listed as a noncurrent liability, Long-term Notes Payable.

[Section 8-4]

PROBLEM 8-5: Calculate the missing amounts in the following independent situations.

	(a)	(b)	(c)	(d)
Dudley Capital 1/1/x1	10,000	50,000	20,000	36,000
New Investment during 19x1	5,000	?	2,000	7,000
Net Income (Loss) 19x1	(6,000)	15,000	?	(2,000)
Withdrawals	2,000	4,000	10,000	?
Dudley Capital 12/31/x1	?	75,000	27,000	35,000

Answer: The ending capital balance is equal to beginning capital + new investment + net income − withdrawals. This formula can be used to solve for the missing numbers.

(a) End. Cap. = Beg. Cap. + Investment + Net Income − Withdrawals
    X   =   10,000 +   5,000   + (−6,000) −   2,000
    X   =   7,000

The Ending Capital Balance was $7,000

Notes: When a number appears in a parenthesis in accounting it is to be interpreted as being a negative number. Negative net income is the same as a loss.

(b) End. Cap = Beg. Cap. + Investment + Net Income − Withdrawals
  75,000 =   50,000 +   X   + 15,000 −   4,000

Solving for X:

$$X = 75,000 - 50,000 - 15,000 + 4,000 = 14,000$$

The amount of new investment was $14,000.

(c) End. Cap. = Beg. Cap. + Investment + Net Income − Withdrawals
  27,000 =   20,000 + 2,000   +   X   −   10,000

Solving for X:

$$X = 27,000 - 20,000 - 2,000 + 10,000 = 15,000$$

The net income for the year was $15,000.

(*d*) End. Cap. = Beg. Cap. + Investment + Net Income - Withdrawals

| 35,000 | = | 36,000 | + | 7,000 | + | (-2,000) | - | X |

Solving for X:

$$X = 36,000 + 7,000 - 2,000 - 35,000 = 6,000$$

Withdrawals during the year totaled $6,000.

[Section 8-5]

PROBLEM 8-6: Mr. Doe is contemplating the purchase of full ownership of the BYME Company. An examination of the most recent balance sheet indicates that the total assets of the business are $100,000. Total liabilities are $56,000 and the owners' equity totals $44,000. Mr. Doe has offered to pay $44,000 for the firm. The owner of the business has just indicated that she has another offer of $75,000. Mr. Doe has come to you. He wants to know how it is possible that a business with an equity of $44,000 might be worth $75,000 to another buyer. He also wants to know what things he should consider before he decides whether to submit a higher offer.

Answer: Mr. Doe is reading more into the balance sheet than is there. Assets on the balance sheet are valued in relation to what the company paid for them. The balance sheet does not measure the current worth of the assets. The equity figure does not indicate the amount of cash that would be left for the owner if the assets were sold and the liabilities paid off. The equity figure does not indicate what the company is worth. A buyer of a business rarely makes the purchase with the intention of liquidating the assets. The buyer generally intends to operate the business to earn a profit. The other bidder has estimated what he/she feels the assets are worth and has also estimated the future profit potential of the business. The $75,000 offer reflects that buyer's evaluation of the value of the net assets and their use in an established business. The balance sheet does not provide a measure of the current worth of assets nor does it provide profit projections. Mr. Doe must make these subjective calculations for himself before he can decide whether or not to submit a higher offer.

[Section 8-8]

PROBLEM 8-7: Van Deryt Company prepared the following balance sheet at December 31, 19x1. (Values shown represent million dollars)

Van Deryt Company
Balance Sheet
December 31, 19x1

ASSETS		LIABILITIES	
Current Assets	$ 5	Current Liabilities	$ 4
Noncurrent Assets	25	Noncurrent Liabilities	20
		Total Liabilities	$24
		OWNERS' EQUITY	
		Van Deryt, Capital	$ 6
Total Assets	$30	Total Liabilities and Equity	$30

(*a*) Compute the debt ratio. What does this ratio tell you?
(*b*) Compute the equity ratio. What does this ratio tell you?
(*c*) Compute the current ratio. What does this ratio tell you?

Answer:

(a) Debt Ratio = (Total Liabilities/Total Assets) (100)
   Debt Ratio = [(4 + 20)/(30)](100) = 80%
   80% of XYZ Corporation's assets were financed by creditors.
(b) Equity Ratio = (Total Equity/Total Assets) (100)
   Equity Ratio = (6/30)(100) = 20%
   20% of XYZ Corporation's assets were financed by the owners.
(c) Current Ratio = Current Assets/Current Liabilities
   Current Ratio = 5/4 = 1.25
   The XYZ Corporation has 1.25 times as many current assets as it has current liabilities.

[Section 8-9]

The following information is for use in Problems 8-8 through 8-10.

	a	b	c
Current Assets	?	5,000	8,000
Noncurrent Assets	50,000	12,000	?
Total Assets	75,000	?	?
Current Liabilities	20,000	?	?
Noncurrent Liabilities	?	?	15,000
Total Liabilities	60,000	?	21,000
Total Equity	?	6,000	?
Total Liabilities + Equity	75,000	?	28,000
Working Capital	?	3,000	?

PROBLEM 8-8: Compute the missing amounts in Case A.

Answer:

Answering this question requires an understanding of the relationship of items on the balance sheet. The following relationships are important:

Total Assets = Total Liabilities + Equity
Working Capital = Current Assets − Current Liabilities
Total Assets = Current Assets + Noncurrent Assets
Total Liabilities = Current Liabilities + Noncurrent Liabilities

The approach to answering the question requires fitting the pieces together in whatever order the problem allows.
We know that:

Total Assets = Current Assets + Noncurrent Assets

Therefore: 75,000 = CA + 50,000
   CA = 25,000

We know that:

Total Liabilities = Current + Noncurrent Liabilities

Therefore: 60,000 = 20,000 + NCL
   NCL = 40,000

We know that:

Total Assets = Total Liabilities + Equity

Therefore: 75,000 = Total Liabilities + Equity
And: 75,000 = 60,000 + Equity
   Equity = 15,000

We know that:

$$\text{Working Capital} = \text{Current assets} - \text{Current liabilities}$$

Therefore: WC = 25,000 − 20,000
    WC = 5,000
               [Sections 8-1 through 8-4, 8-6]

PROBLEM 8-9: Compute the missing amounts in Case B.

Answer:

We know that:

$$\text{Total Assets} = \text{Current} + \text{Noncurrent Assets}$$

Therefore: TA = 5,000 + 12,000 = 17,000
We know that:

$$\text{Working Capital} = \text{Current Assets} - \text{Current Liabilities}$$

Therefore: 3,000 = 5,000 − CL
    CL = 2,000
We know that:

$$\text{Total Assets} = \text{Total Liabilities} + \text{Equity}$$

Therefore: Total Liabilities + Equity = 17,000
And: TL + 6,000 = 17,000
And: TL = 11,000
We know that:

$$\text{Total Liabilities} = \text{Current} + \text{Noncurrent Liabilities}$$

Therefore: 11,000 = 2,000 + NCL
    NCL = 9,000
               [Sections 8-1 through 8-4, 8-6]

PROBLEM 8-10: Compute the missing amounts in Case C.

Answer:

We know that:

$$\text{Total Assets} = \text{Total Liabilities} + \text{Equity} = 28,000$$

Therefore: Total Assets = 28,000
And: 21,000 + Equity = 28,000
    Equity = 7,000
We know that:

$$\text{Total Assets} = \text{Current} + \text{Noncurrent Assets}$$

Therefore: 28,000 = 8,000 + NCA
    NCA = 20,000

We know that:

$$\text{Total Liabilities} = \text{Current} + \text{Noncurrent Liabilities}$$

Therefore: 21,000 = CL + 15,000
    CL = 6,000
We know that:

$$\text{Working Capital} = \text{Current Assets} - \text{Current Liabilities}$$

Therefore: WC = 8,000 − 6,000
    WC = 2,000
               [Sections 8-1 through 8-4, 8-6]

The answers to Problems 8-8 through 8-10 are summarized below:

	a	b	c
Current Assets	25,000	5,000	8,000
Noncurrent Assets	50,000	12,000	20,000
Total Assets	75,000	17,000	28,000
Current Liabilities	20,000	2,000	6,000
Noncurrent Liabilities	40,000	9,000	15,000
Total Liabilities	60,000	11,000	21,000
Equity	15,000	6,000	7,000
Total Liabilities + Equity	75,000	17,000	28,000
Working Capital	5,000	3,000	2,000

PROBLEM 8-11: Shown below is a list of accounts and their respective balances. From it, prepare the balance sheet for Forberg Studios for the year ended December 31, 19x4, in account form.

Accumulated Depreciation — Office Equipment	$ 19,830
Land	20,000
Building	140,000
Prepaid Insurance	4,560
Capital Stock	100,000
Office Supplies	4,060
Merchandise Inventory	59,700
Notes Receivable (due in 5 yrs.)	10,880
Accounts Receivable (net)	20,000
Cash	32,950
Accumulated Depreciation — Building	29,400
Office Equipment	51,750
Accounts Payable	22,420
Salaries Payable	2,000
Mortgage Note Payable	25,000
Retained Earnings	?

Answer:

Forberg Studios
Balance Sheet
For the Year Ended December 31,19x4

ASSETS

Current Assets:

Cash	$ 32,950
Accounts Receivable (net)	20,000
Merchandise Inventory	59,700
Office Supplies	4,060
Prepaid Insurance	4,560
Total Current Assets	$121,270

Long-term Assets:

Notes Receivable	$ 10,880

Plant, Property, and Equipment:

Land	$ 20,000
Building (net of $29,400 accumulated depreciation)	110,600
Office Equipment (net of $19,830 accumulated depreciation)	31,920
Total Plant, Property, and Equipment	$162,520
Total Assets	$294,670

LIABILITIES

Current Liabilities:

Accounts Payable	$ 22,420
Salaries Payable	2,000
Total Current Liabilities	$ 24,420

Long-term Liabilities:

Mortgage Note Payable	25,000
Total Liabilities	$ 49,420

STOCKHOLDERS' EQUITY

Capital Stock	$100,000
Retained Earnings	145,250
Total Stockholders' Equity	$245,250
Total Liabilities and Stockholders' Equity	$294,670

[Sections 8-2 through 8-5]

PROBLEM 8-12: Shown below is a list of accounts and their respective balances for Myra Merchandising Company. Prepare the balance sheet for the year ended December 31, 19x4 in report form.

Salaries Payable	$ 2,900
Myra Gray, Capital	137,954
Accounts Receivable (net)	7,859
Prepaid Insurance	360
Accumulated Depreciation — Equipment	3,845
Notes Payable (due in 4 months)	10,000
Cash	60,000
Merchandise Inventory	26,697
Supplies	433
Building	110,000
Mortgage Note Payable	30,000
Accumulated Depreciation — Building	50,000
Common Stock—Jason Co. (long-term)	12,000
Accounts Payable	22,650
Equipment	40,000

Answer:

Myra Merchandising Company
Balance Sheet
For the Year Ended December 31, 19x4

ASSETS

Current Assets:

Cash	$60,000		
Accounts Receivable	7,859		
Merchandise Inventory	26,697		
Supplies	433		
Prepaid Insurance	360		
Total Current Assets		$ 95,349	

Long-term Investments:

Common Stock — Jason Company		12,000	

Plant, Property, and Equipment:

Building (net of $50,000 accumulated depreciation)	$60,000		
Equipment (net of $3,845 accumulated depreciation)	36,155		
Total Plant, Property, and Equipment		96,155	
Total Assets			$203,504

LIABILITIES

Current Liabilities:

Accounts Payable	$22,650		
Notes Payable	10,000		
Salaries Payable	2,900		
Total Current Liabilities		$ 35,550	

Long-term Liabilities:

Mortgage Note Payable		30,000	
Total Liabilities		$ 65,550	

OWNER'S EQUITY

Myra Gray, Capital		$137,954	
Total Liabilities and Owner's Equity			$203,504

[Sections 8-2 through 8-5]

9 STATEMENT OF CHANGES IN FINANCIAL POSITION (SCFP)—WORKING CAPITAL BASIS

THIS CHAPTER IS ABOUT

- ☑ **The Purpose of the SCFP**
- ☑ **Defining Funds as Working Capital**
- ☑ **The SCFP Format**
- ☑ **Working Capital from Operations**
- ☑ **Other Sources of Working Capital**
- ☑ **Uses of Working Capital**
- ☑ **The "All Financial Resources" Concept**
- ☑ **The T Account Worksheet**
- ☑ **Schedule of Changes in Working Capital Accounts**

9-1. The Purpose of the SCFP

The statement of changes in financial position (SCFP) shows the *sources and uses* of a company's funds during an accounting period. The statement also explains the *changes in funds* between the beginning and end of a period. Both these purposes are illustrated in the SCFP equation

$$\text{SCFP EQUATION} \quad \begin{array}{c} \text{Funds generated} \\ \text{during the} \\ \text{accounting period} \end{array} - \begin{array}{c} \text{Funds used} \\ \text{during the} \\ \text{accounting period} \end{array} = \begin{array}{c} \text{Change in funds} \\ \text{over the} \\ \text{accounting period} \end{array}$$

All firms whose stock is traded on the open market are required to prepare a SCFP. Investors and creditors need to know if a firm's sources of funding are internal or external. They need to know if the firm is selling off its assets to generate funds. They also need to know how the firm is using funds. All this information is given on the SCFP.

9-2. Defining Funds as Working Capital

The FASB has traditionally allowed for two definitions of funds: either cash or working capital. Working capital is equal to current assets less current liabilities; current meaning expected to be turned into cash or settled within one year or an operating cycle, whichever is longer. Current assets include cash, short-term marketable securities and notes receivable, accounts receivable, inventory, and prepaid items. Current liabilities include accounts payable, short-term notes payable, special payables, and unearned income. In this chapter, we will discuss the preparation of the SCFP with working capital as the definition of funds. In Chapter 10, we will continue the discussion of the SCFP using cash as the definition of funds. SFAC. No. 5 appears to suggest that the FASB is moving toward a single cash definition of funds, but no specific guidelines have been published as of the printing of this book.

A. Preparation of the SCFP using working capital as funds is difficult.

Our accounting system is not designed to give us the information needed to prepare the SCFP easily. It was designed more for the preparation of the income statement, statement of retained earnings, and the balance sheet. Most thinking is not done in terms of working capital which means we have to "shift gears", in a manner of speaking, before preparing the SCFP. Preparation of the SCFP is therefore more difficult for us than preparation of other financial statements.

B. Changes in working capital can be explained through the balance sheet accounts.

One of the objectives of the SCFP is to explain the change in working capital over an accounting period. This can be done through information found on the balance sheet. Exhibit 9-1 illustrates this point.

EXHIBIT 9-1: Explaining Changes in Working Capital

$$WC = CA - CL$$
$$TA = CA + NCA$$
$$TL = CL + NCL$$
$$TA = TL + E$$

Therefore:
$$TA = (CL + NCL) + E$$
$$CA + NCA = CL + NCL + E$$
$$CA - CL = NCL + E - NCA$$

Hence:
$$WC = NCL + E - NCA$$

Since
$$WC = CA - CL = NCL - NCA + E$$
$$\Delta WC = \underbrace{\Delta CA - \Delta CL}_{\substack{\textbf{current} \\ \textbf{balance sheet} \\ \textbf{accounts}}} = \underbrace{\Delta NCL - \Delta NCA + \Delta E}_{\substack{\textbf{noncurrent} \\ \textbf{balance sheet} \\ \textbf{accounts}}}$$

Legend   CA — current assets   TA — total assets
         NCA — noncurrent assets   TL — total liabilities
         CL — current liabilities   E — equity
         NCL — noncurrent liabilities   Δ — mathematical symbol for change

You can see from this exhibit that: the change in working capital equals the change in current assets minus the change in current liabilities. We can explain the change in working capital by looking at the change in all noncurrent balance sheet accounts. Exhibit 9-1 tells us that:

3. Increases in noncurrent liabilities (such as long-term borrowing) are a source of working capital
4. Increases in noncurrent assets (such as purchases of equipment) are a use of working capital
5. Increases in equity (such as additional investments by owners) are a source of working capital

If these statements are logical to you, you are well on your way to understanding the fundamentals of preparing a SCFP on a working capital basis.

EXAMPLE 9-1: Now Corporation's balance sheets for the years 19x1 and 19x2 revealed the following selected amounts:

	19x2	19x1	Change
Current Assets	45,000	30,000	+15,000
Current Liabilities	26,000	20,000	+ 6,000

The change in working capital from 19x1 to 19x2 can be computed from these current balance sheet accounts.

$$\Delta WC = \Delta CA - \Delta CL$$

$$\Delta WC = (+15{,}000) - (+6{,}000) = +9{,}000$$

The calculations show that working capital increased by $9,000 during the time period.

EXAMPLE 9-2: Position Corporation's balance sheets for 19x2 and 19x3 showed the following selected figures:

	19x3	19x2	Change
Noncurrent Assets	13,000	15,000	− 2,000
Noncurrent Liabilities	16,000	6,000	+ 10,000
Equity	19,000	22,000	− 3,000

The change in working capital can be computed as follows:

$$\Delta WC = \Delta NCL - \Delta NCA + \Delta E$$

$$\Delta WC = (+10{,}000) - (-2{,}000) + (-3{,}000) = +9{,}000$$

The calculations show that working capital increased by $9,000 during the time period. The general sources of working capital were an increase in noncurrent liabilities (such as borrowing on long-term arrangements) and a decrease in noncurrent assets (such as selling equipment). Both factors had a positive effect on the change in working capital. The general use of working capital was a decrease in equity (such as dividends declared.)

EXAMPLE 9-3: Position Corporation's comparative balance sheet for the years 19x1 and 19x2 revealed the following selected amounts:

	19x2	19x1	Change
Noncurrent Assets	15,000	10,000	+ 5,000
Noncurrent Liabilities	6,000	20,000	−14,000
Equity	22,000	16,000	+ 6,000

The change in working capital over 19x2 can be computed by looking at the changes in the noncurrent balance sheet accounts.

$$\Delta WC = \Delta NCL - \Delta NCA + \Delta E$$

$$\Delta WC = (-14{,}000) - (5{,}000) + (6{,}000) = -13{,}000$$

Working Capital decreased by $13,000 during 19x2. The general source of working capital was an increase in equity. We know this because the change in equity was a positive factor in the calculation of the change in working capital. Equity increases when the firm earns profits and when owners make additional contributions to the business. The firm used working capital to retire noncurrent debt and acquire noncurrent assets. We know this because these two factors had a negative effect on the change in working capital.

9-3. SCFP Format

The general format of the SCFP shows the sources of funds less uses of funds. In the Source of Funds section, net funds generated *by operations* are reported separately from funds generated by *other sources*. Exhibit 9-2 shows the major sections of the SCFP.

EXHIBIT 9-2: Sample SCFP

XYZ Company
Statement of Changes in Financial Position
For the Year Ended 12/31/x1

Sources of Funds:
  Operations
    Net Income   XXX
    Adjustments to Net Income:
      For revenue that does not
        provide funds   XX
      For expenses that do not
        use funds   XX   XXX
    Total Funds From Operations   XXX
  Other Sources
    Sale of long-term assets.   XXX
    Issuance of stock.   XXX
    Issuance of new long-term debt . . .   XXX
    Total Funds From Other Sources. . .   XXX
  Total Sources   XXX

Uses of Funds:
  Purchase of long-term assets.   XXX
  Payment of dividends   XXX
  Retirement of long-term debt   XXX
  Retirement of stock.   XXX
  Total Uses   XXX
Net Change in Funds.   XXX

9-4. Working Capital from Operations

The first section of the SCFP requires a calculation of the working capital generated by the operations of the company. Operations in this context consist of normal production and the sale of goods and services. Determination of the amount of working capital generated from operations is probably the most difficult part of preparing the SCFP.

A. Net income is a good starting point for computing working capital generated from operations.

For most transactions, the amount of change in working capital generated from operations equals the amount of its affect on net income earned. Most revenue increases or generates working capital. When a firms sells goods it receives current assets (such as cash or accounts receivable) equal to the amount of revenue recognized on the sale. Likewise, expenses use up current assets (such as cash), thereby decreasing or using up working capital equal to the amount of the expense. Since net income summarizes the revenue and expenses during an accounting period, it must also summarize the change in working capital from operations for most transactions.

EXAMPLE 9-4: Amiable Company sold merchandise for $50,000 in cash and $70,000 on credit. The company also incurred the following expenses:

Cost of goods sold	—	$40,000
Wages	—	$ 5,000
Interest Expense (payable within 6 months)	—	$ 2,000
Prepaid Insurance expired	—	$ 1,000

By reconstructing the journal entries used to record these activities, it can be shown that the amount of working capital generated equals the revenue recognized and the amount of working capital used equals the expenses incurred.

Cash (WC)	50,000	
Sales (Revenue)		50,000
Accounts Receivable (WC)	70,000	
Sales (Revenue)		70,000
Cost of Goods Sold (Expense)	40,000	
Inventory (WC)		40,000
Wage Expense	5,000	
Cash (WC)		5,000
Interest Expense........................	2,000	
Interest Payable (WC)		2,000
Insurance Expense......................	1,000	
Prepaid Insurance (WC)................		1,000

Debits to Cash and Accounts Receivable increase the amount of current assets thereby increasing the amount of working capital. The credit entries either decrease a current asset and thereby decrease working capital or increase current liabilities which also decrease working capital.

B. Net income must be adjusted for revenue that does not generate an equal amount of working capital.

Net income accurately measures the change in working capital if only current balance sheet accounts are affected when the sale is made. Not all revenue earned, however, affects only current balance sheet accounts. Noncurrent assets change when sales are made on long-term credit terms. Adjustments must be made to profits to exclude revenue which affects noncurrent balance sheet accounts.

EXAMPLE 9-5: Patience, Unlimited reported a profit of $2,000,000 for the year. During the year, the firm sold $500,000 in services to Getrich Company in exchange for a note receivable payable in five years. The entry to record this transaction indicates that no working capital was created.

Notes Receivable (NCA)	500,000	
Sales		500,000

Even though the $500,000 sale was appropriately included in the calculation of net income, it should not be included in computing working capital because it affects a noncurrent account. The working capital generated from operations was actually $1,500,000 not $2,000,000. Therefore, the $500,000 in revenue must be subtracted from net income as an adjustment in computing working capital. This point is illustrated in the section of Patience, Unlimited's SCFP below

Sources of Funds:	
Operations	
Net Income.............................	$2,000,000
Adjustment to Net Income:	
Sales on Long-term Credit	(500,000)
Total Funds From Operations	$1,500,000

C. Net income must be adjusted for expenses that do not use working capital.

Some expenses do not use working capital. Depreciation expense, for example, neither decreases a current asset nor does it increase a current liability. It is accumulated in an account used to adjust the value of a noncurrent asset on the balance sheet. Expenses that will not be paid in the near future likewise do not use working capital.

EXAMPLE 9-6: Mighty Machine Company incurred the following expenses among others during the accounting period: depreciation expense of $6,000 and income tax expense of

$5,000 which was credited to the deferred tax account because the firm did not expect to pay this amount in the near future. The entries to record these expenses were

Depreciation Expense.	6,000	
Accumulated Depreciation.		6,000
Income Tax Expense.	5,000	
Deferred Taxes (NCL)		5,000

In both cases, the expense did not effect a current asset or liability and therefore did not affect working capital. They were, however, subtracted from revenue in computing net income for the period. These two expenses must be added back as an adjustment to net income in computing working capital as shown below in Mighty Machine Company's SCFP.

Sources of Funds:			
Operations			
Net Income from Operations		$75,000	
Adjustments to Net Income:			
Depreciation Expense.	6,000		
Deferred Taxes.	5,000	11,000	
Total Funds from Operations.			$86,000

The working capital from operations is greater than the profit reported because some of the expenses included affected noncurrent balance sheet accounts.

EXAMPLE 9-7: Smadeit Company reported net income of $45,000. Examination of the income statement and balance sheet for the year revealed the following:

1. Depreciation expense was $5,000
2. Amortization of patent expense was $800.
3. $2,000 of sales were made on long-term credit (note receivable)

The journal entries to record these events would have been as follows

Depreciation Expense.	5,000	
Accumulated Depreciation.		5,000
Amortization Expense.	800	
Patent		800
Note Receivable (long-term)	2,000	
Sales		2,000

In each case the revenue or expense affected a noncurrent balance sheet account. Therefore the net income must be adjusted by subtracting the revenue and adding back the expenses. The Sources of Funds—Operations section of the SCFP would appear as follows

Sources of Funds:			
Operations			
Net Income		$45,000	
Adjustments to Net Income:			
Sales (long-term credit)	$(2,000)		
Depreciation Expense.	5,000		
Amortization Expense.	800		
		3,800	
Total Funds from Operations.			$48,800

9-5. Other Sources of Working Capital

Working capital may be generated from activities other than normal production and the sale of goods and services. Common "other sources" of working capital include the sale of long-term assets, new long-term borrowings, and the issuance of stock.

A. Sale of long-term assets presents the greatest potential difficulty in computing other sources of working capital.

The sale of long-term assets presents the greatest potential difficulty in computing other sources of working capital because the amount of working capital generated *will not equal the amount of gain or loss on the sale* but will equal instead the total selling price. Working capital generated by the sale of long-term assets should be reported as Other Sources not as part of Working Capital from Operations.

EXAMPLE 9-8: STS Company sold a building which originally cost the company $100,000. The accumulated depreciation on the building on the date of sale was $57,000. The building was sold for $82,000. The entry to record the sale was as follows:

Cash (WC)	82,000	
Accumulated Depreciation	57,000	
Building		100,000
Gain.		39,000

Note that the only working capital account affected is Cash. Therefore, the amount of working capital generated is $82,000, the selling price of the equipment. This amount must be reported as an Other Source of working capital. The gain of $39,000 was included in net income. This gain must be subtracted as an adjustment to net income in computing working capital from operations.

EXAMPLE 9-9: XYZ Company sold a parcel of land that originally cost $50,000 for $40,000. The entry to record the sale was as follows

Cash (WC)	40,000	
Loss	10,000	
Land.		50,000

Working capital generated from the sale of the land would be $40,000, the selling price of the land, even though the sale was at a $10,000 loss to the company. The loss on the sale was debited in computing net income. The loss must be added back as an adjustment to net income in computing working capital from operations.

B. Borrowing by issuing a long-term debt is also recorded in the Other Sources section of the SCFP.

Borrowing by issuing a short-term debt has no affect on working capital. On the one hand, a current asset is increased and, on the other, a current liability is increased. However, if a company issues long-term debt, a current asset is increased and a noncurrent liability is increased. The net affect on working capital is equal to the increase in the current asset.

EXAMPLE 9-10: K & L Company borrowed cash on two separate occasions: once, by issuing a long-term note payable for $10,000; and another time, by issuing a short-term note for $5,000. The entries to record these activities were as follows

Cash (WC)	10,000	
Note Payable (long-term).		10,000
Cash (WC)	5,000	
Note Payable (short-term) (WC)		5,000

Remember
$$\Delta WC = \Delta CA - \Delta CL$$
$$\Delta WC = (+10,000) - (0) = +10,000$$
$$\Delta WC = (+5,000) - (+5,000) = 0$$

The long-term borrowing increased working capital by $10,000, the short-term borrowing had no effect. Another way to look at the two situations is that in the first case, K & L Company has $10,000 more available to "work with" to meet its current debts. In the second case, the company has $5,000 more available but it also has $5,000 more debt to meet.

C. The issuance of new stock or an increase in equity will often be listed in the Other Sources section of the SCFP.

The issuance of stock for cash increases a company's current assets. It also increases equity which is a noncurrent balance sheet account. Therefore the net affect on working capital is equal to the increase in the current asset. An increase in equity such as the additional investment of cash by an owner, also increases a current asset and increases equity. Working capital is increased by the amount of the investment.

EXAMPLE 9-11: WSX Corporation was expecting financial difficulty. To meet all its current obligations as they came due, the company sold long-term marketable securities that cost $15,000 for $32,000. It also took out a long-term loan of $10,000 and issued 500 new shares of stock @ $40. Each of these events increased the firm's working capital and would be reported on the company's SCFP as follows:

Other Sources	
Sale of long-term securities	$32,000
Increase in long-term debt	10,000
Issuance of stock.	20,000
Total Funds from Other Sources	62,000

9-6. Uses of Working Capital

The firm uses working capital to purchase long-term assets, retire long-term debt, redeem stock, and pay cash dividends. The uses of funds are shown in a separate section, summed, and deducted from the total sources to explain the change in funds over the period.

EXAMPLE 9-12: XYZ Corporation acquired $100,000 of new equipment during 19x1. It retired $400,000 of long-term debt and paid cash dividends to stockholders of $250,000. These items will be reported as uses of working capital on the SCFP. Analysis of the entries made to record the transactions shows that in each case working capital was used up as a result of the event.

Equipment	100,000	
Cash (WC)		100,000
Long-term Notes Payable	400,000	
Cash (WC)		400,000
Dividends (Retained Earnings)	250,000	
Cash (WC)		250,000

In each case working capital is reduced by the amount of the credit to the accounts that are a part of working capital.

EXAMPLE 9-13: XYZ Company's balance sheet indicated that the equipment account began the year with a balance of $100,000. It ended the year with a balance of $125,000. Investigation revealed that equipment that cost $55,000 with accumulated depreciation of $25,000 was sold at a gain of $5,000. How would these events be reported on a SCFP?

The gain on the sale of the equipment would be subtracted from net income in determining the working capital from operations. An analysis of the entries implied gives clues to the way in which the sale of equipment and the acquisition of equipment would be reported. This problem is tricky because you are not given information on the cost of the new equipment purchased. You must determine this amount by looking at the equipment T account.

Equipment

1/1/ (Balance)	100,000	(Sale of Equipment)	55,000
(Acquisitions)	?		
12/31 (Balance)	125,000		

The amount of equipment acquired can be found by determining the missing debit in the equipment account. We know that

$$\text{Ending Balance} = \text{Beg. Balance} + \text{Acquisitions} - \text{Sales of Equipment}$$
$$125,000 = 100,000 + X - 55,000$$
$$X = 80,000$$

The firm acquired \$80,000 of new equipment during the year. The entries implied by the information given in this example are:

Cash (WC)	35,000	
Accumulated Depreciation	25,000	
Equipment		55,000
Gain on Sale		5,000
(Cash received = book value of equipment sold + gain = \$55,000 − 25,000 + 5,000 = 35,000)		
Equipment	80,000	
Cash (WC)		80,000

The cash acquired from selling used equipment will appear as an Other Source of working capital. The cash expended on the purchase of new equipment will be shown as a use of working capital.

9-7. The "All Financial Resources" Concept

The FASB requires that the SCFP reveal information about all major financing transactions even if they do not affect working capital. This is often called the "all financial resources" concept. Common types of other-financing transactions include conversion of long-term debt or preferred stock to common stock, purchase of long-term assets by issuing long-term debt or stock, refinancing of long-term debt with long-term debt. These transactions may be included as separate section on the statement called Changes in Financial Position Which Did Not Affect Net Working Capital or as a source and use of funds.

EXAMPLE 9-14: XYZ Corporation acquired land by issuing \$500,000 of long-term bonds payable to the former owners of the property. During the year, \$200,000 of XYZ Corporation's convertible bonds were turned in for common stock. These transactions represent other important financing transactions. They do not affect working capital, but they will still be reported on the SCFP. An analysis of the entries made reveals that no working capital accounts are affected.

Land	500,000	
Bonds Payable		500,000
Convertible Bonds Payable	200,000	
Common Stock		200,000

In this case, each transaction will be reported as both an other source and a use of working capital.

Other Sources
    Issuance of bonds to acquire land. 500,000
    Issuance of stock to retire convertible bonds 200,000
    Total Funds From Other Sources. 700,000

Uses of Funds:
    Acquisition of land with bonds payable 500,000
    Retirement of convertible bonds by issuing common stock 200,000
    Total Uses 700,000

9-8. The T Account Worksheet

The T account worksheet provides a systematic method of preparing a SCFP. T accounts are prepared with opening and closing balances for all *non-working capital* (noncurrent) balance sheet accounts. The beginning and ending amount of working capital is computed using a large Working Capital account. Information provided on the income statement and from the problem allow the preparer to reconstruct the likely entries which will explain the change in the balances in the non-current (or non-working capital) accounts. Since the change in working capital can always be explained by the change in the non-working capital balance sheet accounts, the process of reproducing the activity in noncurrent balance sheet accounts will supply all the information required to prepare a statement of changes in financial position. For convenience, entries made in the worksheet Working Capital account are separated according to the sections on the statement. The T account worksheet is a device for preparing the SCFP. The accounts and entries shown do not become a part of the company's permanent books. The worksheet may be preserved to show how the SCFP was prepared, but the sheet is merely a tool to aid in the statement preparation.

The steps in using the worksheet method are shown below. The sample problem that follows illustrates the use of the T account worksheet.

STEPS IN USING A T ACCOUNT WORKSHEET TO PREPARE A SCFP

1. Set up T accounts for Working Capital and all noncurrent balance sheet accounts.
2. Compute beginning and ending working capital from the balance sheets for the previous and current year.
3. Enter beginning and ending balances in all the T accounts.
4. Using information on the income statement and other information provided in the problem, reproduce the entries implied to explain the change in the balances in the non-current balance sheet accounts.
5. When all changes in non-current balance sheet accounts are explained, the change in the working capital account should also have been explained. (Check to see that the entries in the accounts fully explain the change in working capital).
6. Prepare the SCFP from the information in the working capital account.

What information do you need in order to prepare a statement of changes in financial position? You need the balance sheets for this year and the previous year in order to establish the change in the balances in non-current accounts. You will need information from the income statement, and also information about dividends paid and certain other kinds of transactions which should be provided in the problem.

9-9. Schedule of Changes in Working Capital Accounts

The FASB requires that a schedule showing the change in each working capital account be presented along with the SCFP when funds are defined as working capital. The schedule is used as a check for the calculations in the SCFP. The schedule make take many forms, one of which is illustrated in Exhibit 9-3 included in Example 9-15.

EXAMPLE 9-15: XYZ Corporation reported the following on its income statement for the year ended 12/31/x1.

XYZ Corporation
Income Statement
For the Year Ended 12/31/x1

Sales		$200,000
Expenses and (Gains):		
Cost of Goods Sold	$108,000	
Wages	44,000	
Rent	8,000	
Depreciation	22,000	
Interest	4,000	
Gain on Sale of Equipment	(2,000)	
Total Expenses and (Gains)		184,000
Net Income Before Income Taxes		$ 16,000
Income Taxes:		
Current	$ 3,000	
Deferred	1,000	4,000
Net Income		$ 12,000

The statement of retained earnings indicated that $6,000 of dividends were paid. Investigation revealed that the company sold equipment that originally cost $25,000 and had accumulated depreciation of $20,000. Long-term notes totaling $2,000 were settled by issuing common stock. The comparative balance sheet for 19x0 and 19x1 is presented below.

XYZ Corporation
Comparative Balance Sheet
12/31/x1 and 12/31/x0

Assets	19x1	19x0	Change
Cash	10,000	8,000	2,000
Accounts Receivable	35,000	24,000	11,000
Inventory	40,000	30,000	10,000
Prepaid Rent	2,000	4,000	(2,000)
Equipment	100,000	95,000	5,000
Accumulated Depreciation	(36,000)	(34,000)	(2,000)
Total Assets	151,000	127,000	24,000
Liabilities and Equity			
Accounts Payable	38,000	25,000	13,000
Short-term Notes Payable	10,000	0	10,000
Long-term Notes Payable	34,000	45,000	(11,000)
Deferred Income Tax	6,000	5,000	1,000
Common Stock	15,000	10,000	5,000
Retained Earnings	48,000	42,000	6,000
Total Liabilities & Equity	151,000	127,000	24,000

Step 1: You should first set up a large Working Capital account and a T account for all non-working capital accounts shown on the balance sheets.

Step 2: The beginning and ending balances in the large working capital account should be computed.

Current Assets include Cash, Accounts Receivable, Inventory, and Prepaid Rent.

Current Liabilities include Accounts Payable and Short-term Notes Payable.

Beg WC = (8,000 + 24,000 + 30,000 + 4,000) − (25,000 + 0) = 41,000
End WC = (10,000 + 35,000 + 40,000 + 2,000) − (38,000 + 10,000) = 39,000

Step 3: The beginning and ending balances for 19x1 should be entered in each account. Remember, the beginning balance for 19x1 is simply the ending balance from 19x0. The T account worksheet is presented below with the beginning and ending balances entered into each account.

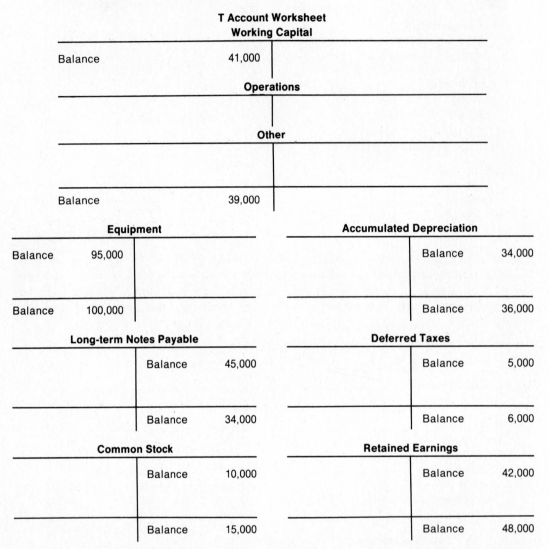

T Account Worksheet

Working Capital

Balance	41,000		

Operations

Other

Balance	39,000		

Equipment			**Accumulated Depreciation**	
Balance	95,000		Balance	34,000
Balance	100,000		Balance	36,000

Long-term Notes Payable			**Deferred Taxes**	
	Balance	45,000	Balance	5,000
	Balance	34,000	Balance	6,000

Common Stock			**Retained Earnings**	
	Balance	10,000	Balance	42,000
	Balance	15,000	Balance	48,000

Step 4: Using the information in the income statement and the other information provided, the following entries are implied in explaining the change in the account balances.

(a) WC-Operations............................ 12,000
    Retained Earnings.....................   12,000 → net income
       Profit is the primary source of WC-Operations.

(b) WC-Operations............................ 22,000
    Accumulated Depreciation...............   22,000
       Profit adjustment for an expense not using WC.

(c) WC-Operations............................ 1,000
    Deferred Income Taxes   1,000
       Adjust profit for expense not using WC.

(d) Retained Earnings 2,000
    WC-Operations   2,000
       Adjust profit for gain on sale of equipment which will be accounted for as an other source of WC.

(e) Cash (WC-Other)	7,000	
Accumulated Depreciation	20,000	
Equipment		25,000
Gain on Sale of Equipment (R.E.)		2,000
Record sale of equipment as WC-Other.		
(f) Equipment	30,000	
Cash (WC-Other)		30,000
Equipment purchase is use of WC. Amount of purchase is equal to debit required to explain ending balance in the Equipment account.		
(g) Long-term N/P	11,000	
Common Stock		2,000
Cash (WC-Other)		9,000
Retirement of long-term debt for cash is a use of WC.		
Retirement of long-term debt for common stock is an other major financing transaction.		
(h) Dividends (Retained Earnings)	6,000	
Cash (WC-Other)		6,000
Dividends are a use of WC.		
(i) Cash (WC-Other)	3,000	
Common Stock		3,000
Cash received for issued stock is an other source of WC.		

After these implied entries have been posted to the T account worksheet, the accounts would appear as follows:

T Account Worksheet

Working Capital

Balance	41,000	

Operations

(a) profit	12,000		(d) gain on sale	2,000
(b) depreciation	22,000			
(c) deferred taxes	1,000			

Other

Sources			Uses	
(e) sale of equipment	7,000		(f) equipment purchased	30,000
(i) common stock issued	3,000		(g) Note Payable retired	9,000
			(h) dividends	6,000
Balance	39,000			

Equipment						**Accumulated Depreciation**				
Balance	95,000								Balance	34,000
(f)	30,000	(e)		25,000		(e)	20,000		(b)	22,000
Balance	100,000								Balance	36,000

Long-term Notes Payable					**Deferred Taxes**				
			Balance	45,000				Balance	5,000
(g)	11,000							(c)	1,000
			Balance	34,000				Balance	6,000

Common Stock					Retained Earnings		
Balance	10,000					Balance	42,000
(g)	2,000	(d)	2,000			(a)	12,000
(i)	3,000	(h)	6,000			(e)	2,000
Balance	15,000					Balance	48,000

Steps 5 and 6: Check each account to be sure that all balances are accounted for. When all balance changes are accounted for, the information in the Working Capital account can be used to prepare the Statement of Changes in Financial Position.

EXHIBIT 9-3: Statement of Changes in Financial Position

XYZ Corporation
Statement of Changes in Financial Position
For the Year Ended 12/31/x1

Sources of Funds:
  Operations

Net Income	$12,000		
Adjustments to Net Income:			
Depreciation Expense	22,000		
Deferred Income Taxes	1,000		
Gain on Sale of Equipment	(2,000)		
Total Funds From Operations		$33,000	
Other Sources			
Sale of equipment	$ 7,000		
Common stock issued for cash	3,000		
Common stock issued to retire long-term note payable	2,000		
Total Funds From Other Sources . . .		12,000	
Total Sources		$ 45,000	
Uses of Funds:			
Equipment purchased	$30,000		
Retirement of long-term note payable for cash	9,000		
Dividends	6,000		
Retirement of long-term note payable for stock	2,000		
Total Uses of Funds		47,000	
Net (Decrease) in Funds		$(2,000)	

Schedule of Changes in Working Capital Accounts

Current Assets: Increases (Decreases)

Cash	$ 2,000	
Accounts Receivable	11,000	
Inventory	10,000	
Prepaid Rent	(2,000)	
Net Increase in Current Assets		$21,000

Current Liabilities: Increases (Decreases)

Accounts Payable	13,000	
Short-term Liabilities	10,000	
Net Increase in Current Liabilities . . .		23,000
Net (Decrease) in Working Capital . . .		(2,000)

RAISE YOUR GRADES

Can you explain...?

☑ the purpose of the SCFP
☑ the SCFP equation
☑ the equation for working capital
☑ what is the primary source of working capital from operations
☑ what are some sources of working capital other than operations
☑ what kind of expenses do not use up working capital
☑ what are some other uses of funds
☑ how to handle the sale of a long-term asset at a gain
☑ what is meant by the "all financial resources" concept
☑ what a significant other financing transaction is and how it is reported on the SCFP
☑ what is the purpose of the schedule of changes in working capital accounts
☑ the steps in preparing a T account worksheet

SUMMARY

1. The purpose of the SCFP is to show the sources and uses of funds during an accounting period and to explain changes in the funds.
2. The SCFP equation states that funds generated during an accounting period less the funds used is equal to the change in funds over the accounting period.
3. The FASB allows two definitions of funds, cash and working capital.
4. Working capital is equal to current assets less current liabilities
5. $\Delta WC = \Delta CA - \Delta CL = \Delta NCL - \Delta NCA + \Delta E$
6. The primary source of working capital from operations is net income.
7. Net income must be adjusted for revenue that does not generate an equal amount of working capital.
8. When preparing the SCFP, net income must be adjusted for expenses that do not use up an equal amount of working capital.
9. Other sources of working capital include sale of long-term assets, new long-term borrowing, and the issuance of stock.
10. Some uses of working capital are the purchase of long-term assets, the retirement of long-term debts, redemption of stock, and the payment of dividends and taxes.
11. The FASB requires that the SCFP reveal information about all significant financing transactions even if they do not affect working capital. This is commonly referred to as the "all financial resources" concept.
12. Financing activities that do not affect working capital include conversion of long-term debt or preferred stock to common stock, the purchase of long-term assets with long-term debt, or refinancing long-term debt with long-term debt. All these activities are reported as both sources and uses of funds on the SCFP. They may also be reported in a separate section.
13. The schedule of changes in working capital accounts is required by the FASB as a supplement to the SCFP, when funds are defined as working capital.
14. The schedule of changes in working capital accounts provides a check for the calculations in the SCFP.

RAPID REVIEW

1. The basic equation of a SCFP is _____ .

2. Which of the following are other sources of working capital. There may be more than one correct answer.
   (a) XYZ borrows funds by issuing a long-term bond payable.
   (b) A widget company sells a widget at a profit.
   (c) A building is sold at a $100,000 loss. The selling price of the building was $1,000,000.
   (d) XYZ Company incurs $100,000 of depreciation expense.
   (e) XYZ Company borrows funds by issuing a short-term note payable.

3. How will the other items in Question 2 be included on a SCFP?

4. XYZ Company reported a net loss of $5,000. Included in the net loss was $17,000 of depreciation expense, and a net loss of $2,000 on the sale of a building. The company borrowed $15,000 by issuing a long-term note payable. What was the Working Capital From Operations for the firm?

5. XYZ Company reported a net income of $7,000. Included in the net income was $6,000 of depreciation expense. The building was sold at a $3,000 profit for $20,000. What was the working capital from operations, the other sources of working capital, and total sources of working capital?

6. Which of the following is a separately reportable use of working capital?
   (a) Company retires a short-term note payable.
   (b) Company buys inventory.
   (c) Company buys treasury stock.
   (d) Company sells a building at a loss.

7. Which of the following would be considered an other major financing transaction?
   (a) Company issues stock in return for cash.
   (b) Company issues stock in return for inventory.
   (c) Company issues stock in return for services received.
   (d) Company issues stock in return for a building.

8. In what section on a SCFP will the following appear? The sections are Working Capital From Operations, Other Sources, and Uses of Funds. Funds are defined as working capital.
   (a) Depreciation Expense
   (b) Funds from sale of long-term bonds payable
   (c) Retirement of common stock
   (d) Dividends paid
   (e) Funds from sale of noncurrent marketable securities sold at a loss

9. XYZ Company's comparative balance sheets indicated that noncurrent assets increased by $10,000, noncurrent liabilities increased by $4,000, and equity increased by $8,000 during the year. By how much did working capital change?

10. XYZ Company lists net income of $50,000, depreciation expense of $12,000, and gain on the sale of long-term marketable securities held as an investment of $4,000. The marketable securities were originally purchased at a cost of $10,000. The firm purchased long-term marketable securities to hold as an investment costing $13,000, issued $15,000 of long-term notes payable, and retired common stock at a cost of $3,000.
    (a) The Working Capital From Operations is _____ .

    (b) The Other Sources total _____ .

    (c) The Uses of Funds total _____ .

    (d) The Change in Working Capital is _____ .

11. What information do you need to prepare a SCFP?

12. Indicate whether each of the following is true or false.
    (*a*) A gain on the sale of a building is added back to profit in calculating working capital from operations.
    (*b*) Sale of an airplane by an airline transport company would be an other source of working capital.
    (*c*) Purchase of an airplane by an airline transport company would reduce working capital from operations.
    (*d*) Depreciation expense is shown as a use of funds.
    (*e*) Issuing shares of stock for cash is an other source of funds.
    (*f*) Sale of treasury stock is an other source of funds.

13. ZXC Company reported $40,000 of net income. Included in the net income was $10,000 depreciation expense, $3,000 of deferred taxes, and a net gain on the sale of land of $7,000. What was the Working Capital from Operations for the year?

14. OPL Company sold a building which originally cost $40,000 at a gain of $10,000. The depreciation accumulated on the building to the date of sale was $28,000. How much working capital was generated from the sale of the building?

Answers:

1. Funds Generated During the Accounting Period − Funds Used During the Accounting Period = Change in Funds Over the Accounting Period [Section 9-1]
2. a, c [Section 9-5]
3. (*b*) WC generated is included in profit in WC-Operations
   (*d*) Add as an adjustment to profit in calculating WC-Operations
   (*e*) No effect on Working Capital
   [Section 9-4]
4. (−5,000) + 17,000 + 2,000 = 14,000 [Sections 9-4 and 9-5]
5. WC − Operations = 7,000 + 6,000 − 3,000 = 10,000
   Other Source = 20,000
   Total Sources = 10,000 + 20,000 = 30,000 [Sections 9-4 and 9-5]
6. c [Section 9-6]
7. d [Section 9-7]
8. (*a*) WC-Operations
   (*b*) Other Sources
   (*c*) Uses
   (*d*) Uses
   (*e*) Other Sources, loss added back in computing WC-Operations
   [Sections 9-4, 9-5 and 9-6]
9. 4,000 − 10,000 + 8,000 = +2,000 [Section 9-2]
10. (*a*) 50,000 + 12,000 − 4,000 = 58,000
    (*b*) 10,000 + 4,000 + 15,000 = 29,000
    (*c*) 13,000 + 3,000 = 16,000
    (*d*) 58,000 + 29,000 − 16,000 = 71,000
    [Sections 9-4, 9-5 and 9-6]
11. The beginning and ending balance sheets, an income statement and sometimes other information. [Section 9-8]
12. (*a*) False
    (*b*) True
    (*c*) False
    (*d*) False
    (*e*) True
    (*f*) True [Sections 9-4, 9-5, and 9-6]
13. 40,000 + 10,000 + 3,000 − 7,000 = 46,000 [Section 9-5]
14. 40,000 − 28,000 + 10,000 = 22,000 [Section 9-5]

SOLVED PROBLEMS

PROBLEM 9-1: TUE Company reported net income of $120,000 for 19x1. The income statement revealed depreciation expense of $35,000, deferred taxes of $10,000 and a net gain on the sale of land of $16,000. The income statement and balance sheets also revealed that $1,000 of the bad debt expense charged to the year reduced the net amount of long-term notes receivable. Of the company's revenue, $4,000 came from its share of profits earned by ABC Company which was accounted for by the equity method. When income from investments is accounted for by the equity method the entry to record the income is as follows:

Investment in ABC Co. Stock	4,000	
Equity in Earnings of ABC Co.		4,000
Investment in ABC Co. Stock is a long-term asset account.		

The account Investment in ABC Co. Stock is a long-term asset account, and equity in earnings of ABC Co. is a revenue account. Prepare the Working Capital From Operations section of the SCFP.

Answer:

Sources of Funds:	
Operations	
Net Income.	$120,000
Adjustments to Net Income:	
Depreciation expense	35,000
Deferred taxes	10,000
Gain on sale of land	(16,000)
Bad debt expense on long-term note receivable	1,000
Equity in earnings of ABC Co.	(4,000)
Total Funds From Operations	$146,000

Depreciation and deferred taxes are added back because they are expenses that do not use up working capital. The gain on the sale of the land is subtracted because the working capital generated by the sale will be accounted for in the other sources section of the statement. Bad debt expense on long-term notes receivable is added back because the expense reduces long-term assets rather than current assets. It is an expense that does not use up working capital. The equity in the earnings of the ABC Co. is deducted because this is revenue that did not generate working capital. The entry made to record the equity in the earnings of ABC increased a long-term investment account, not a current asset account. **[Section 9-4]**

PROBLEM 9-2: CSF Company's income statement showed net income of $45,000 during 19x1. Depreciation expense was $12,000. Of the sales made $3,000 were on long-term credit and increased the balance in the long-term notes receivable account. The company sold land which originally cost $50,000 for $42,000. The company paid off a $10,000 long-term note payable by signing a new long-term note for the same amount at a different interest rate. The company paid $40,000 to acquire 1,000 shares of its own stock which it is holding as treasury stock. Dividends of $25,000 were paid. Prepare a SCFP for CSF Company. Use working capital as the definition of funds.

CSF Company
Statement of Changes in Financial Position
For Year Ended 12/31/x1

Sources of Funds:		
Operations		
Net Income	$45,000	
Adjustments to Net Income:		
Depreciation Expense	12,000	
Sales made on long-term credit	(3,000)	
Loss on sale of land	8,000	
Total Funds From Operations		$ 62,000
Other Sources of Funds:		
Sale of land	$42,000	
Issuance of long-term notes payable to refinance		
long-term debt	10,000	
Total Funds From Other Sources		52,000
Total Sources of Funds		$114,000
Uses of Funds:		
Purchase of Treasury Stock	$40,000	
Dividends	25,000	
Retirement of long-term note payable by		
issuing new long-term note	10,000	
Total Uses of Funds		75,000
Net Increase in Funds		$ 39,000

[Section 9-8]

PROBLEM 9-3: Refer to the statement of changes in financial position prepared in Exhibit 9-3 of the text of this chapter. What observations can you make about the company from the information presented in this statement?

Answer: While XYZ Corporation earned a profit of $12,000, it generated $33,000 of working capital from operations. Depreciation expense was a large expense deducted in the computation of net income that did not use funds. The company generated a considerable amount of the funds it needed internally. (It should be noted that many tax shelter investments are made in firms that show little or no net income but which generate a positive fund flow. The net loss is deducted on the investor's tax return reducing the taxes paid on other income. However, the fund flow from the operation is positive, providing funds for investment in other projects.)

The firm generated funds from the sale of equipment, (selling price was $7,000) and from issuing common stock. Common stock was also issued to retire a long-term note payable. The firm used funds to purchase new equipment and pay dividends. We can see that this firm is expanding. The equipment purchased during the year exceeded the value of the equipment sold. **[Sections 9-4 through 9-7]**

PROBLEM 9-4: Many of the rules in accounting emphasize substance over form in reporting the results of transactions. The SCFP must report significant other financing transactions even though they do not affect the amount of funds the company has. Describe some of the transactions that are labeled significant other financing transactions. Why is their substance such that they should be reported as both sources and uses of funds?

Answer: The category of other significant financing transactions includes transactions such as:

(a) Conversion of long-term debt to stock.
(b) Conversion of preferred stock to common stock.
(c) Refinancing of a long-term note with another long-term note.
(d) Financing the acquisition of a long-term asset by issuing either long-term debt or stock.

These transactions could be viewed as both a source and a use of funds. The conversion of debt could be viewed as two simultaneous transactions. In the first, the company obtains cash from the bondholders by issuing stock to them. In the second, the company uses the cash received for the stock to settle the long-term debt. It just happens that in this special case the people who provide funds for the stock issued are the same people who are paid when the debt is retired.

All of the other transactions can be viewed in a similar manner. They are all transactions that raise funds and then simultaneously use them.   **[Section 9-7]**

PROBLEM 9-5: BBB Company began and ended the accounting period with the following balances in selected accounts.

	Beginning Balance	Ending Balance
Accumulated Depreciation	$40,000	$48,000
Equipment	100,000	102,000

During the year, the firm sold equipment which originally cost $30,000 at a net gain of $6,000. Depreciation expense for the year was $18,000. What amount of funds was generated, by the sale of the equipment? What amount of funds was used to purchase equipment?

Answer: The funds used to purchase equipment equal the purchase price of new equipment. The amount of funds generated from the sale of a long-term asset is equal to the selling price of the asset. Answering this question requires some sleuthing through the accounts. We have information from the accumulated depreciation and equipment accounts that will allow us to answer the question.

Equipment

1/1/x1 (Balance)	100,000		
(Aquisitions)	?	Dispositions	30,000
12/31/x1 (Balance)	102,000		

The firm must have used funds to acquire $32,000 of new equipment because the balance in the Equipment account increased by $2,000 in a year in which equipment which originally cost $30,000 was sold.

Accumulated Depreciation

		1/1/x1 (Balance)	40,000
Accum. Depreciation on Equip. Sold	?	Depn. Expense	18,000
		12/31/x1 (Balance)	48,000

The accumulated depreciation on the equipment sold must have been $10,000. The debits into the accumulated depreciation must have been $8,000 less than the credits because the balance increased by $8,000. The book value of the equipment sold (cost − accumulated depreciation) was $20,000 which equals the $30,000 cost of equipment sold less accumulated depreciation of $10,000. The equipment was sold at a gain of $6,000. The equipment must have been sold for $6,000 more than its book value. The selling price was $26,000 ($20,000 + $6,000). The equipment sold provided funds of $26,000.   **[Section 9-4]**

PROBLEM 9-6: Compute the change in working capital given the information below?

	19x1	19x0
Noncurrent Assets	15,000	10,000
Noncurrent Liabilities	12,000	8,000
Equity	8,000	9,000

Answer:

$$\Delta\,WC = \quad \Delta\,NCL \quad - \quad \Delta\,NCA \quad + \quad \Delta\,E$$
$$\Delta\,WC = (12{,}000 - 8{,}000) - (15{,}000 - 10{,}000) + (8{,}000 - 9{,}000)$$
$$\Delta\,WC = \quad\quad -2{,}000$$

[Section 9-1]

PROBLEM 9-7: GRE Company prepared the following comparative balance sheet for 12/31/x0 and 12/31/x1.

GRE Company
Comparative Balance Sheets
12/31/x1 and 12/31/x0

	12/31/x1	12/31/x0
Cash	$19,000	$16,000
Accounts Receivable.	24,000	26,000
Inventory	12,000	15,000
Long-term Notes Receivable	3,000	0
Investment in Jones Co (Long-term).	8,000	6,000
Equipment	30,000	20,000
Accumulated Depreciation.	(8,000)	(7,000)
Total Assets	$88,000	$76,000
Accounts Payable.	$20,000	$14,000
Wages Payable.	3,000	2,000
Long-term Notes Payable	21,000	10,000
Common Stock	15,000	5,000
Retained Earnings	29,000	45,000
Total Liabilities and Equity.	$88,000	$76,000

The company reported the following net income in 19x1.

GRE Company
Income Statement
For Year Ended 12/31/x1

Sales		$105,000
Equity in Earnings of Jones Company		2,000
Total Revenue		$107,000
Expenses and Losses:		
Cost of Goods Sold	$85,000	
Wages Expense.	15,000	
Depreciation Expense	5,000	
Loss on Sale of Equipment.	6,000	
Total Expenses and Losses		$111,000
Net (Loss).		(4,000)

The original cost of the equipment sold was $15,000. The company accepted a long-term note in payment for $3,000 of goods sold. Set up a T account worksheet and use it to prepare a statement of changes in financial position for GRE Company using working capital as your definition of funds.

Answer: The T account worksheet and implied entries appear below:

(a) Retained Earnings	4,000	
WC-Operations		4,000
A net loss provides negative WC-Operations		
(b) WC-Operations.	5,000	
Accumulated Depreciation.		5,000
Depreciation is an expense that does not use WC.		

(c)	WC-Operations...................	6,000	
	Loss on Sale of Equipment (R.E.).........		6,000
(d)	Investment in Jones Co................	2,000	
	WC-Operations......................		2,000
	Equity in Earnings of Jones Co. is revenue that does not produce WC.		
(e)	Cash (WC-Other).....................	5,000	
	Accumulated Depreciation..............	4,000	
	Loss on Sale of Equipment (R.E.)...........	6,000	
	Equipment..........................		15,000
	To record the sale of equipment which gives WC-Other.		
(f)	Equipment..........................	25,000	
	Cash (WC-Other).....................		25,000
(g)	Long-term Notes Receivable.............	3,000	
	WC-Operations......................		3,000
	To reduce WC-Operations for revenue not providing WC.		
(h)	Cash (WC-Other).....................	11,000	
	Long-term Notes Payable...............		11,000
	New Long-term debt is an other source of WC.		
(i)	Cash (WC-Other).....................	10,000	
	Common Stock......................		10,000
	Issuance of new stock is an other source of WC.		
(j)	Dividends (Retained Earnings)............	12,000	
	Cash (WC-Other).....................		12,000
	Dividends are a use of WC.		

T Account Worksheet

Working Capital

Balance	41,000	

Operations

(b) depreciation	5,000		(a) net loss	4,000
(c) loss on sale	6,000		(d) equity in earnings of Jones Co.	2,000
			(g) Sales on long-term note receivable	3,000

Other

(e) equipment sold	5,000		(f) equipment purchased	25,000
(h) long-term note payable	11,000		(j) dividends	12,000
(i) Common Stock	10,000			
Balance	32,000			

Long-term Note Receivable			**Investment in Jones Co.**		
Balance	0		Balance	6,000	
(g)	3,000		(d)	2,000	
Balance	3,000		Balance	8,000	

Equipment				Accumulated Depreciation			
Balance	20,000					Balance	7,000
(f)	25,000	(e)	15,000	(e)	4,000	(b)	5,000
Balance	30,000					Balance	8,000

Long-term Note Payable				Common Stock			
		Balance	10,000			Balance	5,000
		(h)	11,000			(i)	10,000
		Balance	21,000			Balance	15,000

Retained Earnings			
		Balance	45,000
(a)	4,000		
(e)	6,000	(c)	6,000
(j)	12,000		
		Balance	29,000

The statement of changes in financial position will appear as follows:

GRE Company
Statement of Changes in Financial Position
For Year Ended 12/31/x1

Sources of Funds:		
Operations:		
Net (Loss)	(4,000)	
Adjustments to Net (Loss)		
Depreciation Expense	5,000	
Loss on Sale of Equipment	6,000	
Equity on Earnings of Jones Co.	(2,000)	
Sales made on long-term credit	(3,000)	
Total Funds From Operations		$ 2,000
Other Sources		
Sale of equipment	5,000	
Increase in long-term Notes Payable	11,000	
Issuance of common stock	10,000	
Total Funds From Other Sources		26,000
Total Sources		$ 28,000
Uses of Funds:		
Purchase of Equipment	$25,000	
Dividends	12,000	
Total Uses		37,000
Net (Decrease) in Funds		$(9,000)

Schedule of Changes in Working Capital Accounts

Current Assets: Increases (Decreases)		
Cash	$ 3,000	
Accounts Receivable	(2,000)	
Inventory	(3,000)	
Net (Decrease) in Current Assets		$(2,000)
Current Liabilities: Increases (Decreases)		
Accounts Payable	$ 6,000	
Wages Payable	1,000	
Net Increase in Current Liabilities		$ 7,000
Net (Decrease) in Working Capital		$(9,000)

[Section 9-9]

PROBLEM 9-8: What can you say about GRE Company from the information that appears in the statement of changes in financial position? (Refer to Problem 9-7).

Answer: GRE Company is obtaining the funds it needs externally. The firm generated only $2,000 of its funds from operations. The firm used funds to purchase equipment, thereby increasing long-term assets. It used $12,000 to pay dividends to the stockholders. The $12,000 dividend payment may be excessive given the profit and fund generation performance of the company. The firm appears to be borrowing money in order to make dividend payments.   **[Section 9-9]**

PROBLEM 9-9: MUN Company began and ended the accounting period with the following balances in selected accounts.

	Beginning Balance	Ending Balance
Accumulated Depreciation	140,000	130,000
Trucks	200,000	215,000

During the year, the firm sold a truck which originally cost $50,000 at a net gain of $4,000. Depreciation expense for the year was $10,000. What amount of funds was generated by the sale of the equipment? What amount of funds was used to purchase equipment?

Answer: The funds used to purchase a truck equals the purchase price of the new truck. The amount of funds generated from the sale of a long-term asset is equal to the selling price of the asset. Answering this question requires some sleuthing through the accounts. We have information from the accumulated depreciation and truck accounts that will allow us to answer the question.

Truck

1/1/x1 Balance	200,000		
(Acquisitions)	?	Dispositions	50,000
12/31/x1 (Balance)	215,000		

The firm must have used funds to acquire a $65,000 truck because the balance in the Truck account increased by $15,000 in a year in which a truck which originally cost $50,000 was sold.

Accumulated Depreciation

		1/1/x1 (Balance)	140,000
Accum. Depreciation on Equip. Sold ?		Depn. Expense	10,000
		12/31/x1 (Balance)	130,000

The accumulated depreciation on the equipment sold must have been $20,000. The debits into the accumulated depreciation must have been $10,000 more than the credits because the balance decreased by $10,000. The book value of the equipment sold (cost − accumulated depreciation) was $30,000 which equals the $50,000 cost of equipment sold less accumulated depreciation of $20,000. The equipment was sold at a gain of $4,000. The equipment must have been sold for $4,000 more than its book value. The selling price was $34,000 ($30,000 + $4,000). The equipment sold provided funds of $34,000.   **[Section 9-4]**

PROBLEM 9-10: Compute the change in working capital given the information below?

	19x2	19x1
Current Assets	25,000	10,000
Current Liabilities	16,000	10,000

Answer:

Δ WC = ΔCA   − ΔCL

Δ WC = (25,000 − 10,000) − (16,000 − 10,000)

Δ WC =   +9,000   **[Section 9-1]**

PROBLEM 9-11: MOM Company prepared the following comparative balance sheet for 12/31/x4 and 12/31/x5.

MOM Company
Comparative Balance Sheets
12/31/x5 and 12/31/x4

	12/31/x5	12/31/x4
Cash	$ 34,000	$19,000
Accounts Receivable	15,000	26,000
Inventory	9,000	12,000
Long-term Notes Receivable	13,000	10,000
Investment in Hess Co (Long-term)	12,000	6,000
Equipment	40,000	30,000
Accumulated Depreciation	(12,000)	(10,000)
Total Assets	$111,000	$93,000
Accounts Payable	$ 17,000	$20,000
Wages Payable	8,000	7,000
Long-term Notes Payable	26,000	20,000
Common Stock	15,000	15,000
Retained Earnings	45,000	31,000
Total Liabilities and Equity	$111,000	$93,000

The company reported the following net income in 19x1.

MOM Company
Income Statement
For the Year Ended 12/31/x1

Sales		$244,000
Equity in Earnings of Hess Company		6,000
Total Revenue		$250,000
Expenses and Losses:		
Cost of Goods Sold	$190,000	
Wages Expense	11,000	
Depreciation Expense	9,000	
Loss on Sale of Equipment	9,000	
Total Expenses and Losses		$219,000
Net Income		$ 31,000

The original cost of the equipment sold was $30,000. The company accepted a long-term note in payment for $3,000 of goods sold. Set up a T account worksheet. Reconstruct the implied journal entires to explain the change in working capital and post these transactions to the T account worksheet.

Answer: The T account worksheet and implied entries appear below:

(a) WC-Operations		31,000	
Retained Earnings			31,000
A net income provides WC-Operations			
(b) WC-Operations		9,000	
Accumulated Depreciation			9,000
Depreciation is an expense that does not use WC.			

(c)	WC-Operations.		9,000	
	Loss on Sale of Equipment (R.E.)			9,000
(d)	Investment in Hess Co.		6,000	
	WC-Operations			6,000
	Equity in Earnings of Jones Co. is revenue that does not produce WC.			
(e)	Cash (WC-Other)		14,000	
	Accumulated Depreciation		7,000	
	Loss on Sale of Equipment (R.E.).		9,000	
	Equipment			30,000
	To record the sale of equipment which gives WC-Other			
(f)	Equipment		40,000	
	Cash (WC-Other).			40,000
(g)	Long-term Notes Receivable		3,000	
	WC-Operations			3,000
	To reduce WC-Operations for revenue not providing WC.			
(h)	Cash (WC-Other)		6,000	
	Long-term Notes Payable.			6,000
	New long-term debt is an other source of of WC.			
(i)	Dividends (Retained Earnings)		17,000	
	Cash (WC-Other).			17,000
	Dividends are a use of WC.			

T Account Worksheet

Working Capital

Balance	30,000	

Operations

(a) net income	31,000	(d) equity in earnings of	
(b) depreciation	9,000	Hess Co.	6,000
(c) loss on sale	9,000	(g) sales on long-term	
		notes receivable	3,000

Other

(e) equipment sold	14,000	(f) equipment purchased	40,000
(h) long-term N/P	6,000	(i) dividends	17,000
Balance	33,000		

Long-term Note Receivable				Investment in Hess Co.		
Balance	10,000			Balance	6,000	
(g)	3,000			(d)	6,000	
Balance	13,000			Balance	12,000	

Equipment				Accumulated Depreciation			
Balance	30,000					Balance	10,000
(f)	40,000	(e)	30,000	(e)	7,000	(b)	9,000
Balance	40,000					Balance	12,000

Long-term Note Payable				Common Stock		
		Balance	20,000		Balance	15,000
		(h)	6,000			
		Balance	26,000		Balance	15,000

Retained Earnings			
		Balance	31,000
(e)	9,000	(a)	31,000
(i)	17,000	(c)	9,000
		Balance	45,000

[Section 9-9]

PROBLEM 9-12: From the information in Problem 9-11, prepare a SCFP.

Answer: The statement of changes in financial position will appear as follows:

MOM Company
Statement of Changes in Financial Position
For the Year Ended 12/31/x1

Sources of Funds:			
Operations			
Net Income	$31,000		
Adjustment to Net Income			
Depreciation Expense	9,000		
Loss on Sale of Equipment	9,000		
Equity on Earnings of Hess Co.	(6,000)		
Sales made on long-term credit	(3,000)		
Total Funds from Operations		$40,000	
Other Sources of Funds:			
Sale of Equipment	14,000		
Increase in long-term Notes Payable	6,000		
Total Funds From Other Sources			
Total Sources		20,000	
		$60,000	
Uses of Funds:			
Purchase of Equipment	$40,000		
Dividends	17,000		
Total Uses of Funds		57,000	
Net Change in Working Capital		$ 3,000	

Schedule of Changes in Working Capital Accounts

Current Assets: Increases (Decreases)		
Cash	$15,000	
Accounts Receivable	(11,000)	
Inventory	(3,000)	
Net Increase in Current Assets		$ 1,000
Current Liabilities: Increase (Decrease)		
Accounts Payable	$(3,000)	
Wages/Payable	1,000	
Net Increase in Current Liabilities		$ (2,000)
Net Increase in Working Capital		$ 3,000

[Section 9-9]

10 STATEMENT OF CHANGES IN FINANCIAL POSITION: CASH BASIS

THIS CHAPTER IS ABOUT

☑ **Defining Funds as Cash**

☑ **Sources of Cash**

☑ **Uses of Cash**

☑ **Other Significant Financing Transactions**

☑ **The Cash Basis T Account Worksheet**

10-1. Defining Funds as Cash

The statement of changes in financial position (SCFP) may be prepared on a *cash basis*; that is, using cash as the definition funds. The statement describes the sources and uses of cash in order to explain the change in the Cash account during the period.

A. Using cash as the definition of funds provides more relevant information.

The FASB has indicated the financial reports should present more information about the amounts, timing, and uncertainty of cash flows than they have in the past. This concern suggests that using cash as the definition of funds may be more relevant to the user in making decisions than the working capital definition (Chapter 9). SFAC No. 5 suggests that in the future a cash flow statement will be required. Although specific guidelines have not been issued, the SCFP on a cash basis provides cash flow information and may replace the SCFP on a working capital basis.

B. A change in cash funds may be explained by the changes in all noncash balance sheet accounts.

Exhibit 10-1 shows that the net change in cash funds (the Cash account) may be explained by looking at the changes in all noncash accounts on the balance sheet.

EXHIBIT 10-1: Finding the Net Changes in Cash.

$$TA = TL + E$$
$$TA = Cash + Noncash\ Assets$$

Therefore: $Cash + Noncash\ Assets = TL + E$

$$Cash = TL + E - Noncash\ Assets$$

Hence $\Delta Cash = \Delta TL + \Delta E - \Delta Noncash\ Assets$

Legend:

TA = Total Assets   E = Equity

TL = Total Liabilities Δ = Mathematical symbol for change

EXAMPLE 10-1: QRS Company's balance sheets for 12/31/x1 and 12/31/x2 show the following selected figures:

	19x2	19x1	Change
Noncash Assets	13,000	15,000	−2,000
Total Liabilities	9,000	7,000	+2,000
Equity	11,000	14,000	−3,000

[handwritten: $\Delta WL = \Delta NCL - \Delta NCA + \Delta E$]

The net change in cash funds (the Cash account) was

$$\Delta Cash = \Delta TL + \Delta E - \Delta NCA$$
$$= 2,000 + (-3,000) - (-2,000) = 1,000$$

The net change in cash funds (the Cash account) was an increase of $1,000. This change was the result of increases in cash funds due to borrowing (the increase in liabilities) and to selling assets (the decrease in noncash assets), and a decrease in cash funds due to a net loss, payments to the owners, or both (the decrease in equity).

EXAMPLE 10-2: QRS Company's balance sheets for 12/31/x0 and 12/31/x1 show the following selected figures:

	19x1	19x0	Change
Noncash Assets	15,000	12,000	+3,000
Total Liabilities	7,000	5,000	+2,000
Equity	14,000	8,000	+6,000

The net change in cash funds (the Cash account) was

$$\Delta Cash = \Delta TL + \Delta E - \Delta NCA$$
$$= 2,000 + 6,000 - 3,000 = 5,000$$

The net change in cash funds (the Cash account) was an increase of $5,000. This change was the result of increases in cash funds due to borrowing (the increase in liabilities) and to profits, additional investments, or both (the increase in equity), and a decrease in cash funds due to purchasing noncash assets (the increase in noncash assets).

10-2. Sources of Cash

Cash may be generated through normal business operations or from other sources. For any given transaction, you can analyze the effect on the Cash account by looking at the corresponding journal entry. If the Cash account is debited, the transaction increases cash. If the Cash account is credited, the transaction decreases cash.

A. Cash is generated by operations.

Cash may be generated through normal business operations as the firm buys, sells, and produces services for its customers. When the SCFP is prepared on the cash basis, it is assumed that a good first measure of the cash thus generated is net income. However, this net income must be adjusted when the revenue it is based on does not equal actual cash collections, or when the expenses it is based on do not equal actual cash payments.

1. *Adjustments to net income when revenue does not equal cash collections.* The net income reported on the income statement is based on revenue earned, which may be different from the amount of cash actually collected from customers (revenue only generates cash if it is collected during the same accounting period). Thus on the SCFP net income must be adjusted when revenue is greater than or less than actual cash collections. Exhibit 10-2 describes the four basic types of transactions where this is the case, along with the adjustment to net income that must be made for each type.

EXHIBIT 10-2: Adjustments to Net Income for Revenue

Transaction	Explanation	Adjustment
Increase in Accounts Receivable	Revenue was earned but not collected from customers	Subtract the amount of increase
Decrease in Accounts Receivable	Cash was collected from customers on account in excess of revenue earned	Add the amount of decrease
Increase in Unearned Revenue	Cash was collected for revenue to be earned in a later period	Add the amount of increase
Decrease in Unearned Revenue	Revenue was earned for which cash had already been collected in an earlier period	Subtract the amount of decrease

EXAMPLE 10-3: In 19x1, EFG Company's income statement reported revenue of $500,000 and a net income of $75,000. However, the firm's actual cash collections were less than that reported revenue. In fact, $25,000 was earned but not collected from credit customers (increasing Accounts Receivable by that amount), and another $4,000 in earnings had already been collected in an earlier period (the actual earning of this money causing a decrease of $4,000 in Unearned Revenue during the current period). The entries implied by these changes are as follows:

Accounts Receivable	25,000	
Revenue.		25,000
Sales on credit		
Unearned Revenue.	4,000	
Revenue		4,000
Revenue earned		

Since the firm's cash collections in 19x1 were less than its reported revenue, its cash flow from operations must have been less than the reported net income of $75,000. On the firm's SCFP the necessary adjustments to net income would be as follows:

Sources of Funds:			
Operations			
Net Income		$75,000	
Adjustments to Net Income:			
Increase in accounts receivable. .	$(25,000)		
Decrease in unearned revenue . .	(4,000)	(29,000)	
Total Cash from Operations			$46,000

EXAMPLE 10-4: In 19x4, OPR Company's income statement reported a net income of $80,000. Revenue earned during the year was reported as $350,000. However, the firm's actual cash collections were greater than this reported revenue. It collected $15,000 from customers on account (decreasing Accounts Receivable by that amount), and it collected $7,000 from customers for merchandise to be delivered later (increasing Unearned Revenue by that amount). The entries implied by these changes are as follows:

Cash	15,000	
Accounts Receivable.		15,000
Cash	7,000	
Unearned Revenue		7,000

Since the firm's cash collections were greater than its reported revenue, its cash flow from operations must have been greater than the reported net income of $80,000. On the firm's SCFP, the necessary adjustments to net income would be as follows:

Sources of Funds:		
Operations		
Net Income		$80,000
Adjustments to Net Income:		
Decrease in accounts receivable .	$15,000	
Increase in unearned revenue . . .	7,000	22,000
Total Cash from Operations		$102,000

2. *Adjustments to net income when expenses do not equal cash payments.* Net income must also be adjusted for expenses where there is no cash payment, such as depreciation expense, and when the expense reported on the income statement is greater than or less than the actual cash payment. Exhibit 10-3 describes the basic types of transactions where this is the case, along with the adjustment to net income that must be made for each type.

EXHIBIT 10-3: Adjustments to Net Income for Expenses

Transaction	Explanation	Adjustment
Increase in Inventory	Amount of inventory purchased exceeded the cost of goods sold	Subtract the amount of increase
Decrease in Inventory	Amount of inventory purchased was less than the cost of goods sold	Add the amount of decrease
Increase in Accounts Payable	Part of the cost of goods sold was inventory purchased on credit	Add the amount of increase
Decrease in Accounts Payable	Cash payments exceeded purchases	Subtract the amount of decrease
Decrease in prepaid accounts	No cash expenditure for expense	Add the amount of decrease
Increase in depreciation expense	No cash expenditure for expense	Add the amount of increase
Increase in all other short-term payables	No cash expenditure	Add the amount of increase

EXAMPLE 10-5: On its income statement, XYZ Corporation reported a cost of goods sold of $400,000. Net income totaled $92,000. However, there were situations where expenses were different from actual cash payments. Of the total cost of good sold, $12,000 will not actually be paid until a later period (increasing Accounts Payable by that amount), and $5,000 of inventory had already been paid for in an earlier period (decreasing Inventory by that amount). The entries implied by these changes are as follows:

Cost of Goods Sold.	400,000	
Accounts Payable		12,000
Inventory		5,000
Cash		383,000

Since actual cash payments were less than the reported cost of goods sold, cash flow from operations must have been greater than the reported net income of $92,000. On the firm's SCFP, the necessary adjustments to net income would be as follows:

Sources of Funds:		
Operations		
Net Income		$92,000
Adjustments to Net Income:		
Increase in accounts payable . . .	$12,000	
Decrease in inventory	5,000	17,000
Total Cash from Operations		$109,000

EXAMPLE 10-6: XYZ Company reported net income of $40,000 for the year. However, it also had situations where expenses were different from actual cash payments. Insurance expense was reported as $1,500, but actual payments were lower because some of the insurance used reduced the balance in the Prepaid Insurance account from $2,000 to $1,400. Depreciation expense was $3,900 this expense involved no actual cash payment. The entries to record these transactions were as follows:

Insurance Expense	1,500	
Prepaid Insurance		600
Cash		900
Depreciation Expense	3,900	
Accumulated Depreciation		3,900

Since the cash disbursed for insurance was less than the reported insurance expense, and because no cash was disbursed for depreciation expense, cash flow from operations must have been greater than the reported net income of $40,000. On the firm's SCFP, the necessary adjustments to net income would be as follows:

Sources of Funds:		
Operations		
Net Income		$40,000
Adjustments to Net Income:		
Decrease in prepaid insurance . .	$ 600	
Depreciation expense	3,900	4,500
Total Cash from Operations		$44,500

EXAMPLE 10-7: XYZ Company's income statement reported net income of $100,000 for the year ended 12/31/x1. However, some of the expenses shown on that statement—$75,000 in depreciation expense and $12,000 of deferred income taxes involved no actual cash payments. Selected beginning and ending balances for some of the firm's balance sheet accounts were as follows:

[handwritten annotations: for assts when change gives debit entry, subtract for SCFP / for liab + OE when change gives debit, add for SCFP]

	19x2	19x1	Change
Accounts Receivable (net*)	50,000	39,000	+11,000
Prepaid Rent	6,000	9,000	− 3,000
Inventory	72,000	68,000	+ 4,000
Accounts Payable	52,000	60,000	− 8,000
Current Taxes Payable	5,000	3,000	+ 2,000
Unearned Revenue	8,000	4,000	+ 4,000
Deferred Taxes	52,000	40,000	+12,000

* accounts receivable net of allowance for uncollectible accounts.

On the firm's SCFP, the necessary adjustments to net income would be as follows:

Sources of Funds:			
Operations			
Net Income		$100,000	
Adjustments to Net Income:			
(a) Depreciation Expense.	$75,000		
(b) Increase in Accounts			
Receivable (net)	(11,000)		
(c) Decrease in Prepaid Rent	3,000		
(d) Increase in Inventory	(4,000)		
(e) Decrease in Accounts			
Payable	(8,000)		
(f) Increase in Unearned			
Revenue	4,000		
(g) Deferred Income Taxes.	12,000		
(h) Decrease in Taxes			
Payable	2,000	73,000	
Total Funds from Operations			$173,000

The adjustments can be explained as follows:

(a) *Depreciation expense* is added back to net income since there was no actual cash disbursement for this expense.

(b) *The $11,000 increase in net Accounts Receivable* indicates that revenue was earned but not collected. Therefore this amount must be subtracted from net income in order not to overstate cash collections.

(c) *The $3,000 decrease in Prepaid Rent* indicates that part of the rent expense incurred was paid for in a prior period. It must be added back since no actual cash disbursement was made for this amount in 19x1.

(d) *The $4,000 increase in Inventory* indicates that the inventory purchased was not all used as part of cost of goods sold. This amount is subtracted.

(e) *The $8,000 decrease in Accounts Payable* indicates that cash payments exceeded purchases of supplies and inventory. This amount is subtracted from net income since the computation of net income thus understated the cash actually spent for purchases.

(f) *The $4,000 increase in Unearned Revenue* (indicating that the firm collected more cash than it actually earned in revenue during the period because some customers paid for merchandise in advance) is added to net income since the revenue figure used to compute net income thus understated actual cash collections.

(g) *Deferred income taxes* will be paid at a later date and involve no current cash outlay. Tax expense overstates cash expended so the deferred taxes must be added back to compute cash from operations.

(h) *The increase in taxes payable* means that the company did not pay all of its current tax expense during the year. Some will be paid for in the next year. Current tax expense overstates cash outlays for taxes by the amount of the increase in taxes payable. Therefore the adjustment adds the increase in taxes payable to profits to compute cash from operations.

Note that the cash generated from operations ($173,000) exceeded the reported profits ($100,000). This is possible because many of the firm's expenses involved no actual cash payments and because the firm was able to collect some cash in advance from customers.

B. Cash may also be generated from other sources.

Other sources of cash include the sale of long-term assets, an increase in long-term borrowing, and the sale of investments. The cash generated from any of these activities is equal to the *cash received* by the firm, not any recorded gain or loss.

EXAMPLE 10-8: XYZ Company sold equipment that originally cost $40,000 when accumulated depreciation was $30,000. The company received $8,000. The entry to record this sale provides the information needed to prepare the SCFP.

Cash	8,000	
Accumulated Depreciation	30,000	
Loss on Sale	2,000	
Equipment		40,000

The $2,000 loss on the sale would be added back to net income in the calculation of cash from operations. The sale provided an other source of cash of $8,000. (*Note:* a sale can generate cash even if the asset is sold at a loss.)

EXAMPLE 10-9: XYZ Company borrowed $500,000 from the bank, signing a long-term note payable. The company also issued 1,000 shares of new stock for $60,000 in cash. The SCFP would report these transactions as other sources of cash, as follows:

Other Sources:	
Increase in Long-term Notes Payable	500,000
Issued 1,000 shares of common stock	60,000
Total Funds from Other Sources	560,000

10-3. Uses of Cash

In addition to paying the expenses of operations, firms commonly use cash to purchase long-term assets, to retire debts or stock, to buy treasury stock, and to pay dividends. The uses of cash are very similar to the uses of working capital presented in Chapter 9. The uses of cash are reported in a separate section of the SCFP. Total uses are subtracted from total sources to compute the change in cash over the accounting period.

10-4. Other Significant Financing Transactions

The FASB requires that the SCFP report other significant financing transactions even if they do not affect the amount of cash. Examples include acquisition of long-term assets by issuing stock or debt, conversion of bonds to stock, and the sale of long-term assets in return for a long-term receivable. Other significant financing transactions are reported as either both a source and use of funds or in a separate section of the SCFP called Changes in Financial Position Which Do Not Affect Working Capital. We will use the first of these approaches in the solutions to problems presented in this text.

10-5. The Cash Basis T Account Worksheet

The same method is used to produce a SCFP on a cash basis as was used when working capital was the definition of funds. The master account in the worksheet will be the Cash account. The change in the cash account will be explained when the changes in the balances in all non-cash balance sheet accounts has been explained. The accounts shown on the worksheet and the analytical entries recorded will not be entered on the books. The worksheet is only used as a tool for preparing the SCFP.

EXAMPLE 10-10: XYZ Company prepared the following comparative balance sheets and income statement. The firm acquired new equipment costing $10,000 signing a long-term note payable for the entire amount.

XYZ Company
Comparative Balance Sheets
12/31/x1 and 12/31/x0

	19x1	19x0	Change
Cash	$ 18,000	$ 14,000	+$ 4,000
Accounts Receivable (net).	22,000	20,000	+ 2,000
Inventory	52,000	58,000	− 6,000
Prepaid Insurance	1,000	0	+ 1,000
Long-term Notes Receivable	3,000	5,000	− 2,000
Equipment	40,000	35,000	+ 5,000
Accumulated Depreciation	(10,000)	(8,000)	(+ 2,000)
Total Assets	126,000	124,000	+ 2,000
Accounts Payable.	20,000	16,000	+ 4,000
Taxes Payable	2,000	3,000	− 1,000
Wages Payable.	7,000	5,000	+ 2,000
Long-term Notes Payable	30,000	20,000	+ 10,000
Bonds Payable	10,000	30,000	− 20,000
Common Stock	15,000	10,000	+ 5,000
Retained Earnings	42,000	40,000	+ 2,000
Total Liabilities and Equity	126,000	124,000	+ 2,000

XYZ Company
Income Statement
For the Year Ended 12/31/x1

Sales		$100,000
Expenses and (Gains)		
Cost of Goods Sold	$60,000	
Wage Expense	15,000	
Insurance Expense	1,200	
Rent Expense	1,800	
Depreciation Expense	4,000	
(Gain) on Sale of Equipment.	(3,000)	
Total Expenses		$ 79,000
Net Income Before Taxes.		21,000
Income Taxes		8,000
Net Income		$ 13,000

The T account worksheet and implied entries to explain the change in cash are presented below:

(a)	Cash-Operations	13,000		
	Retained Earnings.		13,000	
	Profit is first component of cash from operations.			

Adjustments to Net Income for Cash From Operations

(b)	Cash-Operations	4,000		
	Accumulated Depreciation.		4,000	
	Adjust profit for depreciation expense which does not use cash.			
(c)	Retained Earnings	3,000		
	Cash-Operations.		3,000	
	Remove gain from cash-operations. Gain will be accounted for as an other source of cash.			

(d) Accounts Receivable .... | 2,000 |
    Cash-Operations...................... | | 2,000
        Cash from Operations is reduced by revenue not collected in cash which increases Accounts Receivable.

(e) Cash-Operations .... | 6,000 |
    Inventory .... | | 6,000
        Part of Cost of Goods Sold did not involve an outlay of cash because the size of the inventory was reduced.

(f) Prepaid Insurance .... | 1,000 |
    Cash-Operations...................... | | 1,000
        Payments to insurance companies exceeded insurance expense. Some of the payments increased the balance in prepaid insurance.

(g) Cash-Operations .... | 4,000 |
    Accounts Payable .... | | 4,000
        Some expenses increased Accounts Payable rather than using up cash.

(h) Taxes Payable .... | 1,000 |
    Cash-Operations...................... | | 1,000
        Payments for taxes were greater than tax expense because some of the payments reduced Taxes Payable.

(i) Cash-Operations .... | 2,000 |
    Wages Payable........................ | | 2,000
        Wage payments were less than wages expense. Some of this year's wages will be paid next year.

Other Sources and Uses of Cash

(j) Cash-Other .... | 2,000 |
    Long-term Notes Receivable .... | | 2,000
        Cash received in payment on the note.

(k) Equipment........................... | 10,000 |
    Long-term Notes Payable. .... | | 10,000
        Equipment was purchased on long-term credit. This is an other significant financing transaction.

(l) Accumulated Depreciation .... | 2,000 |
    Cash .... | 6,000 |
        Equipment .... | | 5,000
        Gain on Sale (Retained Earnings). .... | | 3,000
        Accounts for equipment sold. Dr. to accumulated depreciation is amount to explain change in account balance. Cr. to the equipment account explains the change in that account balance. Dr. to cash balances entry.

(m) Bonds Payable....................... | 20,000 |
    Cash-Other.......................... | | 20,000
        Cash was used to retire bonds.

(n) Cash-Other .... | 5,000 |
    Common Stock .... | | 5,000
        Issued Common Stock.

(o) Dividends (Retained Earnings)	11,000	
Cash-Other.		11,000
Dividends amount balances the Retained Earnings account.		

T Account Worksheet

Sources   **Cash**   *Uses*

Balance	14,000	

Operations

(a) profit	13,000	(c) gain on sale of equip.	3,000
(b) depreciation	4,000	(d) increase in Accounts	
(e) decrease in inventory	6,000	Receivable	2,000
(g) increase in Accounts		(f) increase in Prepaid	
Payable	4,000	Insurance	1,000
(i) increase in Wages Payable	2,000	(h) decrease in Taxes	
		Payable	1,000

Other

(j) decrease in long-term		(m) Bonds retired	20,000
notes receivable	2,000	(o) dividends	11,000
(l) sale of equipment	6,000		
(n) Common stock issued	5,000		

	18,000	
Balance		

Accounts Receivable		
Balance	20,000	
(d)	2,000	
Balance	22,000	

Inventory		
Balance	58,000	
		(e) 6,000
Balance	52,000	

Prepaid Insurance		
Balance	0	
(f)	1,000	
Balance	1,000	

Long-term Note Receivable		
Balance	5,000	
		(j) 2,000
Balance	3,000	

Equipment		
Balance	35,000	
(k)	10,000	(l) 5,000
Balance	40,000	

Accumulated Depreciation		
	Balance	8,000
(l) 2,000	(b)	4,000
	Balance	10,000

Accounts Payable		
	Balance	16,000
	(g)	4,000
	Balance	20,000

Taxes Payable		
	Balance	3,000
(h) 1,000		
	Balance	2,000

Wages Payable		
	Balance	5,000
	(i)	2,000
	Balance	7,000

Long-term Notes Payable		
	Balance	20,000
	(k)	10,000
	Balance	30,000

Bonds Payable				Common Stock		
		Balance	30,000			Balance	10,000
(m)	20,000					(n)	5,000
		Balance	10,000			Balance	15,000

Retained Earnings			
		Balance	40,000
(c)	3,000	(a)	13,000
(o)	11,000	(l)	3,000
		Balance	42,000

The statement of changes in financial position is presented below.

XYZ Company
Statement of Changes in Financial Position — Cash Basis
For the Year Ended 12/31/x1

Sources of Funds:
  Operations
    Net Income $13,000
    Adjustments to Net Income:
      Depreciation.   4,000
      Decrease in Inventory   6,000
      Increase in Accounts Payable   4,000
      Increase in Wages Payable   2,000
      Gain on Sale of Equipment . . . .   (3,000)
      Increase in Accounts Receivable (net) . . . .   (2,000)
      Increase in Prepaid Insurance . . . .   (1,000)
      Decrease in Taxes Payable . . . .   (1,000)
    Cash From Operations $22,000

Other Sources
  Reduction in Long-term Notes Receivable   2,000
  Sale of Equipment.   6,000
  Common Stock Issued   5,000
  Long-term Notes Payable Issued for Equipment.   10,000
Total Sources $45,000

Uses of Funds:
  Retirement of Bonds Payable. $20,000
  Dividends   11,000
  Purchase of Equipment with Notes Payable.   10,000
  Total Uses of Funds.   41,000
Net Increase in Cash. . . . . $ 4,000

No schedule of changes in working capital accounts is required when the SCFP is prepared on the cash basis. All of the changes in working capital accounts are mentioned on the face of the statement so no further explanation is required.

RAISE YOUR GRADES

Can you explain . . . ?

☑ how the change in cash funds can be determined by looking at the changes in noncash balance sheet accounts

☑ why accountants might prefer to prepare the SCFP on the cash basis

☑ why an increase in Accounts Receivable is subtracted from net income in computing cash from operations

☑ why an increase in Unearned Revenue is added to net income in computing cash from operations

☑ why an increase in Inventory is subtracted from net income in computing cash from operations

☑ why an increase in Accounts Payable is added to net income in computing cash from operations

☑ what kinds of transactions are reported as other sources of cash

☑ what kinds of transactions are considered to be other significant financing transactions

☑ where other significant financing transactions appear on the SCFP—cash basis

SUMMARY

1. The SCFP may be prepared using cash as the definition of funds.
2. The SCFP (cash basis) describes the sources and uses of cash in order to explain the change in the Cash account during the accounting period.
3. The net change in cash funds during an accounting period may be explained by the changes in all noncash balance sheet accounts:

$$\Delta Cash = \Delta TL + \Delta E - \Delta Noncash\ Assets$$

4. When the SCFP is prepared on the cash basis, it is assumed that net income is a good first measure of the funds generated by operations.
5. The net income reported on the income statement is based on revenue earned, not on the amount of cash actually collected from customers.
6. When computing cash from operations, net income must be adjusted when the revenue it is based on does not equal actual cash collections, and when the expenses it is based on do not equal actual cash payments.
7. Revenue does not equal actual cash collections if there are increases or decreases in Accounts Receivable or Unearned Revenue. In each case, the actual cash collected is greater than or less than the amount reported as revenue on the income statement.
8. Expenses do not equal actual cash payments if there are increases or decreases in Accounts Payable or Inventory, or if there are changes in prepaid items. In each case, the actual cash disbursed is greater than or less than the amount reported as expenses on the income statement.
9. Depreciation expense and deferred income taxes do not involve actual cash disbursements. Therefore, the total amount of these expenses must be added back to net income when computing cash from operations.
10. Other sources of cash include the sale of long term assets, an increase in long-term borrowing, and the sale of investments. The cash generated from these activities is equal to the amount of cash received by the firm, not the amount of any reported gain or loss.
11. Uses of cash include purchases of long-term assets, the retirement of debts and stocks, purchases of treasury stock, and payments of dividends.
12. Other significant financing transactions are reported as either both a source and use of funds or in a separate section called Changes in Financial Position which Do Not Affect Cash.

RAPID REVIEW

1. The general equation for explaining the change in the cash account is _____ .
2. If noncash assets decrease by $100, liabilities increase by $50, and equity decreases by $40, what is the change in the Cash account?

3. C & L Company reports a $200 profit. Accounts Receivable (net) decreased by $50, Inventory increased by $75, and Accounts Payable decreased by $25. How much cash was generated from operations?

4. WLG Company reports a $500 profit. Accounts Receivable (net) increased by $80, Prepaid Insurance decreased by $20, Inventory decreased by $50, and Accounts Payable increased by $70. In addition, the company incurred a depreciation expense of $200. How much cash was generated from operations?

5. M & D Company sold used equipment for $5,000 in cash. The equipment originally cost $12,000 but has since depreciated $8,000. The company reported a gain of $1,000 on this sale on its income statement. What will be the amount reported as an "other source" of funds on the SCFP?

6. R & W Company sold equipment which originally cost $5,000. Accumulated depreciation on the equipment was $3,500. The company reported a $200 loss on the sale. How much cash was generated from the sale of the equipment?

7. XYZ Company reports profits of $700. Depreciation expense was $400. Accounts Payable increased by $50. Long-term Notes Payable increased by $300 and the company paid dividends of $100. How much cash was generated from operations?

8. In Question 7, what were the other sources of cash?

9. In Question 7, what was the change in cash?

10. How will each of the following be treated on the SCFP? Use the key below in answering.

A = + adjustment to profit in computing cash from operations

C = other source of funds

B = − adjustment to profit in computing cash from operations

D = use of funds

(a) Purchase of controlling interest in another company by issuing $500,000 of common stock
(b) Decrease in inventory of $40,000
(c) Issuance of stock worth $500 by firm
(d) Payment of dividends amounting to $5,000
(e) Increase in Accounts Receivable (net) of $60,000
(f) Decrease in Prepaid Rent of $20,000
(g) Issuance of $5,000 long-term bond payable
(h) Acquisition of building by issuing a long-term mortgage payable
(i) Purchase of $5,000 of company's own treasury stock

Answers:

1. ΔCash = ΔTL + ΔE − ΔNoncash Assets [Section 10-1]
2. ΔCash = $50 + (−$40) − (−$100) = $110 [Section 10-1]
3. $200 + $50 − $75 − $25 = $150 [Section 10-2]
4. $500 − $80 + $20 + $50 + $70 + $200 = $760 [Section 10-2]
5. $5,000 [Section 10-2]
6. $5,000 − $3,500 − $200 = $1,300 [Section 10-2]
7. $700 + $400 + $50 = $1,150 [Section 10-2]
8. $300 [Section 10-2]
9. $1,150 + $300 − $100 = $1,350 [Sections 10-2, 10-3, and 10-4]
10. (a) C and D   (f) A
    (b) A   (g) C
    (c) C   (h) C and D
    (d) D   (i) D
    (e) B
    [Sections 10-2 through 10-5]

SOLVED PROBLEMS

PROBLEM 10-1: Complete the following chart and then answer the question below.

ACCOUNT	TYPE OF ACCOUNT	CHANGE IN BALANCE	ADJUSTMENT TO NET INCOME ON SCFP (+/−)
Accounts Receivable	Asset	+	−
Accounts Receivable	Asset	−	+
Prepaid Rent	Asset	+	−
Prepaid Rent	Asset	−	+
Inventory	Asset	+	−
Inventory	Asset	−	+
Accounts Payable	Liability	+	+
Accounts Payable	Liability	−	−
Unearned Revenue	Liability	+	+
Unearned Revenue	Liability	−	−
Wages Payable	Liability	+	+
Wages Payable	Liability	−	−

Answer:

ACCOUNT	TYPE OF ACCOUNT	CHANGE IN BALANCE	ADJUSTMENT TO NET INCOME ON SCFP (+/−)
Accounts Receivable	Asset	+	−
Accounts Receivable	Asset	−	+
Prepaid Rent	Asset	+	−
Prepaid Rent	Asset	−	+
Inventory	Asset	+	−
Inventory	Asset	−	+
Accounts Payable	Liability	+	+
Accounts Payable	Liability	−	−
Unearned Revenue	Liability	+	+
Unearned Revenue	Liability	−	−
Wages Payable	Liability	+	+
Wages Payable	Liability	−	−

[Section 10-2]

PROBLEM 10-2: Based on the completed chart, devise a rule for explaining the direction of the adjustment required to account for the changes in the balances of accounts like Accounts Receivable, Accounts Payable, etc.

Answer:
Rule: For asset accounts, the adjustment to net income is the reverse of the direction of change in the account balance. If the asset account increases in balance, the adjustment decreases cash from operations. If the asset account decreases, the adjustment increases cash from operations.

  For liability accounts, the adjustment to net income is in the same direction as the change in the balance of the account. If the liability account's balance increases (decreases), the adjustment increases (decreases) cash from operations.   **[Section 10-2]**

PROBLEM 10-3: A change in any account balance does not necessarily mean an adjustment to net income is required in computing cash from operations. Devise a rule for deciding what kinds of accounts should be considered when making adjustment to net income on the SCFP.

Answer: The accounts whose balance changes are reported as adjustments, fall into two categories.

1. *Current Assets and Current Liabilities.* A change in the balance of a current asset (other than cash) or a current liability is generally reported as an adjustment to net income in computing cash from operations.
2. *Expenses that do not involve cash outlays.* Expenses, such as depreciation and deferred taxes do not involve cash. Therefore an adjustment must be made to net income for the overstatement of expenses. Information about these expenses is found on the income statement.   **[Section 10-2]**

PROBLEM 10-4: What is the difference in the kinds of accounts that are most commonly reported as adjustments to net income on the SCFP (cash basis) and those reported as other sources and uses?

Answer: The types of accounts that most commonly appear as adjustments to net income in computing cash from operations are current asset and current liability accounts. The type of accounts shown as other sources and uses tend to be noncurrent asset, noncurrent liability, and equity accounts. There are exceptions to this rule. The adjustment to net income for depreciation, for example, involves the accumulated depreciation account-a negative long-term asset account. Adjustments to profits to remove gains and losses on the sale of long-term assets involve the retained earnings account.

[Sections 10-2 through 10-4]

PROBLEM 10-5: XYZ reported a net income of $100,000. The income statement revealed depreciation expense of $40,000; deferred taxes of $6,000; and a gain on the sale of a building of $20,000. Selected current balance sheet accounts showed the following changes:

Accounts Receivable (net)	+8,000
Inventory	+2,000
Prepaid Insurance	−1,000
Accounts Payable	+4,000
Wages Payable	− 500
Unearned Revenue	+1,500

Show the SCFP-Cash Basis through the computation of Cash From Operations in good form.

Answer:

Sources of Funds:		
Operations		
Net Income		$100,000
Adjustments to Net Income:		
Depreciation Expense.	$40,000	
Deferred Taxes	6,000	
Gain on sale of Building	(20,000)	
Increase in Accounts Receivable		
(net)	(8,000)	
Increase in Inventory	(2,000)	
Decrease in Prepaid Insurance . .	1,000	
Increase in Accounts Payable . . .	4,000	
Decrease in Wages Payable	(500)	
Increase in Unearned Revenue . .	1,500	22,000
Total Cash From Operations		$122,000

[Section 10-2]

PROBLEM 10-6: J&B Company reported net income of $150,000. The income statement revealed that depreciation expense was $60,000; the company paid $5,000 of previously deferred taxes. Selected account balance changes from the current section of the balance sheet were as follows:

Accounts Receivable (net)	−13,000
Interest Receivable	+ 1,000
Inventory	− 5,000
Accounts Payable	− 8,000
Interest Payable	+ 2,000
Current Taxes Payable	+ 1,000

In addition the firm borrowed $200,000 by selling long-term bonds. $100,000 of new stock was issued for cash. $400,000 of new equipment was purchased.

Prepare a SCFP-Cash Basis through Cash From Operations.

Answer:

Sources of Funds		
Operations:		
Net Income		$150,000
Adjustments to Net Income:		
Depreciation Expense.	$60,000	
Reduction in Deferred Taxes	(5,000)	
Decrease in Accounts Receivable	13,000	
Increase in Interest Receivable . .	(1,000)	
Decrease in Inventory	5,000	
Decrease in Accounts Payable. . .	(8,000)	
Increase in Interest Payable	2,000	
Increase in Taxes Payable.	1,000	67,000
Cash From Operations		$217,000

The remaining information in the problem refers to transactions that would be reported as other sources and uses of funds. **[Section 10-2]**

PROBLEM 10-7: ILS Company sold equipment with an original cost of $150,000 during the year. The gain on the sale of the equipment was $20,000. Depreciation expense for the year was $100,000. The balance in the equipment account increased by $220,000 and the balance in the accumulated depreciation account increased by $30,000. Determine the other sources and uses of funds from equipment transactions.

Answer: Answering this problem requires that you reproduce the activity in the equipment and accumulated depreciation accounts. You do not need to know the beginning and ending balances if you know the change in balance. You can set up the accounts with $0 as the beginning balance and the indicated change in balance as the ending balance.

Equipment

Beginning Balance	0		
Acquisitions	?	Dispositions	150,000
Ending Balance	220,000		

The acquisitions of equipmemt must have totaled $370,000 in order to explain the $220,000 increase in the equipment account balance. Purchases of equipment represent a $370,000 use of funds.

Accumulated Depreciation

		Beginning Balance	0
Accumulated Depreciation		Depreciation Expense	100,000
on Equipment Sold	?		
		Ending Balance	30,000

The accumulated depreciation on the equipment sold must have been $70,000 to explain the change in the accumulated depreciation balance of $30,000. The entry to record the sale of equipment must have been:

Cash	100,000	
Accumulated Depreciation	70,000	
Equipment		150,000
Gain on Sale		20,000

The equipment was sold for $100,000 in order to show a gain on the sale of $20,000. The $100,000 received from selling equipment will be shown as an other source of funds:

PROBLEM 10-8: XYZ Company prepared the following income statement and comparative balance sheets on 12/31/x1:

XYZ Company
Income Statement
For the Year Ended 12/31/x1

Sales		$250,000
Interest Revenue		10,000
Total Revenue		$260,000
Expenses:		
Cost of Goods Sold	$170,000	
Wages	50,000	
Depreciation Expense	35,000	
Bad Debt Expense	6,000	
Interest Expense	3,000	
Loss on Sale of Equipment	8,000	
Total Expenses		$272,000
Net (Loss)		$ (12,000)

XYZ Company
Comparative Balance Sheet
12/31/x1 and 12/31/x0

	12/31/x1	12/31/x0	Change
Cash	20,000	25,000	−5,000
Accounts Receivable (net)	45,000	37,000	8,000
Interest Receivable	3,000	2,000	+1,000
Inventory	28,000	32,000	−4,000
Long-term Investment	10,000	7,000	+3,000
Equipment	75,000	60,000	+15,000
Accumulated Depreciation	(12,000)	(9,000)	(+3,000)
Total Assets	169,000	154,000	+15,000
Accounts Payable	30,000	25,000	+5,000
Interest Payable	2,000	4,000	−2,000
Wages Payable	5,000	4,000	+1,000
Bonds Payable	50,000	40,000	+10,000
Common Stock	30,000	15,000	+15,000
Retained Earnings	52,000	66,000	−14,000
Total Liabilities and Equity	169,000	154,000	+15,000

Other Information: Equipment with a book value of $70,000 was sold during the year. Common stock was issued to acquire some of the new equipment.

Reconstruct the implied journal entries to explain the change in Cash.

Answer:

(*a*) Retained Earnings 12,000

  Cash-Operations...................... 12,000

   The net loss reduces Cash-Operations.

Adjustments to Net Income to Compute Cash-Operations

(*b*) Accounts Receivable (net)............... 8,000

  Cash-Operations...................... 8,000

   The increase in Accounts Receivable reduces Cash-Operations.

(*c*) Interest Receivable.................... 1,000

  Cash-Operations...................... 1,000

   The increase in interest receivable reduces Cash-Operations.

(*d*) Cash-Operations 4,000

  Inventory 4,000

   The decrease in inventory increases Cash-Operations.

(*e*) Cash-Operations 5,000

  Accounts Payable 5,000

   The increase in Accounts Payable increases Cash-Operations.

(*f*) Interest Payable...................... 2,000

  Cash-Operations...................... 2,000

   The decrease in interest payable decreases Cash-Operations.

(*g*) Cash-Operations 1,000

  Wages Payable...................... 1,000

   The increase in wage payable increases Cash-Operations.

(h)	Cash-Operations	35,000	
	Accumulated Depreciation		35,000
	Depreciation expense uses no cash and increases Cash-Operations.		
(i)	Cash-Operations	8,000	
	Loss on Sale (Retained Earnings)		8,000
	Remove the loss from the Cash-Operations section.		

Other Sources and Uses of Funds

(j)	Cash-Other	62,000	
	Accumulated Depreciation	32,000	
	Loss on Sale (Retained Earnings)	8,000	
	Equipment		102,000
	To account for the sale of the equipment.		

The debit to Accumulated Depreciation balances that account. The credit to Equipment is computed from information given in the problem. The book value of equipment sold was $70,000 which equals its cost minus accumulated depreciation. Accumulated depreciation on equipment sold was $32,000. Therefore:

$$\text{Book Value} = 70,000 = \text{Cost} - 32,000$$
$$\text{Cost} = \$102,000$$

The debit to the Loss account comes from information on the income statement. The debit to the cash account balances the entry.

(k)	Equipment	117,000	
	Common Stock		15,000
	Cash-Other		102,000
	Debit to equipment balances the equipment account.		
(l)	Long-term Investment	3,000	
	Cash-Other		3,000
(m)	Cash-Other	10,000	
	Bonds Payable		10,000
(n)	Dividends (Retained Earnings)	2,000	
	Cash-Other		2,000
	Debit to dividends balances the retained earnings account.		

PROBLEM 10-9: From the information given in Problem 10-8, record the beginning and ending balances in the T account worksheet. Then record the implied entries.

Answer: Cash Account is on next page.

Accounts Receivable (net)

Balance	37,000	
(b)	18,000	
Balance	45,000	

Interest Receivable

Balance	2,000	
(c)	1,000	
Balance	3,000	

Inventory

Balance	32,000		
		(d)	4,000
Balance	28,000		

Cash

Balance	25,000	

Operations

(d)	decrease in inventory	4,000	(a)	net loss	12,000
(e)	increase in Accounts		(b)	increase in Accounts	
	Payable	5,000		Receivable	8,000
(g)	increase in Wages Payable	1,000	(c)	increase in Interest	
(h)	depreciation expense	35,000		Receivable	1,000
(i)	loss on sale of equip.	8,000	(f)	decrease in Interest	
				Payable	2,000

Other

(j)	sale of equipment	62,000	(k)	purchase of equipment	102,000
(m)	sale of bond payable	10,000	(l)	purchase of long-term	
				investment	3,000
			(n)	dividends	2,000

Balance	20,000	

Long-term Investment

Balance	7,000	
(l)	3,000	
Balance	10,000	

Equipment

Balance	60,000		
(k)	117,000	(j)	102,000
Balance	75,000		

Accumulated Depreciation

		Balance	9,000
(j)	32,000	(h)	35,000
		Balance	12,000

Accounts Payable

		Balance	25,000
		(e)	5,000
		Balance	30,000

Interest Payable

		Balance	4,000
(f)	2,000		
		Balance	2,000

Wages Payable

		Balance	4,000
		(g)	1,000
		Balance	5,000

Bonds Payable

		Balance	40,000
		(m)	10,000
		Balance	50,000

Common Stock

		Balance	15,000
		(k)	15,000
		Balance	30,000

Retained Earnings

		Balance	66,000
(a)	12,000	(i)	8,000
(j)	8,000		
(n)	2,000		
		Balance	52,000

PROBLEM 10-10: From the information in Problems 10-8 and 10-9, prepare the statement of changes in financial position using cash as the definition of funds.

Answer:

XYZ Company
Statement of Changes in Financial Position — Cash Basis
For the Year Ended 12/31/x1

Sources of Funds		
Operations		
Net (Loss)		(12,000)
Adjustments to Net (Loss):		
Decrease in Inventory	4,000	
Increase in Accounts Payable	5,000	
Increase in Wages Payable	1,000	
Depreciation Expense	35,000	
Loss on Sale of Equipment	8,000	
Increase in Accounts Receivable	(8,000)	
Increase in Interest Receivable	(1,000)	
Decrease in Interest Payable	(2,000)	42,000
Cash from Operations.		30,000
Other Sources:		
Sale of Equipment		62,000
Bonds Payable Issued		10,000
Common Stock Issued to Purchase Equipment........		15,000
Total Sources		117,000
Uses of Funds:		
Purchase of Equipment With Cash	$102,000	
Purchase of Long-term Investment	3,000	
Dividends	2,000	
Purchase of Equipment with Stock	15,000	
Total Uses of Funds.		122,000
Net (Decrease) in Cash		(5,000)

PROBLEM 10-11: Explain how a firm like the XYZ Company in Problem 10-8 can suffer a $12,000 net loss, not pay any income taxes, and still generate funds from operations and other sources totaling $117,000.

Answer: A firm can show a net loss and still generate a positive cash flow. Many expenses do not use cash. Depreciation expense is an example of an expense that does not use cash. A firm can generate cash flow in excess of net income by delving into its inventory and by not paying its bills. The firm can borrow additional sums of money increasing its debt. It can issue more shares of stock. Cash can be raised by selling off assets. By the same token, profitable firms may have poor cash flow if they prepay their expenses, purchase large amounts of assets, or fail to collect from their customers. **[Section 10-2]**

PROBLEM 10-12: Daniels Corporation received a 5 year extension on a short-term note payable. The note was for $150,000. How would this transaction be reflected on an SCFP prepared with working capital as the definition of funds and one with cash as the definition of funds?

Answer: Working capital is increased by $150,000. The entry for this transaction would have been as follows:

Notes Payable (WC)	150,000	
Notes Payable (long-term)		150,000

The current liability, Notes Payable (short-term), is a working capital account. Working capital increased because the firm entered into an agreement for long-term debt. The increase in long-term notes payable is an "other source" of working capital.

This transaction will be reported differently on a SCFP (cash basis). The reduction in short-term notes payable will be reported as a negative adjustment to net income in determining cash from operations. The increase in long-term debt will be shown as an "other source" of cash. The net result will properly show no net change in cash because the cash account was not affected by the transaction. **[Section 10-4]**

EXAMINATION II(CHAPTERS 6 THROUGH 10)

I. Multiple Choice

1. Slick Merchandising Firm sold goods with a ticketed price of $5,000 to a customer on credit. The customer returned $500 of the merchandise because it was the wrong color. The firm's past experience indicates that 5% of its net credit sales will prove to be uncollectible. How much revenue will the firm recognize on this sale net of bad debt expense?
   (a) $4,750
   (b) $4,500
   (c) $4,275
   (d) $4,250
   (e) none of the above

2. Depreciation is an example of an expense that
   (a) is specifically matched to related revenue
   (b) is charged off in a systematic way even though it cannot necessarily be specifically matched to related revenue.
   (c) is charged off in the accounting period in which it is paid because it cannot be specifically matched to its related revenue
   (d) all of the above
   (e) none of the above

3. The order in which sections of the income statement appear is
   (a) continuing operations, extraordinary items, effect of accounting changes, discontinued operations, EPS.
   (b) continuing operations, discontinued operations, effect of accounting changes, extraordinary items, EPS.
   (c) continuing operations, effect of accounting changes, discontinued operations, extraordinary items, EPS.
   (d) continuing operations, discontinued operations, extraordinary items, effect of accounting changes, EPS.
   (e) continuing operations, EPS, discontinued operations, EPS, extraordinary item, EPS, effect of accounting changes, EPS.

4. Mortimer is the owner of two separate businesses. The first is organized as a sole proprietorship. Its profits were $100,000. Mortimer withdrew $32,000 from the firm. The second business is organized as a corporation. The corporation earned before tax profits of $120,000 and paid $30,000 in income taxes. Mortimer removed $21,000 from the corporation in the form of dividends. How much business income will Mortimer report on his income tax return assuming that none of the dividends or business income is subject to any special exclusions under the tax laws.
   (a) $53,000   (d) $121,000
   (b) $220,000   (e) $190,000
   (c) $122,000

5. Which of the following disposals would you report in the discontinued operations section of the income statement?
   (a) sale of the wooden toy factory by a full-line toy maker that is going to concentrate on plastic toys instead
   (b) sale of the wooden toy factory in California so that the firm can move wooden toy manufacturing to Thailand
   (c) sale of the wooden toy factory because it is outdated and the firm plans to modernize in a different location

(*d*) sale of the wooden toy division by a conglomerate company that will no longer be in the toy business

(*e*) all of the above would be reported in the discontinued operations section

6. On March 1, 19x1, Alpha Corporation approved a plan to dispose of Beta Division. The Beta Division had lost $4,000 after taxes during the first two months of 19x1. It is expected that Beta would lose an additional $5,000 after taxes, while operating during the phase-out period and that the firm would lose $45,000 after taxes on the sale of Beta's assets. The income statement would show a loss from operations of Beta division as a part of the discontinued operations section of

(*a*) $4,000

(*b*) $5,000

(*c*) $45,000

(*d*) $50,000

(*e*) $54,000

7. Indicate which of the following events should be reported in the extraordinary items section of the income statement:

(*a*) writeoff of extraordinarily large amount of receivables due to change in eligibility of farmers to receive government loans

(*b*) frost damage to crop located in area where frosts occur every few years

(*c*) extraordinarily large net income due to strike at a competitor's plant

(*d*) loss on exchange of foreign currency due to unprecedented rise in the value of the US dollar

(*e*) loss of plant in Outer Tangelo when the Tangelian Government expropriated the property

8. Earnings per share figures must be presented for which of the following?

(*a*) discontinued operations

(*b*) cumulative effect of change in accounting principle

(*c*) income before extraordinary item

(*d*) extraordinary item

(*e*) all of the above

9. Microchip Corporation's operating cycle requires eight months. On 12/31/x1, the firm has the following liabilities outstanding: $10,000 note payable due 9/6/x2; $25,000 of accounts payable due 1/30/x2; and a $6,000 note payable with $2,000 due on 10/5/x2 and $4,000 due on 10/5/x3. Current liabilities total

(*a*) $10,000

(*b*) $25,000

(*c*) $35,000

(*d*) $41,000

(*e*) $37,000

Questions 10 through 13 refer to the following information

On 12/31/x1, Smokey Joe's Charcoal Company presented the following summarized balance sheet.

Smokey Joe's Charcoal Company
Balance Sheet
12/31/x1

Current Assets	$30,000	Current Liabilities	$20,000
Noncurrent Assets.	80,000	Noncurrent Liabilities	60,000

10. Smokey Joe's Charcoal Company has a current ratio equal to

(*a*) 1.50

(*b*) .75

(*c*) 1.38

(*d*) 1.33

(*e*) .67

11. Smokey Joe's has an equity ratio equal to
    (a) .73
    (b) 1.38
    (c) .75
    (d) .27
    (e) .18

12. Smokey Joe's has a debt ratio equal to
    (a) .75
    (b) .67
    (c) .73
    (d) 1.00
    (e) .55

13. Smokey Joe's has working capital equal to
    (a) $10,000
    (b) $20,000
    (c) $30,000
    (d) $50,000
    (e) $60,000

14. The following must be added back to net income in calculating working capital provided by operations on a statement of changes in financial position.
    (a) increase in wages payable
    (b) decrease in accounts receivable
    (c) depreciation expense
    (d) decrease in deferred taxes
    (e) gain on sale of long-term asset

15. The following must be subtracted from net income in calculating working capital provided by operations on a statement of changes of financial position.
    (a) depreciation expense
    (b) decrease in long-term debt
    (c) increase in deferred income taxes
    (d) loss on sale of long-term asset
    (e) none of the above

16. The following is an example of an other source of funds on a statement of changes in financial position working capital basis.
    (a) sale of long-term bonds payable
    (b) sale of common stock
    (c) sale of property
    (d) borrowing money and issuing a long-term note payable
    (e) all of the above.

17. The following is an example of a use of funds on a statement of changes in financial position working capital basis.
    (a) sale of long-term bonds payable
    (b) depreciation expense
    (c) purchase and retirement of preferred stock
    (d) loss on sale of property
    (e) all of the above

18. The following is an example of an "other important financing transaction" that must be reported on the statement of changes in financial position even though it does not affect working capital.
    (a) company buys building paying cash
    (b) company buys property by issuing new common stock
    (c) company sells an airplane and receives cash
    (d) company retires $5,000,000 of long-term bonds at a gain
    (e) all of the above are other important financing transactions

19. An item which must be added back to net income in computing cash generated by operations on a statement of changes in financial position is

   (a) an increase in accounts receivable
   (b) an increase in prepaid insurance
   (c) an increase in unearned revenue
   (d) a decrease in accounts payable
   (e) increase in inventory

20. An item which must be subtracted from net income in computing cash generated by operations on a statement of changes in financial position is
   (a) decrease in accounts payable
   (b) decrease in inventory
   (c) bad debt expense
   (d) depreciation expense
   (e) decrease in prepaid insurance

Questions 21 and 25 relate to the following information:

The Machinery and Accumulated Depreciation accounts give the information below for the year:

	Beginning Bal.	Ending Bal.
Machinery	$700,000	$750,000
Accumulated Depreciation	210,000	240,000

Net Income for the year was $205,000 and machinery costing $40,000 and having a book value of $15,000 was sold at a gain of $12,000. Depreciation expense for the year was $55,000.

21. The accumulated depreciation on the machinery that was sold was
   (a) $30,000
   (b) $25,000
   (c) $15,000
   (d) $3,000
   (e) cannot be determined from the information given

22. The selling price of the machinery was
   (a) $27,000
   (b) $15,000
   (c) $25,000
   (d) $12,000
   (e) cannot be determined from the information given

23. Assuming that there were no other transactions that would require the adjustment of net income on the statement of changes in financial position, the working capital provided from operations would be
   (a) $260,000
   (b) $205,000
   (c) $272,000
   (d) $248,000
   (e) none of the above

24. Assuming that there were no other relevant transactions that should be reported on the statement of changes in financial position, total working capital provided would equal
   (a) $260,000
   (b) $275,000
   (c) $260,000
   (d) $248,000
   (e) none of the above

25. In this problem, cash provided by operations would be
   (a) greater than the working capital provided by operations
   (b) less than the working capital provided by operations
   (c) equal to the working capital provided by operations
   (d) impossible to determine from the information given

II. Problems

1. Abbadabba Corporation's board of directors voted to dispose of the firm's Heavy Metal Division. On March 31, 19x1, the firm adopted a plan for disposal, calling for the sale of all of the division's assets. It is estimated that the sale of the assets will be completed by March 31, 19x2. During the first three months of 19x1, the Heavy Metal Division showed a before tax loss of $60,000. It is estimated that the division will incur further before tax losses of $100,000 before the disposal is completed. The firm anticipates that the assets will be sold at a loss of $75,000 before tax considerations, and that the firm will have to make severance payments to employees of $80,000. The firm's tax rate is 40%. How could this information be presented on the March 31, 19x1 quarterly income statement?

2. XYZ Corporation presented the following income statement and comparative balance sheets:

XYZ Corporation
Income Statement
For the Year Ended 12/31/x1

Sales		$180,000
Less Expenses:		
Cost of Goods Sold	$75,000	
Wage Expense	20,000	
Rent Expense	2,400	
Bad Debt Expense	1,800	
Interest Expense	400	
Depreciation Expense	6,500	
Total Expenses		$106,100
Net Income Before Taxes		$ 73,900
Income Taxes		25,600
Net Income		$ 48,300

XYZ Corporation
Balance Sheet
12/31/x0 and 12/31/x1

	12/31/x1	12/31/x0
Assets:		
Cash	$ 9,800	$ 8,000
Accounts Receivable (net)	29,500	26,600
Inventory	18,500	20,200
Long-term Investment in MES	5,000	0
Equipment	25,000	20,000
Accumulated Depreciation	(9,400)	(8,100)
Total Assets	$78,400	$66,700
Liabilities:		
Accounts Payable	$24,000	$21,600
Wages Payable	4,100	5,200
Long-term Note Payable	28,000	20,000
Common Stock	5,000	5,000
Retained Earnings	17,300	14,900
	$78,400	$66,700

The firm sold equipment that originally cost $10,000 and had a book value of $4,800 at the time of the sale at no gain or loss. Dividends declared and paid totaled $45,900. Prepare a statement of changes in financial position on a cash basis for the year ended 12/31/x1.

ANSWERS TO EXAMINATION II

Multiple Choice Questions

1. c	6. a	11. d	16. e	21. b
2. b	7. e	12. c	17. c	22. a
3. d	8. c	13. a	18. b	23. d
4. d	9. e	14. c	19. c	24. b
5. d	10. a	15. e	20. a	25. d

Problem 1

Discontinued Operations:

Loss from operations of Heavy Metal Division (net of $24,000 of income tax benefits)	$ 36,000
Loss on disposal of Heavy Metal Division including provision for loss of $60,000 net of tax benefits on operations during the phase out period	153,000*
Total loss from discontinued operation	$189,000

*Loss on Disposal includes:

Loss on operations during phase out period	$100,000
Loss on sale of assets	75,000
Severance pay.	80,000
	$255,000
Tax benefit (40%).	102,000
Loss on disposal	$153,000

Problem 2

XYZ Corporation
Statement of Changes in Financial Position
(Cash Basis)
For the Year Ended 12/31/x1

Sources of Funds:		
Operations:		
Net Income		$48,300
Adjustments to Net Income:		
Depreciation Expense.	$ 6,500	
Increase in Accounts Receivable (net)	(2,900)	
Decrease in Inventory	1,700	
Increase in Accounts Payable	2,400	
Decrease in Wages Payable	(1,100)	
Total Adjustments		$ 6,600
Cash Provided by Operations		$54,900
Other Sources:		
Sale of Equipment.		4,800
Long term Notes Payable		8,000
Total Cash Provided		$67,700
Uses of Cash:		
Purchase of Equipment	$15,000	
Dividends Paid	45,900	
Investment in Long-term MES.	5,000	
Total Uses of Cash		$65,900
Increase in Cash.		$ 1,800

11 COMPOUND INTEREST CONCEPTS

THIS CHAPTER IS ABOUT

☑ **Simple Interest**
☑ **Compound Interest**
☑ **The Effect of Compounding Interest**
☑ **The Future Value of a Single Sum**
☑ **The Present Value of a Single Sum**

11-1. Simple Interest

The simple interest formula computes interest for a specified *single period of time*. The formula for calculating simple interest is

SIMPLE INTEREST FORMULA   Interest = Principal × Interest Rate × Time
or
$$i = P \times r \times t$$

The interest rate is stated on an annual basis and time is stated in years.

EXAMPLE 11-1: Borrower Corporation signs a note agreeing to pay back the principal of $4,000 plus 10% interest at the end of a five year period. The amount of interest to be paid at the end of the five year period is computed as follows:

$$i = P \times r \times t$$
$$i = \$4,000 \times .10 \times 5$$
$$i = \$2,000$$

At the end of the five year period, Borrower Corporation will pay the lender the $4,000 principal plus $2,000 in interest or a total of $6,000.

EXAMPLE 11-2: Tenkotte Corporation signs a note agreeing to pay back the principal of $3,000 plus 10% interest at the end of a nine month period. The amount of interest to be paid at the end of the nine month period is computed as follows

$$i = P \times r \times t$$
$$i = \$3,000 \times .10 \times 9/12 = \$225$$

Tenkotte Corporation would pay interest equal to 10% of the principal if the money were borrowed for one year. However, since Tenkotte Corporation only uses the money for 9/12ths of the year, it only owes 9/12ths of the full year's 10% interest.

11-2. Compound Interest

The compound interest formula computes interest for two or more periods of time. At the end of the first period, the interest is computed based on the principal. The interest for the next period(s) is computed on the principal plus any unpaid interest from the previous period(s). Thus, after the first period, interest is being paid on interest (compounded).

EXAMPLE 11-3: Peoples Bank agrees to pay Jean Bissell 10% interest compounded annually (once a year) on her $1,000 savings account balance. The interest would be compounded over the next five years as follows

Year	Beginning Balance	Interest Earned for Year	Ending Balance (Beginning Balance + Interest)
1	$1,000	$1,000 × .10 × 1 = $100	$1,100
2	$1,100	$1,100 × .10 × 1 = $110	$1,210
3	$1,210	$1,210 × .10 × 1 = $121	$1,331
4	$1,331	$1,331 × .10 × 1 = $133	$1,464
5	$1,464	$1,464 × .10 × 1 = $146	$1,610

Therefore, Peoples Bank is agreeing to pay back $1,610, if Jean Bissell puts $1,000 in a savings account for a five year period.

11-3. The Effect of Compounding Interest

The effect of compounding interest is far greater than most people realize. When interest is compounded annually, the interest amount is added to the principal at the end of each year. Since the interest for the next year is computed on this larger amount, it becomes larger too. Whereas the simple interest rate produces the same amount of interest each year because the interest is computed on the same amount each year.

EXAMPLE 11-4: Citizens Bank agrees to pay Linda Allen 10% simple interest on her $1,000 savings account balance. The interest to be paid at the end of a five year period would be computed as follows:

$$i = P \times r \times t$$
$$i = \$1,000 \times .10 \times 5 = \$500$$

Both Linda Allen and Jean Bissell (Example 11-3) are being offered a 10% interest rate; but, by getting a compounded interest rate, Jean will be earning $110 more. This is the result after only five years. If the two women kept their accounts for thirty years, Jean Bissell would have $17,449, whereas Linda Allen would only have $4,000.

11-4. Future Value of a Single Sum

If you want to know how much would be in an account after a certain period of time if the account balance is compounded once a year at a given rate, you would have to calculate the future value of a single sum (your account balance).

A. The future value of a single sum can be computed using the compound interest formula.

The formula for computing the future value of a single sum is as follows

FUTURE VALUE OF A SINGLE SUM (compound interest formula)

$$FV = PV(1 + r)^n$$

where: FV = future value of a single sum
PV = present value of the single sum
r = interest rate per period
n = number of periods of time

The crucial constraints of using the formula are

1. the interest must be computed at the *end* of the period
2. the interest must be compounded *only once* per period
3. the interest *rate* must remain *constant* over the investment period
4. the length of each *period* must remain *constant*

EXAMPLE 11-5: Bill Lee places $5,000 in an account paying 12% interest compounded once a year for five years. Bill computes the future value of the $5,000 account as follows

$$FV = (\$5,000)(1 + .12)^5$$
$$FV = \$5,000 \times 1.76234$$
$$FV = \$8,812$$

B. Adjustments must be made to information used in the compound interest formula, if interest is compounded more than once a year.

Banks and other financial institutions quote interest rates as *annual* rates and give additional information about the frequency of compounding. For example, if a bank quotes an interest rate of 12% compounded quarterly, it means that it will give you 12% interest for the year; but, interest will be figured four times a year. If the interest is computed four times per year and it will total 12% at the end of the year, then the interest rate used each time must be 3% (12% ÷ 4). Thus, when using the compound interest formula, the number of periods (n) would equal four and the interest rate (r) would equal 3% not 12%.

EXAMPLE 11-6: Mark Sears places $5,000 in an account paying 12% interest compounded *semiannually* (twice per year) for five years. Mark computes the future value of the $5,000 account as follows:

$$FV = (\$5,000)(1 + .06)^{10}$$
$$FV = \$5,000 \times 1.79085$$
$$FV = \$8,954$$

Notice that, since the interest is computed twice a year, the number of periods is ten not five and the interest rate is 6% not 12%.

C. The future value of a single sum can be found by using a Future Value of $1 table.

A Future Value of $1 table shows the amount to which $1 would grow, if invested at certain interest rates for certain periods of time. Exhibit 11-1, page 195, is such a table. To read the table, you simply read down the periods column until you find the number of periods you need. You then read across the row until you come to the column headed with the interest rate you need. The figure shown will be the value of $1 invested for that number of periods at that interest rate.

EXAMPLE 11-7: Ina Spaeth place $5,000 in an account paying 12% interest compounded quarterly for five years. Ina uses the Future Value of $1 table to compute the future value of her account. Since the interest will be computed four times per year for five years, the number of periods to (n) is equal to twenty. The interest rate (r) is equal to 3% (12% ÷ 4). Looking across the row for 20-period investments to the 3% interest column, she finds that $1 will grow to be $1.80611. She therefore computes that her investment will grow to 5,000 times that much.

$$FV = \$9,031 \times 1.58687 = \$14,331$$

EXAMPLE 11-8: After the five-year investment period, Ina Spaeth has the opportunity to invest in a preferred customer account that offers 16% compounded semiannually for three years. Looking again at the Future Value of $1 table, Ina finds that $1 compounded for 6 periods at 8% interest will grow to $1.58687. Since her account will have grown to $9,031 by the beginning of this new investment period, she computes the future value of the account as follows

$$FV = \$9,031 \times 1.58687 = \$14,331$$

This amount could be computed in one step. The $5,000 investment would grow to ($5,000 × 1.80611) at the end of five years. This amount would be multiplied by 1.58687

FUTURE VALUE TABLE OF $1

$$FV = \$1(1 + r)^n$$

Periods (n)	1%	2%	2.5%	3%	4%	5%	6%	8%	10%	12%	16%	20%	24%	Periods (n)
1	1.01000	1.02000	1.02500	1.03000	1.04000	1.05000	1.06000	1.08000	1.10000	1.12000	1.16000	1.20000	1.24000	1
2	1.02010	1.04040	1.05062	1.06090	1.08160	1.10250	1.12360	1.16640	1.21000	1.25440	1.34560	1.44000	1.53760	2
3	1.03030	1.06121	1.07689	1.09273	1.12486	1.15762	1.19102	1.25971	1.33100	1.40493	1.56090	1.72800	1.90662	3
4	1.04060	1.08243	1.10381	1.12551	1.16986	1.21550	1.26248	1.36049	1.46410	1.57352	1.81064	2.07360	2.36421	4
5	1.05101	1.10408	1.13141	1.15927	1.21665	1.27628	1.33823	1.46933	1.61051	1.76234	2.10034	2.48832	2.93163	5
6	1.06152	1.12616	1.15969	1.19405	1.26532	1.34009	1.41852	1.58687	1.77156	1.97382	2.43640	2.98598	3.63522	6
7	1.07214	1.14869	1.18869	1.22987	1.31593	1.40710	1.50363	1.71382	1.94872	2.21068	2.82622	3.58318	4.50767	7
8	1.08286	1.17166	1.21840	1.26677	1.36857	1.47745	1.59385	1.85093	2.14359	2.47596	3.27841	4.29982	5.58951	8
9	1.09369	1.19509	1.24886	1.30477	1.42331	1.55132	1.68948	1.99900	2.35795	2.77308	3.80296	5.15978	6.93099	9
10	1.10462	1.21899	1.28008	1.34392	1.48024	1.62889	1.79085	2.15892	2.59374	3.10585	4.41144	6.19174	8.59443	10
11	1.11567	1.24337	1.31209	1.38423	1.53945	1.71033	1.89830	2.33164	2.85312	3.47855	5.11726	7.43008	10.65709	11
12	1.12683	1.26824	1.34489	1.42576	1.60103	1.79586	2.01220	2.51817	3.13843	3.89598	5.93603	8.91610	13.21479	12
13	1.13809	1.29361	1.37851	1.46853	1.66507	1.88664	2.13293	2.71962	3.45227	4.36349	6.88579	10.69932	16.38634	13
14	1.14947	1.31948	1.41297	1.51259	1.73168	1.97893	2.26090	2.93719	3.79750	4.88711	7.98752	12.83918	20.31906	14
15	1.16097	1.34587	1.44830	1.55797	1.80094	2.07893	2.39656	3.17217	4.17725	5.47357	9.26552	15.40702	25.19563	15
16	1.17258	1.37279	1.48451	1.60471	1.87298	2.18287	2.54035	3.42594	4.59497	6.13039	10.74800	18.48843	31.24259	16
17	1.18430	1.40024	1.52162	1.65285	1.94790	2.29201	2.69277	3.70002	5.05447	6.86604	12.46768	22.18611	38.74081	17
18	1.19615	1.42825	1.55966	1.70243	2.02582	2.40662	2.85434	3.99602	5.55992	7.68997	14.46251	26.62333	48.03860	18
19	1.20811	1.45681	1.59865	1.75351	2.10685	2.52695	3.02560	4.31570	6.11591	8.61276	16.77652	31.94800	59.56786	19
20	1.22019	1.48595	1.63862	1.80611	2.19112	2.65339	3.20714	4.66096	6.72750	9.64629	19.46076	38.33760	73.86415	20
21	1.23239	1.51567	1.67958	1.86029	2.27877	2.78596	3.39956	5.03383	7.40025	10.80385	22.57448	46.00512	91.59155	21
22	1.24472	1.54598	1.72157	1.91610	2.36992	2.92526	3.60354	5.43654	8.14027	12.10031	26.18640	55.20614	113.57352	22
23	1.25716	1.57690	1.76461	1.97359	2.46472	3.07152	3.81975	5.87146	8.95430	13.55235	30.37622	66.24737	140.83116	23
24	1.26973	1.60844	1.80873	2.03279	2.56330	3.22509	4.04893	6.34118	9.84973	15.17863	35.23642	79.49685	174.63064	24
25	1.28243	1.64061	1.85394	2.09378	2.66584	3.38635	4.29187	6.84848	10.83471	17.00006	40.87424	95.39622	216.54199	25
26	1.29526	1.67342	1.90029	2.15659	2.77247	3.55567	4.54938	7.39635	11.91818	19.04007	47.41412	114.47546	268.51207	26
27	1.30821	1.70689	1.94780	2.22129	2.88337	3.73346	4.82235	7.98806	13.10999	21.32488	55.00038	137.37055	332.95497	27
28	1.32129	1.74102	1.99650	2.28793	2.99870	3.92013	5.11169	8.62711	14.42099	23.88387	63.80044	164.84466	412.86416	28
29	1.33450	1.77584	2.04641	2.35657	3.11865	4.11614	5.41839	9.31727	15.86309	26.74993	74.00851	197.81359	511.95156	29
30	1.34785	1.81136	2.09757	2.42726	3.24340	4.32194	5.74349	10.06266	17.44940	29.95992	85.84988	237.37631	634.81993	30
31	1.36133	1.84759	2.15001	2.50008	3.37313	4.53803	6.08810	10.86767	19.19434	33.55511	99.58586	284.85158	787.17672	31
32	1.37494	1.88454	2.20376	2.57508	3.50806	4.76494	6.45339	11.73708	21.11378	37.58173	115.51959	341.82189	976.09913	32
33	1.38869	1.92223	2.25885	2.65234	3.64838	5.00319	6.84059	12.67605	23.22515	42.09153	134.00273	410.18627	1210.36292	33
34	1.40258	1.96068	2.31532	2.73191	3.79432	5.25335	7.25103	13.69013	25.54767	47.14252	155.44317	492.22352	1500.85002	34
35	1.41660	1.99989	2.37321	2.81386	3.94609	5.51602	7.68609	14.78534	28.10244	52.79962	180.31407	590.66823	1861.05403	35
36	1.43077	2.03989	2.43254	2.89828	4.10393	5.79181	8.14725	15.96817	30.91268	59.13557	209.16432	708.80187	2307.70699	36
37	1.44508	2.08069	2.49335	2.98523	4.26809	6.08141	8.63609	17.24563	34.00395	66.23184	242.63062	850.56225	2861.55667	37
38	1.45953	2.12230	2.55568	3.07478	4.43881	6.38548	9.15425	18.62528	37.40434	74.17966	281.45151	1020.67470	3548.33027	38
39	1.47412	2.16474	2.61957	3.16703	4.61637	6.70475	9.70351	20.11530	41.14478	83.08122	326.48376	1224.80964	4399.92954	39
40	1.48886	2.20804	2.68506	3.26204	4.80102	7.03999	10.28572	21.72452	45.25926	93.05097	378.72116	1469.77157	5455.91262	40

EXHIBIT 11-1

after three more years at the new interest rate. Therefore, the final balance could be computed as follows

$$FV = \$5{,}000 \times 1.80611 \times 1.58687 = \$14{,}330^*$$

* Slight difference due to rounding

EXAMPLE 11-9: Sly Salesman promises Mr. Naive that he will give Naive $18,000 in ten years if Naive will invest $10,000 in Sly's Slick Operation today. Mr. Naive is so impressed at the prospect of nearly doubling his money that he jumps at the chance.

If Mr. Naive had looked at a Future Value of $1 table he would see that $1 would grow to $1.80611 at the end of 20 periods at 3% interest. Therefore, $10,000 would become $18,061 if it were invested for 10 years at 6% interest compounded semiannually. When interest rates are in the double digits, 6% interest is not much to get excited about. Even if Mr. Naive only got 10% compounded semiannually, he would make twice as much interest. The future value of the investment would equal $26,534 ($10,000 × 2.65339).

11-5. The Present Value of a Single Sum

If you want to know how much you would have to invest in an account now to have a certain amount after a given period of time if interest is compounded at a given rate during this period, you would have to calculate the present value of a single sum (your goal amount).

A. The present value of a single sum can be computed from a formula derived from the compound interest formula.

The formula for computing the present value of a single sum is derived from the compound interest formula as follows:

**PRESENT VALUE OF
A SINGLE SUM**
$$FV = PV(1 + r)^n$$
$$PV = FV/(1 + r)^n$$

The same crucial constraints apply to the use of this formula as those applied to the use of compound interest formula.

EXAMPLE 11-10: Investor Corporation wishes to have $5,000 at the end of three years. The corporation can invest its money in an account that pays 10% interest compounded annually. Investor Corporation needs to know how much money to place in the account now to reach its $5,000 goal. Using the present value of a single sum formula, the initial investment is calculated as follows:

$$PV = (\$5{,}000)/(1 + .10)^3$$
$$PV = \$3{,}757$$

If the corporation places $3,757 in an account paying 10% interest compounded annually, the balance will grow to $5,000 by the end of the third year. We can prove this by looking at the table below.

Year	Beginning Balance	Interest Earned for Year	Ending Balance (Beginning Balance + Interest)
1	$3,757	($3,757)(.10)(1) = $376	$4,133
2	$4,133	($4,133)(.10)(1) = $413	$4,546
3	$4,546	($4,546)(.10)(1) = $455	$5,001*

*Difference due to rounding

B. Adjustments must be made to information used in the present value formula, if interest is compounded more than once a year.

Just as with the compound interest formula, the values of *r* and *n* must be adjusted when interest is to be compounded more than once per year. Remember, the present value of a single sum formula is just a restatement of the compound interest formula.

C. The present value of a single sum can be found by using a Present Value of $1 table.

A Present Value of $1 table shows the amount that must be invested now at a certain interest rate to have $1 at the end of a certain number of periods. Exhibit 11-2, page 198, is such a table. It is read in exactly the same manner as the Future Value of $1 table.

EXAMPLE 11-11: XYZ Corporation wants to purchase some new equipment. The corporation has the choice of paying $6,000 for the equipment now or paying $10,000 for it at the end of five years. If the company decides to pay for the equipment in five years, it has the opportunity to invest the $6,000 elsewhere and get 12% interest compounded annually.

Looking at the Present Value of $1 table, XYZ Corporation sees that $.56743 must be invested now to have $1 at the end of five years, therefore the corporation will need to set aside only $5,674 to have $10,000. The firm would prefer to invest $5,674 currently in a 12% investment allowing $10,000 to accumulate by the end of five years than to give up $6,000 to pay cash for the equipment.

RAISE YOUR GRADES

Can you explain ... ?

☑ how to compute simple interest for a single period of time
☑ what is meant by compounding interest
☑ what is the effect of compounding interest
☑ how to compute the future value of a single sum
☑ what adjustments must be made to information used in the compound interest formula when interest is compounded more than once a year
☑ what the numbers on the Future Value of $1 table represent
☑ how to compute the present value of a single sum
☑ what the numbers on the Present Value of $1 table represent

---

SUMMARY

1. The formula for calculating simple interest is $i = P \times r \times t$.
2. Interest is stated on an annual basis and time is stated in years when using the simple interest formula.
3. The compound interest formula computes interest for two or more periods of time.
4. When computing compound interest, interest is figured on the principal plus any unpaid interest from previous periods.
5. The formula for computing the future value of a single sum is $FV = PV(1 + r)^n$.
6. When computing the future value of a single sum, the interest must be added at the end of the period and compounded only once per period.
7. When computing the future value of a single sum using the compound interest formula, the interest rate must remain constant over the investment period.
8. When computing the future value of a single sum using the compound interest formula, the length of each period must remain constant.

PRESENT VALUE TABLE OF $1

$$PV = \frac{\$1}{(1 + r)^n}$$

Periods (n)	1%	2%	2.5%	3%	4%	5%	6%	8%	10%	12%	16%	20%	24%	Periods (n)
1	.99010	.98039	.97561	.97087	.96154	.95238	.94340	.92593	.90909	.89286	.86207	.83333	.80645	1
2	.98030	.96117	.95181	.94260	.92456	.90703	.89000	.85734	.82645	.79719	.74316	.69444	.65036	2
3	.97059	.94232	.92860	.91514	.88900	.86384	.83962	.79383	.75131	.71178	.64066	.57870	.52449	3
4	.96098	.92385	.90595	.88849	.85480	.82270	.79209	.73503	.68301	.63552	.55229	.48225	.42297	4
5	.95147	.90573	.88385	.86261	.82193	.78353	.74726	.68058	.62092	.56743	.47611	.40188	.34111	5
6	.94205	.88797	.86230	.83748	.79031	.74622	.70496	.63017	.56447	.50663	.41044	.33490	.27509	6
7	.93272	.87056	.84127	.81309	.75992	.71068	.66506	.58349	.51316	.45235	.35383	.27908	.22184	7
8	.92348	.85349	.82075	.78941	.73069	.67684	.62741	.54027	.46651	.40388	.30503	.23257	.17891	8
9	.91434	.83676	.80073	.76642	.70259	.64461	.59190	.50025	.42410	.36061	.26295	.19381	.14428	9
10	.90529	.82035	.78120	.74409	.67556	.61391	.55839	.46319	.38554	.32197	.22668	.16151	.11635	10
11	.89632	.80426	.76214	.72242	.64958	.58468	.52679	.42888	.35049	.28748	.19542	.13459	.09383	11
12	.88745	.78849	.74356	.70138	.62460	.55684	.49697	.39711	.31863	.25668	.16846	.11216	.07567	12
13	.87866	.77303	.72542	.68095	.60057	.53032	.46884	.36770	.28966	.22917	.14523	.09346	.06103	13
14	.86996	.75788	.70773	.66112	.57748	.50507	.44230	.34046	.26333	.20462	.12520	.07789	.04921	14
15	.86135	.74301	.69047	.64186	.55526	.48102	.41727	.31524	.23939	.18270	.10793	.06491	.03969	15
16	.85282	.72845	.67362	.62317	.53391	.45811	.39365	.29189	.21763	.16312	.09304	.05409	.03201	16
17	.84438	.71416	.65720	.60502	.51337	.43630	.37136	.27027	.19784	.14564	.08021	.04507	.02581	17
18	.83602	.70016	.64117	.58739	.49363	.41552	.35034	.25025	.17986	.13004	.06914	.03756	.02082	18
19	.82774	.68643	.62553	.57029	.47464	.39573	.33051	.23171	.16351	.11611	.05961	.03130	.01679	19
20	.81954	.67297	.61027	.55368	.45639	.37689	.31180	.21455	.14864	.10367	.05139	.02608	.01354	20
21	.81143	.65978	.59539	.53755	.43883	.35894	.29416	.19866	.13513	.09256	.04430	.02174	.01092	21
22	.80340	.64684	.58086	.52189	.42196	.34185	.27751	.18394	.12285	.08264	.03819	.01811	.00880	22
23	.79544	.63416	.56670	.50669	.40573	.32557	.26180	.17032	.11168	.07379	.03292	.01509	.00710	23
24	.78757	.62172	.55288	.49193	.39012	.31007	.24698	.15770	.10153	.06588	.02838	.01258	.00573	24
25	.77977	.60953	.53939	.47761	.37512	.29530	.23300	.14602	.09230	.05882	.02447	.01048	.00462	25
26	.77205	.59758	.52623	.46369	.36069	.28124	.21981	.13520	.08391	.05252	.02109	.00874	.00372	26
27	.76440	.58586	.51340	.45019	.34682	.26785	.20737	.12519	.07628	.04689	.01818	.00728	.00300	27
28	.75684	.57437	.50088	.43708	.33348	.25509	.19563	.11591	.06934	.04187	.01567	.00607	.00242	28
29	.74934	.56311	.48866	.42435	.32065	.24295	.18456	.10733	.06304	.03738	.01351	.00506	.00195	29
30	.74192	.55207	.47674	.41199	.30832	.23138	.17411	.09938	.05731	.03338	.01165	.00421	.00158	30
31	.73458	.54125	.46511	.39999	.29646	.22036	.16425	.09202	.05210	.02980	.01004	.00351	.00127	31
32	.72730	.53063	.45377	.38834	.28506	.20987	.15496	.08520	.04736	.02661	.00866	.00293	.00102	32
33	.72010	.52023	.44270	.37703	.27409	.19987	.14619	.07889	.04306	.02376	.00746	.00244	.00083	33
34	.71297	.51003	.43191	.36604	.26355	.19035	.13791	.07305	.03914	.02121	.00643	.00203	.00067	34
35	.70591	.50003	.42137	.35538	.25342	.18129	.13011	.06763	.03558	.01894	.00555	.00169	.00054	35
36	.69892	.49022	.41109	.34503	.24367	.17266	.12274	.06262	.03235	.01691	.00478	.00141	.00043	36
37	.69200	.48061	.40107	.33498	.23430	.16444	.11579	.05799	.02941	.01510	.00412	.00118	.00035	37
38	.68515	.47119	.39128	.32523	.22529	.15661	.10924	.05369	.02673	.01348	.00355	.00098	.00028	38
39	.67837	.46195	.38174	.31575	.21662	.14915	.10306	.04971	.02430	.01204	.00306	.00082	.00023	39
40	.67165	.45289	.37243	.30656	.20829	.14205	.09722	.04603	.02209	.01075	.00264	.00068	.00018	40

EXHIBIT 11-2

9. If a bank quotes an interest rate of 12% compounded quarterly, the number of periods (n) used in the compound interest formula would be four times the number of years of investment; the interest rate (r) would be 3% (12% ÷ 4). .

10. The Future Value of $1 table shows the amount to which $1 would grow if invested at certain interest rates for certain periods of time.

11. The formula for computing the present value of a single sum is $PV = FV/(1 + r)^n$.

12. The Present Value of $1 table shows the amount that must be invested now at a certain compound interest rate to have $1 at the end of a certain number of periods.

RAPID REVIEW

1. What would be the simple interest earned on a $10,000 investment in an account that yields 12% interest for eight years?

2. What is the future value of a $10,000 investment in an account that yields 12% interest compounded annually for eight years? (Use the compound interest formula.)

3. In the following cases, what would be the number of periods and relevant interest rates used in solving the compound interest formula?
   (a) 8% compounded quarterly for seven years
   (b) 20% compounded semiannually for nine years
   (c) 18% compounded monthly for two years

4. Would you prefer to invest in an account that yields 12% compounded monthly or quarterly, all other conditions being equal?

5. What is the future value of an $800 investment in an account that yields 12% interest compounded quarterly for six years? (Use the Future Value of $1 table.)

6. Using the Future Value of $1 table, you will find that $1 placed in account that yields 10% interest compounded semiannually for four years will grow to approximately
   (a) $4.30   (b) $1.22   (c) $1.48   (d) $1.46

7. Using the Future Value of $1 table, you will find that $200,000 placed in an account that yields 12% interest compounded quarterly for five years will grow to approximately
   (a) $352,465   (b) $358,170   (c) $331,854   (d) $361,222

8. Using the Present Value of $1 table, you will find that $_____ invested in an account that yields 12% interest compounded annually now will grow to $100,000 in fifteen years.
   (a) $18,270   (b) $17,411   (c) $56,743   (d) $41,199

9. Using the Present Value of $1 table, you will find that $_____ invested in an account that yields 10% interest compounded quarterly now will grow to $200,000 in four years.
   (a) $124,920   (b) $134,724   (c) $135,368   (d) $136,602

10. Using the Present Value of $1 table, you will find that $_____ invested in an account that yields 10% interest compounded semiannually now will grow to $10,000 in nine years.
   (a) $4,100   (b) $4,155   (c) $4,241   (d) $4,018

Answers:

1. $10,000 × .12 × 8 = $9,600 [Section 11-1]
2. ($10,000)(1 + .12)^8 = $24,760 [Section 11-4A]
3. (a) 28 periods; 2% interest
   (b) 18 periods; 10% interest
   (c) 24 periods; 1.5% interest
      [Section 11-4B]
4. 12% compounded monthly [Section 11-3]
5. $800 × 2.03279 = $1,626 [Section 11-4C]

6. (c) [Section 11-4C]
7. (d) [Section 11-4C]
8. (a) [Section 11-5C]
9. (b) [Section 11-5C]
10. (b) [Section 11-5C]

SOLVED PROBLEMS

In the problems that follow, use the tables provided in this text. Also, assume there is no penalty for early payment of a debt.

PROBLEM 11-1: Marguerite Moran signs a note agreeing to pay back the principal of $5,000 plus 15% simple interest at the end of a four year period. What will be the amount she owes in four years?

Answer: i = $5,000 × .15 × 4 = $3,000; $5,000 + $3,000 = $8,000   [Section 11-1]

PROBLEM 11-2: Peggy Royal signs a note agreeing to pay back the principal of $7,000 plus 12% simple interest at the end of a five year period. There is a 5% penalty if the note is not paid on time; the penalty being computed on both the principal and interest. What will be the amount Peggy owes after five years, if she does *not* pay on time?

Answer: i = $7,000 × .12 × 5 = $4,200
        $7,000 + $4,200 = $11,200
        penalty = $11,200 × .05 = $560
        total amount due = $11,200 + $560 = $11,760   [Section 11-1]

PROBLEM 11-3: Suppose that Peggy Royal in Problem 11-2 decided to pay of the note in thirty months not four years. What would be the amount she pays?

Answer: i = $7,000 × .12 × $3\frac{1}{2}$ = $2.940
        $7,000 + $2,940 = $9,940   [Section 11-1]

PROBLEM 11-4: Dave Lafferty invests $10,000 in an account that pays 16% interest compounded annually for four years? Using the Future Value of $1 table, find the value of the account at the end of the four years.

Answer: 1.81064 is the factor for r = 16% and n = 4
        FV = $10,000 × 1.81064 = $18,106   [Section 11-4C]

PROBLEM 11-5: Pat Raftery invests $20,000 in an account that pays 16% interest compounded semiannually for four years. Pat decides to withdraw her money early. Using the Future Value of $1 table, find the value of the account after 42 months (7 six-month periods).

Answer: 1.71382 is the factor for r = 8% and n = 7
        $20,000 × 1.71382 = $34,276   [Section 11-4C]

PROBLEM 11-6: Candi Appell invests $6,000 in an account that pays 12% interest compounded semiannually for five years. After five years, the account balance will be rolled over into a preferred customer account which pays 16% interest compounded quarterly. What will be the balance in Candi's account after ten years?

Answer: 1.79085 is the factor for r = 6% and n = 10
        $6,000 × 1.79085 = $10,745
        2.19112 is the factor for r = 4% and n = 20
        $10,745 × 2.19112 = $23,544   [Section 11-4C]

PROBLEM 11-7: BFP Corporation wishes to have $1,000,000 at the end of three years. The corporation can invest its money in an account that pays 12% interest compounded monthly. How much money should BFP invest in the account now to reach its $1,000,000 goal?

Answer: .69892 is the factor for r = 1% and n = 36
$1,000,000 × .69892 = $698,920   **[Section 11-5C]**

PROBLEM 11-8: WHHS Corporation just received a check for $10,000 from an investment they made five years ago. The investment was $5,536. At what rate of interest was the investment compounded and for what periods?

Answer: Looking at the Present Value of $1 table, .55368 is the factor for r = 3% and n = 20. If there were 20 periods in 5 years, the interest must have been compounded quarterly. If so, the annual interest rate must have been 12%.   **[Section 11-5B]**

PROBLEM 11-9: Tiffany Loges signs a note agreeing to pay back the principal of $7,500 plus 13% simple interest at the end of a five year period. What will be the amount she owes in five years?

Answer: i = $7,500 × .13 × 5 = $4,875; $7,500 + $4,875 = $12,375   **[Section 11-1]**

PROBLEM 11-10: Tige Ohm signs a note agreeing to pay back the principal of $9,250 plus 10% simple interest at the end of a nine year period. There is a 6% penalty if the note is not paid on time; the penalty being computed on both the principal and interest. What will be the amount Tige owes after nine years, if he does *not* pay on time?

Answer: i = $9,250 × .10 × 9 = $8,325
$9,250 + $8,325 = $17,575
$17,575 × 6% = $1,054.50 = penalty
total amount due = $17,575 + $1,054.50 = $18,629.50   **[Section 11-1]**

PROBLEM 11-11: Suppose that Tige Ohm in Problem 11-10 decided to pay off the note in ninety months not nine years. What would be the amount he pays?

Answer: i = $9,250 × .10 × 90/12 = $6,937.50
total payment = $9,250 + $6,937.50 = $16,187.50   **[Section 11-1]**

PROBLEM 11-12: Mike Zackery invests $25,000 in an account that pays 12% interest compounded annually for six years. Using the Future Value of $1 table, find the value of the account at the end of the six years.

Answer: 1.97382 is the factor for r = 12 and n = 6
FV = $25,000 × 1.97382 = $49,345.50   **[Section 11-4C]**

PROBLEM 11-13: Susan Cobb invests $8,000 in an account that pays 10% interest compounded semiannually for four years. She decides to withdraw her money early. Using the Future Value of $1 table, find the value of the account after 30 months.

Answer: 1.27628 is the factor for r = 5% and n = 5
$8,000 × 1.27628 = $10,210.24   **[Section 11-4C]**

PROBLEM 11-14: IS Corporation wishes to have $2,500,000 at the end of nine years. The corporation can invest its money in an account that pays 16% interest compounded quarterly. How much money should IS invest in the account now to reach its $2,500,000 goal?

Answer: .24367 is the factor for r = 4% and n = 36
$2,500,000 × .24367 = $609,175   **[Section 11-5C]**

12 ANNUITIES

THIS CHAPTER IS ABOUT

☑ **Annuities**
☑ **The Future Value of an Ordinary Annuity**
☑ **The Future Value of an Annuity Due**
☑ **The Present Value of an Ordinary Annuity**
☑ **The Present Value of an Annuity Due**

12-1. Annuities

An annuity is a series of equal deposits or withdrawals that occur over equal time periods with interest being compounded at a constant rate at the end of each period. These deposits or withdrawals are often called **rents.** If the rents occur at the end of each period, the annuity is called an **ordinary annuity** or an annuity in arrears. If the rents occur at the beginning of the period, the annuity is called an **annuity due** or an annuity in advance.

12-2. The Future Value of an Ordinary Annuity

Determining the future value of an ordinary annuity follows the same basic principles as finding the future value of a single sum. We can see this by reviewing the activity in the account below. A deposit of $100 is made to the account at the end of each year. The bank pays 10% interest compounded annually.

Year	Beginning Balance	+	Interest	+	Deposit (Year End)	=	Ending Balance
1	$ 0		$ 0 × .10 × 1 = $ 0		$100		$100
2	$100		$100 × .10 × 1 = $10		$100		$210
3	$210		$210 × .10 × 1 = $21		$100		$331

The account will have a balance of $331 at the end of the third year immediately after the third deposit is made. Interest in each year is computed on the beginning balance in the account. No interest is earned on the deposit until the following period, since the deposit is made at the *end* of the current period.

A. The future value of an ordinary annuity is equal to the sum of the future values of the individual deposits (single sums).

The ending balance in the account mentioned above could be explained as the future value of a single sum, $100, with 10% interest compounded annually for two years plus another compounded for one year plus yet another compounded for zero years. The third deposit is made on the day the final balance is computed and therefore it doesn't earn any interest. However, it still contributes $100 to the final balance. The time-line below illustrates this concept.

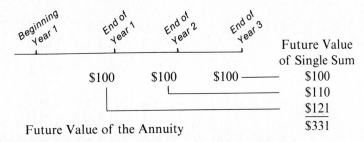

Future Value of the Annuity

The distinguishing feature of an ordinary annuity is that the last deposit earns no interest.

B. The future value of an ordinary annuity can be found by using the Future Value of an Ordinary Annuity of $1 table.

The Future Value of an Ordinary Annuity of $1 table shows the final balance in an account if $1 is deposited at the end of the period for "n" periods with interest being compounded at rate "r" at the end of each period. Exhibit 12-1, page 204, is such a table. The numbers from this table can only be used if

1. the amount of each rent remains constant
2. the length of each period remains constant
3. the interest rate remains constant
4. interest is compounded once each period

EXAMPLE 12-1: Mr. and Mrs. Saver wish to deposit $1,000 at the end of each quarter into an account that pays 8% interest compounded quarterly for five years. Mr. Saver wants to know how much will be in the account at the end of the fifth year, before they make a decision.

Mrs. Saver knows that they are dealing with an ordinary annuity because the deposits will be made at the end of the period. The annuity involves twenty rents (5 years × 4) and an interest rate of 2% (8% ÷ 4). Looking at the Future Value of an Ordinary Annuity of $1 table, Mrs. Saver finds that a balance will grow to $24.29737, if rents of $1 are made for 20 periods at 2% interest. She then concludes that a $1,000 investment would grow to

$$\$1,000 \times 24.29737 = \$24,297$$

EXAMPLE 12-2: Mr. Retiree wishes to have $50,000 in his savings account when he retires in ten years. He will make a deposit at the end of each six months between now and the day he retires. His account pays 12% interest compounded semiannually.

Mr. Retiree will be making 20 deposits into an account that pays 6% each six months. The last deposit will be made on the day he retires. The Future Value of an Ordinary Annuity of $1 indicates that under these conditions $1 would grow to $36.78559. Therefore,

$$\$50,000 = \text{semiannual deposit} \times 36.78559$$
$$or \text{ semiannual deposit} = \$50,000 \div 36.78559 = \$1,359$$

Therefore, if Mr. Retiree deposits $1,359 into an account at the end of each six months, he will have $50,000 by the time he retires. Mr. Retiree knows that he is dealing with an ordinary annuity because the last deposit earns no interest.

12-3. The Future Value of an Annuity Due

If rents are made at the beginning of each period, the annuity is called an annuity due or an annuity in advance. The future value of an annuity due differs from that of an ordinary annuity in that *all* deposits will earn interest. By changing the account in Section 12-2 into an annuity due account, we can see the difference this additional interest makes.

FUTURE VALUE OF AN ORDINARY ANNUITY OF $1 TABLE

$$FV = \frac{(1+i)^n - 1}{i}$$

Periods (n)	1%	2%	2.5%	3%	4%	5%	6%	8%	10%	12%	16%	20%	24%	Periods (n)
1	1.00000	1.00000	1.00000	1.00000	1.00000	1.00000	1.00000	1.00000	1.00000	1.00000	1.00000	1.00000	1.00000	1
2	2.01000	2.02000	2.02500	2.03000	2.04000	2.05000	2.06000	2.08000	2.10000	2.12000	2.16000	2.20000	2.24000	2
3	3.03010	3.06040	3.07562	3.09090	3.12160	3.15250	3.18360	3.24640	3.31000	3.37440	3.50560	3.64000	3.77760	3
4	4.06040	4.12161	4.15252	4.18363	4.24646	4.31013	4.37462	4.50611	4.64100	4.77933	5.06650	5.36800	5.68422	4
5	5.10101	5.20404	5.25633	5.30914	5.41632	5.52563	5.63709	5.86660	6.10510	6.35285	6.87714	7.44160	8.04844	5
6	6.15202	6.30812	6.38774	6.46841	6.63298	6.80191	6.97532	7.33593	7.71561	8.11519	8.97748	9.92992	10.98006	6
7	7.21354	7.43428	7.54743	7.66246	7.89829	8.14201	8.39384	8.92280	9.48717	10.08901	11.41387	12.91590	14.61528	7
8	8.28567	8.58297	8.73612	8.89234	9.21423	9.54911	9.89747	10.63663	11.43589	12.29969	14.24009	16.49908	19.12294	8
9	9.36853	9.75463	9.95452	10.15911	10.58280	11.02656	11.49132	12.48756	13.57948	14.77566	17.51851	20.79890	24.71245	9
10	10.46221	10.94972	11.20338	11.46388	12.00611	12.57789	13.18079	14.48656	15.93742	17.54874	21.32147	25.95868	31.64344	10
11	11.56683	12.16872	12.48347	12.80780	13.48635	14.20679	14.97164	16.64549	18.53117	20.65458	25.73290	32.15042	40.23787	11
12	12.68250	13.41209	13.79555	14.19203	15.02581	15.91713	16.86994	18.97713	21.38428	24.13313	30.85017	39.58050	50.89495	12
13	13.80933	14.68033	15.14044	15.61779	16.62684	17.71298	18.88214	21.49530	24.52271	28.02911	36.78620	48.49660	64.10974	13
14	14.94742	15.97394	16.51895	17.08632	18.29191	19.59863	21.01507	24.21492	27.97498	32.39260	43.67199	59.19592	80.49608	14
15	16.09690	17.29342	17.93193	18.59891	20.02359	21.57856	23.27597	27.15211	31.77248	37.27971	51.65951	72.03511	100.81514	15
16	17.25786	18.63929	19.38022	20.15688	21.82453	23.65749	25.67253	30.32428	35.94973	42.75328	60.92503	87.44213	126.01077	16
17	18.43044	20.01207	20.86473	21.76159	23.69751	25.84037	28.21288	33.75023	40.54470	48.88367	71.67303	105.93056	157.25336	17
18	19.61475	21.41231	22.38635	23.41444	25.64541	28.13238	30.90565	37.45024	45.59917	55.74971	84.14072	128.11667	195.99416	18
19	20.81090	22.84056	23.94601	25.11687	27.67123	30.53900	33.75999	41.44626	51.15909	63.43968	98.60323	154.74000	244.03276	19
20	22.01900	24.29737	25.54466	26.87037	29.77808	33.06595	36.78559	45.76196	57.27500	72.05244	115.37975	186.68800	303.60062	20
21	23.23919	25.78332	27.18327	28.67649	31.96920	35.71925	39.99273	50.42292	64.00250	81.69874	134.84051	225.02560	377.46477	21
22	24.47159	27.29898	28.86286	30.53678	34.24797	38.50521	43.39229	55.45676	71.40275	92.50258	157.41499	271.03072	469.05632	22
23	25.71630	28.84496	30.58443	32.45288	36.61789	41.43048	46.99583	60.89330	79.54302	104.60289	183.60138	326.23686	582.62984	23
24	26.97346	30.42186	32.34904	34.42647	39.08260	44.50200	50.81558	66.76476	88.49733	118.15524	213.97761	392.48424	723.46100	24
25	28.24320	32.03030	34.15776	36.45926	41.64591	47.72710	54.86451	73.10594	98.34706	133.33387	249.21402	471.98108	898.09164	25
26	29.52563	33.67091	36.01171	38.55304	44.31174	51.11345	59.15638	79.95442	109.18177	150.33393	290.08827	567.37730	1114.63363	26
27	30.82089	35.34432	37.91200	40.70963	47.08421	54.66912	63.70577	87.35077	121.09994	169.37401	337.50239	681.85276	1383.14570	27
28	32.12910	37.05121	39.85980	42.93092	49.96758	58.40258	68.52811	95.33883	134.20994	190.69889	392.50277	819.22331	1716.10067	28
29	33.45039	38.79223	41.85630	45.21885	52.96629	62.32271	73.63980	103.96594	148.63093	214.58275	456.30322	984.06797	2128.96483	29
30	34.78489	40.56808	43.90270	47.57542	56.08494	66.43885	79.05819	113.28321	164.49402	241.33268	530.31173	1181.88157	2640.91639	30
31	36.13274	42.37944	46.00027	50.00268	59.32834	70.76189	84.80168	123.34587	181.94342	271.29261	616.16161	1419.25788	3275.73632	31
32	37.49407	44.22703	48.15028	52.50276	62.70147	75.29882	90.88978	134.21354	201.13777	304.84772	715.74746	1704.10946	4062.91304	32
33	38.86901	46.11157	50.35403	55.07784	66.20953	80.06377	97.34316	145.95062	222.25154	342.42945	831.26706	2045.93135	5039.01217	33
34	40.25770	48.03380	52.61289	57.73018	69.85791	85.06696	104.18375	158.62667	245.47670	384.52098	965.26979	2456.11762	6249.37509	34
35	41.66028	49.99448	54.92821	60.46208	73.65222	90.32031	111.43478	172.31680	271.02437	431.66350	1120.71295	2948.34115	7750.22511	35
36	43.07688	51.99437	57.30141	63.27594	77.59831	95.83632	119.12087	187.10215	299.12681	484.46312	1301.02703	3539.00937	9611.27913	36
37	44.50765	54.03425	59.73395	66.17422	81.70225	101.62814	127.26812	203.07032	330.03949	543.59869	1510.19135	4247.81125	11918.98612	37
38	45.95272	56.11494	62.22730	69.15945	85.97034	107.70954	135.90421	220.31595	364.04343	609.83053	1752.82197	5098.37350	14780.54279	38
39	47.41225	58.23724	64.78298	72.23423	90.40915	114.09502	145.05846	238.94122	401.44778	684.01020	2034.27348	6119.04820	18328.87306	39
40	48.88637	60.40198	67.40255	75.40126	95.02550	120.79977	154.76197	259.05652	442.59256	767.09142	2360.75724	7343.85784	22728.80260	40

EXHIBIT 12-1

Year	Beginning Balance	+	Deposit (Beg. Yr)	+	Interest	=	Ending Balance
1	$ 0		$100		$100 × .10 × 1 = $10		$110
2	$110		$100		$210 × .10 × 1 = $21		$231
3	$231		$100		$231 × .10 × 1 = $33		$364

The account earns $33 more when the rents are made at the beginning of the period than when rents were made at the end of the period. This could become a substantial difference when investing larger amounts at higher rates for longer periods of time.

A. The future value of an annuity due is equal to the sum of the future values of the individual deposits (single sums).

The accuracy of this statement is illustrated in the time-line below.

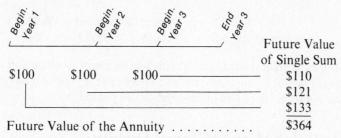

Future Value of the Annuity $364

The distinguishing feature of an annuity due is that interest is earned on the last deposit.

B. The future value of an annuity due can be found by adjusting information found on the Future Value of an Ordinary Annuity of $1 table.

Most textbooks do not have tables for annuities due. However, by using the equation below, information given in the Future Value of an Ordinary Annuity of $1 table can be adjusted and used to find the future value of an annuity due.

$$\text{Future Value of an Annuity Due for "n" periods} = \text{Future Value of an Ordinary Annuity of "n + 1" periods} - 1 \text{ rent}$$

An annuity due of three rents earns three periods of interest. An ordinary annuity of three rents only earns interest for two periods. At the end of three periods the two types of annuities would have the following balances:

Annuities Due	Ordinary Annuities
3 periods' interest + 3 rents	2 periods' interest + 3 rents
after four periods	
4 periods' interest + 4 rents	3 periods' interest + 4 rents

From this you can see that an annuity due for 3 periods yields the same final balance as an ordinary annuity for four (or three + 1) periods minus one rent. Therefore, when trying to find the future value of an annuity due using the Future Value of an Ordinary Annuity of $1 table, you must use the factor for "n + 1" periods — $1 (one rent).

EXAMPLE 12-3: Mr. and Mrs. Saver (Example 12-1) have decided to deposit $1,000 at the *beginning* rather than the end of each quarter. The accounts pays 8% interest compounded quarterly for five years. Mr. Saver is curious about how much more they will earn.

Mrs. Saver knows that they are now dealing with an annuity due because the deposits will be made at the beginning of the period and the last deposit will earn interest. Again, the annuity involves twenty rents and an interest rate of 2%. Looking at the Future Value of an Ordinary Annuity of $1 table, Mrs. Saver finds the factor in the table for *twenty-one* rents at an interest rate of 2%. The table indicates that twenty-one rents of $1 each will grow to $25.78332 immediately after the last deposit is made. She then subtracts $1 (one rent) to find the future value of an annuity due of 20 rents, $24.78332. Since Mr. and

Mrs. Saver are depositing $1,000, their account will grow to

$$\$1,000 \times 24.78332 = \$24,783$$

This is $486 more than would accumulate if deposits were made at the end of the period.

EXAMPLE 12-4: Mr. Retiree (Example 12-2) still wishes to have $50,000 in his account when he retires in ten years. However, he now plans to make his deposits at the *beginning* of each six-month period with the last deposit being made six months before retirement. The account pays 12% interest compounded semiannually.

Mr. Retiree will now be dealing with annuity due. The last deposit will earn interest. The Future Value of an Ordinary Annuity of $1 table indicates that $1 rents deposited for twenty-one periods into an account that pays 6% interest will grow to $39.99273. Therefore, an annuity due for twenty periods would grow to $38.99273 ($39,99273 − $1). Using the equation, Mr. Retiree finds that

$$\$50,000 = \text{semiannual deposit} \times 38.99273$$
$$\text{semiannual deposit} = \$50,000 \div 38,99273 = \$1,282$$

Mr. Retiree would have to deposit $1,282 at the beginning of each period to have $50,000 in his savings account when he retires. This is $77 less per six-month period than he would have to pay if he made his deposits at the end of the period.

12-4. Present Value of an Ordinary Annuity

As stated in the definition of an annuity, a rent may be a deposit or a withdrawal. In dealing with withdrawals, the principles are the reverse of what we have discussed thus far in this chapter. Rather than computing what you will *end up* with after making a certain number of deposits, you must compute what you must *start with* to accomodate a certain number of withdrawals. Rather than computing future values, you must compute present values.

A. The present value of an ordinary annuity is equal to the sum of the present values of the individual withdrawals (single sums).

Suppose that we want to withdraw $100 at the end of each of three years from an account that pays 10% interest compounded annually. We do not need to deposit $300 now in order to make these withdrawals because the funds left in the account will be earning interest. We actually need to deposit an amount that will grow to $100 in one year plus an amount that will grow to $100 in two years plus yet another that will grow to $100 at the end of three years. The time-line below illustrates this concept.

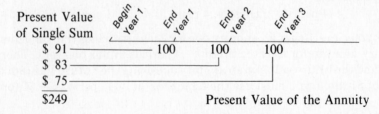

Approximately $249 must be deposited into the account to accommodate the three withdrawals.

We can prove the accuracy of these numbers by following the activity in the account.

Year	Beginning Balance	+	Interest	−	Withdrawal	=	Ending Balance
1	$249		$249 × .10 × 1 = $25		$100		$174
2	$174		$174 × .10 × 1 = $17		$100		$ 91
3	$ 91		$ 91 × .10 × 1 = $ 9		$100		0

B. The present value of an ordinary annuity can be found by using the Present Value of an Ordinary Annuity of $1 table.

The Present Value of an Ordinary Annuity of $1 table shows the amount that must be deposited today to accommodate withdrawals of $1 at the end of each period for "n" periods from an account that earns "r" rate of interest compounded once each period. Exhibit 12-2, page 208, is such a table. The unadjusted numbers in the table can only be used if

1. the withdrawals occur at the *end* of the period
2. the amount of the withdrawal remains constant
3. the length of the period remains constant
4. the interest rate remains constant

EXAMPLE 12-5: Sally Setaside wishes to withdraw $500 at the end of each month from an account that pays 12% interest compounded monthly for the next three years. Sally needs to know how much to deposit in her account today to meet her goal and have a zero balance in her account after the last withdrawal.

Again we are dealing with an ordinary annuity because the withdrawals will be made at the *end* of the period. There will be 36 monthly withdrawals and an interest rate of 1%. The Present Value of an Ordinary Annuity of $1 table indicates that $30.10751 must be deposited today to accommodate 36 withdrawals of $1 under these circumstances. If Sally is to withdraw $500 at the end of each month she must deposit

$$\$500 \times 30.10751 = \$15,054$$

EXAMPLE 12-6: XYZ Corporation sells tractors on a long-term payment plan. The buyer agrees to pay $1,000 now and $400 per month for two years. The first monthly payment is to be made one month from the date of sale. The current interest rate is 24% compounded monthly.

The selling price of the tractor is equal to the present value of the $1,000 down payment plus the present value of the 24 monthly payments. The Present Value of an Ordinary Annuity of $1 table indicates $18.91393 is the present value of 24 monthly payments of $1 when the interest rate per period is 2%. Therefore the present value of 24 monthly payments of $400 must be

$$\$400 \times 18.91393 = \$7,566$$

The present value of the $1,000 down payment is $1,000 since it is being made today. Therefore the selling price of the tractor is $8,566 ($7,566 + $1,000).

EXAMPLE 12-7: Ms. Investor wishes to purchase a $1,000 bond from Borrower Corporation. The bond will mature in ten years and pay 12% compounded semiannually. Ms. Investor wants to know how much she should pay for the bond today in order to have earned a return of 16% interest compounded semiannually on her investment after the ten years are up.

The $1,000 bond will pay 12% semiannually or $60 ($1,000 × .12 × $\frac{1}{2}$) every six months for the next ten years. Ms. Investor must figure what amount deposited in an account earning 16% compounded semiannually will provide for withdrawals of $60 every six months for ten years. According to the Present Value of an Ordinary Annuity of $1 table, if she deposited $9.81815 she would be able to withdraw $1 each six months. This factor is found in the Present Value of an Ordinary Annuity of $1 table for r = 8% and n = 20. Therefore, she figures that if she deposits $589 ($60 × 9.81815) she could obtain $60 every six months. The right to receive $60 each six months for 10 years, therefore has a present value of $589.

Ms. Investor must also figure what amount she would have to deposit now in an account that earns 16% compounded semiannually to obtain $1,000 after ten years. According to the Present Value of $1 table $.21455 would grow to $1 under these conditions. Therefore $215 ($1,000 × .21455) would grow to $1,000 when invested at 8% per period for 20 periods.

PRESENT VALUE OF AN ORDINARY ANNUITY OF $1

$$PV = \frac{1 - \dfrac{1}{(1+i)^n}}{i}$$

Periods (n)	24%	20%	16%	12%	10%	8%	6%	5%	4%	3%	2.5%	2%	1%
1	0.80645	0.83333	0.86207	0.89286	0.90909	0.92593	0.94340	0.95238	0.96154	0.97087	0.97561	0.98039	0.99010
2	1.45682	1.52778	1.60523	1.69005	1.73554	1.78326	1.83339	1.85941	1.88609	1.91347	1.92742	1.94156	1.97040
3	1.98130	2.10648	2.24589	2.40183	2.48685	2.57710	2.67301	2.72325	2.77509	2.82861	2.85602	2.88388	2.94099
4	2.40428	2.58873	2.79818	3.03735	3.16987	3.31213	3.46511	3.54595	3.62990	3.71710	3.76197	3.80773	3.90197
5	2.74538	2.99061	3.27429	3.60478	3.79079	3.99271	4.21236	4.32948	4.45182	4.57971	4.64583	4.71346	4.85343
6	3.02047	3.32551	3.68474	4.11141	4.35526	4.62288	4.91732	5.07569	5.24214	5.41719	5.50813	5.60143	5.79548
7	3.24232	3.60459	4.03857	4.56376	4.86842	5.20637	5.58238	5.78637	6.00205	6.23028	6.34939	6.47199	6.72819
8	3.42122	3.83716	4.34359	4.96764	5.33493	5.74664	6.20979	6.46321	6.73274	7.01969	7.17014	7.32548	7.65168
9	3.56550	4.03097	4.60654	5.32825	5.75902	6.24689	6.80169	7.10782	7.43533	7.78611	7.97087	8.16224	8.56602
10	3.68186	4.19247	4.83323	5.65022	6.14457	6.71008	7.36009	7.72173	8.11090	8.53020	8.75206	8.98259	9.47130
11	3.77569	4.32706	5.02864	5.93770	6.49506	7.13896	7.88687	8.30641	8.76048	9.25262	9.51421	9.78685	10.36763
12	3.85136	4.43922	5.19711	6.19437	6.81369	7.53608	8.38384	8.86325	9.38507	9.95400	10.25776	10.57534	11.25508
13	3.91239	4.53268	5.34233	6.42355	7.10336	7.90378	8.85268	9.39357	9.98565	10.63496	10.98318	11.34837	12.13374
14	3.96160	4.61057	5.46753	6.62817	7.36669	8.24424	9.29498	9.89864	10.56312	11.29607	11.69091	12.10625	13.00370
15	4.00129	4.67547	5.57546	6.81086	7.60608	8.55948	9.71225	10.37966	11.11839	11.93794	12.38138	12.84926	13.86505
16	4.03330	4.72956	5.66850	6.97399	7.82371	8.85137	10.10590	10.83777	11.65230	12.56110	13.05500	13.57771	14.71787
17	4.05911	4.77463	5.74870	7.11963	8.02155	9.12164	10.47726	11.27407	12.16567	13.16612	13.71220	14.29187	15.56225
18	4.07993	4.81219	5.81785	7.24967	8.20141	9.37189	10.82760	11.68959	12.65930	13.75351	14.35336	14.99203	16.39827
19	4.09672	4.84350	5.87746	7.36578	8.36492	9.60360	11.15812	12.08532	13.13394	14.32380	14.97889	15.67846	17.22601
20	4.11026	4.86958	5.92884	7.46944	8.51356	9.81815	11.46992	12.46221	13.59033	14.87747	15.58916	16.35143	18.04555
21	4.12117	4.89132	5.97314	7.56200	8.64869	10.01680	11.76408	12.82115	14.02916	15.41502	16.18455	17.01121	18.85698
22	4.12998	4.90943	6.01133	7.64465	8.77154	10.20074	12.04158	13.16300	14.45112	15.93692	16.76541	17.65805	19.66038
23	4.13708	4.92453	6.04425	7.71843	8.88322	10.37106	12.30338	13.48857	14.85684	16.44361	17.33211	18.29220	20.45582
24	4.14281	4.93710	6.07263	7.78432	8.98474	10.52876	12.55036	13.79864	15.24696	16.93554	17.88499	18.91393	21.24339
25	4.14742	4.94759	6.09709	7.84314	9.07704	10.67478	12.78336	14.09394	15.62208	17.41315	18.42438	19.52346	22.02316
26	4.15115	4.95632	6.11818	7.89566	9.16095	10.80998	13.00317	14.37519	15.98277	17.87684	18.95061	20.12104	22.79520
27	4.15415	4.96360	6.13636	7.94255	9.23722	10.93516	13.21053	14.64303	16.32959	18.32703	19.46401	20.70690	23.55961
28	4.15657	4.96967	6.15204	7.98442	9.30657	11.05108	13.40616	14.89813	16.66306	18.76411	19.96489	21.28127	24.31644
29	4.15853	4.97472	6.16555	8.02181	9.36961	11.15841	13.59072	15.14107	16.98371	19.18845	20.45355	21.84438	25.06579
30	4.16010	4.97894	6.17720	8.05518	9.42691	11.25778	13.76483	15.37245	17.29203	19.60044	20.93029	22.39646	25.80771
31	4.16137	4.98245	6.18724	8.08499	9.47901	11.34980	13.92909	15.59281	17.58849	20.00043	21.39541	22.93770	26.54229
32	4.16240	4.98537	6.19590	8.11159	9.52638	11.43500	14.08404	15.80268	17.87355	20.38877	21.84918	23.46833	27.26959
33	4.16322	4.98781	6.20336	8.13535	9.56943	11.51389	14.23023	16.00255	18.14765	20.76579	22.29188	23.98856	27.98969
34	4.16389	4.98984	6.20979	8.15656	9.60857	11.58693	14.36814	16.19290	18.41120	21.13184	22.72379	24.49859	28.70267
35	4.16443	4.99154	6.21534	8.17550	9.64416	11.65457	14.49825	16.37419	18.66461	21.48722	23.14516	24.99862	29.40858
36	4.16486	4.99295	6.22012	8.19241	9.67651	11.71719	14.62099	16.54685	18.90828	21.83225	23.55625	25.48884	30.10751
37	4.16521	4.99412	6.22424	8.20751	9.70592	11.77518	14.73678	16.71129	19.14258	22.16724	23.95732	25.96945	30.79951
38	4.16549	4.99510	6.22779	8.22099	9.73265	11.82887	14.84602	16.86789	19.36786	22.49246	24.34860	26.44064	31.48466
39	4.16572	4.99592	6.23086	8.23303	9.75696	11.87858	14.94907	17.01704	19.58448	22.80822	24.73034	26.90259	32.16303
40	4.16590	4.99660	6.23350	8.24378	9.77905	11.92461	15.04630	17.15909	19.79277	23.11477	25.10278	27.35548	32.83469

EXHIBIT 12-2

As a result, Ms. Investor should be willing to pay $804 ($589 + $215) if she wants to earn 16% compounded semiannually.

12-5. The Present Value of an Annuity Due

The principles behind finding the present value of an annuity due are similar to those for finding the present value of an ordinary annuity. The only difference is that the withdrawals for the annuity due are made at the *beginning* of the period rather than at the end.

A. The present value of an annuity due is equal to the sum of the present values of the individual withdrawals (single sums).

Suppose that we now wish to withdraw $100 at the beginning of each year from an account that pays 10% interest compounded annually. We know that we must have $100 on hand to accommodate the first withdrawal. We also need an amount that will grow to $100 after one year and another that will grow to $100 after two years. The timeline below illustrates this concept.

Present Value of Single Sum

	Begin Year 1	Begin Year 2	Begin Year 3	End Year 3
	$100	$100	$100	$0

$100 ──────
$ 91 ──────
$ 83 ──────
─────
$274

Approximately $274 must be deposited into the account for the withdrawals to be made at the beginning of the year. We can prove the accuracy of these numbers by again following the activity in the account.

Year	Beginning Balance	− Withdrawal	+ Interest	= Ending Balance
1	$274	$100	$174 × .10 × 1 = $17	$191
2	$191	$100	$ 91 × .10 × 1 = $ 9	$100
3	$100	$100	0	0

B. The present value of an annuity due can be found by adjusting information found on the Present Value of an Ordinary Annuity of $1 table.

By using the equation below, information given in the Present Value of an Ordinary Annuity of $1 table can be adjusted and used to find the present value of an annuity due.

$$\text{Present Value of an Annuity Due for "n" periods} = \text{Present Value of an Ordinary Annuity of "n − 1" periods} + 1 \text{ rent}$$

Since the first withdrawal on an annuity due is made at the beginning of the period it does not have a chance to earn interest. Therefore, an annuity due for three periods would only earn interest for two periods. An ordinary annuity however would earn interest for all three periods. At the end of three periods the two types of annuities would have the following balances:

Annuity Due	Ordinary Annuity
2 periods' interest + 3 rents	3 periods' interest + 3 rents

after four periods

3 periods' interest + 4 rents	4 periods' interest + 4 rents

From this you can see that an ordinary annuity for four(n) periods yields the same final balance as an ordinary annuity for three (n − 1) periods + one rent.

EXAMPLE 12-8: Gary Goodson wishes to start an account from which his elderly mother can withdraw $500 a month. The account pays 12% interest compounded monthly for the next three years. He wants his mother to begin withdrawing money immediately.

Gary is allowing his mother thirty-six withdrawals and an interest rate of 1% per period. Looking at the Present Value of an Ordinary Annuity of $1 table, Gary finds the factor for *thirty-five* withdrawals of $1 at an interest rate of 1%, $29.40858. To this figure he adds one rent, $1. Therefore, $30.40858 must be deposited now for *thirty-six* withdrawals of $1 to be made on an annuity due. Since Gary's mother will be withdrawing $500, Gary must deposit $15,204 ($500 × 30.40858).

EXAMPLE 12-9: Dakor Company sells furniture and draperies on a long-term payment plan. The buyer agrees to pay $400 now and $400 per month for the next 23 months. The current interest rate is 24% compounded monthly.

The selling price of the furniture and draperies is equal to the present value on an annuity due with *twenty-four* payments of $400 and an interest rate of 2% per period. Looking at the Present Value of an Ordinary Annuity of $1 table, the company finds that $18.29220 must be deposited now to accommodate *twenty-three* payments of $1 from an ordinary annuity. Therefore, $19.29220 must be deposited to make twenty-four payments of $1 from an annuity due. Since the payments in the buyers case are $400, the present value of the annuity due must be $7,717 ($400 × $19.29220). This would also be the selling price of the furniture.

RAISE YOUR GRADES

Can you explain . . . ?

☑ what an annuity is
☑ what the difference is between an ordinary annuity and an annuity due
☑ how many times interest is earned in computing the future value of an ordinary annuity of ten rents
☑ what the numbers in a Future Value of an Ordinary Annuity of $1 table tell you
☑ how many times interest is earned in computing the future value of an annuity due of ten rents
☑ what the numbers in the Present Value of an Ordinary Annuity of $1 table tell you
☑ how to use a Present Value of an Ordinary Annuity of $1 table to compute the present value of an annuity due
☑ how to use the Future Value of an Ordinary Annuity of $1 table to compute the future value of an annuity due

SUMMARY

1. An annuity is a series of equal deposits or withdrawals that occur over equal periods with interest being compounded at a constant rate at the end of each period.
2. The deposits or withdrawals in an annuity are called rents.
3. If the rents occur at the end of each period, the annuity is called an ordinary annuity.
4. If the rents occur at the beginning of the period, the annuity is called an annuity due.
5. The future value of an annuity is equal to the sum of the future values of the individual rents.

6. The Future Value of an Ordinary Annuity of $1 table shows the final balance in an account if $1 is deposited at the end of the period for "n" periods with interest being compounded at rate "r" at the end of each period.

7. The numbers from the Future Value of an Ordinary Annuity of $1 table can only be used if the amount of each rent, the length of each period, and the interest rate remain constant.

8. The future value of an annuity due for "n" periods equals the future value of an ordinary annuity of "n + 1" periods — one rent.

9. The present value of an annuity is equal to the sum of the present value of the individual rents.

10. The Present Value of an Ordinary Annuity of $1 table shows the amount that must be deposited today to accommodate withdrawals of $1 at the end of "n" periods if the account earns "r" rate of interest compounded once each period.

11. The present value of an annuity due for "n" periods is equal to the present value of an ordinary annuity for "n − 1" periods + one rent.

RAPID REVIEW

The following information pertains to Questions 1 through 7.

XYZ Corporation deposits $100,000 at the end of each six months into a trust fund that pays 10% compounded semiannually for the next fifteen years. The trust fund will be used to retire bonds worth $7,000,000 immediately after the last deposit is made.

1. Does this situation concern
   (a) the future value of an ordinary annuity
   (b) the future value of an annuity due
   (c) the present value of an annuity due
   (d) none of the above

2. The relevant interest rate to be used in locating a factor from the proper table is _____.

3. The number of periods to be used in locating a factor on the proper table is _____.

4. The future value of this annuity is _____.

5. Will there be enough in the fund to retire the bonds? (yes/no)

6. Assuming that the deposits are made at the beginning of the period, what would be the future value of this annuity?

7. Assuming that the deposits were made at the beginning of the period, would there be enough money in the fund to retire the bonds?

The following information pertains to Questions 8–12.

Seller Corporation sells equipment on a long-term payment plan. Buyer Company agrees to pay $600 per month for three years beginning 30 days from the date of sale. The current interest rate is 12% compounded monthly. (The seller is recording the sale.)

8. Does this situation concern
   (a) the future value of an ordinary annuity
   (b) the future value of an annuity due
   (c) the present value of an ordinary annuity
   (d) the present value of an annuity due

9. The relevant interest rate to be used in locating a factor from the proper table is _____.

10. The number of periods to be used in locating a factor on the proper table is _____.

11. The selling price of the equipment would be _____.

12. If the monthly payments started on the date of the sale, what would be the selling price of the equipment?

Answers:

1. (a) [Section 12-2]
2. 5% [Section 12-2B]
3. 30 [Section 12-2B]
4. $6,643,885 [Section 12-2B]
5. no
6. $6,976,189 [Section 12-3B]
7. no
8. (c) [Section 12-4]
9. 1% [Section 12-4B]
10. 36 [Section 12-4B]
11. $18,065 [Section 12-4B]
12. $18,245 [Section 12-5B]

SOLVED PROBLEMS

PROBLEM 12-1: Compute the future value of the following annuities:

(a) $1,000 deposited at the end of each quarter in an account paying 12% interest compounded quarterly for four years.

(b) $1,000 deposited at the beginning of each quarter in an account paying 16% interest compounded quarterly for four years.

(c) $1,000 deposited at the end of each month in an account paying 12% interest compounded monthly for two years.

(d) $1,000 deposited at the beginning of each six months in an account paying 10% interest compounded semiannually for six years.

Answer: You must use the Future Value of an Ordinary Annuity of $1 table to answer these questions

(a) FV = $1,000 × 20.15688 = $20,157; r = 3% and n = 16
(b) FV = ($1,000)(23.69751 − 1) = $22,698; r = 4% and n + 1 = 17
(c) FV = $1,000 × 26.97346 = $26,973; r = 1% and n = 24
(d) FV = ($1,000)(17.71298 − 1) = $16,713; r = 5% and n + 1 = 13

[Section 12-2 and 12-3]

PROBLEM 12-2: Compute the current balance required in each of these accounts, if the balance is zero after the last withdrawal.

(a) $1,000 withdrawn at the end of each quarter from an account that earns 12% interest compounded quarterly for four years.

(b) $1,000 withdrawn at the beginning of each quarter from an account paying 16% interest compounded quarterly for four years.

(c) $1,000 withdrawn at the end of each month from an account earning 12% interest compounded monthly for two years.

(d) $1,000 withdrawn at the beginning of each six months from an account earning 10% interest compounded semiannually for six years.

Answer: You must use the Present Value of an Ordinary Annuity of $1 table to answer these questions.

(a) PV = $1,000 × 12.56110 = $12,561; r = 3% and n = 16
(b) PV = ($1,000)(11.11839 + 1) = $12,118; r = 4% and n − 1 = 15
(c) PV = $1,000 × 21.24339 = $21,243; r = 1% and n = 24
(d) PV = ($1,000)(8.30641 + 1) = $9,306; r = 5% and n − 1 = 11

[Sections 12-4 and 12-5]

PROBLEM 12-3: CDE Company wishes to deposit an amount at the end of each quarter to an account that pays 12% interest compounded quarterly for eight years. How much must be deposited at the end of each quarter in order for the account to have a $1,000,000 balance immediately after the last deposit is made?

Answer: This problem is asking you to find the rent for an ordinary annuity with a future value of $1,000,000. Using the Future Value of an Ordinary Annuity of $1 table with $r = 3\%$ and $n = 32$

$$FV = \text{Amount of deposit} \times \text{Factor from table}$$
$$\$1,000,000 = \text{Amount of deposit} \times 52.50276$$
$$\text{Amount of deposit} = \$1,000,000 \div 52.50276 = \$19,047$$

Therefore, the firm must deposit $19,047 in the account at the end of each quarter for eight years to have $1,000,000 immediately after the last deposit is made.   **[Section 12-2B]**

PROBLEM 12-4: How large must the deposits be in Problem 12-3, if they are made at the *beginning* of each quarter?

Answer: The problem is now dealing with an annuity due. The future value of an annuity due is equal to the future value of a similar ordinary annuity of one additional period minus one rent.

$$FV = \text{Amount of deposit} \times \text{Adjusted factor from table}$$
$$\$1,000,000 = (\text{Amount of deposit})(55.07784 - 1)$$
$$\text{Amount of deposit} = \$1,000,000 \div 54.07784 = \$18,492$$

Therefore the firm must only deposit $18,492 in the account each quarter if the deposits are made at the beginning of the quarter.   **[Section 12-3B]**

PROBLEM 12-5: Mr. Toorich has just deposited $1,000,000 in a trust fund for his grandson as a 21st birthday present. The terms of the fund are that a withdrawal is to be made at the end of each quarter from the fund which earns 10% compounded quarterly for 10 years. The fund will be depleted upon the last withdrawal. What will be the amount of each quarterly withdrawal?

Answer: This problem deals with an ordinary annuity. Using the Present Value of an Ordinary Annuity of $1 with $r = 2.5\%$ and $n = 40$

$$PV = \text{Amount of withdrawal} \times \text{Factor from table}$$
$$\$1,000,000 = \text{Amount of withdrawal} \times 25.10278$$
$$\text{Amount of withdrawal} = \$1,000,000 \div 25.10278 = \$39,836$$

Therefore the grandson will receive a $39,836 allowance quarterly from his trust fund for a ten year period.   **[Section 12-4]**

PROBLEM 12-6: Carol has the opportunity to purchase a $1,000 bond. The bond will mature in seven years and pay $50 interest semiannually. What should Carol pay for the bond if she wishes to make a return on her investment of 8% compounded semiannually?

Answer: Computing the value of the bond requires the use of the Present Value of $1 table and the Present Value of an Ordinary Annuity of $1 table. In both cases $r = 4\%$ and $n = 14$.

Using the Present Value of $1 table, the current worth of $1,000 to be received in 7 years is:

$$PV = \$1,000 \times .57748 = \$577$$

Using the Present Value of an Ordinary Annuity of $1 table, the current worth of the fourteen interest payments is:

$$PV = \$50 \times 10.56312 = \$528$$

Therefore, if Carol pays $1,105 ($577 + $528) for the bond, she will make an 8% return on her investment over seven years.   **[Sections 11-5 and 12-4]**

PROBLEM 12-7: Joe Shmoe has consistently allowed his employer to withhold $100 per month more than he owes the federal government in income taxes. Joe then files his tax return early in January and receives a $1,200 tax refund which he uses for an early February vacation in the Bahamas. How much would Joe have to spend on his vacation if he adjusted his withholding to exactly the amount of taxes owed, and invested his increased monthly take-home pay at 12% compounded monthly?

Answer: This is a future value of an annuity due problem. The annuity is an annuity due because the last payment into the account is made on December 31. The last deposit earns interest until withdrawn at the end of January, or beginning of February to pay for the vacation. What is the future value of an annuity due of twelve $100 deposits if the account into which the deposits are made earns 1% per period?

$$FV = (\$100)(13.80933 - 1) = \$1,281$$

Use the factor from a Future Value of an Ordinary Annuity table for r = 1% and n = 13. This factor must be adjusted when used to compute the future value of an annuity due. Joe would have $1,281 to spend on his vacation if, beginning on January 31, he deposited his $100 of increased take-home pay into the account and did this for twelve months. One month after the last deposit was made he would have a balance of $1,281 in the account.

[Section 12-3]

PROBLEM 12-8: Compute the future value of the following annuities:

(a) $3,500 deposited at the end of each quarter in an account paying 16% interest compounded quarterly for four years.
(b) $5,400 deposited at the beginning of each quarter in an account paying 12% interest compounded quarterly for four years.
(c) $1,800 deposited at the end of each month in an account paying 12% interest compounded monthly for two years.
(d) $9,100 deposited at the beginning of each six months in an account paying 16% interest compounded semiannually for six years.

Answer: You must use the Future Value of an Ordinary Annuity of $1 table to answer these questions.

(a) FV = $3,500 × 21.82453 = $76,385.85; r = 4% and n = 16
(b) FV = $5,400 × (21.76159 − 1) = $112,112.59; r = 3% and n + 1 = 17
(c) FV = $1,800 × 26.97346 = $48,552.23; r = 1% and n = 24
(d) FV = $9,100 × (21.49530 − 1) = $186,507.23; r = 8% and n + 1 = 13

[Sections 12-2 and 12-3]

PROBLEM 12-9: Compute the current balance in each of these accounts, if the balance will be zero after the last withdrawal.

(a) $1,900 withdrawn at the end of each quarter from an account that earns 8% interest compounded quarterly for four years.
(b) $5,000 withdrawn at the beginning of each quarter from an account paying 8% interest compounded quarterly for four years.
(c) $7,200 withdrawn at the end of each month from an account earning 12% interest monthly for three years.
(d) $7,600 withdrawn at the beginning of each six months from an account earning 16% interest compounded semiannually for eight years.

Answer: You must use the Present Value of an Ordinary Annuity of $1 table to answer these questions.

(a) PV = $1,900 × 13.57771 = $25,797.65; r = 2% and n = 16
(b) PV = $5,000 × (12.84926 + 1) = $69,246.30; r = 2% and n − 1 = 15
(c) PV = $7,200 × 30.10751 = $216,774.07; r = 1% and n = 36
(d) PV = $7,600 × (8.55948 + 1) = $72,652.05; r = 8% and n − 1 = 15

[Sections 12-4 and 12-5]

PROBLEM 12-10: FSL Company wishes to deposit an amount at the end of each quarter to an account that pays 20% interest compounded quarterly for eight years. How much must be deposited at the end of each quarter in order for the account to have a $3,500,000 balance immediately after the last deposit is made?

Answer: This problem is asking you to find the rent for an ordinary annuity with a future value of $3,500,000. Using the Future Value of an Ordinary Annuity of $1 table with r = 5% and n = 32.

$$FV = \text{Amount of deposit} \times \text{Factor from table}$$
$$\$3,500,000 = \text{Amount of deposit} \times 75.29683$$
$$\text{Amount of deposit} = \$3,500,000 \div 75.29882 = \$46,482.70$$

Therefore, the firm must deposit $46,482.70 in the account at the end of each quarter for eight years to have $3,500,000 after the last deposit is made.   **[Section 12-2B]**

PROBLEM 12-11: How large must the deposits be in Problem 12-10 if they are made at the *beginning* of each quarter?

Answer: The problem is now dealing with an annuity due. The future value of an annuity due is equal to the future value of a similar ordinary annuity of one additional period minus one rent.

$$FV = \text{Amount of deposit} \times \text{Adjusted factor from table}$$
$$\$3,500,000 = (\text{Amount of deposit})(80.06377 - 1)$$
$$\text{Amount of deposit} = \$3,500,000 \div 79.06377 = \$44,268.06$$

Therefore the firm must only deposit $44,268.06 in the account each quarter if the deposits are made at the beginning of the quarter.   **[Section 12-3B]**

PROBLEM 12-12: Mr. Forsite has just deposited $1,000,000 in a retirement account, money which he inherited from a rich aunt. The terms of the fund are that a withdrawal is to be made at the end of each six months from the fund which earns 20% compounded semiannually for 15 years. The fund will be depleted upon the last withdrawal. What will be the amount of each quarterly withdrawal?

Answer: This problem deals with an ordinary annuity. Using the Present Value of an Ordinary Annuity of $1 with r = 10% and n = 30.

$$PV = \text{Amount of withdrawal} \times \text{Factor from table}$$
$$\$1,000,000 = \text{Amount of withdrawal} \times 9.42691$$
$$\text{Amount of withdrawal} = \$1,000,000 \div 9.42691 = \$106,079.30$$

Therefore Mr. Forsite would receive $106.079.30 every six months for the next 15 years.
          [Section 12-4]

13 CASH

THIS CHAPTER IS ABOUT

☑ **Cash Accounts**
☑ **Internal Control of Cash**
☑ **Accounting for the Petty Cash Fund**
☑ **The Bank Reconciliation Statement**
☑ **Deposits in Transit and Outstanding Checks**

13-1. Cash Accounts

Most companies will keep several cash accounts. The most common types are

- **Cash on Hand** — used to account for undeposited cash receipts
- **Petty Cash** — used to account for funds kept on hand to make small or "petty" disbursements
- **Cash in Bank** — used to account for cash kept in a checking account. There should be one account kept for each checking account maintained by the company.

The cash balance shown on the balance sheet is the sum of the balances in each of these cash accounts.

13-2. Internal Control of Cash

Cash is the most liquid (easily transferable) asset. It is also the asset most likely to be stolen unless precautions, such as internal control, are taken to prevent theft.

A. There are six general principles of internal control.

There are six general principles of internal control that apply to the protection of all assets. They are listed for you in Exhibit 13-1.

EXHIBIT 13-1: General Principles of Internal Control

1. Employ competent and trustworthy personnel, giving them clear lines of authority and responsibility.
2. Provide for adequate segregation of duties.
3. Set up well defined procedures for authorization of transactions.
4. Maintain adequate documents and records.
5. Provide for adequate physical control over assets and records.
6. Provide for independent checks on performance.

B. Each of the six general principles of internal control can be applied to cash.

1. *Trustworthy Personnel.* Proper cash control begins with the employment of competent and trustworthy personnel. Trustworthy is an especially important characteristic since the employee may be handling or accounting for large sums of money.

2. *Segregation of duties*. The duties of the persons who handle cash and those who account for cash must be clearly separate. The person who has custody of the cash should not have access to the accounting records. The person who authorizes payments from the cash account should not sign the checks. When the duties are separated, theft can only occur if two or more employees work together (collusion).

3. *Proper authorization*. Only a limited number of people in a company should have the power to authorize cash disbursements. Some companies require more than one person to authorize cash disbursements over a certain amount. No cash disbursement should be made unless the proper authorization has been given.

4. *Adequate documents and records*. The company should maintain a set of documents and records to justify each cash disbursement and receipt. These records should generally be kept on prenumbered forms and the sequence of forms accounted for. (No form should be discarded even if damaged or completed incorrectly. The form should have the word "Void" written across it and filed for future reference.) Disbursements should be made on prenumbered checks. The checks should be securely stored and all checks should be accounted for on a periodic basis. Control over access to blank checks and forms prevents unauthorized disbursements.

5. *Adequate physical control*. Cash should be deposited on a timely basis. At no point in time should large sums of money be left in a place of easy access. Cash registers and drawers with locks or vaults in which cash and blank checks can be kept are important devices to maintain physical control over cash.

6. *Independent checks on performance*. A person *not* associated with daily cash transactions should check the records for the handling of cash. Customers should also be used as an independent check. Cash registers should have a display screen that shows the amounts entered and the total to the customer. Cash register receipts or some other form of receipt should be given to the customer with each transaction. Rotation of personnel to different recordkeeping jobs can uncover irregularities also.

EXAMPLE 13-1: A clerk in a department store rings up a $10 purchase on the cash register as $8. When the customers pays the $10, the clerk places $8 in the cash register drawer and pockets the other $2.

This theft would be less likely to occur if the cash register had a display screen to show that only $8 had been charged or if the customer were given a cash register receipt. To get customers to ask for a receipt stores will require a receipt before a refund is given for returned goods. They will also display signs that a purchase is free if the clerk fails to give a receipt or if a red star appears on the receipt.

EXAMPLE 13-2: A cashier in the credit department receives cash from a customer as payment on an overdue account. The cashier pockets the cash and writes the balance of the account off as a bad debt expense.

This type of theft would not have occurred if there had been adequate separation of duties. The person handling money should not be in charge of accounting records. Write-offs of bad debts should also require authorization by someone without access to cash.

EXAMPLE 13-3: During an audit, it is discovered that XYZ Corporation has paid Thalmeier Advertising Agency twice; once, when the invoice arrived with the shipment of catalogs and a second time, when the agency sent an end-of-month billing which did not show credit for the earlier payment.

Double payments can be avoided if there is a specific procedure for authorizing payments. The procedure would require that the invoice from the supplier be matched with the receiving report from the warehouse verifying the receipt of all the catalogs in good condition. A person would then match the two reports and authorize the payment. Another person would write the check. Some firms would require that yet another person match the amount of the check to the payment authorization. The invoice and receiving report would then be marked "PAID" so that they could not be used to justify another payment.

EXAMPLE 13-4: A robber held up the Surefoot Shoe store taking $14,000, a full week's receipts, from the till.

A loss of this magnitude could be avoided if cash were deposited on a daily basis. Procedures to safeguard cash require that cash be held in a secure place. For most businesses the preferred secure place is the bank. Taxi drivers, pizza delivery persons, and many all night stores indicate that the cash on hand will never exceed a small sum.

13-3. Accounting for the Petty Cash Fund

Many firms keep limited amounts of cash on hand to pay small expenses. This limited amount of cash is called the petty cash fund. The petty cash fund eliminates the need for writing numerous checks for insignificant amounts of money.

A. The petty cash fund is established by debiting Petty Cash and crediting Cash.

The entry a company would make to establish a petty cash fund of $200 would be as follows

Petty Cash	200	
Cash		200

Total cash has not changed. The amount of cash is merely being accounted for in two separate cash accounts. The $200 will be placed in a box or drawer until authorized disbursements are to be made.

B. Disbursements from the petty cash fund are documented by petty cash vouchers.

Before disbursements are made from the petty cash fund, the custodian in charge of the fund will fill out a prenumbered form indicating the person to whom money is being given and the reason. This prenumbered form is called a petty cash voucher. The person receiving the funds will sign the voucher to verify the amount disbursed. All vouchers must be accounted for on a regular basis.

C. The petty cash fund is replenished by debiting the individual expenses and crediting Cash.

Periodically the fund must be replenished and the disbursements from the fund accounted for. The fund is usually replenished at the end of the accounting period or when the balance in the fund falls near or below a predetermined amount. The entry to replenish the fund would debit the expenses indicated on the petty cash vouchers and credit cash for the amount needed to replenish the cash in the fund.

EXAMPLE 13-5: GHJ Corporation has established a petty cash fund of $200. During the last month disbursements were made for stamps ($47), taxi service ($28), and coffee and pastries for a week of meetings ($18). The entry to record this activity in the petty cash fund and to replenish the fund would be

Postage Expense	47	
Transportation Expense	28	
Entertainment Expense	18	
Cash		93

The accountant would then void and file the petty cash vouchers and place $93 in the drawer to replenish the fund.

D. The Cash Short or Over account is used to account for small errors in the balance of the petty cash fund.

A small amount of cash may be unaccounted for in the petty cash fund. This is usually due to an error in making change. Small errors in accounting for cash in the petty cash fund are recorded in the Cash Short or Over account. However, if shortages occur frequently, further investigation may be necessary.

EXAMPLE 13-6: Suppose that in Example 13-5, only $105 remained in the petty cash drawer instead of $107. The entry to record the activity in the petty cash fund and to replenish the fund would be

Postage Expense	47	
Transportation Expense	28	
Entertainment Expense.	18	
Cash Short or Over.	2	
Cash		95

The accountant would void and file the petty cash vouchers but place $95 in the drawer to replenish the fund to its original $200 balance.

Cash Short or Over is debited when the fund is short of cash and credited when the fund has more cash than expected given the receipts in the drawer. The account is reported as an expense if it has a debit balance. It is recorded as revenue if it has a credit balance.

13-4. The Bank Reconciliation Statement

A separate Cash in Bank account should be maintained in the company books for each checking account the company has established. At the end of each month, the company will receive a statement reporting the activity in the account according to the bank's records. The bank reconciliation statement is a formal report that explains the difference in the balance per the bank statement (bank balance) and the balance per the company's books (book balance). This will determine the correct balance in the Cash in Bank account.

A. The difference between the bank balance and the book balance is due to a lack of information on the part of the bank and the company.

Several activities may have occurred in the account that only the bank knows about or only the company knows about.

1. *Deposits in Transit.* The company may make a deposit on the day the bank's statement is prepared. The bank may not record this deposit until the following day.
2. *Outstanding Checks.* Checks may have been written by the company which have not yet been presented at the bank for payment.
3. *Service Charges.* The bank will deduct fees for services rendered in handling the account. The company is not aware of these charges until the bank statement is received.
4. *Collections.* Some banks will act as a collection agent for depositors. If a collection is made during the month, the company may not know until the bank statement is received.
5. *Errors.* Amounts may be deducted from or added to the balance of an account by mistake. Errors may also occur in addition or subtraction. These types of errors could occur on the part of the bank or the company.

B. Adjustments must be made to both the book balance and bank balance to determine the correct balance in the Cash in Bank account.

Adjustments must be made to the bank balance for activities that occured during the month which the bank did not record. Adjustments must also be made to the book balance for activities that occured which the company was not aware of.

1. *Deposits in Transit*. Since deposits in transit are additions to the Cash in Bank account balance which the bank has yet to record, they should be added to the bank balance.
2. *Outstanding Checks*. Since outstanding checks are deductions from the Cash in Bank account balance which the bank has not yet recorded, they should be deducted from the bank balance.
3. *Service Charges*. Since service charges are deductions from the Cash in Bank account balance which the company was unaware of and has not yet recorded, the service charge must be deducted from the book balance.
4. *Collections*. Collections are additions to the Cash in Bank account that do not appear in the book balance and therefore must be added to the book balance.

The adjusted bank balance should equal the adjusted book balance. This is the correct balance for the Cash in Bank account. Entries must be made to correct the balance in the Cash in Bank account for any adjustments made to the book balance.

C. The bank reconciliation statement follows one general format.

The general format of the bank reconciliation statement is shown in Exhibit 13-2.

EXHIBIT 13-2: Bank Reconciliation Statement Format

Name of Company
Bank Reconciliation Statement
Date

Balance per Bank Statement		xxxx
Add:		
Deposits in Transit.	xxx	
Bank Errors (which when corrected will increase the bank balance)	xxx	xxx
		xxxx
Deduct:		
Outstanding Checks.	xxx	
Bank Errors (which when corrected will decrease the bank balance)	xxx	xxx
Adjusted Bank Balance		xxxx
Balance per Books		xxxx
Add:		
Collections	xxx	
Book Errors (which when corrected will increase the book balance)	xxx	xxx
		xxxx
Deduct:		
Service Charges	xxx	
Book Errors (which when corrected will decrease the book balance)	xxx	xxx
Adjusted Book Balance		xxxx

EXAMPLE 13-7: At the end of March, 19x4, Control Corporation shows a balance in its Cash in Bank account of $4,200. The firm receives a bank statement, dated March 28, 19x4,

that indicates the balance in the account is $5,500. In attempting to explain the difference in the two account balances, the internal auditor finds the following:

(a) On March 29, $1,200 was deposited to the account. Since the deposit was made after the date of the statement, it is classified as a deposit in transit.

(b) The bank charged Control Corporation $50 for special services that it actually performed for another company whose account number is almost identical to Control Corporation's account number. This is a bank deduction that was made in error and must be added back to the bank balance.

(c) As of the March 28 statement date, checks totaling $2,250 had not been presented for payment. These are classified as outstanding checks.

(d) The bank collected a note for Control Corporation. The *collection* consisted of the $300 principal, $85 interest receivable recognized in 19x3, $20 interest earned in 19x4. From this total of $405, the bank deducted a $5 collection fee. Therefore $400 must be added to the book balance.

(e) Control Corporation made an error in recording Check #421. The check was written for $36 to pay a utility bill. The check was recorded in the books as $63. Since the firm deducted more from the account than it should, the difference must be added back to the book balance.

(f) The corporation had new checks printed. The bank charged $17 for this service. The service charge must be deducted from the Cash in Bank account on the company's books.

(g) The bank recorded a deposit of a check for $110. On March 20, the check was returned for "not sufficient funds." Since this amount was added to the balance in the account but will not be received, it was deducted from the bank balance. The firm must make the same deduction on its books.

The internal auditor then prepared a bank reconciliation statement as follows:

Control Corporation
Bank Reconciliation Statement
March 31, 19x4

Balance per Bank		$5,500
Add:		
Deposits in Transit	$1,200	
Bank Error	50	1,250
		6,750
Deduct:		
Outstanding Checks		2,250
Adjusted Bank Balance		$4,500
Balance per Books		$4,200
Add:		
Note Receivable Collected	$ 400	
Error in Recording Check #421	27	427
		$4,627
Deduct:		
Service Charge	$ 17	
NSF Check	110	127
Adjusted Book Balance		$4,500

The correct balance in the Cash in Bank account would therefore be $4,500.

EXAMPLE 13-8: Now that the internal auditor for Control Corporation knows the correct balance in the Cash in Bank account, the books must be adjusted to reflect this amount. Adjustments are needed for the following items

(a) *Note Receivable Collected*

Cash in Bank	400	
Miscellaneous Expense (fee)	5	
Notes Receivable		300
Interest Receivable		85
Interest Revenue		20

(b) *Error in Recording Check #421*

Cash in Bank	27	
Utilities Expense		27

(c) *Service Charge*

Miscellaneous Expense	17	
Cash in Bank		17

(d) *NSF Check* (now an account receivable because $110 must be collected to replace the check)

Accounts Receivable	110	
Cash in Bank		110

The Cash in Bank account will have the correct balance after these entries have been posted to the account.

Cash in Bank

Balance	4,200	(c)	17
(a)	400	(d)	110
(b)	27		
Balance	4,500		

D. The bank reconciliation statement is a form of internal control over cash.

In preparing the bank reconciliation statement, the auditor is making a periodic check on cash transactions and how they were handled. This is an excellent means on internal control over cash. The auditor should be someone who has no responsibility for handling or recording cash.

13-5. Deposits in Transit and Outstanding Checks

Accounting texts often ask you to demonstrate your understanding of deposits in transit and outstanding checks by giving you the information you need to compute these figures in a round about way.

EXAMPLE 13-9: CVB Corporation's March 31 bank reconciliation statement indicated that there were deposits in transit totaling $620. During April the bank credited the corporation's account with deposits of $2,880. The corporation's books indicated that deposits totaling $2,690 were made during the month of April. Compute the amount of deposits in transit that would appear on the April 30 bank reconciliation.

Of the $2,880 deposits recorded by the bank in April, $620 in deposits would be those that were in transit at the end of March. This means that $2,260 ($2,880 − $620) are deposits that were made in April. However the corporation made deposits totaling $2,690. This means that $430 ($2,690 − $2,260) in deposits have not been recorded by the bank and are therefore in transit as of the end of April.

EXAMPLE 13-10: RTY Corporation's September 30 bank reconciliation statement indicated that there were outstanding checks totaling $1,850. During October the bank deducted checks totaling $8,720. The corporation's books indicate that checks totaling $8,630 were written during the month of October. Compute the amount of outstanding checks that would be reported on the October 31 bank reconciliation statement.

Of the checks that were outstanding in October, $1,850 were written in September and $8,630 were written in October. These two amounts would total $10,480. Of this amount only $8,720 were actually paid. This means that checks totaling $1,760 have yet to be paid and are therefore outstanding at the end of the month.

RAISE YOUR GRADES

Can you explain . . . ?

☑ what are the three most common types of cash accounts
☑ what are the six general principles of internal control
☑ how segregation of duties can make theft of cash more difficult
☑ how theft of cash can still occur with segregation of duties
☑ what is meant by proper authorization
☑ how physical control can be maintained over cash
☑ what are some of the independent checks on performance
☑ what is the purpose of a petty cash fund
☑ what entry is made to establish the petty cash fund
☑ how disbursements are made from the petty cash fund
☑ what entry is made to replenish the petty cash fund
☑ what is the purpose of the bank reconciliation statement
☑ what situations require adjustment to the bank balance
☑ what situations require adjustments to the book balance
☑ what are deposits in transit
☑ what are outstanding checks

SUMMARY

1. The three most common types of cash accounts are cash on hand, the petty cash fund, and cash in bank.
2. Cash is the most liquid of assets and the asset most likely to be stolen.
3. Proper cash control begins with the employment of competent and trustworthy personnel.
4. The duties of the persons who handle cash and those who account for cash must be clearly separate.
5. Only a limited number of people in a company should have the power to authorize cash disbursements.
6. The company should maintain a set of documents and records to justify each cash disbursement and receipt.
7. Cash should be deposited on a timely basis.
8. Independent checks should be made on employee performance.
9. The petty cash fund is a limited amount of cash on hand used to pay small expenses.

10. The petty cash fund is established by debiting Petty Cash and crediting Cash.
11. Disbursements from the petty cash fund are documented by petty cash vouchers.
12. The petty cash fund is replenished by debiting the individual expenses and crediting Cash.
13. The Cash Short or Over account is used to account for small errors in the balance of the petty cash fund.
14. If the Cash Short or Over account has a debit balance it is reported as an expense. If it has a credit balance it is reported as revenue.
15. The bank reconciliation statement is a formal report that explains the difference between the bank balance and the book balance of the Cash in Bank account.
16. Adjustments are made to both the book balance and the bank balance to determine the correct balance in the Cash in Bank account.
17. Once the correct balance for the Cash in Bank account has been determined, the books must be adjusted to reflect this amount.
18. The bank reconciliation process is a form of internal control over cash.
19. Deposits in transit are deposits that have been made but not yet recorded by the bank.
20. Outstanding checks are checks that have been written but not yet presented at the bank for payment.

RAPID REVIEW

1. Indicate whether the following statements relating to the internal control over cash are true or false.
   (a) Customers can independently check the cash handling activities of a sales clerk.
   (b) A good internal control system can prevent all thefts by employees even if they work together.
   (c) Most businesses consider locking money in a cash register drawer just as safe as putting the money in the bank.
   (d) Once an invoice is paid it should be thrown away so that it may not be used to document another disbursement of cash.
   (e) The person who authorizes disbursements should also write the checks to be sure that they are made out correctly.

2. Prepare the entry to establish a $200 petty cash fund.

3. The petty cash fund established in Question 2 has $48 in petty cash vouchers and $157 in cash. The Cash Short or Over account will be (debited/credited) for $_____ when the fund is replenished.

4. Outstanding checks (increase/decrease) the (bank/book) balance on a bank reconciliation statement.

5. Recording a check written for $55 as $44 results in a error which when corrected will (increase/decrease) the (bank/book) balance on a bank reconciliation statement in the amount of $_____.

6. Deposits in transit (increase/decrease) the (bank/book) balance on a bank reconciliation statement.

7. Bank service charges (increase/decrease) the (bank/book) balance on a bank reconciliation statement.

8. Who should prepare the bank reconciliation statement?

9. The January 31 bank reconciliation statement indicated that there were deposits in transit totaling $400. During February the bank credited the account with deposits totaling $2,500. The company's books indicated that deposits totaling $2,600 were actually made during the month of February. Compute the amount of deposits in transit that would appear on the February 28 bank reconciliation statement.

10. The March 31 bank reconciliation statement indicated that there were checks outstanding totaling $250. During April the bank deducted checks totaling $2,150. The firm's books indicate that checks totaling $2,300 were written during the month of April. Compute the amount of checks outstanding that would be reported on the April 30 bank reconciliation statement.

Answers:

1. (*a*) true
   (*b*) false
   (*c*) false
   (*d*) false
   (*e*) false
   [Section 13-2B]
2. Petty Cash | 200 |
      Cash | | 200
   [Section 13-3A]
3. credited; $5 [Section 13-3D]
4. decrease; bank [Section 13-4B]
5. decrease; book; $11 [Section 13-4A]
6. increase; bank [Section 13-4B]
7. decrease; book [Section 13-4B]
8. Someone who does not handle or account for cash [Section 13-4D]
9. $500 which equals $2,600 − ($2,500 − $400) [Section 13-5]
10. $400 which equals ($250 + $2,300) − $2,150 [Section 13-5]

SOLVED PROBLEMS

PROBLEM 13-1: TYU Corporation establishes a petty cash fund of $150. By the end of the month the fund contains $82 in cash and the following petty cash vouchers

001	Postage	$ 8.00
002	Supplies	$12.00
003	Entertainment Advance	$20.00
004	Postage	$ 6.00
005	Coffee (Miscellaneous)	$ 6.00
006	Taxi Fare (Travel)	$ 9.00
007	Entertainment Advance	$ 5.00

Prepare the entries to establish the petty cash fund and to replenish it.

Answer:

Petty Cash	150	
Cash		150
Postage Expense	14	
Supplies	12	
Entertainment Expense.	25	
Miscellaneous Expense	6	
Travel Expense	9	
Cash Short or Over.	2	
Cash		68

[Section 13-3]

PROBLEM 13-2: At the end of April, CDE Corporation shows a balance in its Cash in Bank account of $8,670. The firm receives a bank statement, dated April 28, 19x1, that indicates the balance in the account is $8,280. In attempting to explain the difference in the two account balances, the internal auditor finds the following

(a) On April 29, $2,005 was deposited to the account.
(b) As of the April 28 statement date, checks totaling $880 had not been presented for payment.
(c) The bank incorrectly deducted $420 from the account for Check #2265 which was actually written for $440.
(d) The bank collected a note for CDE Corporation. The collection consisted of the $1,100 principal plus $100 interest receivable. From this total of $1,200, the bank deducted a $5 collection fee.
(e) The bank recorded a deposit of a check for $445. On April 25, the check was returned for not sufficient funds. In addition to deducting the amount of the check, the bank charged an additional $5 penalty fee.
(f) The corporation had new checks printed. The bank charged $30 for this service.

Prepare the bank reconciliation statement for CDE Corporation as of the end of April.

Answer:

CDE Corporation
Bank Reconciliation Statement
April 30, 19x1

Balance per Bank		$ 8,280
Add: Deposits in Transit		2,005
		$10,285
Deduct:		
Outstanding Checks	$880	
Bank Error	20	900
Adjusted Bank Balance		$ 9,385
Balance per Books		$ 8,670
Add: Note Receivable Collected		1,195
		$ 9,865
Deduct:		
NSF Check	$450	
Service Charge	30	480
Adjusted Book Balance		$ 9,385

[Section 13-4]

PROBLEM 13-3: Now that you know the correct balance for the Cash in Bank account in Problem 13-2, prepare the entries to adjust the books to reflect this amount.

Answer:

Cash in Bank	1,195	
Miscellaneous Expense	5	
Notes Receivable		1,100
Interest Revenue		100

Accounts Receivable		450		
Cash in Bank			450	
Miscellaneous Expense		30		
Cash in Bank			30	

[Section 13-4C]

PROBLEM 13-4: You have been called in by Jo Jones, the bookkeeper for Happy Daze Corporation. Jo has prepared the bank reconciliation statement below but has been unable to get the adjusted bank balance to equal the adjusted book balance.

Happy Daze Corporation
Bank Reconciliation Statement
June 30, 19x1

Balance per Bank		$4,200
Add: Deposits in Transit		320
		$4,530
Deduct: Outstanding Checks		
#380	$ 35	
#400	180	
#423	90	
#425	20	325
Adjusted Bank Balance		$4,205
Balance per Books		$3,790
Add:		
Note Receivable Collected	$300	
Error in Recording Check #301	10	310
		$4,100
Deduct:		
Service Charge	$ 20	
NSF Check	90	110
Adjusted Book Balance		$3,980

In attempting to explain the difference in the two account balances, you find the following:

(a) On June 29, $320 was deposited to the account. The deposit was made after the date of the bank statement.

(b) As of the June 28 statement date, the following checks had not been presented for payment: #400 for $180; #422 for $75; #423 for $90; #425 for $20.

(c) The bank collected a note for Happy Daze Corporation. The note was for $290. From this amount, the bank deducted a $10 collection fee.

(d) The bank charged $20 for services for the month.

(e) The bank recorded a deposit of a check for $95. On June 22, the check was returned for not sufficient funds. In addition, the bank deducted a $5 penalty fee.

(f) Check #380 for $35 was voided, but the amount was not added back to the checking account balance on the firm's books.

(g) Happy Daze Corporation made an error in recording Check #421. The check was recorded for $100 but actually written for $110.

(h) The balance per the bank statement was $4,200 and the balance per the company books was $3,970.

Prepare the bank reconciliation statement correctly. What errors did the bookkeeper make?

Answer:

Happy Daze Corporation
Bank Reconciliation Statement
June 30, 19x1

Balance per Bank		$4,200
Add: Deposits in Transit		320
		$4,520
Deduct: Outstanding Checks		
#400	$180	
#422	75	
#423	90	
#425	20	365
Adjusted Bank Balance		$4,155
Balance per Books		$3,970
Add:		
Note Receivable Collected	$280	
Voided Check #380	35	315
		$4,285
Deduct:		
Service Charge	$ 20	
NSF Check	100	
Error in Recording Check #301	10	130
Adjusted Book Balance		$4,155

The bookkeeper made the following errors:

1. The balance per bank and deposits in transit were incorrectly totaled.
2. The voided check was incorrectly included as an outstanding check.
3. Outstanding Check #422 was omitted.
4. The $10 collection fee on the note receivable should have been deducted from the proceeds not added.
5. The voided check was not added back to the book balance.
6. The penalty fee for the NSF check was deducted from the amount of the check rather than added to it in computing the deduction from the book balance.
7. The error in recording Check #301 was added to rather than subtracted from the book balance.
8. The balance per books was incorrectly stated.

[Section 13-4]

PROBLEM 13-5: On January 27, 19x1, Careful Corporation received its bank statement. A comparison of the information on the statement and information on the books as of January 31 indicates the following:

	Per Bank	Per Books
Balance 1/1/x1	$4,180	$3,850
January Deposits	1,840	1,420
Checks Paid Out	(3,490)	(3,680)
Service Charge	(20)	
Balance 1/26/x1	$2,510	
Balance 1/31/x1		$1,590

On 12/31/x0, deposits in transit totaled $770 and outstanding checks totaled $1,100. Prepare a bank reconciliation statement for 1/31/x1.

Answer: Deposits in transit = $1,420 − ($1,840 − $770) = $350
Outstanding checks = ($3,680 + $1,100) − $3,490 = $1,290

Careful Corporation
Bank Reconciliation Statement
1/31/x1

Balance per Bank	$2,510
Add: Deposits in Transit	350
	$2,860
Deduct: Outstanding Checks	1,290
Adjusted Bank Balance	$1,570
Balance per Books	$1,590
Deduct: Service Charge	20
Adjusted Book Balance	$1,570

[Sections 13-4 and 13-5]

PROBLEM 13-6: Miller Hardware Store had grown so much in the last few years that the owner could no longer handle all the bookkeeping duties and management responsibilities. As a result, Mr. Miller quickly hired a staff to assist him. Mr. Miller had little time to investigate the background of people he hired. A few months later he notice a gradual decline in the company profits even though business seemed better than ever. You were asked to investigate the situation. In doing so, you found that the responsibilities of the office staff are as follows:

(a) Ms. Lightfingers is in charge of cash receipts. The salesclerks bring their cash drawers to her at the end of the day. Ms. Lightfingers then counts the money, compares the figures to the cash register tapes, records the amount of cash receipts in the company books, and throws the cash register tapes away. She deposits the money in the bank on Friday and prepares the bank reconciliation statement monthly.
(b) Mr. Shifty is the office manager. He supervises the staff and authorizes cash payments. Mr. Shifty also prepares delivery reports for goods arriving at the firm.
(c) Mrs. Shifty, Mr. Shifty's wife, records cash disbursements and writes the checks.
(d) Mr. Autovit is the Mr. Shifty's secretary. He handles correspondence and filing. To keep his files neat, Mr. Autovit discards all delivery reports after they have been verified and all invoices after they have been paid by dropping them into the trash. By doing this he feels those items needing further processing will be easier to find.

What principles of internal control over cash does this office setup violate?

Answer:

(a) *Trustworthy Personnel.* Mr. Miller should have carefully investigated the background of his employees especially those who would deal with the firm's cash.
(b) *Segregation of duties.* Mrs. Lightfingers should not handle cash if she is also responsible for the accounting records and bank reconciliation. Likewise, Mrs. Shifty should not write checks if she also records cash disbursements. Having a husband and wife with the collective power to authorize cash disbursements and write checks could lead to collusion. Mr. Shifty should not be certifying delivery and authorizing payments.
(c) *Proper Authorization.* Mr. Shifty should not be authorizing payments. He also certifies delivery of goods. He is in an excellent position to document a nonexistent delivery and collect for the phantom goods.
(d) *Adequate documents and records.* By discarding the cash register tapes, there is no way for anyone to verify Ms. Lightfinger's work. After Mr. Autovit discards the delivery reports and paid invoices, there is no documentation for cash payments. If these documents are not voided, they could be used to justify duplicate payments.
(e) *Adequate Physical Control.* Cash should be deposited in the bank daily to avoid having large sums which might be stolen.

(*f*) *Independent Checks on Performance.* There are no independent checks built into this system. Mr. Miller should reconcile the bank statement. He should authorize payments and provide for adequate supervision of his employees.

[Section 13-2]

PROBLEM 13-7: Explain why it would be difficult for small firms to segregate duties as recommended by the principles of internal control. What can a small firm do to discourage embezzlement of funds by employees?

Answer: Small firms have few employees. It is therefore difficult to separate duties. One employee may be assigned a number of tasks to fill his/her working day. The firm should utilize as many independent checks as possible. Customers should be encouraged to monitor the amounts rung up on the cash register. The owner should prepare deposits and personally authorize disbursements. The owner should reconcile the bank account. If there are several employees, they may be rotated from job to job. It may be possible to separate duties by hiring part-time employees. Care must always be taken to hire competent and trustworthy persons.

[Section 13-2]

PROBLEM 13-8: Smedley has embezzled thousands of dollars from Trusting Company by submitting bills for payment for goods never received by the firm. The payments go to a fictitious company and Smedley cashes the checks sending the money to a Carribean bank account. Smedley makes out the checks and signs them himself. What steps could Trusting Company take to avoid this kind of theft?

Answer: The procedure for authorizing payments should require that a receiving report be matched to an invoice for goods. The receiving report should be filled out by the warehouse as the goods arrive and are inspected. No payment should be made without both documents. The person who signs the checks should not be the person who authorizes payment. Another person should review the documents and the check to make sure all procedures have been followed. Duties have not been adequately segregated creating an environment where theft can be accomplished without collusion by employees.

[Section 13-2]

PROBLEM 13-9: You are asked to reconcile a bank account for a good buddy who has noticed that a business he owns seems to have suddenly become less profitable. The August 31, 19x1 Bank Reconciliation Statement for Friend's Company appears below. The statement was prepared by the cashier.

Friend's Company
Bank Reconciliation Statement
August 31, 19x1

Balance per Bank		$14,880
Add: Deposits in Transit		2,850
		$17,830
Deduct: Outstanding Checks:		
#8430	$860	
#8471	240	
#8480	180	1,180
Adjusted Bank Balance		$16,650
Balance per Books		$17,400
Deduct:		
Unrecorded Bank Credit	$720	
Service Charge	30	750
Adjusted Book Balance		$16,650

Your buddy is certain that the cash left in the vault at the end of the month should have created a greater month end deposit than is reported as deposits in transit on the bank reconciliation statement.

You investigate and discover that the cashier has not listed all of the outstanding checks. In addition to those shown on the statement, Check #7480 for $1,620 is still outstanding. Check #8480 was written for $380. You call the bank and find that the only deposit made since the cutoff date of the bank statement was on August 30th for $2,550. The service charge on the bank statement was $20.

Prepare a correct bank reconciliation and determine the amount of funds missing.

Answer:

Friend's Company
Bank Reconciliation Statement
August 31, 19x1

Balance per Bank		$14,880
Add: Deposits in Transit		2,550
		$17,430
Deduct: Outstanding Checks		
#7480	$1,620	
#8430	860	
#8471	240	
#8480	380	3,100
Adjusted Bank Balance		$14,330
Balance per Books		$17,400
Add: Unrecorded Bank Credit		720
		$18,120
Deduct: Service Charge.		20
Adjusted Book Balance		$18,100

The adjusted bank balance indicates what the company really has in the bank to spend. The company has an adjusted bank balance of $14,330. The adjusted book balance indicates what the company should have in the bank. The adjusted book balance is $18,100. The difference between the two amounts represents money that has disappeared. The expropriated funds total ($18,100 − $14,330) = $3,770. This amount must be deducted from the adjusted book balance to make the book balance correspond with the adjusted bank balance. **[Section 13-4]**

PROBLEM 13-10: Explain how the abstraction of funds was covered up on the original bank reconciliation statement. What could be done to avoid this kind of loss?

Answer: The abstraction was covered up as follows:

Overstatement of Deposits in Transit	$ 300
Misadded Beg. Bal plus Deposits in Transit	100
Did not Include all Outstanding Checks	1,620
Understated Check #8480	200
Misadded Reported Outstanding Checks	100
Deducted Unrecorded Credit rather than adding	1,440
Overstated Service Charge	10
Total Funds Taken	$3,770

The firm should segregate responsibilities. The person who handles the cash should not prepare the bank reconciliation statement. The firm apparently had $6,320 in the vault, enough to accommodate a $2,550 end of month deposit and an abstraction of $3,770. The firm should deposit its funds in the bank on a timely basis. **[Sections 13-3 and 13-4]**

PROBLEM 13-11: At the end of June, Cha-Cha Company shows a balance in its Cash in Bank account of $1,770. The firm receives a bank statement, dated June 28, 19x1, that indicates the balance in the account is $4,250. In attempting to explain the difference in the two account balances, the internal auditor finds the following

(*a*) On June 29, $1,100 was deposited to the account.

(*b*) As of the June 28 statement date, checks totaling $589 had not been presented for payment.

(*c*) The bank incorrectly deducted $135 from the account for Check #362 which was actually written for $153.

(*d*) The bank collected a note for Cha-Cha Company. The collection consisted of the $2,900 principal plus $174 interest receivable. From this total of $3,074, the bank deducted a $31 collection fee.

(*e*) The bank recorded a deposit of a check for $62. On June 12, the check was returned for not sufficient funds. In addition to deducting the amount of the check, the bank charged an additional $5 penalty fee. The bank charged $3 for June's services.

Prepare the bank reconciliation statement for Cha-Cha Company as of the end of June.

Answer:

Cha-Cha Company
Bank Reconciliation Statement
April 30, 19x1

Balance per Bank..............................		$4,250
Add: Deposits in Transit		1,100
		5,350
Deduct:		
Outstanding Checks.........................	$589	
Bank Error	18	607
Adjusted Bank Balance		$4,743
Balance per Books		$1,770
Add: Note Receivable Collected...................		3,043
		$4,813
Deduct:		
NSF Check	$ 67	
Service Charge............................	3	70
Adjusted Book Balance		$4,743

[Section 13-4]

PROBLEM 13-12: Now that you know the correct balance for the Cash in Bank account in Problem 13-11, prepare the entries to adjust the books to reflect this amount.

Answer:

Cash in Bank	3,043	
Miscellaneous Expense	31	
Notes Receivable		2,900
Interest Revenue....................		174
Accounts Receivable	67	
Cash in Bank		67
Miscellaneous Expense	3	
Cash in Bank		3

[Section 13-4C]

14 ACCOUNTS RECEIVABLE

THIS CHAPTER IS ABOUT

☑ **The Definition and Valuation of Accounts Receivable**
☑ **Discounts**
☑ **The Gross Method of Valuing Sales and Accounts Receivable**
☑ **The Net Method of Valuing Sales and Accounts Receivable**
☑ **Accounting for Bad Debts**
☑ **The Allowance Method of Accounting for Bad Debts**

14-1. The Definition and Valuation of Accounts Receivable

Amounts owed to a firm by its customers are called **accounts receivable**. Some customers may choose to pay these amounts before they are due in exchange for a price reduction or discount. Others may not be able to pay at all. To report a more accurate value of Accounts Receivable, the amount owed should be adjusted for anticipated discounts and bad debt losses. Therefore, Accounts Receivable are valued at their **net realizable value**, the amount of cash the firm actually expects to collect.

14-2. Discounts

Firms often reduce the price of goods (services) for customers who pay early. This reduction in price is called a **discount**. The terms of these discounts will vary from firm to firm.

A. The terms of discount are communicated at the time of sale.

At the time of sale, the customer is given the terms of discount. An example of such terms is 2/10, n/30. This discount indicates that the customer can take a 2% discount if payment is made within *ten* days (2/10), otherwise the balance is due within *thirty* days (n/30). Terms may be as complex as 5/5, 2/10, n/30, in which the customer also has the option of paying within five days and receiving a 5% discount.

B. The annual interest rate that is implied by a discount is surprising to most people.

The annual interest rate that corresponds to a 2/10, n/30 discount, is surprisingly high. If the 2% discount is lost because the bill is not paid within ten days, the buyer is in effect borrowing money from the seller. The buyer borrows the money for an additional twenty days, the 11th to the 30th day, by postponing the bill. Paying a penalty of 2% to borrow money for twenty days is the same as paying more than 36% to borrow money for a year.

EXAMPLE 14-1: XYZ Corporation buys $1,000 of goods under the terms 2/10, n/30. If the bill is paid within ten days the amount remitted will be

$$\$1,000 - (\$1,000 \times .02) = \$980$$

If the firm pays on the 30th day, it must remit $1,000. The additional $20 is an interest charge for borrowing $980 for twenty days. Remembering that

$$i = P \quad \times r \times t$$
$$\$20 = \$980 \times r \times 20/360$$
$$\text{thus} \quad r = 36.7\%$$

(*Note:* When computing interest for days, the year is often assumed to be 360 days to make calculations easier. Passing up a discount from a seller under the terms 2/10, n/30 is the same as borrowing money elsewhere at a 36.7% annual interest rate.)

14-3. The Gross Method of Valuing Sales and Accounts Receivable

The gross method of valuing accounts receivable assumes that most customers *will not* pay within the discount period. They will lose the discount and pay the full amount of the bill. Therefore, the related sale is also recorded at the full, undiscounted amount. If the bill is paid within the discount period, the Sales Discounts account is debited for the amount of the discount.

EXAMPLE 14-2: Seller Corporation uses the gross method of accounting for accounts receivable and sales. On March 1, the firm sold $1,000 of goods, terms 2/10, n/30, to Mr. Jones. On March 30, Mr. Jones paid for the goods. The entries to record the sale and the receipt of the cash payment are shown below.

3/1	Accounts Receivable............	1,000	
	Sales		1,000
3/30	Cash	1,000	
	Accounts Receivable		1,000

The firm's expectations under the gross method are realized. The customer does not take advantage of the discount and the firm collects the full $1,000. The entries in this situation are straightforward.

EXAMPLE 14-3: Now suppose that Mr. Jones in Example 14-2 *does* pay within the discount period. The entries to record the sale and the receipt of the cash payment would be as follows:

3/1	Accounts Receivable............	1,000	
	Sales		1,000
3/10	Cash	980	
	Sales Discounts	20	
	Accounts Receivable		1,000

The Sales Discounts account is a negative (contra) revenue account. It is deducted from Sales in calculating net sales on the income statement.

14-4. The Net Method of Valuing Sales and Accounts Receivable

The net method of valuing accounts receivable assumes that most customers *will* pay within the discount period. They will get the discount and pay the reduced price. Therefore, the related sale is recorded at the selling price less the discount. The assumption is that since the discount will most likely be taken, valuing the account at the greater undiscounted amount will overstate its net realizable value. If the bill is not paid within the discount period, the Sales Discount Lost account is credited for the amount of the discount.

EXAMPLE 14-4: DTA Corporation uses the net method of valuing accounts receivable and sales. On March 1, the firm sold $1,000 of goods, terms 2/10, n/30, to Mr. Smith. On March 10, Mr. Smith pays for the goods. The entries to record the sale and the receipt of the cash payment are shown below.

3/1	Accounts Receivable	980	
	Sales		980
3/10	Cash	980	
	Accounts Receivable		980

The firm's expectations under the net method are realized. The customer takes advantage of the discount and the firm collects $980. The entries in this situation are straightforward.

EXAMPLE 14-5: Now assume that Mr. Smith in Example 14-4 *does not* pay for the merchandise within the discount period. The entries to record the sale and the receipt of the cash payment would be as follows:

3/1	Accounts Receivable	980	
	Sales		980
3/30	Cash	1,000	
	Accounts Receivable		980
	Sales Discounts Lost		20

The Sales Discounts Lost account is an interest or "other revenue" account. The balance in this account is reported as interest income on the income statement. Payment outside the discount period requires recognition of the interest earned for lending money to the customer from March 10 through March 30.

A. The net method correctly values the sale.

Most academic accountants would say that the net method of valuing sales represents the substance of the transaction. The amount of the sale in Examples 14-2 through 14-5 is really $980, the amount of cash the firm would accept on the date of sale in exchange for the merchandise. By allowing the discount period to lapse, the customer is borrowing money from the seller and the seller is receiving interest revenue from the buyer. The net method correctly identifies this extra amount as interest revenue.

B. The Sales Discounts Lost account provides more important information than does the Sales Discount account.

The Sales Discounts Lost account reveals the discounts *not* taken. The Sales Discounts account reports the discounts that *are* taken. Since companies offer discounts to encourage customers to pay quickly, they want to know if the discount offered is adequate incentive. Customers will choose to forego the discount if the implied interest rate being charged by the seller is lower than the interest rate charged by other sources. When a large number of customers ignore the discount, the seller knows that the funding being provided is cheaper than that being offered elsewhere. The Sales Discounts Lost account alerts the seller to this and therefore gives the important information needed to evaluate the discount policy.

C. Most businesses use the gross method of valuing sales and accounts receivable.

Although academic accountants prefer the net method, most businesses use the gross method. The entries made under the gross method are probably more easily understood by the majority of people.

14-5. Accounting for Bad Debts

Bad debts should be anticipated and the value of accounts receivable should be reduced by the estimate of uncollectible accounts.

A. There are two general methods of accounting for bad debts: the direct write-off method and the allowance method.

The direct write-off method makes no attempt to anticipate bad debts. Uncollectible accounts are written off as an expense in the accounting period when the account is determined to be uncollectible. The allowance method requires that the accountant estimate bad debts in the accounting period when the credit sales are made. The estimate is based on the company's own experience or that of similar companies. The expense is recognized in the period of sale and an allowance for uncollectible accounts is set up. The allowance account is a contra asset account and is deducted from Accounts Receivable on the balance sheet. When an account is determined to be uncollectible, the allowance account and the Accounts Receivable are both reduced by the amount of the uncollectible account's balance. The general entries for both methods are shown below.

DIRECT WRITE-OFF METHOD

Date of Sale	Accounts Receivable.	xxx	
	Sales		xxx
End of Period	No adjusting entry		
Date Account Identified as Uncollectible	Bad Debt Expense	xxx	
	Accounts Receivable		xxx

ALLOWANCE METHOD

Date of Sale	Accounts Receivable.	xxx	
	Sales		xxx
End of Period	Bad Debt Expense	xxx	
	Allowance for Uncollectible Accounts		xxx
Date Account Identified as Uncollectible	Allowance for Uncollectible Accounts	xxx	
	Accounts Receivable		xxx

B. GAAP requires that the allowance method be used whenever possible.

Generally accepted accounting principles require that, whenever possible, the allowance method for accounting for bad debts be used. There are several reasons.

1. The theoretical objection to the direct write-off method centers around its failure to match the bad debt expense to its related revenue. The bad debt expense is charged in the accounting period when an account is determined to be uncollectible. The related sale may have occurred in a previous accounting period. The revenue from the credit sale is recognized in one period, but the expense associated with extending the credit is recognized in a later period. The matching principle has been violated.

2. The direct write-off method tends to value accounts receivable higher than the expected net realizable value. Not all accounts will be collected. The value of the accounts should be reduced by anticipated uncollectibles.

3. The allowance method does attempt to match bad debt expense to its related revenue. The expense is recognized in the period when the sale is made. The allowance for uncollectible accounts reduces the value placed on accounts receivable on the balance sheet. No expense is recognized in the accounting period when the account is actually identified as uncollectible because an allowance has already been made for this event.

14-6. The Allowance Method of Accounting for Bad Debts

When using the allowance method for accounting for bad debts, estimates may be based on Sales or Accounts Receivable.

A. The estimate of bad debt expense can be based upon sales.

One way to estimate the amount of bad debt expense is to find the relationship between bad debts and the amount of credit sales. When this method is used, the estimate of bad debt expense will equal some percentage of credit sales. The percentage will be based upon the past experience of the firm or of similar firms.

EXAMPLE 14-6: TRS Corporation sold $1,000,000 of merchandise on credit during March. At the end of March, the balance in Accounts Receivable was $200,000. The credit balance in Allowance for Uncollectible Accounts was $800. The firm estimates that 2% of credit sales will eventually prove to be uncollectible. The adjusting entry to record the bad debt expense is

Bad Debt Expense ($1,000,000 × .02).........	20,000	
Allowance for Uncollectible Accounts		20,000

The amount of bad debt expense that will appear on the income statement for the period is $20,000. The credit balance in the allowance account will be $20,800. Accounts Receivable will be reported on the balance sheet as follows:

Accounts Receivable.........................	200,000	
Less: Allowance for Uncollectible Accounts	20,800	$179,200

Estimating bad debt expense as a percentage of credit sales is often called the **income statement method**. It is an income statement method because the calculation establishes the desired balance for the bad debt expense account on the income statement. No effort is made to reach a particular balance in the allowance account.

B. The estimate of bad debt expense can be based upon accounts receivable.

Based upon past experience, the firm may know that a given percentage of its accounts receivable will prove uncollectible. The object of the adjusting entry for bad debts is to correct the balance in the allowance account. The balance in the allowance account should equal the predetermined percentage of accounts receivable. Bad debt expense is therefore determined by computing the amount that must be added to the balance in the allowance account to achieve the desired balance.

EXAMPLE 14-7: ABC Corporation sold $1,000,000 of merchandise during March. The ending balance in Accounts Receivable was $200,000. The credit balance in the allowance account was $800. The firm estimates that 9% of its accounts will not be collected. The desired balance in the allowance account is therefore $18,000 ($200,000 × .09). The account currently has a balance of $800. Therefore, $17,200 ($18,000 − $800) must be added to the account balance through an adjusting entry for bad debts to give the allowance account its desired balance. The bad debt adjusting entry would be

Bad Debt Expense	17,200	
Allowance for Uncollectible Accounts		17,200

Accounts Receivable will be reported on the balance sheet as follows:

Accounts Receivable.	$200,000	
Less: Allowance for Uncollectible Accounts	18,000	$182,000

Estimating bad debt expense as a percentage of accounts receivable is often called the **balance sheet method**. It is called the balance sheet method because it emphasizes proper valuation of accounts receivable on the balance sheet.

C. The information in the accounting problem will tell you which method of estimating bad debt expense to use.

The information in the problem gives you clues as to which method of estimating bad debt expense is appropriate. The income statement method is used when bad debt experience is stated as a percentage of credit sales. The balance sheet method is used when bad debt experience is stated as a percentage of accounts receivable.

EXAMPLE 14-8: DFG Corporation ends the accounting period with $400,000 in Accounts Receivable. Before adjusting entries are posted the credit balance in the Allowance for Uncollectible Accounts equals $6,200. Credit sales were $1,500,000 and DFG Corporation estimates that 1.5% of its credit sales will not be collected.

The problem suggests that you use the income statement method because bad debt experience is stated in terms of credit sales. Bad debt expense will equal $22,500 ($1,500,000 × .015). The ending balance in the allowance account is not considered in the calculations of bad debt expense.

EXAMPLE 14-9: CDE Corporation ended the accounting period with $320,000 in Accounts Receivable. Before adjusting entries were made, there was a $450 debit balance in Allowance for Uncollectible Accounts. Credit sales totaled $850,000. The firm estimates that 3% of its outstanding accounts will never be collected.

This problem tells you to use the balance sheet method. Bad debt experience is stated as a percentage of accounts receivable. You are given information to compute the desired ending balance for the allowance account. Allowance for Uncollectible Accounts should have a credit balance of $9,600 ($320,000 × .03). The account has a debit balance of $450. Therefore, $10,050 ($9,600 + $450) should be credited to the allowance account to achieve the desired credit balance. Bad debt expense must equal this $10,050 amount.

RAISE YOUR GRADES

Can you explain . . . ?

☑ how accounts receivable are valued
☑ what the terms 2/10, n/30 mean
☑ how the gross method values accounts receivable on the date of sale
☑ how the net method values accounts receivable on the date of sale
☑ the direct write-off method of accounting for bad debts
☑ the allowance method of accounting for bad debts
☑ how to estimate the amount of bad debt expense using the income statement method
☑ how to estimate the amount of bad debt expense using the balance sheet method

SUMMARY

1. Accounts receivable are amounts owed to a firm by its customers.
2. Accounts receivable are valued at their net realizable value, the amount of cash the firm actually expects to collect.
3. A discount of 1/12, n/45 means a customer can take a 1% discount, if payment is made within twelve days; otherwise, the balance must be paid within forty-five days.
4. Buyers who fail to take advantage of a discount are in effect borrowing money from the seller to finance the purchase.
5. The terms 2/10, n/30 impose a 36.7% annual interest charge upon customers who choose to let the discount period lapse.
6. The gross method of valuing sales and accounts receivable assumes that most customers will not pay within the discount period.
7. The gross method values the sale and account receivable at the full, undiscounted amount.
8. The gross method debits the Sales Discounts account when the discount is taken by the customer. The Sales Discounts account is a contra (negative) revenue account which is deducted from Sales in computing net sales on the income statement.
9. The net method of valuing the sale and account receivable assumes that most customers will pay within the discount period.
10. The net method values the sale and the accounts receivable at the gross sales price minus the discount.
11. The net method credits a Sales Discounts Lost account when the customer pays after the discount period has lapsed. This account is an "other" revenue or interest revenue account on the income statement.
12. The net method is theoretically preferable because it records the sale at the cash sale price; it does not overvalue the account receivable; it identifies sales discounts lost as interest revenue; and it provides information that is useful in evaluating the firm's discount policy.
13. Most businesses use the gross method of valuing sales because the entries are more easily understood by most people.
14. The direct write-off method recognizes bad debt expense in the accounting period when an account is identified as being uncollectible.
15. The allowance method requires that the accountant estimate bad debt expense in the accounting period the related credit sale is made.
16. The allowance method creates an allowance for uncollectible accounts which is deducted from Accounts Receivable in valuing the accounts on the balance sheet.
17. The allowance method is required by the GAAP because, unlike the direct write-off method, it matches bad debt expense with its related revenue, and attempts to value accounts receivable at net realizable value.
18. The amount of bad debt expense may be estimated as a percentage of credit sales. This approach to estimating bad debt expense is called the income statement method.
19. The amount of bad debt expense may be estimated based on accounts receivable. This approach to estimating bad debt expense is called the balance sheet method.
20. The balance sheet method requires an adjustment to the allowance account. The pre-adjustment balance in the allowance account must be considered in determining the amount of the adjustment required.

RAPID REVIEW

1. Net realizable value equals _____ .
2. The terms 5/10, 1/20, n/45 means _____ .
3. On March 1, Ms. Boswell buys $200 of goods, terms 2/10, n/60. She should remit _____ if she pays within ten days.
4. The seller in Question 3 is, in effect, charging an annual interest rate of _____ .

5. When the gross method of valuing sales and accounts receivable is used, (Sales Discounts/Sales Discounts Lost) is (debited/credited) when the discount is (taken/lost).

6. When the net method of valuing sales and accounts receivable is used, (Sales Discounts/Sales Discounts Lost) is (debited/credited) when the discount is (taken/lost).

7. Mr. Golstone buys $400 of goods, terms 2/10, n/30. He pays within the discount period. Prepare the journal entry made to record the receipt of the payment, if the firm is using the gross method of valuing sales and accounts receivable.

8. Prepare the journal entry to record the payment by Mr. Goldstone (refer to Question 7 above), if the firm is using the net method of valuing sales and accounts receivable.

9. Now assume that Mr. Goldstone (refer to Question 7 above) waits for 30 days to pay. Prepare the journal entry to record the receipt of payment if the firm used the gross method of valuing sales and accounts receivable.

10. Refer to Question 9 above. Prepare the journal entry to record the receipt of payment, if the firm uses the net method of valuing sales and accounts receivable.

Questions 11-14 refer to the following information:

XYZ Corporation sold $50,000 of goods on credit during April. The balance in the Accounts Receivable account on April 30 was $10,400. Before adjustments, there was a credit balance of $200 in Allowance for Uncollectible Accounts.

11. Prepare the journal entry to record bad debt expense for the month of April, if the firm estimates that 1% of credit sales will prove to be uncollectible.

12. Refer to Question 11 above. Accounts Receivable will be valued at _____ on the balance sheet.

13. Prepare the entry to record bad debt expense for the month of April, if the firm estimates that 8% of the accounts receivable will prove to be uncollectible.

14. Refer to Question 13 above. Accounts Receivable will be valued at _____ on the balance sheet.

15. XYZ Corporation estimates that 4% of its accounts receivable will prove to be uncollectible. The firm is using the (income statement/balance sheet) method of estimating bad debt expense.

Answers:

1. The amount of cash the firm actually expects to collect for an account receivable. [Section 14-1]

2. Take a 5% discount, if you pay within ten days; take a 1% discount, if you pay within twenty days; or pay the net amount in forty-five days. [Section 14-2A]

3. $200 × .98 = $196 [Section 14-2A]

4. $4 = ($196 × r × 50/360) or r = 14.7% [Section 14-2B]

5. Sales Discounts; debited; taken [Section 14-3]

6. Sales Discounts Lost; credited; lost [Section 14-4]

7.
Cash ($400 × .98)...................	392	
Sales Discounts......................	8	
Accounts Receivable...............		400

[Section 14-3]

8.
Cash.............................	392	
Accounts Receivable...............		392

[Section 14-4]

9.
Cash.............................	400	
Accounts Receivable...............		400

[Section 14-3]

10. Cash	400	
Accounts Receivable		392
Sales Discounts Lost		8

[Section 14-4]

11. Bad Debt Expense ($50,000 × .01)	500	
Allowance for Uncollectible Accounts		500

[Section 14-6A]

12. $10,400 − ($200 + $500) = $9,700 [Section 14-6A]

13. Bad Debt Expense [($10,400 × .08) − $200]	632	
Allowance for Uncollectible Accounts		632

[Section 14-6B]

14. $10,400 − ($632 + $200) = $9,568 [Section 14-6B]
15. balance sheet [Section 14-6C]

SOLVED PROBLEMS

PROBLEM 14-1: During August, QRS Corporation sold $1,000,000 of goods, terms 3/5, n/45. During the month, the firm collected $698,400 from credit customers paying within the discount period. The firm collected $180,000 from credit customers not taking advantage of the discount.
(a) Show the entries to record the credit sales and collections from the credit customers, if the firm uses the gross method of valuing sales.
(b) Show the entries to record the credit sales and collections, if the firm uses the net method of valuing sales.
(c) Which method is theoretically better? Why?

Answer:

(a) Accounts Receivable	1,000,000	
Sales		1,000,000

Cash	698,400	
Sales Discounts	21,600	
Accounts Receivable		720,000*

* $698,400 = Gross accounts receivable × .97
Therefore, Gross accounts receivable = $698,400 ÷ .97 = $720,000

Cash	180,000	
Accounts Receivable		180,000

(b) Accounts Receivable ($1,000,000 × .97)	970,000	
Sales		970,000

Cash	698,400	
Accounts Receivable		698,400

Cash	180,000	
Sales Discounts Lost ($180,000 × .03)		5,400
Accounts Receivable		174,600

(c) Most academic accountants would say that the net method of valuing sales represents the substance of the transaction. The amount of the sales is really $970,000, the amount of cash the firm would accept on the date of sale in exchange for the merchandise. By allowing the discount period to lapse, the customer is borrowing money from the seller and the seller is collecting interest revenue from the buyer. The net method correctly identifies this extra amount as interest revenue. The gross method overstates the net realizable value by including the interest revenue which may never be collected.

[Sections 14-2 through 14-4]

PROBLEM 14-2: Doctors Corporation provides its services under the terms 5/0, n/60. What is the annual interest rate that the firm is in effect charging those customers that wish to be billed?

Answer: Answering the question may be easier if you insert some hypothetical numbers. If the doctor charged you $100, you could remit $95 immediately to settle the account. The extra $5 is the interest for borrowing the $95 for sixty days. The annual interest charge would be computed as

$$i = P \times r \times t$$
$$\$5 = \$95 \times r \times 60/360$$
$$r = 31.6\%$$

Be sure to understand why the amount borrowed in this problem is $95 and not $100. The doctor actually charged $95 for services rendered. The doctor was willing to accept $95, if the bill were paid immediately.   **[Section 14-2]**

PROBLEM 14-3: Explain why the direct write-off method is not acceptable under the GAAP.

Answer: The theoretical objection to the direct write-off method centers around its failure to match bad debt expense to its related revenue. The bad debt expense is charged in the accounting period when an account is determined to be uncollectible. The related sale may have occurred in a previous accounting period. Therefore, the revenue from the credit sale is recognized in one period and the expense of extending the credit is recognized in another. The direct write-off method also tends to value accounts receivable at more than their net realizable value. Not all of the accounts included will be collected.

[Section 14-6A]

PROBLEM 14-4: During 19x1, XYZ Corporation sold $1,000,000 of goods, terms 1/10, n/60. The Sales Discounts Lost account totaled $9,800 for the year. What can the firm learn from this information?

Answer: The total discount amount available on 19x1 sales was $10,000 ($1,000,000 × .01). The balance in the Sales Discounts Lost account indicates that very few customers chose to take advantage of the discount. The financing charge that XYZ is in effect making must be less than the interest rate that is being charged elsewhere.

For example, using a $1,000 account, the amount that could be remitted within the discount period would be $990 ($1,000 × .99). The annual interest rate being charged to the customer for not paying within the discount period is computed as follows:

$$\$10 = \$990 \times r \times 50/360$$
$$r = 7.3\%$$

The 7.3% interest rate must be below the market rate of interest. The firm should raise its discount to encourage faster payments by customers and avoid lending money at a 7.3% interest rate.   **[Sections 14-2B and 14-4B]**

Problems 14-5 through 14-7 refer to the following information:

NJI Corporation sold $1,000,000 of goods on credit during June, terms 2/15, n/45. The beginning balance in Accounts Receivable was $280,000. Credits to Accounts Receivable totaled $750,000 during the month. One third of the amount came from customers who missed the discount period. In addition, $6,000 of accounts were written off as un-collectible during the month. The credit balance in Allowance for Uncollectible Accounts at the beginning of the month was $14,000.

PROBLEM 14-5: Prepare the entries to record the sales and cash receipts from customers, if the firm uses the gross method of valuing sales and accounts receivable. Prepare the entry to record the write-off.

Answer:

Accounts Receivable	1,000,000	
Sales		1,000,000
Cash	740,000	
Sales Discounts (2/3 × $750,000 × .02)	10,000	
Accounts Receivable		750,000
Allowance for Uncollectible Accounts	6,000	
Accounts Receivable		6,000

[Sections 14-3 and 14-5]

PROBLEM 14-6: Show the adjusting entry to record bad debt expense, if the firm described in Problem 14-5 estimates that 2% of credit sales will prove to be uncollectible. What will be the value of Accounts Receivable on the June 30 balance sheet?

Answer:

Bad Debt Expense ($1,000,000 × .02)	20,000	
Allowance for Uncollectible Accounts		20,000

By June 30, Accounts Receivable and Allowance for Uncollectible Accounts will show the following activity:

Accounts Receivable			
Balance	280,000		
Credit Sales	1,000,000	Received on Account	750,000
		Accounts Written Off	6,000
Balance	524,000		

Allowance for Uncollectible Accounts			
		Balance	14,000
Accounts Written Off	6,000	Bad Debt Expense	20,000
		Balance	28,000

Accounts Receivable will appear on the balance sheet as follows:

Accounts Receivable	$524,000	
Less: Allowance for Uncollectible Accounts	28,000	$496,000

[Section 14-6]

PROBLEM 14-7: Now assume that bad debt expense is estimated to be 5% of the outstanding accounts receivable. Prepare the entry to record the adjustment for bad debt expense. What will be the value of Accounts Receivable on the June 30 balance sheet.

Answer:

Bad Debt Expense ($524,000 × .05) − $8,000 . . .	18,200	
Allowance for Uncollectible Accounts		18,200

The activity in Accounts Receivable will be the same as in Problem 14-6. Allowance for Uncollectible Accounts will appear as follows:

Allowance for Uncollectible Accounts

		Balance	14,000
Accounts Written Off	6,000	Bad Debt Expense	18,200
		Balance	26,200

Accounts Receivable will appear on the balance sheet as follows:

Accounts Receivable...............................	$524,000	
Less: Allowance for Uncollectible Accounts	26,200	$497,800

[Section 14-6]

PROBLEM 14-8: GHI Corporation began the accounting period with a balance in Accounts Receivable of $325,000. Allowance for Uncollectible Accounts had a credit balance of $13,000. During the year, the firm sold $1,500,000 of goods on credit. Accounts totaling $15,400 were determined to be uncollectible and written off. Collections from customers totaled $1,380,000. The firm estimates that 4% of its outstanding accounts receivable will prove to be uncollectible. Prepare the entries to record the above information.

Answer:

Accounts Receivable	1,500,000	
Sales		1,500,000
Allowance for Uncollectible Accounts.........	15,400	
Accounts Receivable..................		15,400
Cash	1,380,000	
Accounts Receivable................		1,380,000

Accounts Receivable balance = $325,000 + $1,500,000 − $15,400 − $1,380,000
= $429,600

Allowance for Uncollectible Accounts balance = $13,000 − $15,400 = −$2,400

This means the account now has a *debit* balance.

Desired balance in Allowance for Uncollectible Accounts = $429,600 × .04 = $17,184

Therefore, bad debt expense = $2,400 + $17,184 = $19,584

Bad Debt Expense	19,584	
Allowance for Uncollectible Accounts.......		19,584

[Sections 14-5A and 14-6B]

PROBLEM 14-9: BNM Corporation is just beginning business. The owner of the business wishes to report favorable earnings. She is deciding upon accounting methods to be used to record transactions.

(a) If the owner's wish is to maximize the reported profits, what accounting method should she use for valuing sales and accounts receivable? Why?

(b) What general method should the owner use for accounting for bad debts? Why? How could the owner justify using this method?

Answer:

(a) The owner would choose the gross method of valuing sales and accounts receivable. This method reports a higher value for sales by including the finance charge in sales revenue before it is earned. This method also places a higher value on Accounts Receivable on the balance sheet.

(b) The owner would choose to use the direct write-off method to account for bad debt expense. Since the expense is not recognized until an account is determined to be uncollectible, it is unlikely that the owner will recognize any such expense in the first year of operations. The owner thus minimizes an expense and maximizes profits.

Even though the GAAP does not allow the direct write-off method, the owner could justify using the method by contending that the business is new and has no past experience on which to base a reasonable estimate of bad debts. Also, since the company is new, the amount that would be written off and that allowed for would, in any case, be small and not *materially* affect either net income or total assets. The direct write-off method could be used under the exception principle.

[**Sections 14-5 and 14-6**]

Problems 14-10 through 14-12 refer to the following information:

Grandma Corporation sold $850,000 of goods on credit during November, terms 2/10, n/30. The beginning balance in Accounts Receivable was $132,650. Credits to Accounts Receivable totaled $165,150. One third of the amount came from customers who missed the discount period. In addition, $1,921 of accounts were written off as uncollectible during the month. The credit balance in Allowance for Uncollectible Accounts at the beginning of the month was $5,791.

PROBLEM 14-10: Prepare the entries to record the sales and cash receipts from customers, if the firm uses the gross method of valuing sales and accounts receivable. Prepare the entry to record the write-off.

Answer:

Accounts Receivable	850,000	
Sales		850,000
Cash	162,948	
Sales Discounts (2/3 × $165,150 × .02)	2,202	
Accounts Receivable		165,150
Allowance for Uncollectible Accounts	1,921	
Accounts Receivable		1,921

[**Sections 14-3 and 14-5**]

PROBLEM 14-11: Show the adjusting entry to record bad debt expense, if the firm described in Problem 14-10 estimates that 2% of credit sales will prove to be uncollectible. What will be the value of Accounts Receivable on the November 30 balance sheet?

Answer:

Bad Debt Expense ($850,000 × .02)	17,000	
Allowance for Uncollectible Accounts		17,000

By November 30, Accounts Receivable and Allowance for Uncollectible Accounts will show the following activity:

Accounts Receivable

Balance	132,650		
Credit Sales	850,000	Received on Account	165,150
		Accounts Written off	1,921
Balance	815,579		

Allowance for Uncollectible Accounts

		Balance	5,791
Accounts Written Off	1,921		
		Bad Debt Expense	17,000
		Balance	20,800

Accounts Receivable will appear on the balance sheet as follows:

Accounts Receivable.	$815,579	
Less Allowance for Uncollectible Accounts	20,800	$794,779

[Section 14-6]

PROBLEM 14-12: Now assume that bad debt expense is estimated to be 4% of the outstanding accounts receivable. Prepare the entry to record the adjustment for bad debt expense. What will be the value of Accounts receivable on the November 30 balance sheet.

Answer:

Bad Debt Expense [($815,579 × .04) − $3,870 . .	28,753	
Allowance for Uncollectible Accounts		28,753

The activity in Accounts Receivable will be the same as in Problem 14-6. Allowance for Uncollectible Accounts will appear as follows:

Allowance for Uncollectible Accounts

		Balance	5,791
Accounts Written Off	1,921		
		Bad Debt Expense	28,753
		Balance	32,623

Accounts Receivable will appear on the balance sheet as follows:

Accounts Receivable.	815,579	
Less: Allowance for Uncollectible Accounts	32,623	782,956

[Section 14-6]

15 SHORT-TERM NOTES RECEIVABLE

THIS CHAPTER IS ABOUT

☑ **Defining Notes**
☑ **Types of Notes**
☑ **Accounting for Interest-bearing Notes**
☑ **Accounting for Non Interest-bearing Notes**
☑ **Discounting Notes**
☑ **Discount Rates vs Interest Rates**

15-1. Defining Notes

A note is a formal "IOU" upon which the borrower agrees to pay a specified sum of money on a specified future date. The note should contain all the information to identify who will pay (maker), the total amount to be re-paid (maturity value), and the date upon which payment will be made (date of maturity).

15-2. Types of Notes

A note can be classified in two categories: interest-bearing and non interest-bearing. With the interest-bearing format, the note specifies on its face the principal amount (the amount actually received by the borrower) plus interest stated at an annual percentage rate. With the non interest-bearing format, the note simply shows its maturity amount. The specified amount is equal to the principal plus whatever interest would be charged over the life of the note but no reference is made to them as separate amounts.

EXAMPLE 15-1: On 3/1/x1, Lender Corporation lent $1,000 to Borrower Corporation. Borrower signed an interest-bearing note agreeing to pay back $1,000 plus 12% interest in 3 months. This note contains all of the information required:

Maturity Date	6/1/x1
Principal	$1,000
Interest ($1,000 $\times$ .12 $\times$ 3/12)	$ 30
Maturity Value	$1,030

The maturity date will be three months after the date on which the note is signed and the $1,000 is received by the borrower. Interest can be computed from the interest rate information given on the face of the note. The maturity value of the note is equal to the principal plus the interest to maturity.

EXAMPLE 15-2: On 3/1/x1, B & B Corporation lent $1,000 to H & M Corporation. H & M signed a note agreeing to pay $1,030 to B & B, three months from the date the note was signed. The note signed by the borrower is in the non interest-bearing format. This does not mean that no interest is being charged. It means only that the interest portion of the amount paid upon maturity is not separated from the principal portion on the face of the note.

We know from the description given:

Maturity Date	6/1/x1
Principal	$1,000
Interest	$ 30
Maturity Value	$1,030

The lender and borrower in Example 15-1 and 15-2 have committed themselves to equal agreements. Both notes result in $1,000 being lent out and $1,030 returned in three months. Since the two notes are really exactly the same, the accounting entries to record each note must result in the same value for the note on the balance sheet and the same amount of interest revenue on the income statement.

15-3. Accounting for Interest-bearing Notes

Only the principal amount of an interest-bearing note is recorded on the date the note is accepted. The entries to recognize interest are made as the interest is earned. On the balance sheet, the note is valued at the amount of principal plus any interest that has been earned.

EXAMPLE 15-3: TRS Corporation accepted a $100,000 note from ABC Corporation in settlement of a $100,000 account receivable. The note specifies that ABC Corporation will pay $100,000 plus 15% interest in 3 months. The note is signed on 1/1/x1. TRS Corporation closes its books monthly.

The entries to record the acceptance of the note, the adjustments for interest revenue, and the final payment of the note appear below.

1/1/x1	Notes Receivable	100,000	
	Accounts Receivable		100,000
1/31/x1	Interest Receivable*	1,250	
	Interest Revenue		1,250
2/28/x1	Interest Receivable*	1,250	
	Interest Revenue		1,250
3/31/x1	Interest Receivable*	1,250	
	Interest Revenue		1,250
4/1/x1	Cash	103,750	
	Notes Receivable		100,000
	Interest Receivable		3,750

($100,000)(.15)(1/12)

The following summary shows how the note will be reported on the income statement and balance sheet each month it is outstanding.

	1/1/x1	1/31/x1	2/28/x1	3/31/x1
Income Statement:				
Interest Revenue	NA	$ 1,250	$ 1,250	$ 1,250
Balance Sheet:				
Notes Receivable	$100,000	$100,000	$100,000	$100,000
Interest Receivable	0	1,250	2,500	3,750
Total	$100,000	$101,250	$102,500	$103,750

Short-Term Notes Receivable 249

15-4. Accounting for Non Interest-bearing Notes

When a non interest-bearing note is accepted, Notes Receivable is debited for the maturity value of the note. Since the maturity value includes "interest" on the principal amount which has not yet been earned, an entry must be made to show that the value shown in Notes Receivable is overstated. This is done by crediting a negative (or contra) asset account called Discount on Notes Receivable. The amount shown in this account represents that amount of unearned interest included in the balance of the Notes Receivable account. As interest is earned the Discount on Notes Receivable account is debited and Interest Revenue is credited.

EXAMPLE 15-4: WCD Corporation accepted a $103,750 non interest-bearing note from K & W Corporation in settlement of a $100,000 account receivable. The note matures in 3 months from 1/1/x1, the date it was signed. The entry to record the acceptance of the note is

1/1/x1	Notes Receivable..............	103,750	
	Accounts Receivable...........		100,000
	Discount on Notes Receivable		3,750

The note is debited to Notes Receivable at its face value of $103,750. The firm is not owed $103,750 on 1/1/x1. Of the maturity value, $3,750 is really interest that will be earned over the life of the note. None of that interest has been earned as of 1/1/x1, so the balance in the Discount on Notes Receivable account is $3,750. If a balance sheet were prepared on 1/1/x1, the note would be valued at its maturity amount of $103,750 less the balance in the discount account of $3,750. Its net value would be $100,000 ($103,750 − $3,750).

The adjusting entries to record the earning of interest revenue during January, February, and March are as follows:

1/31/x1	Discount on Notes Receivable ($3,750/3)	1,250	
	Interest Revenue............		1,250
2/28/x1	Discount on Notes Receivable	1,250	
	Interest Revenue.............		1,250
3/31/x1	Discount on Notes Receivable	1,250	
	Interest Revenue.............		1,250

WCD Corporation will earn $3,750 in interest over the three-month life of the note or $1,250 per month. The adjusting entries recognize the interest revenue earned and reduce the balance in the discount account. Recall that the discount account contains any interest included in Notes Receivable that has not been earned. The balance in the discount account must be reduced as the interest included on the face of the note is earned.

The entry on 4/1/x1, the date the note matures, is as follows:

4/1/x1	Cash	103,750	
	Notes Receivable		103,750

By 4/1/x1, the day the note matures, all of the $3,750 of interest included in the maturity value of the note has been earned. The adjusting entries at the end of each month have written the balance in the discount account down to zero. The book value of the note is $103,750 ($103,750 − $0).

A summary of the information that appears on the income statement and balance sheet appears below.

	1/1/x1	1/31/x1	2/28/x1	3/31/x1
Income Statement:				
Interest Revenue	NA	$ 1,250	$ 1,250	$ 1,250
Balance Sheet:				
Notes Receivable	$103,750	$103,750	$103,750	$103,750
Less Discount on Notes Receivable	3,750	2,500	1,250	0
Net Value for Notes Receivable	$100,000	$101,250	$102,500	$103,750

Compare the income statement and balance sheet results from Example 15-4 with those from Example 15-3. The two notes are really the same. They both involve settlement of a $100,000 account receivable. Both charge $3,750 in interest for the three-month period. The accounting entries result in the same amount of interest revenue in each month and the same total asset figures at the end of each month.

15-5. Discounting Notes

A business may need cash prior to the maturity date of a note receivable. At times like this, the business may decide to sell the note receivable for cash. This is known as **discounting the note**. The note is sold for an amount less than the maturity value and the seller is usually required to guarantee payment of the note, if the maker fails to do so. When such a guarantee is given, the note is said to be **discounted with recourse**.

A. When a note is discounted, the seller is charged a fee.

Since the seller receives an amount less than the maturity value of the note, the buyer is, in essence, charging the seller a fee. This fee is called the **discount**. The amount received by the seller is called the **proceeds**. The formulas for calculating the discount and proceeds are as follows:

$$D = MV \times DR \times T$$
$$P = MV - D$$

where:		
	D — amount of discount	T — time between discount
	MV — maturity value of note	and maturity date
	DR — discount rate	P — proceeds

B. Discounting a note creates a contingent liability for the seller.

When a note receivable is discounted with recourse, the amount of the note is transferred from the Notes Receivable account to a contingent liability account called Notes Receivable Discounted. The account is a contingent liability because responsibility for the note is dependent or contingent on payment by the maker of the note. The balance in the Notes Receivable Discounted account is subtracted from Notes Receivable in reporting the value of Notes Receivable on the balance sheet.

C. The difference between the proceeds from the sale of a note receivable and its book value is recorded as interest revenue or expense.

The book value of an interest-bearing note on the discount date is equal to the balance in Notes Receivable plus any interest receivable that has been recognized. The book value of a non interest-bearing note is the balance in Notes Receivable less the balance in the Discount on Notes Receivable account. On the date the note is discounted, Cash is debited for the amount of proceeds and Notes Receivable Discounted is credited for amount originally debited to Notes Receivable. Amounts contained in the Interest Revenue or Discount on Notes Receivable account must be eliminated. If the seller receives more for the note than its book value, Interest Revenue is credited for the difference. If the seller receives less than the book value of the note, Interest Expense is debited.

EXAMPLE 15-5: On 2/1/x1, XYZ Corporation accepted a 12%, nine-month, $10,000 note from a customer in payment of an account receivable. This is an interest-bearing note because the amount of interest is stated separately. The note will mature on 11/1/x1. The maturity value of the note is equal to

$$MV = \$10,000 + (\$10,000 \times .12 \times 9/12) = \$10,900$$

On 5/1/x1, XYZ Corporation discounts the note at the bank. The bank charges a discount rate of 14%. The proceeds from discounting the note will be:

$$D = MV \times DR \times T$$
$$D = \$10,900 \times .14 \times 6/12 = \$763$$
$$P = MV - D = \$10,900 - \$763 = \$10,137$$

On 5/1/x1, XYZ Corporation will receive $10,137 for the note. The note is discounted after three months so there are 6 months remaining in the discount period. The discount rate was 14% and the maturity value of the note is equal to $10,900, its face value plus interest to maturity.

The entries to record all of this information are shown below.

2/1/x1	Notes Receivable	10,000	
	Accounts Receivable		10,000
5/1/x1	Cash	10,137	
	Notes Receivable Discounted		10,000
	Interest Revenue		137

D. The term "discount" is used in three completely different ways in accounting for notes.

The term "discount" is used in three ways in accounting for notes:

1. *Discount on Notes Receivable.* This title refers to the account that reports the balance of unearned interest revenue on non interest-bearing notes.
2. *Notes Receivable Discounted.* This title refers to the contingent liability account that reflects the value of notes sold and for which the company is still held responsible until the maker pays the buyer.
3. *Discount.* The maturity value of a note sold less the proceeds from the sale.

It is very important not to confuse these terms.

E. When a note is sold, the seller is responsible for the note until payment is made by the maker.

When a note has been sold, the buyer will approach the maker of the note for payment on the maturity date.

1. *If the maker remits payment*, the seller is notified that the contingent liability no longer exists. Notes Receivable Discounted is debited to remove the contingent liability and Notes Receivable is credited to remove the asset.
2. *If the maker defaults*, the buyer will present the note to the seller for payment. The seller must cover the note. It will then be the seller's problem to seek payment from the maker of the note.

EXAMPLE 15-6: Assume that the maker of the note in Example 15-5 pays the note off when it matures. The bank will inform XYZ Corporation that the contingent liability no longer exists. XYZ Corporation will make the following entry to remove the note from the books.

| 11/1/x1 | Notes Receivable Discounted . . . . . | 10,000 | |
| | Notes Receivable . . . . | | 10,000 |

If the maker of the note defaults, the bank will present the note to XYZ Corporation for payment. XYZ Corporation will have to pursue the maker for reimbursement. XYZ Corporation will make the following entries to record the dishonor of the note by the maker:

Notes Receivable Discounted	10,000	
Notes Receivable		10,000
Accounts Receivable	10,900	
Cash		10,900

XYZ Corporation will pay $10,900 cash, the maturity value of the note, to the bank and will seek to collect from the maker of the note.

EXAMPLE 15-7: On 4/1/x1, Wolverton Corporation accepted a $12,000, ninety-day note in payment of an $11,000 account receivable. The note was immediately discounted, with recourse, at the bank. The discount rate charged by the bank was 18%.

The note in this example is a non interest-bearing note. The maturity value of the note is $12,000. The note will mature on 6/29/x1, ninety calendar days from 4/1/x1. The bank will not give Wolverton Corporation $12,000 for the note. The proceeds will equal $12,000 (its maturity value) minus the amount of the discount charged by the bank.

$$\text{Proceeds} = \$12,000 - (\$12,000 \times .18 \times 90/360) = \$11,460$$

The entries to record the acceptance of the note, its discounting and subsequent payment by the maker would be:

4/1/x1	Notes Receivable	12,000	
	Discount on Notes Receivable . . .		1,000
	Accounts Receivable		11,000
	To record acceptance of note.		
	Cash	11,460	
	Discount on Notes Receivable	1,000	
	Notes Receivable Discounted		12,000
	Interest Revenue		460
	To record discounting of note.		
6/29/x1	Notes Receivable Discounted	12,000	
	Notes Receivable		12,000
	To record payment by maker of note.		

EXAMPLE 15-8: On 7/1/x1, Riddick Company accepted a $5,000, 6%, 120-day note in settlement of an account receivable. Ten days later, the firm discounted the note with recourse at the bank. The bank's discount rate was 16%. On 10/28/x1, the maturity date of the note, the maker of the note defaulted. Record all the entries that would have been made pertaining to this note.

The maturity value of the interest-bearing note is

$$MV = \text{Principal} + \text{Interest}$$
$$MV = \$5,000 + (\$5,000 \times .06 \times 120/360) = \$5,100$$

The proceeds from the note are

$$\text{Proceeds} = \$5,100 - (\$5,100)(.16)(110/120) = \$4,352$$

The entry to record the acceptance of the note, the discounting of the note, and the default by the maker are

7/1/x1	Notes Receivable	5,000	
	Accounts Receivable		5,000
	To record acceptance of note.		

7/11/x1	Cash	4,352	
	Interest Expense	648	
	Notes Receivable Discounted . . .		5,000
	To record discounting of note.		
10/28/x1	Notes Receivable Discounted	5,000	
	Notes Receivable		5,000
	Accounts Receivable	5,100	
	Cash		5,100
	To record dishonor of note by the maker		

15-6. Discount Rates vs Interest Rates

When a firm charges a certain discount rate, it is charging *more* than that rate in interest. The discount rate understates the real interest rate because the discount rate is applied to the maturity value of note; the interest rate is applied to the principal amount of the loan.

EXAMPLE 15-9: EBI Corporation discounts its own $10,000, six-month note at the bank which charges an 18% discount rate. In this example, the EBI Corporation signs a note at the bank agreeing to pay the bank $10,000 in six months. The bank gives EBI Corporation $10,000 less the discount amount for the note. The proceeds from the note will equal

$$\text{Proceeds} = \$10,000 - (10,000)(.18)(6/12) = \$9,100$$

The maturity value of this note is the $10,000 that will be paid by EBI Corporation upon maturity. The discount rate is 18%. The bank will wait six months to be paid, so the length of time in the discount period is 6/12ths of a year.

EBI Corporation receives $9,100 now and must repay $10,000 in six months. Banks often lend money out in this manner. The 18% discount rate is the equivalent of a 19.8% interest rate. Substituting the information into the interest formula we find the following:

$$i = p \quad \times r \times t$$
$$\$900 = \$9,100 \times r \times 6/12$$
$$r = 19.8\%$$

The bank is really charging a 19.8% annual interest rate on a loan of $9,100 for six months.

RAISE YOUR GRADES

Can you explain . . . ?

☑ what is a note
☑ what is the format of an interest-bearing note
☑ what is the format of a non interest-bearing note
☑ how to account for an interest-bearing note
☑ how to account for a non interest-bearing note
☑ what is meant by discounting a note receivable with recourse
☑ what is the difference between a discount rate and the interest rate
☑ how to compute the proceeds from a discounted note
☑ how to account for a discounted note
☑ what a contingent liability is
☑ three terms that include the word discount

SUMMARY

1. A note is a formal "IOU" upon which the borrower agrees to pay a specified sum of money on a specified future date.
2. An interest-bearing note specifies on its face the principal amount plus an annual rate of interest.
3. A non interest-bearing note simply states a specified maturity amount on its face.
4. When an interest-bearing note is accepted, Notes Receivable is debited for the principal amount.
5. When a non interest-bearing note is accepted, Notes Receivable is debited for the maturity value and Discount on Notes Receivable is credited for the amount of unearned interest included in the maturity value.
6. As interest is earned on an interest-bearing note, Interest Receivable is debited and Interest Revenue is credited.
7. As interest is earned on a non interest-bearing note, Discount on Notes Receivable is debited and Interest Revenue is credited.
8. When an interest-bearing note is paid upon maturity, Cash is debited and Notes Receivable and Interest Receivable are credited.
9. When a non interest-bearing note is paid, Cash is debited and Notes Receivable is credited.
10. Selling a note receivable before its maturity date is called discounting the note.
11. When a note is discounted with recourse, the seller remains contingently liable to the buyer until the maker of the note settles the debt.
12. Proceeds equal the amount the seller receives in return for the discounted note.
13. The discount is the difference between the maturity value of the note and its selling price.
14. When a note is discounted, Cash is debited and Notes Receivable Discounted is credited. The remainder of the entry depends upon the relationship of the proceeds to the book value of the note.
15. When the maker of a Note Receivable pays off the note, the seller debits Notes Receivable Discounted and Notes Receivable is credited.
16. The difference between the book value of a note as of the discount date and the proceeds from the sale of the note is charged to either Interest Revenue or Interest Expense.
17. If a maker of a note that has been discounted defaults, the seller must pay the buyer and seek the maker of the note for payment.
18. When a discounted note is defaulted, Notes Receivable is credited for the value of the note and Notes Receivable Discounted is debited. Next Accounts Receivable is debited and Cash is credited.
19. Discount rates are not the same as interest rate.
20. Discounts are based on the maturity value of a note and interest rates are based on the principal amount.

RAPID REVIEW

1. "I will pay $1,500 on June 30, 19x5." If this promise were formally placed on the face of a note, the note would be classified as (interest-bearing/non interest-bearing).
2. Assume the maker of the note described in Question 1 received $1,250 on July 1, 19x4, the day the note was signed.
   (a) The maturity value of the note is _____.
   (b) The principal amount is _____.
   (c) The interest amount over the life of the note is _____.
   (d) The annual interest rate charged on this loan is _____.
3. "I will pay $1,250 plus 20% interest on June 30, 19x5." If this promise were formally placed on the face of a note, the note would be classified as (interest-bearing/non interest-bearing).

4. Assume the maker of the note described in Question 3 received $1,250 on July 1, 19x4, the day the note was signed.
   (a) The maturity value of the note is _____.
   (b) The principal amount is _____.
   (c) The interest amount over the life of the note is _____.
   (d) The annual interest rate charged on this loan is _____.

5. Would the lender prefer that a borrower sign the note described in Question 1 or Question 3 given that $1,250 is given to the borrower in each case?

6. Prepare the entry to record the lender's acceptance of the note described in Question 1 given that $1,250 is provided to the borrower on 7/1/x4.

7. Prepare the entry to record the lender's acceptance of the note described in Question 3 given that $1,250 is provided to the borrower on 7/1/x4.

8. What will be the book value of the note recorded in Question 6 on 7/1/x4 immediately after the loan is made?

9. What will be the book value of the note recorded in Question 7 on 7/1/x4 immediately after the loan is made?

10. The lender discounts the note described in Question 1 at the bank four months after accepting it. The bank charges a 15% discount rate. The proceeds from discounting the note will be _____.

Answers:

1. non interest-bearing [Section 15-2]
2. (a) $1,500
   (b) $1,250
   (c) $1,500 − $1,250 = $250
   (d) $250 = $1,250 × r × 1; r = 20% [Section 15-2]
3. interest-bearing [Section 15-2]
4. (a) $1,250 + ($1,250 × .20 × 1) = $1,500
   (b) $1,250
   (c) $1,250 × .20 × 1 = $250
   (d) 20% [Section 15-2]
5. The lender will be indifferent. The amount lent out equals $1,250, and the amount returned in one year equals $1,500 in both cases. [Section 15-4]
6. Notes Receivable   1,500
      Discount on Notes Receivable   250
      Cash   1,250
   [Section 15-4]
7. Notes Receivable   1,250
      Cash   1,250
   [Section 15-3]
8. $1,500 − $250 = $1,250 [Section 15-4]
9. $1,250 [Section 15-3]
10. $1,500 − ($1,500 × .15 × 8/12) = $1,350 [Section 15-5]

SOLVED PROBLEMS

PROBLEM 15-1: On October 1, 19x1, Beach Corporation accepts a $2,000, nine-month, 16% note from Harper Company in payment of an account receivable. Prepare the entries to record the acceptance of this note, the adjustments required on 12/31/x1, and the payment of the note by the maker on 7/1/x2. Show how Notes Receivable and any accumulated interest would appear on the 12/31/x1 balance sheet.

Answer:

10/1/x1	Notes Receivable	2,000	
	Accounts Receivable		2,000
12/31/x1	Interest Receivable		
	($2,000 × .16 × 3/12)	80	
	Interest Revenue		80
7/1/x2	Cash [$2,000 + ($2,000 × .16 × 9/12)]	2,240	
	Notes Receivable		2,000
	Interest Receivable.		80
	Interest Revenue		160

The note and its accumulated interest would appear on the balance sheet as follows:

Notes Receivable	$2,000
Interest Receivable	80

[Section 15-3]

PROBLEM 15-2: Restate Problem 15-1 by describing the note in a non interest-bearing format.

Answer: On October 1, 19x1, Beach Corporation accepts a note in which Harper Company agrees to pay $2,240 in nine months as settlement of a $2,000 account receivable. Prepare the entries to record the acceptance of this note, the adjustments required on 12/31/x1, and the payment of the note by the maker on 7/1/x2. Show how Notes Receivable and any accumulated interest would appear on the 12/31/x1 balance sheet.

[Section 15-2]

PROBLEM 15-3: Prepare the entries requested in your answer to Problem 15-2.

Answer:

10/1/x1	Notes Receivable	2,240	
	Discount on Notes Receivable . .		240
	Accounts Receivable		2,000
12/31/x1	Discount on Notes Receivable		
	($240/9)(3).	80	
	Interest Revenue		80
7/1/x2	Discount on Notes Receivable	160	
	Interest Revenue		160
	Cash	2,240	
	Notes Receivable.		2,240

Notes Receivable will appear on the 12/31/x1 balance sheet as

Notes Receivable	$2,240	
Less Discount on Notes Receivable	160	$2,080

The balance in the Notes Receivable account equals the principal amount plus the total interest charged. The Discount on Notes Receivable account reduces the balance in Notes Receivable by the amount of interest not yet earned. **[Section 15-4]**

PROBLEM 15-4: On 11/1/x1, WLG Corporation accepts a $6,000, eight-month 15% note from a customer in settlement of an account receivable.

(*a*) When does this note mature?
(*b*) What is the maturity value of the note?
(*c*) How much interest revenue would WLC Corporation recognize on 12/31/x1?

(d) What value would appear on the 12/31/x1 balance sheet with regard to this note?

(e) How much interest revenue would WLC Corporation recognize on this note in 19x2?

(f) What would the proceeds be if the note were discounted at 20% on 1/1/x1?

Answers:

(a) The note matures on 7/1/x2.

(b) MV = $6,000 + ($6,000 × .15 × 8/12) = $6,600

(c) $6,000 × .15 × 2/12 = $150

(d) $6,000 + $150 = $6,150

(e) $6,000 × .15 × 6/12 = $450

(f) Proceeds = $6,600 − ($6,600 × .20 × 6/12) = $5,940   **[Sections 15-3 and 15-5]**

PROBLEM 15-5: On 11/1/x1, JEB Corporation accepts a $4,000, 9%, eight-month note in settlement of an account receivable. The company makes all required entries with regard to the note. After three months the firm discounts the note at the bank. The bank charges an 18% discount rate. On the maturity date, 7/1/x2, the maker of the note honors the note. Prepare all the entries with regard to this note, assuming the company closes its books on 12/31/x1.

Answer:

11/1/x1	Notes Receivable.	4,000	
	Accounts Receivable.		4,000
12/31/x1	Interest Receivable		
	($4,000)(.09)(2/12).	60	
	Interest Revenue.		60
2/1/x2	Cash*	3,922	
	Interest Expense	138	
	Notes Receivable Discounted. . . .		4,000
	Interest Receivable.		60
7/1/x2	Notes Receivable Discounted	4,000	
	Notes Receivable		4,000

MV = $4,000 + ($4,000 × .09 × 8/12) = $4,240

P = $4,240 − ($4,240 × .18 × 5/12) = $3,922

[Sections 15-3 and 15-5]

PROBLEM 15-6: On 11/1/x1, Brockman Company accepted a non interest-bearing, eight-month, $4,240 note in settlement of a $4,000 account receivable. After three months, the company discounted the note at the bank. The bank charged an 18% discount rate. On the maturity date, 7/1/x2, the maker of the note defaulted. Prepare all the entries with regard to this note assuming the firm closes its books on 12/31/x1.

Answer:

11/1/x1	Notes Receivable.	4,240	
	Discount on Notes		
	Receivable		240
	Accounts Receivable.		4,000
12/31/x1	Discount on Notes Receivable.	60	
	Interest Revenue*.		60
2/1/x2	Cash**	3,922	
	Discount on Notes		
	Receivable***	180	
	Interest Expense****	138	
	Notes Receivable Discounted. . . .		4,240

7/1/x2	Accounts Receivable	4,240	
	Cash		4,240
	(To record payment to bank for dishonored notes.)		
	Notes Receivable Discounted	4,240	
	Notes Receivable		4,240

Interest Revenue = ($240/8)(2) = $60; $240 of interest will be earned over 8 months. $60 of interest is earned in 2 months.

**Proceeds = MV − Discount Amount*
= $4,240 − ($4,240 × .18 × 5/12) = $3,922

***Discount on Notes Receivable balance = ($240 − $60) = $180*

****Debit to Interest Expense balances the entry.*

[Sections 15-4 and 15-5]

PROBLEM 15-7: On 3/1/x1, you borrow $2,000. Would you rather sign a note agreeing to pay back the $2,000 plus 14.5% interest in nine months or a note agreeing to pay $2,250 in the nine months?

Answer: The maturity value of the interest-bearing note is equal to

$$MV = \$2,000 + (\$2,000 \times .145 \times 9/12) = \$2,217.50$$

The maturity value of the non interest-bearing note is $2,250.

You would prefer to sign the note that requires the smallest amount to be paid at maturity. You would sign the interest-bearing note.   [Section 15-2]

PROBLEM 15-8: You discount a note with a maturity value of $1,000 at the bank. The note matures one year from the day on which it is discounted. The bank uses a 20% discount rate. What interest rate is the bank charging on this loan?

Answer: The proceeds from the note would be:

$$Proceeds = \$1,000 - (\$1,000 \times .20 \times 1) = \$800$$

You receive $800 and pay back $1,000 at the end of one year. This is the equivalent of paying the following interest rate on the $800, one year loan.

$$i = P \times r \times t$$
$$\$200 = \$800 \times r \times 1$$
$$r = \$200 \div \$800 = 25\%$$

You have been charged an interest rate of 25% on a one-year loan of $800.

[Section 15-6]

PROBLEM 15-9: EXE Company accepts a $6,000, sixty-day, 12% note from a customer in settlement of an account receivable. The note is immediately discounted at the bank which charges a 9% discount rate. Show the journal entry to record the discounting of the note.

Answer:

Cash*	6,028.20	
Notes Receivable Discounted.		6,000.00
Interest Revenue.		28.20

MV = $6,000 + ($6,000 × .12 × 60/360) = $6,120

Proceeds = $6,120 − ($6,120 × .09 × 60/360) = $6,028.20

[Section 15-5]

PROBLEM 15-10: On January 1, 19x1, SRW Company accepts a $3,300, five-month, non interest-bearing note in return for a $3,000 loan to a firm. Define the term asked for and compute its value.

(a) What is the maturity value of this note?
(b) What is the principal amount?
(c) What is the amount of interest being charged for the five-month period of the loan?

Answer each of the following questions:

(d) How would acceptance of the note be recorded?
(e) What adjusting entry would be made on 1/31/x1 with regard to this note?
(f) At what value would the note be reported on a 1/31/x1 balance sheet?

Answer:

(a) The maturity value is the amount to be paid when the note matures. The MV = $3,300.
(b) The principal amount is the amount of the loan. The principal amount equals $3,000.
(c) The amount of interest is the difference between the amount paid at maturity and the amount borrowed. The interest amount on this note is $300.
(d) The entry to record the acceptance of the note is

Notes Receivable	3,300	
Discount on Notes Receivable		300
Cash		3,000

(e) The adjusting entry made on 1/31/x1 would recognize interest earned on the note and would reduce the balance in the discount account.

Discount on Notes Receivable ($300/5)	60	
Interest Revenue.		60

(f) The note will be valued at the amount of the Note Receivable less the balance in the Discount on Notes Receivable account. As of 1/31/x1, the note would be valued at

$$\$3,300 - (\$300 - \$60) = \$3,060$$

[Section 15-4]

PROBLEM 15-11: On September 1, 19x8, Sherffield Corporation accepts a $7,600, six-month, 14% note from Loren Company in payment of an account receivable. Prepare the entries to record the acceptance of this note, the adjustments required on 12/31/x8, and the payment of the note by the maker on 3/1/x9. Show how Notes Receivable and any accumulated interest would appear on the 12/31/x8 balance sheet.

Answer:

9/1/x8	Notes Receivable	7,600.00	
	Accounts Receivable.		7,600.00
12/31/x8	Interest Receivable ($7,600 × .14 × 4/12)	354.67	
	Interest Revenue.		354.67
3/1/x9	Cash [$7,600 + ($7,600 × .14 × 6/12)]	8,132.00	
	Notes Receivable		7,600.00
	Interest Receivable		354.67
	Interest Revenue.		177.33

The note and its accumulated interest would appear on the balance sheet as follows

Notes Receivable	$7,600.00
Interest Receivable	354.67

[Section 15-3]

PROBLEM 15-12: Restate Problem 15-11 by describing the note in a non interest-bearing format.

Answer: On September 1, 19x8, Sherffield Corporation accepts a note in which Loren Company agrees to pay $8,132 in six months as settlement of a $7,600 account receivable. Prepare the entries to record the acceptance of this note, the adjustments required on 12/31/x8, and the payment of the note by the maker on 3/1/x9. Show how Notes Receivable and any accumulated interest would appear on the 12/31/x8 balance sheet.

[Section 15-2]

EXAMINATION III (CHAPTERS 11 THROUGH 15)

I. Multiple Choice

Questions 1 through 10 may require the use of present and future value tables. *Answers are rounded to nearest dollar.*

1. Mortimer places $5,000 in an investment for five years. The investment pays 10% simple interest for five years. At the end of five years, the balance in Mortimer's account will equal
   - (a) $5,000
   - (b) $2,500
   - (c) $8,053
   - (d) $7,500
   - (e) $18,954

2. Smiley puts $6,000 in an account that pays 8% compounded quarterly. How much will Smiley have in his account at the end of five years?
   - (a) $8,400
   - (b) $8,816
   - (c) $8,916
   - (d) $8,881
   - (e) none of the above

3. How much must Ima Saver put into an account that pays 12% compounded semiannually in order to have $10,000 at the end of four years?
   - (a) $6,355
   - (b) $6,274
   - (c) $6,232
   - (d) $10,000
   - (e) none of the above

4. Jones can invest $5,000 today in an account that pays 10% compounded semiannually. At the end of five years, he can reinvest the balance in an account paying 16% compounded quarterly for an additional five years. How much will be in the account at the end of ten years?
   - (a) $12,339
   - (b) $17,845
   - (c) $17,644
   - (d) $17,688
   - (e) none of the above

5. The amount that must be deposited into an account today in order to have a desired amount at some future time will
   - (a) increase when interest rates increase all other things equal
   - (b) increase when the future amount desired decreases all other things equal
   - (c) increase when the number of time periods of investment increases all other things equal
   - (d) increase when the interest rates decrease all other things equal
   - (e) none of the above is correct

6. XYZ Corporation must make semiannual deposits into a sinking fund to retire $1,000,000 of bonds at the end of five years. If the sinking fund pays 8% interest compounded semiannually, what must the size of each of the ten deposits be so that the firm can retire the bond issue immediately after making the last deposit?
   - (a) $123,291
   - (b) $250,456
   - (c) $170,456
   - (d) $83,291
   - (e) none of the above

7. Customer A agrees to pay $500 per month for two years for a Gizmo. The payments begin immediately. The customer would normally have to pay 24% compounded monthly to borrow money. What is the selling price of a Gizmo?
   (a) $9,262
   (b) $9,457
   (c) $9,646
   (d) $10,262
   (e) none of the above

8. The present value of an annuity is greater when
   (a) the interest rate is higher all other things equal
   (b) when the annuity is an annuity due rather than an ordinary annuity all other things equal
   (c) when the number of payments is reduced all other things equal
   (d) when the amount of each rent is reduced all other things equal
   (e) none of the above

9. How much will be in an account at the end of ten years, if $10,000 is deposited in the account at the beginning of each year and the account pays 10% compounded annually?
   (a) $145,795
   (b) $159,374
   (c) $175,312
   (d) $185,312
   (e) none of the above

10. Which of the following statements is correct?
    (a) Interest is added ten times to an ordinary annuity of ten rents
    (b) Interest is added ten times to an annuity due of ten rents
    (c) Interest is added nine times to an annuity due of ten rents
    (d) Interest is added eleven times to an annuity due of ten rents
    (e) none of the above is correct

11. Careful Company established a petty cash fund of $200. In replenishing the petty cash fund at the end of the year, the accountant found $27 in the drawer and signed receipts for expenses totaling $169. The entry to record the replenishment of the fund would
    (a) debit Petty Cash for $169
    (b) debit Cash Short and Over for $4
    (c) credit Petty Cash for $173
    (d) credit Cash Short and Over for $4
    (e) credit various expense accounts for $169

Questions 12 through 15 refer to the following information:

In preparing a bank reconciliation for the month of October, the following information is available:

From September 30 Bank Reconciliation:	
Deposits in Transit	$ 400
Outstanding Checks	290
From Company Books:	
Deposits made during October	4,850
Checks written during October	4,150
Book Balance October 31	1,800
Check #5003 recorded at	170
From Bank Statement:	
Deposits credited to account during October	5,100
Checks paid during October	4,050
Service Charge	40
Balance per Bank Statement October 31	2,030
Check #5003 was written for	140

12. Deposits in transit on October 31 were
(a) $650
(b) $250
(c) $150
(d) $0
(e) none of the above

13. Outstanding checks on October 31 totaled
(a) $0
(b) $100
(c) $130
(d) $190
(e) $390

14. The error in recording check #5003 would be
(a) added to the book balance
(b) added to the bank balance
(c) subtracted from the book balance
(d) subtracted from the bank balance
(e) none of the above

15. The adjusted book and bank balance would be
(a) $1,690
(b) $1,790
(c) $1,730
(d) $2,090
(e) none of the above

Questions 16 and 17 relate to the following information:

During 19x1, *the first year of operations*, the Jones and Company sold goods with a gross selling price of $900,000 terms 2/10, n/30. The gross selling price of goods that were returned was $85,000. The firm received $490,000 from customers paying within the discount period and $220,000 from customers who paid after the discount period had expired.

16. What will the balance in Accounts Receivable be at the end of the period, if Jones and Company uses the gross method of accounting for sales and accounts receivable?
(a) $95,000
(b) $105,000
(c) $180,000
(d) $190,000
(e) none of the above

17. What will the balance in Accounts Receivable be at the end of the period, if Jones and Company uses the net method of accounting for sales and accounts receivable?
(a) $176,400
(b) $102,900
(c) $93,100
(d) $87,000
(e) none of the above

Questions 18 through 20 relate to the following information:

Selected information for Easy Credit Corporation is presented below.

Credit Sales	$1,500,000
Accounts written off as uncollectible	35,000
Accounts Receivable balance 1/1/x1	540,000
Payments received on account	1,400,000
Allowance for Uncollectible Accounts balance 1/1/x1	27,000

18. If Easy Credit uses the direct writeoff method of accounting for bad debts the bad debt expense for 19x1 would be
(a) $35,000

(b) $27,000

(c) $100,000

(d) $640,000

(e) none of the above

19. If Easy Credit uses the allowance method of accounting for bad debts and estimates that 5% of accounts receivable will become uncollectible, the bad debt expense for 19x1 would be

(a) $5,000

(b) $30,250

(c) $32,000

(d) $38,250

(e) none of the above

20. If Easy Credit uses the allowance method of accounting for bad debts and estimates that 2% of credit sales will prove uncollectible, bad debt expense will equal

(a) $22,000

(b) $30,000

(c) $38,000

(d) $65,000

(e) none of the above

21. On 10/1/x1, Chelsey Corporation accepted a $5000, 10%, six-month note from Soho Company as full payment of a $5,000 account receivable. Chelsey closes its books on 12/31/x1. Chelsey would make an adjusting entry regarding the note that

(a) debits Cash for $123

(b) debits Interest Revenue for $125

(c) debits Interest Receivable for $125

(d) credits Interest Payable for $83.33

(e) credits Interest Revenue for $83.33

22. On 10/1/x1, Jones and Company accepts a $5,500, six-month note in exchange for $5,000 cash. The value assigned to this note on the 12/31/x1 balance sheet will be

(a) $5,500

(b) $5,250

(c) $5,000

(d) $0 because the note is non-interest bearing

(e) none of the above

Questions 23 through 25 refer to the information below.

Micromedia Corporation accepted a $10,000, 10%, 18-month note from a customer in payment for Micromedia's latest model microscan. On 2/1/x1, the note was accepted. On 8/1/x1, Micromedia discounted the note at the bank. The discount rate charged by the bank was 12%.

23. The maturity value of the note was

(a) $11,200

(b) $11,000

(c) $11,500

(d) $11,800

(e) none of the above

24. The amount of discount charged by the bank on 8/1/x1 would be

(a) $1,150

(b) $1,200

(c) $1,380

(d) $2,070

(e) none of the above

25. The entry to record the discounting of the note will

(a) credit Interest Revenue for $300

(b) credit Interest Revenue for $350

(c) debit Interest Expense for $570
(d) credit Interest Revenue for $120
(e) none of the above

II. Problems

1. Smedley has the opportunity to purchase an Ibacat Corporation bond. The 10% bond would pay Smedley $1,000 at the end of seven years and pays interest semiannually. Smedley wants to earn 12% compounded semiannually on his investments. How much can Smedley pay for the Ibacat bond so that he will earn the 12% desired return on this investment?

2. Ruff'n Ready Retailer buys merchandise from a supplier that sells under the terms 3/10, n/45. Compute the actual interest rate being charged by the supplier.

3. On 5/1/x1, ABC Corporation accepted a $4,000, six-month note from YES Company. ABC Corporation gave YES Corporation $3,500 on the day the note was signed. ABC Corporation closes its books on 6/30/x1. On 7/1/x1, ABC Corporation discounted the note at the bank which charged a discount rate of 10%. YES Corporation paid the note upon its maturity. Make all of the entries required on the books of ABC Corporation with regard to this note.

ANSWERS TO EXAMINATION III

Multiple Choice Questions

1. d	6. d	11. b	16. a	21. c
2. c	7. c	12. c	17. c	22. b
3. b	8. b	13. e	18. a	23. c
4. b	9. c	14. a	19. d	24. c
5. d	10. b	15. b	20. b	25. d

Problems

Problem 1 Present Value of Cash Payments Discounted at 12%:

PV of $1,000 to be received in 14 periods discounted at
6% per period = 1,000(.44230) $442
PV of ordinary annuity of 14 rents of $50
(1,000)(.10)(1/2), discounted at 6% per
period = $50(9.29498)   465
Amount to pay for bond $907

Problem 2 If firm were to buy merchandise with a gross selling price of $1,000, it would pay $30 for the right to postpone paying $970 for 35 days. This is the equivalent of an interest charge of 31.8%.

$$30 = 970(r)(35/360)$$
$$r = .318 \text{ or } 31.8\%$$

Problem 3 The entries to record the activity surrounding the note are as follows:

5/1/x1	Notes Receivable	4,000	
	Cash		3,500
	Discount on Notes Receivable. . . .		500
	To record acceptance of the		
	note.		

6/30/x1	Discount on Notes Receivable	167	
	Interest Revenue		167
	To record interest revenue earned for two months. $500 of interest is earned over six months therefore (500)(2/6) is earned over two months.		
7/1/x1	Cash.	3,867	
	Discount on Notes Receivable	333	
	Notes Receivable Discounted		4,000
	Interest Revenue		200
	To record discounting of note.*		
11/1/x1	Notes Receivable Discounted.	5,000	
	Notes Receivable.		5,000
	To write off note upon settlement		

* *Maturity Value*	*$4,000*
Discount Amount ($4,000 × .10 × 4/12) .	*133*
Proceeds	*$3,867*

16 INVENTORIES: GENERAL REVIEW

THIS CHAPTER IS ABOUT

☑ **Defining and Classifying Inventories**
☑ **Inventory Systems**
☑ **Costs Included in Inventory**
☑ **Purchase Discounts**
☑ **Counting the Ending Inventory**
☑ **Cost Flow Assumptions**
☑ **Choosing a Cost Flow Assumption**

16-1. Defining and Classifying Inventories

Inventories are goods held for sale or use in production of goods. An inventory may be of raw materials to be used directly in the production of goods (Raw Materials Inventory), goods in production but not yet complete (Work-in-Process Inventory), finished goods held for resale (Finished Goods Inventory), or supplies used by the firm. The total value of the items in an inventory is shown on the balance sheet as a current asset. Manufacturing companies will generally have all four kinds of inventory. Non-manufacturing firms will not have Raw Materials or Work-in-Process Inventories.

16-2. Inventory Systems

Inventory records can be kept on a periodic or perpetual basis. The periodic system involves less record keeping than does the perpetual system but it also provides less information.

A. Under a periodic inventory system, the Inventory account is *not* updated when goods are purchased or sold (used).

A periodic inventory system updates the Inventory account on a periodic basis. Purchases of goods are debited to the Purchases account not to Inventory. No entry is made when goods are sold or used. At the end of the period, a physical count is taken to determine the value of the goods remaining. The balance in the Inventory account is then adjusted to reflect this new amount. The adjustment of the inventory account should be made as an adjusting entry to facilitate preparation of the financial statements.

B. Under a perpetual inventory system, the Inventory account is updated each time goods are purchased or sold (used).

Under a perpetual inventory system, the Inventory account is debited when goods are purchased and credited when goods are sold. Subsidiary records are kept for each inventory item so that the firm knows the quantity of each item that remains in the inventory. The system signals when the stocks are low. At the end of the accounting period, a physical count of the inventory can be checked against the records to determine if goods are missing.

EXAMPLE 16-1: Roby Corporation uses a perpetual inventory system. Its inventory consists of a single item, widgets. The company began the accounting period with fifty widgets that cost $2.00 each. During the period, it acquired 100 additional widgets on credit at a cost of $2.00 each. The firm sold 120 widgets on credit at a selling price of $5.00 each. At the end of the period, the firm counted the inventory and found that 30 widgets remained in stock. The entries to record the inventory activity appear below.

Inventory	200	
Accounts Payable		200
To record the purchase.		
Accounts Receivable	600	
Sales		600
To record the sale.		
Cost of Goods Sold (120 @ $2)	240	
Inventory		240
To record the reduction in inventory.		

When the physical count is made at the end of the period and goods are missing an adjustment must be made to the inventory account. Suppose that only 27 widgets remained instead of the expected 30. The adjustment would be recorded as follows:

| Loss Due to Inventory Shrinkage | 6 | |
| Inventory (3 @ $2) | | 6 |

1. Under the perpetual inventory system, individual inventory records are kept. These records show the number of units received (purchased), issued (sold or used), and the current balance. The running balance on the inventory record allows the firm to reorder those items whose stock has run low. The record also allows the firm to differentiate between those items that are sold and those that disappear for some other reason. A inventory record for the widgets in Example 16-1 is shown in Exhibit 16-1.

EXHIBIT 16-1: Inventory Record

INVENTORY RECORD									
Item Widgets									
	Received			Issued			Balance		
	Units	Unit Cost	Total	Units	Unit Cost	Total	Units	Unit Cost	Total
Beg. Balance							50	$2	$100
Purchase	100	$2	$200				150	$2	$300
Sale				120	$2	$240	30	$2	$ 60
Missing				3	$2	$ 6	27	$2	$ 54

2. Computers can maintain a perpetual inventory system very efficiently. Since the system requires so much record keeping, computers can save a lot of time.

Businesses now have cash registers connected to computers which automatically update records as items are sold. The warehouse can also have terminals to update records as items arrive. The perpetual system is becoming more and more popular as the use of the computer expands.

16-3. Costs Included in Inventory

Inventories include the cost of acquiring or producing items and the cost of transporting the items to the firm's warehouse. Warehousing expenses, expenses of the purchasing department, and interest expense on money borrowed to carry inventory are not included in inventory costs because they are too difficult to allocate individual items.

EXAMPLE 16-2: Frost Corporation acquired 300 gooey ducks for its inventory. The purchase price of each duck was $30. Freight paid on shipping the ducks to the warehouse was $1,200. The total cost of acquiring the ducks was therefore $9,000 (300 × $30) plus $1,200 or $10,200. The unit cost assigned to the ducks in the inventory would be $34 ($10,200 ÷ 300).

16-4. Purchase Discounts

Sometimes sellers offer early payment discounts. These purchase discounts can be accounted for either under a gross or net method. The value of inventory will depend on the method used.

A. The gross method of accounting for purchases does not recognize discounts until they are actually taken.

The gross method of accounting for purchases records items at their full purchase price. Under this method, it is assumed that discounts for the most part will not be taken and thus the full amount reflects the value of inventory.

1. *Periodic inventory system.* The Purchases account is debited for the full purchase price. If payment is made within the discount period, an account titled Purchase Discounts is credited. The Purchase Discount account is a contra purchases account and reduces the value of Net Purchases and therefore Cost of Goods Available for Sale.
2. *Perpetual inventory system.* The Inventory account is debited for the full purchase price. If payment is made within the discount period, Inventory is credited for the amount of the discount. Under this system Inventory is given one valuation if the discount is taken and a higher valuation if the discount is missed. Theoretically, this makes no sense.

EXAMPLE 16-3: Bennett Corporation maintains a periodic inventory system. The firm purchased 100 gizmos at a price of $5 each and under the terms 2/10, n/30. The entries to record the purchase of the gizmos and payment made after the discount period are as follows:

Purchases	500	
Accounts Payable		500
To record the purchase.		
Accounts Payable.	500	
Cash		500
To record the payment.		

EXAMPLE 16-4: Assume that Bennett Corporation in Example 16-3 paid within the discount period. The entry to record the payment would be as follows:

periodic

Accounts Payable.......................	500	
Purchase Discounts (500 × 2%)..........		10
Cash		490

EXAMPLE 16-5: Assume that Bennett Corporation in Example 16-3 maintained a perpetual inventory system. The entry to record the purchase would be as follows:

Inventory.............................	500	
Accounts Payable.....................		500

The entry to record the payment after the discount period would be

Accounts Payable.......................	500	
Cash		500

The entry to record the payment within the discount period would be

perpetual

Accounts Payable.......................	500	
Inventory		10
Cash		490

B. The net method of accounting records purchases at their discounted price.

The net method of accounting for purchases records items at their net purchase price. Under this method it is assumed that discounts for the most part will be taken and therefore the net amount reflects the value at which inventory should be recorded. Under both the periodic and perpetual inventory systems discounts not taken are recorded in an account titled Purchases Discounts Lost which is an interest or other expense account.

EXAMPLE 16-6: Kohli Corporation maintains a periodic inventory system and uses the net method to record purchases. The firm purchases 100 gizmos at a price of $5 each and under the terms 2/10, n/30. The entry to record the purchase would be as follows:

Purchases ($500 × .98)..................	490	
Accounts Payable.....................		490

The entry to record the payment within the discount period would be

Accounts Payable.......................	490	
Cash		490

The entry to record the payment after the discount period would be

Accounts Payable.......................	490	
Purchase Discounts Lost.................	10	
Cash		500

EXAMPLE 16-7: Assume that Kohli Corporation in Example 16-6 maintains a perpetual inventory system. The entry to record the purchase would be

Inventory.............................	490	
Accounts Payable.....................		490

The entry to record payment within the discount period would be

Accounts Payable.	490	
Cash		490

The entry to record payment after the discount period would be

Accounts Payable.	490	
Purchase Discounts Lost	10	
Cash		500

C. The net method of accounting for purchases and purchase discounts is theoretically preferable.

The net method is theoretically preferable because it values inventory at the price the seller is willing to accept in exchange for the merchandise at the time of sale. The extra amount is a fee or interest the seller is charging to allow payment to be made after the discount period.

16-5. Counting the Ending Inventory

Correct inventory valuation requires an accurate count of the items in the inventory which may be more difficult than it appears. Counting all the items in the warehouse is just a start. However, there may be items in the warehouse that do not belong to the company and these items must be excluded from the inventory count. There may also be items that are not in the warehouse that do belong to the company. These items must be included in the count.

A. Goods in transit to the firm *purchased* FOB *shipping point* must be *included* in the inventory count.

When goods are purchased FOB shipping point, the title of the goods is transferred to the buyer as soon as the goods are loaded on the carrier. The goods become a part of the buyer's inventory even though they have not arrived at the warehouse. An accurate count requires that these items be included.

B. Goods in transit to the firm *purchased* FOB *destination* must be *excluded* from the inventory count.

When goods are purchased FOB destination, this means that the title of the goods is transferred to the buyer when the goods reach the warehouse. Since the goods are in transit and have not yet arrived in the warehouse, they must be excluded from the inventory count.

C. Goods in transit which were *sold* FOB *shipping* point must be *excluded* from the inventory count.

Goods in transit which were sold FOB shipping point had their title transferred to the buyer as soon as the goods were loaded on the carrier. These items are no longer a part of inventory and must be excluded from the count.

D. Goods in transit which were *sold* FOB *destination* must be *included* in the inventory count.

When goods are sold FOB destination, the title is not transferred until the items reach the buyer's warehouse. As long as the goods are in transit, they must be included in the inventory count.

E. Goods out on consignment are included in the inventory count.

The title to an item out on consignment is not transferred until the item is sold. Until then, the consignee (person holding the goods) has the right to return the merchandise. Therefore, these items must be included in the inventory count until sold.

F. Goods accepted on consignment are excluded from the inventory count.

The title to goods in the warehouse that have been accepted on consignment remains with the consignor. These goods must be excluded from the inventory count of the consignee.

The firm cannot value its ending inventory by simply counting the goods in the warehouse. The accountant must scrutinize (examine) those goods carefully and reduce the count by any items that do not belong to the firm. Goods accepted on consignment are in the warehouse but do not belong to the firm and cannot be included in ending inventory. Units in transit to and from the company must be examined to determine if the firm holds title to them. Any item in transit to the firm under shipping terms FOB shipping point must be included. Goods sold and in transit terms FOB destination still belong to the firm and must be included. Goods out on consignment must be included.

EXAMPLE 16-8: XYZ Company has the following units in its inventory count

Goods in the warehouse	15,000 units
Goods in Transit to XYZ Company:	
Terms FOB shipping point	500
Terms FOB destination	200
Goods Sold and in Transit to customer:	
Terms FOB shipping point	400
Terms FOB destination	100
Goods Out on Consignment	600
Goods in Warehouse Accepted on Consignment	800

XYZ Company's correct ending inventory count is determined as follows:

Goods in warehouse	15,000 units
Less items in warehouse that do not belong to XYZ:	
Goods accepted on consignment	800
Goods in warehouse that belong to XYZ	14,200 units
Add: Items not in warehouse that belong to XYZ:	
Goods in transit to XYZ terms FOB shipping point	500
Goods in transit sold FOB destination	100
Goods out on consignment	600
Ending Inventory	15,400 units

G. An incorrect inventory count affects both the balance sheet and income statement.

Correct counting of the inventory is very important because the ending inventory figure is reported on the balance sheet and is used to compute the cost of goods sold on the income statement. Errors will have multiple affects on the firm's financial statements.

EXAMPLE 16-9: Hogue Corporation would have reported the following information for 19x1 and 19x2, if ending inventory was correctly measured.

	19x1	19x2
Sales	$20,000	$20,000
Beginning Inventory	5,000	5,000
Ending Inventory	5,000	5,000
Purchases	12,000	12,000

The correct calculations for gross profit on the income statements for both years would be as follows:

Correct Income Statements

	For Years Ended	
	12/31/x1	12/31/x2
Sales	$20,000	$20,000
Beginning Inventory	$ 5,000	$ 5,000
Purchases	12,000	12,000
Cost of Goods Available for Sale	$17,000	$17,000
Less Ending Inventory	5,000	5,000
Cost of Goods Sold	$12,000	$12,000
Gross Profit	$ 8,000	$ 8,000

Assume now that the firm failed to include 100 of the inventory items with a unit cost of $10 in the ending inventory account on 12/31/x1. All the financial statements would be affected by this error. Assuming that the correct ending inventory count was made at the end of 19x2, the calculations of the gross profit on the income statement would be as follows:

Reported Income Statement

	For Years Ended	
	12/31/x1	12/31/x2
Sales	$20,000	$20,000
Beginning Inventory	$ 5,000	$ 4,000
Purchases	12,000	12,000
Cost of Goods Available for Sale	$17,000	$16,000
Less Ending Inventory	4,000	5,000
Cost of Goods Sold	$13,000	$11,000
Gross Profit	$ 7,000	$ 9,000

Understating ending inventory in 19x1 also causes cost of goods sold to be overstated by $1,000 in that year. Gross profit and net income will be understated by $1,000 in 19x1. The understatement of ending inventory in 19x1 means that beginning inventory in 19x2 will be understated by $1,000. Failure to include all items in the count means the current assets would be understated by $1,000, on the 12/31/x1 balance sheet. Understatement of 19x1 profit means that owner's equity would also be understated as of 12/31/x1. The financial ratios would also show incorrect figures as a result, not to mention the SCFP. An error in valuing the ending inventory will translate into one inaccurate balance sheet and two incorrect income statements.

16-6. Cost Flow Assumptions

The value of ending inventory is found by assigning a unit cost to each item in the ending inventory. This is a simple process, if prices remain unchanged. It is more difficult, if prices fluctuate.

EXAMPLE 16-10: Noble Corporation sells one item—shmoos. The firm begins the year with 1,000 shmoos. It acquires 8,000 additional shmoos in three separate purchases. At the end of the year, there are 3,500 shmoos left in the warehouse. A summary of the inventory activity would be as follows:

Total	Units		Unit Cost
Beginning Inventory	1,000	$10	$ 10,000
Purchase # 1	3,000	14	42,000
Purchase # 2	2,000	16	32,000
Purchase # 3	3,000	18	54,000
Available for Sale	9,000		$138,000
Ending Inventory	3,500		
Units Sold	5,500		

Valuation of the 3,500 units in the ending inventory becomes a question of "which units are left in the warehouse?" Are the units that remain $10 units, $14 units, $16 units, $18 units or some combination? Which units remain in the ending inventory? What units did the firm sell? Usually the firm will be unable to specifically identify the units sold and the units remaining. A cost flow assumption must be made.

A. The weighted-average cost flow assumption suggests that the average cost be assigned to the units sold and left in the ending inventory.

The weighted-average cost flow assumption implies that the items in an inventory are sold at random. This means that the items in the ending inventory could include some of the original items from the beginning balance and some from each purchase made during the period. Rather than trying to place a particular cost on each item, the items are assigned an average cost.

1. When an weighted-average cost flow assumption is used with a periodic inventory system, the average unit cost is computed at the end of the period. The formula used to compute the average unit cost is as follows:

AVERAGE UNIT COST $\text{Average unit cost} = \dfrac{\text{Cost of goods available for sale}}{\text{Number of units available for sale}}$

The ending inventory is then computed by multiplying the average unit cost times the number of units in the ending inventory. The cost of goods sold is computed by subtracting the value of the ending inventory from the cost of goods available for sale.

EXAMPLE 16-11: If Noble Corporation in Example 16-10 uses the weighted-average cost flow assumption, it will value ending inventory and cost of goods sold as follows:

$$\text{Average unit cost} = \frac{\$138,000}{9,000} = \$15.3333$$

$$\text{Ending inventory} = 3,500 \times \$15.3333 = \$53,667$$

$$\text{Cost of goods sold} = \$138,000 - \$53,667 = \$84,333$$

The cost of goods sold could also be computed by multiplying the average unit cost times the number of units sold. This is risky because the cost figure is rounded. The value of ending inventory plus the cost of goods sold may not equal the value of the cost of goods available for sale. It is best to compute the cost of goods sold by subtracting ending inventory from the cost of goods available for sale. Use the alternate method as a check.

2. When the weighted-average cost flow assumption is used with a perpetual inventory system, a new average unit cost is computed each time a purchase is made. The average unit cost will therefore change each time a purchase is made at a cost different from the current average unit cost.

EXAMPLE 16-12: Noble Corporation in Example 16-10 uses a perpetual inventory system. The 5,500 units were sold as follows:

1,500 after Purchase #1 but before Purchase #2

2,000 after Purchase #2 but before Purchase #3

2,000 after Purchase #3

The perpetual inventory record would appear as follows:

INVENTORY RECORD

Item _____Shmoos_____

	Received			Issued			Balance		
	Units	Unit Cost $	Total $	Units	Unit Cost $	Total $	Units	Unit Cost $	Total $
Beg Bal							1,000	10	10,000
Pur #1	3,000	14	42,000				4,000	13	52,000
Sale #1				1,500	13	19,500	2,500	13	32,500
Pur #2	2,000	16	32,000				4,500	14.33	64,500
Sale #2				2,000	14.33	28,667	2,500	14.33	35,833
Pur #3	3,000	18	54,000				5,500	16.33	89,833
Sale #3				2,000	16.33	32,666	3,500	16.33	57,167

The value of the ending inventory is computed as $57,167. The cost of goods sold would equal $80,833 ($138,000 − $57,167). The cost of goods sold could also be computed by simply adding each of the cost of the individual sales, $19,500 + $28,667 + $32,666*, which also equals $80,833. (*Again, be careful of errors due to rounding). The values in the ending inventory and cost of goods sold with the perpetual inventory system are different from those with the periodic inventory system because the average unit cost changed with each group of items sold. Therefore, the ending inventory balance was also changed.

B. The First-in, First-out (FIFO) cost flow assumption presumes that the oldest units are sold before the newest units.

As the name implies, this cost flow assumption presumes that the first items into the warehouse are the first out. This assumption probably corresponds to the way most firms actually try to flow goods out of their warehouses. This would be especially true of firms that stocked perishable items. Goods sold are assigned the cost of the oldest inventory available. This leaves the ending inventory to be valued at the most recent costs.

EXAMPLE 16-13: Assume that Noble Corporation in Example 16-10 uses a periodic inventory system and the FIFO cost flow assumption. The value of the ending inventory and cost of goods sold would be computed as follows: The ending inventory consists of the newest 3,500 units so it must contain

$$3000 @ \$18 = \$54,000$$
$$500 @ \quad 16 = \underline{\quad 8,000}$$
$$= \$62,000$$

The cost of goods sold equals CGAS minus the ending inventory

$$CGS = \$138,000 - \$62,000 = \$76,000$$

The cost of goods sold can also be computed by determining which units were sold. The oldest 5,500 units were sold so the cost of goods sold must equal

$$1,000 @ \$10 = \$10,000$$
$$3,000 @ \$14 = \$42,000$$
$$1,500 @ \$16 = \underline{\$24,000}$$
$$\$76,000$$

Since the unit cost figures are not rounded, the cost of goods sold amount should be the same under either approach.

EXAMPLE 16-14: If the Noble Corporation in Example 16-10 uses a perpetual inventory system and the FIFO cost flow assumption, the perpetual inventory record would appear as follows:

INVENTORY RECORD

Item _____ *Shmoos* _____

	Receipts			Issued			Balance		
	Units	Unit Cost $	Total $	Units	Unit Cost $	Total $	Units	Unit Cost $	Total $
Beg Bal							1,000	10	10,000
Pur #1	3,000	14	42,000				1,000 3,000	10 14	10,000 42,000
Sale #1				1,000 500	10 14	10,000 7,000	2,500	14	35,000
Pur #2	2,000	16	32,000				2,500 2,000	14 16	35,000 32,000
Sale #2				2,000	14	28,000	500 2,000	14 16	7,000 32,000
Pur #3	3,000	18	54,000				500 2,000 3,000	14 16 18	7,000 32,000 54,000
Sale #3				500 1,500	14 16	7,000 24,000	500 3,000	16 18	8,000 54,000

The ending inventory is valued at $62,000. Cost of Goods Sold can be found by adding up the cost of issued units and equals $76,000. Since the same units were sold at the same cost under both the periodic and perpetual system, the values for cost of goods sold and ending inventory are identical.

C. The Last-in, First-out (LIFO) cost flow assumption presumes that the newest units are sold before the oldest units.

As the title suggests, the LIFO cost flow assumption suggests that the newest items are the first sold. This means that the most recent prices are used to value the cost of goods sold.

EXAMPLE 16-15: Assume that Noble Corporation in Example 16-10 uses a periodic inventory system and the LIFO cost flow assumption. The ending inventory would contain the oldest 3,500 units. The ending inventory would be assigned the value of

$$1,000 @ \$10 = \$10,000$$
$$2,500 @ \$14 = \underline{35,000}$$
$$\$45,000$$

The cost of goods sold would be equal to the CGAS minus the value placed on the ending inventory.

$$CGS = \$138,000 - \$45,000 = \$93,000$$

The cost of goods sold consists of the 5,500 most recently purchased units.

$$3,000 \ @ \ \$18 = \$54,000$$
$$2,000 \ @ \ \$16 = 32,000$$
$$500 \ @ \ \$14 = \underline{7,000}$$
$$\$93,000$$

EXAMPLE 16-16: Assume that Noble Corporation in Example 16-10 uses a perpetual inventory system and the LIFO cost flow assumption. The perpetual inventory record would appear as follows:

INVENTORY RECORD

Item _____ Shmoos _____

		Receipts			Issues			Balance	
	Units	Unit Cost $	Total $	Units	Unit Cost $	Total $	Units	Unit Cost $	Total $
Beg Bal							1,000	10	10,000
Pur #1	3,000	14	42,000				1,000 3,000	10 14	10,000 42,000
Sale #1				1,500	14	21,000	1,000 1,500	10 14	10,000 21,000
Pur #2	2,000	16	32,000				1,000 1,500 2,000	10 14 16	10,000 21,000 32,000
Sale #2				2,000	16	32,000	1,000 1,500	10 14	10,000 21,000
Pur #3	3,000	18	54,000				1,000 1,500 3,000	10 14 18	10,000 21,000 54,000
Sale #3				2,000	18	36,000	1,000 1,500 1,000	10 14 18	10,000 21,000 18,000

The ending inventory equals $49,000 ($10,000 + $21,000 + $18,000). The cost of goods sold equals $89,000. The values for cost of goods sold are different under the periodic and perpetual inventory systems because different items were assumed to be sold at different costs. Because of this, the items in ending inventory also have different values.

16-7. Choosing a Cost Flow Assumption

Firms may choose any of the cost flow assumptions described in this chapter. Once chosen, the cost flow assumption should not be changed unless the firm can demonstrate that the new assumption better represents the results of activities. There is no rule that says that a firm must choose a cost flow assumption that corresponds to the way goods actually flow out of the warehouse. The firm will make the decision on the basis of the effect the method has on the financial statements and the taxes the company must pay. The tax code requires that the firm use the same cost flow method for reporting to owners as it uses on the tax return.

A. The first consideration in choosing a cost flow assumption is its affect on the value of ending inventory and cost of goods sold.

A review of the ending inventory and cost of goods sold values (Examples 16-11 through 16-16) under a periodic inventory system with each cost flow assumption appears below. Some of the advantages and disadvantages to be considered under each method can be seen from these numbers.

	Ending Inventory	CGS
FIFO	$62,000	$76,000
Average Cost	$53,667	$84,333
LIFO	$45,000	$93,000

The examples occur during a time of rising prices. The results indicate that during such periods

1. LIFO gives the highest cost of goods because the newest, most expensive units are assumed to be sold. It gives the lowest ending inventory figure because the oldest, least expensive units are assumed to remain in the inventory. Therefore, LIFO will also provide the lowest net income because the expense figure is the greatest. Firms which have a high net income prefer LIFO during periods of rising prices because it minimizes the net income and, more importantly, income taxes.
2. FIFO results in the lowest cost of goods sold figure because it assumes the oldest, least expensive units are sold. It maximizes the value placed on ending inventory because the newest, most expensive items remain. Firms attempting to maximize reported profits and total assets might choose FIFO even though the choice increases the income taxes they pay.

B. There are theoretical tradeoffs between LIFO and FIFO.

There are advantages and disadvantages to using either the FIFO or LIFO methods depending on which financial statement the user is relying on for information.

1. LIFO places the most recent unit costs on the income statement as cost of goods sold. The cost of goods sold figure, therefore, more closely reflects the cost of replacing the inventory sold. FIFO places old costs on the income statement which gives a cost of goods sold figure that may greatly understate the cost of replacing the goods sold. A firm must replace what it sells, if it is to continue business. Readers of the income statement want to know if the selling price of the products covers the cost of replacing the items sold plus the other costs incurred by the firm. LIFO gives the more relevant figure for cost of goods sold.
2. FIFO, on the other hand, places the most recent unit costs on the balance sheet as inventory. The value assigned to the inventory more closely reflects the inventory's current value. LIFO accumulates old cost amounts on the balance sheet. If the LIFO method is used for twenty years, it is conceivable some of the inventory may be valued at twenty-year old prices. FIFO gives the more relevant value for inventory on the balance sheet.
3. Footnotes to financial statements should explain the tradeoffs between methods. The footnotes should explain what the cost of goods sold figure would have been if recent purchase costs had been shown when using the FIFO cost flow assumption. Readers can then make their assessment of the real net income for the year. The footnotes should reveal the current value of inventory when using the LIFO cost flow assumption. Readers could then make a true assessment of the current assets held by the firm.

EXAMPLE 16-17: Noble Company in Example 16-10 uses the LIFO cost flow assumption. The firm's reported cost of goods sold was $52,000. The ending inventory totaled $15,000. The notes to the financial statements indicate that ending inventory would have been

$21,000 if current costs had been used to value the ending inventory. What would the CGS have been if the FIFO cost flow assumption had been used?

CGS — LIFO.		$52,000
End. Inv. — Current Costs	$21,000	
End. Inv. — LIFO.	15,000	
Diff. End. Inv.		6,000
CGS — FIFO.		$46,000

The cost flow assumption gives us a method of allocating the cost of goods available for sale between the units that are sold and the units that remain in the ending inventory. If the most recent costs had been placed in the ending inventory (FIFO cost flow assumption), the ending inventory figure would have been $6,000 higher. If the additional $6,000 of the cost of goods available for sale were allocated to ending inventory, then the cost of goods sold would be $6,000 lower. The cost of goods sold would have equaled $46,000 rather than $52,000.

RAISE YOUR GRADES

Can you explain...?

☑ what kind of items may be included in a manufacturing firm's inventory
☑ how inventories are classified on the balance sheet
☑ how a periodic inventory system differs from a perpetual inventory system
☑ what costs are included in inventory
☑ what a purchase discount represents
☑ how the net method of accounting for inventory purchases differs from the gross method
☑ what items are included in an inventory count
☑ what items are excluded from an inventory count
☑ the three cost flow assumptions
☑ why using a LIFO cost flow assumption minimizes income taxes paid during a period of rising prices
☑ how undervaluation of inventory affects the income statement and balance sheet

SUMMARY

1. An inventory may consist of finished goods, raw materials, work-in-process, and supplies.
2. Inventories are classified on the balance sheet as current assets.
3. Under a periodic inventory system, the inventory account is not updated as goods are purchased or sold.
4. Under the periodic inventory system, a Purchases account is debited when goods are purchased. Adjustments are made to the Inventory account only at the end of the period after a physical count has been made.
5. Under a perpetual inventory system, the Inventory account is updated each time goods are purchased or sold.
6. Under a perpetual inventory system, a physical count is taken at the end of the period to verify the balance in the Inventory account.
7. Under the perpetual inventory system, an inventory record is maintained for each type of inventory. This record alerts the firm to low stock levels, unit costs, and quantities of inventory missing.

8. Computers have increased the efficiency of using the perpetual inventory system.

9. Inventories include the costs of acquiring or producing goods and transporting goods to the firm's warehouse.

10. Expenses too difficult to allocate to individual items are not included in inventory.

11. Purchase discounts are offered by sellers in exchange for early payment.

12. The gross method of accounting for purchase discounts assumes that the discount will most likely not be taken.

13. Under the gross method, the Purchases (or Inventory) account is debited for the full purchase price. If the discount is taken the Purchase Discounts (or Inventory) account is credited for the amount of the discount.

14. The net method of accounting for purchase discounts assumes that the discounts will most likely be taken.

15. Under the net method, the Purchases (or Inventory) account is debited for the discounted amount. If the discount is not taken, the Purchase Discount Lost account is debited for the amount of the discount.

16. The net method of accounting for purchase discounts is theoretically preferable because it values inventory at the true selling price of the item. The amount of the discount lost is really interest charged for being allowed to pay after the discount period.

17. Goods purchased FOB shipping point or sold FOB destination must be included in the inventory count while in transit.

18. Goods purchased FOB destination or sold FOB shipping point must be excluded from the inventory count while in transit.

19. Goods out on consignment are included in the inventory count.

20. An incorrect inventory count affects the amount shown for the current assets on the balance sheet.

21. An incorrect inventory count gives rise to incorrect cost of goods sold and net income figures on the income statement.

22. The weighted-average cost flow assumption assigns an average cost to goods sold and remaining in ending inventory.

23. The average unit cost is equal to the cost of goods available for sale divided by the number of units available for sale.

24. The FIFO cost flow assumption suggests that the goods first into the warehouse are the first sold.

25. The LIFO cost flow assumption suggests that the last goods into the warehouse are the first sold.

26. The LIFO cost flow assumption gives the most relevant figure for cost of goods sold.

27. The FIFO cost flow assumption gives the most relevant value of inventory on the balance sheet.

28. Footnotes to financial statements should explain the tradeoffs between methods.

RAPID REVIEW

1. XYZ Corporation acquired merchandise inventory with a gross selling price of $10,000 terms 2/10, n/30. What value will be placed on the inventory acquired if the firm uses the gross method of accounting for purchases and the discount is missed?

2. What value will be placed on the inventory described in Question #1 above, if the gross method is used and payment is made within the discount period?

3. What value will be placed on the inventory described in Question #1 above, if the firm uses the net method and the discount is missed?

4. What value will be placed on the inventory described in Question #1 above, if the firm uses the net method and payment is made within the discount period?

5. The (periodic/perpetual) inventory system provides continuously updated inventory information.

6. The (periodic/perpetual) inventory system provides a continuously updated cost of goods sold figure.

7. The (periodic/perpetual) inventory system is less costly to operate.

8. Indicate which of the following inventory related costs are included in the inventory account:
   (*a*) purchase price
   (*b*) purchasing department salaries
   (*c*) heat for the warehouse
   (*d*) transportation cost to bring goods to the warehouse
   (*e*) purchasing department overhead
   (*f*) cost of telephone calls to hurry a shipment
   (*g*) interest on inventory loan from the bank

9. If ending inventory is overvalued, the cost of goods sold will be (overstated/understated), net income will be (overstated/understated), total assets will be (overstated/understated), and owners' equity will be (overstated/understated) in the year in which the error is made.

10. Goods purchased FOB shipping point and in transit (should/should not) be included in the ending inventory count.

11. Goods sold FOB shipping point and in transit (should/should not) be included in the ending inventory count.

12. Goods on consignment belong to the (consignor/consignee).

Questions 13 through 21 refer to the following information:

XYZ Corporation began the year with 100 thingees at a unit cost of $15 each. The firm made three purchases during the year. The beginning inventory and purchases are described below.

Beginning Inventory	100 @ $15 =	$1,500
Purchase #1	150 @ $16 =	2,400
Purchase #2	75 @ $20 =	1,500
Purchase #3	50 @ $21 =	1,050
	375	$6,450
Units in Ending Inventory	75	
Units Sold	300	

13. The average cost of a unit during the year was _____.

14. If the firm uses a periodic inventory system and a weighted-average cost flow assumption, the value of the ending inventory would be _____.

15. If the firm uses a periodic inventory system and a weighted-average cost flow assumption, the cost of goods sold would be _____.

16. If the firm uses a periodic inventory system and a FIFO cost flow assumption, the value of ending inventory would be _____.

17. If the firm uses a periodic inventory system and a FIFO cost flow assumption, the cost of goods sold would be _____.

18. If the firm uses a periodic inventory system and a LIFO cost flow assumption, the value of ending inventory would be _____.

19. If the firm uses a periodic inventory system and a LIFO cost flow assumption, the cost of goods sold would be _____.

20. Which method maximizes reported profits? Why?

21. Which method minimizes income tax expense? Why?

Answers:

1. $10,000 [Section 16-4A]
2. .98 × $10,000 = $9,800 [Section 16-4A]
3. $9,800 [Section 16-4B]

4. $9,800 [Section 16-4B]
5. perpetual [Section 16-2B]
6. perpetual [Section 16-2B]
7. periodic [Section 16-2A]
8. a; d [Section 16-3]
9. understated; overstated; overstated; overstated [Section 16-5]
10. should [Section 16-5A]
11. should not [Section 16-5C]
12. consignor [Section 16-5E]
13. $6,450/375 = $17.20 [Section 16-6A]
14. $17.20 × 75 = $1,290 [Section 16-6A]
15. $6,450 − $1,290 = $5,160 [Section 16-6A]
16. ($21 × 50) + ($20 × 25) = $1,550 [Section 16-6B]
17. $6,450 − $1,550 = $4,900 [Section 16-6B]
18. $15 × 75 = $1,125 [Section 16-6C]
19. $6,450 − $1,125 = $5,325 [Section 16-6C]
20. FIFO; FIFO gives the lowest CGS. [Section 16-7A]
21. LIFO; LIFO gives the highest CGS and lowest taxable income. [Section 16-7A]

SOLVED PROBLEMS

Problems 16-1 through 16-3 refer to the information below.

XYZ Corporation began the accounting period with 1,500 mightymites which cost $20 each. Mightymite activity is summarized below.

	Units	Unit Cost	Total
Beginning Balance	1,500	$20	$30,000
Sale #1	500		
Purchase #1	1,000	19	19,000
Sale #2	800		
Purchase #2	400	16	6,400
Sale #3	300		

The selling price of units sold is $25. The units are sold and purchased on account. A physical count at the end of the year showed an ending inventory of 1,280 units.

PROBLEM 16-1: Prepare the entries to record the acquisition of inventory, the sales, and the entries at the end of the period to record cost of goods sold and correct the inventory account if the firm uses a periodic inventory system with weighted-average cost flow assumption.

Answer: The entries would be as follows:

Accounts Receivable (500 × $25)	12,500	
Sales		12,500
To record Sale #1.		
Purchases	19,000	
Accounts Payable		19,000
To record Purchase #1.		

Accounts Receivable (800 × $25).	20,000	
Sales		20,000
To record Sale #2.		
Purchases	6,400	
Accounts Payable		6,400
To record Purchase #2.		
Accounts Receivable (300 × $25)	7,500	
Sales		7,500
To record Sale #3.		

End-of-Period Adjustments

Inventory (19,000 + 6,400).	25,400	
Purchases		25,400
To add purchases to inventory account.		
Cost of Goods Sold.	30,948	
Inventory		30,948

Average unit cost = $55,400 ÷ 2,900 = $19.103

Ending inventory = 1,280 × $19.103 = $24,452

Cost of goods sold = $55,400 − $24,452 = $30,948   **[Section 16-2 and 16-6]**

PROBLEM 16-2: XYZ Corporation uses a perpetual inventory system and a weighted-average cost flow assumption. Prepare an inventory record for the mightymites and record the required inventory activity.

INVENTORY RECORD									
Item *Mightymites*									
	Received			**Issues**			**Balance**		
	Units	Unit Cost	Total	Units	Unit Cost	Total	Units	Unit Cost	Total
Balance							1,500	20.00	30,000
Sale #1				500	20.00	10,000	1,000	20.00	20,000
Pur #1	1,000	19.00	19,000				2,000	19.50	39,000
Sale #2				800	19.50	15,600	1,200	19.50	23,400
Pur #2	400	16.00	6,400				1,600	18.625	29,800
Sale #3				300	18.625	5,588	1,300	18.625	24,212
Missing				20	18.625	372	1,280	18.625	23,840

Answer: The entries would appear as follows:

Accounts Receivable	12,500	
Sales		12,500
To record Sale #1.		
Cost of Goods Sold.	10,000	
Inventory		10,000
To record cost of goods sold.		

Inventory	19,000	
Accounts Payable		19,000
To record Purchase #1.		
Accounts Receivable	20,000	
Sales		20,000
To record Sale #2.		
Cost of Goods Sold.	15,600	
Inventory		15,600
To record cost of goods sold.		
Inventory	6,400	
Accounts Payable		6,400
To record Purchase #2.		
Accounts Receivable	7,500	
Sales		7,500
To record Sales #3.		
Cost of Goods Sold.	5,588	
Inventory		5,588
To record cost of goods sold.		

End-of-Period Adjustments

Loss Due to Inventory Shrinkage	372	
Inventory		372
To account for missing units.		

[Sections 16-2 and 16-6]

PROBLEM 16-3: Consider the treatment of missing units in Problems 16-1 and 16-2.

(*a*) How were the missing units accounted for in Problem 16-1?
(*b*) How were the missing units accounted for in Problem 16-2?
(*c*) Which method gives you better information?

Answer:

(*a*) The missing units are not specifically accounted for under a periodic inventory system. All units available for sale which are not left in the ending inventory are assumed to be sold. The cost of the missing units is included in the cost of goods sold.
(*b*) The number of missing units can be identified in a perpetual inventory system. The perpetual records indicated that 1,300 units should remain in the warehouse. Only 1,280 were there. The twenty missing units can be specifically accounted for. In an weighted-average cost, perpetual system, average units are assumed to be missing.
(*c*) The perpetual system provides for a check of inventory procedures. It enables the firm to determine whether "shrinkage" of inventory is a problem requiring management attention. The cost of the missing units is computed. The firm can assess the magnitude of its losses and decide whether more money should be spent to secure the inventory.

[Sections 16-2B and 16-6A]

PROBLEM 16-4: The year-end count of inventory showed that there were 10,250 widgets in the warehouse. The accountant learned that another 400 widgets were in transit from the supplier, terms FOB destination. The firm had sold 620 widgets to a customer in Alaska, terms FOB destination. The 620 widgets were in transit as of year end. Sometimes the company sends widgets out on consignment. As of year end, 110 widgets were stored in the warehouse of a retailer who had agreed to sell them for a 20% commission. How many widgets should the firm include in its ending inventory? Justify your answer.

Answer: The final count of widgets will include the following:

Widgets in Warehouse	10,250
Widgets sold FOB Destination	620
Widgets Out On Consignment	110
Total	10,980

The accountant will NOT include the widgets in transit to the firm terms FOB destination. Title does not pass to the firm until the widgets reach the destination. The widgets in transit to the customer are included in the count because the title does not pass to the buyer until the goods reach the customer's warehouse in Alaska. The goods out on consignment are included in the count because the firm retains title to the goods until they are sold by the consignee. **[Section 16-5]**

Problems 16-5 through 16-7 refer to the information below:

Olympic Athletic Company buys sporting goods merchandise under terms 2/10, n/30. During the month of October, the firm entered into the following transactions:

(*a*) Paid an account payable for goods purchased in September with a gross price of $1,000 within the discount period.

(*b*) Received merchandise with a gross price of $5,000.

(*c*) Received merchandise with a gross price of $3,000.

(*d*) Paid for the merchandise received in Part "b" within the discount period.

(*e*) Paid for the merchandise received in Part "c" outside the discount period.

PROBLEM 16-5: Prepare the journal entries to record the events described above, if the Olympic Athletic Company uses the gross method to account for purchases of inventory. The firm uses a periodic inventory system. Show the end of month balances for purchases, purchase discounts, and the recorded cost of merchandise inventory acquired.

Answer:

Accounts Payable......................	1,000	
Purchase Discounts ($1,000 × .02).........		20
Cash..................................		980
Payment on account less discount.		
Purchases............................	5,000	
Accounts Payable.....................		5,000
To record purchase of inventory.		
Purchases............................	3,000	
Accounts Payable.....................		3,000
To record purchase of inventory.		
Accounts Payable......................	5,000	
Purchase Discount ($5,000 × .02)..........		100
Cash..................................		4,900
Payment on account less discount.		
Accounts Payable......................	3,000	
Cash..................................		3,000
Payment on account.		

Cost of merchandise acquired = Purchases − Purchase Discounts

Cost of merchandise acquired = $8,000 − $120 = $7,880

[Section 16-4A]

PROBLEM 16-6: Discuss the theoretical problems with the gross method of accounting for purchases. Your discussion should center on the valuation of newly acquired inventory and the degree to which the method accurately describes the nature of the transactions.

Answer: The gross method allows for variable valuation of inventory acquired. Inventory is initially recorded at gross selling price. This value is reduced if the discount is taken. Merchandise that is paid for within the discount period is assigned a lower value than is merchandise upon which the discount is lost. It would be difficult to justify such a variable valuation method. Inventory does not lose value because it is promptly paid for. It does not gain value when the seller is not paid. Furthermore, the purchase discounts account contains discounts taken on last month's purchases. The first $20 credited into the account related to a purchase made in the preceding month. It would be difficult to argue that this month's purchases are of less value because a discount was taken on last month's purchases.

When a firm chooses to delay payment beyond the discount period, it is borrowing money from the supplier. The cost of borrowing money is called interest expense. Whenever a firm borrows money from a supplier and pays more than the cash or net price for the product, the extra amount paid should be accounted for as interest expense. The extra amount should not be added to the value of the inventory. If the firm borrowed money from a bank to finance its inventory, the interest expense would not be added to the cost of the purchase. Money borrowed from a supplier should not be treated differently.

[Section 16-4C]

PROBLEM 16-7: Prepare the journal entries to record the events described in Problem 16-5 if the Olympic Athletic Company uses the net method to account for purchases of inventory. The firm uses a periodic inventory system. Show the end-of-month balance for purchases. Where will the Purchase Discounts Lost account appear on the financial statements?

Answer:

Accounts Payable ($1,000 × .98)	980	
Cash		980
Payment on account.		
Purchases ($5,000 × .98)	4,900	
Accounts Payable		4,900
To record purchase.		
Purchases ($3,000 × .98)	2,940	
Accounts Payable		2,940
To record purchase.		
Accounts Payable.	4,900	
Cash		4,900
Payment on account.		
Accounts Payable.	2,940	
Purchase Discount Lost.	60	
Cash		3,000
Payment on account after discount period.		

Total purchases would equal $7,840. The Purchase Discounts Lost account would appear as interest or "other" expense on the income statement.   **[Section 16-4B]**

Problems 16-8 through 16-10 refer to the information below:

The inventory activity for HHJ Corporation for the month of June is summarized below.

Beginning Balance	1,450 @ $45
Purchase #1	850 @ 50
Purchase #2	400 @ 52
Purchase #3	1,000 @ 55
Ending Inventory	1,600

PROBLEM 16-8: HHJ Corporation uses a periodic inventory system. It uses the FIFO cost flow assumption. Value the inventory as of the end of June. Compute the cost of goods sold in two ways.

Answer: When a FIFO cost flow assumption is used, the newest 1,600 units are assumed to be left in the ending inventory. The value of the ending inventory would be

$$
\begin{array}{rl}
1,000 \text{ units @ \$55} = & \$55,000 \\
400 \text{ units @ \$52} = & 20,800 \\
200 \text{ units @ \$50} = & \underline{10,000} \\
& \$85,800
\end{array}
$$

Under a FIFO cost flow assumption we assume the oldest units are sold. We need to know the number of units sold to compute the cost of goods sold directly. The number of units sold can be computed in the following manner:

Beginning Balance	1,450 units
Purchases (850 + 400 + 1,000)	2,250
Units Available For Sale	3,700
Ending Inventory	1,600
Units Sold	2,100

The 2,100 units sold must have included

$$
\begin{array}{rl}
1,450 \text{ units @ \$45} = & \$65,250 \\
650 \text{ units @ \$50} = & \underline{32,500} \\
\text{Cost of Goods Sold} & \$97,750
\end{array}
$$

The cost of goods sold can also be computed by subtracting the ending inventory value from the cost of goods available for sale. The cost of goods available for sale is equal to the beginning inventory plus purchases. A second way to calculate cost of goods sold is shown below.

Beginning Balance (1,450 @ $45)		$65,250
Purchase #1	(850 @ $50)	42,500
Purchase #2	(400 @ $52)	20,800
Purchase #3	(1,000 @ $55)	55,000
Cost of Goods Available for Sale		$183,550
Less Ending Inventory		85,800
Cost of Goods Sold		$ 97,750

[Section 16-6B]

PROBLEM 16-9: HHJ Corporation uses a periodic inventory system. It uses the LIFO cost flow assumption. Value the inventory as of the end of June. Compute the cost of goods sold in two ways.

Answer: The LIFO cost flow assumption presumes that the ending inventory consists of the oldest 1,600 units. The ending inventory would therefore be valued at

$$
\begin{array}{rl}
1,450 \text{ units @ \$45} = & \$65,250 \\
150 \text{ units @ \$50} = & \underline{7,500} \\
\text{Ending Inventory} & \$72,750
\end{array}
$$

The cost of goods sold can be valued directly. The 2,100 units that are assumed to be sold include the newest units and would be valued as follows:

$$
\begin{array}{rl}
1,000 \text{ @ \$55} = & \$ 55,000 \\
400 \text{ @ \$52} = & 20,800 \\
700 \text{ @ \$50} = & \underline{35,000} \\
\text{Cost of Goods Sold} & \$110,800
\end{array}
$$

The cost of goods sold can also be computed by deducting the ending inventory from the cost of goods available for sale.

Cost of Goods Available for Sale	$183,550
Less Ending Inventory	72,750
Cost of Goods Sold	$110,800

[Section 16-6C]

PROBLEM 16-10: Looking at your answers in Problems 16-8 and 16-9, answer the following questions and explain your answers:

(a) Which cost flow assumption probably represents the real flow of goods from the warehouse?
(b) Which cost flow assumption will maximize reported profits.
(c) Which cost flow assumption will minimize the firm's bill for income taxes?
(d) Which cost flow assumption provides the most relevant net income figure if the reader is attempting to decide whether the firm can continue in business?
(e) Which cost flow assumption would give a total asset figure which most closely represents the current value of the assets.

Answer:

(a) Most firms would attempt to ship the oldest units out first so that the firm does not end up holding out-of-date inventory. The FIFO cost flow assumption reproduces this sequence of shipping. It assumes the first goods in are the first goods out — the oldest units are shipped out first.
(b) The firm will maximize its reported profits by minimizing its reported expenses. The cost of goods sold expense is lowest in this problem when the FIFO cost flow assumption is used. Prices are rising. The oldest units have the lowest unit cost. FIFO assumes that the oldest, lowest cost units have been sold. FIFO minimizes the cost of goods sold.
(c) The firm will minimize its income tax bill, if it minimizes its reported profits. Profits are lowest when expenses are highest. LIFO assumes the newest, most costly units are sold. LIFO gives a higher cost of goods sold figure in a period of rising prices, thereby minimizing profits and income taxes.
(d) LIFO measures the cost of goods sold at the most recent prices because the newest, most recently purchased units, are assumed to be the ones sold. The LIFO cost of goods sold figure will more closely approximate the replacement cost of the units sold. The LIFO profit figure tells whether the firm has generated enough revenue to cover the replacement cost of the goods sold. If a firm cannot replace the inventory sold, it cannot continue in business.
(e) The FIFO cost flow assumption assumes that the newest, most recently purchased units are in the inventory. The inventory is valued at recent prices which most closely measure the current value of the inventory the company is holding. The total asset figure will therefore measure the current value of the assets.   [Section 16-7]

PROBLEM 16-11: XYZ Corporation began the year with 400 gizmos at a cost of $30 each. During the year the firm made two purchases of 500 units each. The firm sold 800 units during the year. The ending inventory calculated using the FIFO cost flow assumption equaled $23,500. The ending inventory using the LIFO cost flow assumption equaled $19,000. Compute the unit price paid for each purchase during the year. What would the ending inventory have been if the firm had used a weighted-average cost flow assumption?

Answer: We know the following from the information in the problem. We know that total units available for sale were 1,400 (400 + 500 + 500). Unit sales totaled 800 units. The ending inventory must have been 600 units (1,400 − 800).

When the LIFO cost flow assumption is used, the ending inventory consists of the oldest 600 units. These must include the 400 beginning units plus 200 units from the first purchase. The ending inventory using a LIFO cost flow assumption was $19,000. Therefore,

$$\text{Ending Inventory} = (\$30)(400) + (x)(200) = \$19,000$$
$$(200)(x) = (\$19,000) - (\$12,000)$$
$$(200)(x) = \$7,000$$
$$(x) = \$35$$

The unit cost of the first purchase was $35.

When the FIFO cost flow assumption is used, the ending inventory consists of the newest 600 units. These must include the 500 units most recently purchased (Purchase #2) plus 100 from Purchase #1. We know that the value of the ending inventory using a FIFO cost flow assumption is $23,500. We also know that Purchase #1 was made at a unit cost of $35. Therefore,

$$\text{Ending Inventory} = (x)(500) + (\$35)(100) = \$23,500$$
$$(500)(x) = (\$23,500) - (\$3,500)$$
$$(500)(x) = \$20,000$$
$$(x) = \$40$$

The unit cost of second purchase was $40.

The average cost of a unit in the inventory during the month can be calculated by dividing the cost of goods available for sale by the number of units available for sale.

Beginning Balance	(400 @ $30) =	$12,000
Purchase #1	(500 @ $35) =	17,500
Purchase #2	(500 @ $40) =	20,000
Available for Sale	1,400	$49,500

$$\text{Average Cost} = \$49,500/1,400 = \$35,357$$
$$\text{Ending Inventory} = (\$35.357 \times 600) = \$21,214$$

[Section 16-6A]

PROBLEM 16-12: ZZZ Company began the accounting period with 7,200 snoozers which cost $12 each. Snoozer activity is summarized below.

	Units	Unit Cost	Total
Beginning Balance	7,200	$12	$86,400
Sale #1	800		
Purchase #1	2,000	12.50	25,000
Sale #2	1,800		
Purchase #2	6,400	11	70,400
Sale #3	3,800		

The selling price of units sold is $15. The units are sold and purchased on account. A physical count at the end of the year showed an ending inventory of 9,200 units. Prepare the entries to record the acquisition of inventory, the sales, and the entries at the end of the period to record cost of goods sold and correct the inventory account if the firm uses a periodic inventory system with a weighted-average cost flow assumption.

Answer: The entries would be as follows:

Accounts Receivable (800 × $15)	12,000.00	
Sales		12,000.00
To record Sale #1		
Purchases	25,000.00	
Accounts Payable		25,000.00
To record Purchase #1		

Accounts Receivable (1,800 × $15)	27,000.00	
Sales		27,000.00
To record Sale #2		
Purchases	70,400.00	
Accounts Payable		70,400.00
To record Purchase #2		
Accounts Receivable (3,800 × $15)	57,000.00	
Sales		57,000.00
To record Sale #3		

End-of-Period Adjustments

Inventory (25,000 + 70,400)	95,400.00	
Purchases		95,400.00
To add purchases to inventory account.		
Cost of Goods Sold	74,583.20	
Inventory		74,583.20

Average unit cost = $181,800 ÷ 15,600 = $11.654

Ending inventory = 9,200 × $11.654 = $107,216.80

Cost of goods sold = $181,800 − $107,216.80 = $74,583.20

[Sections 16-2 and 16-6]

17 INVENTORIES: DOLLAR VALUE LIFO AND LCM VALUATION

THIS CHAPTER IS ABOUT

☑ **The Tax Advantages of LIFO**
☑ **Dollar Value LIFO**
☑ **Lower of Cost or Market (LCM) Valuation**
☑ **The Use of LCM for Tax Purposes**

17-1. The Tax Advantages of LIFO

Many firms adopt the LIFO cost flow assumption because the firm will pay less income tax under certain conditions. The LIFO income tax bill will be lower so long as prices are rising and the quantity of inventory is not depleted.

A. The tax benefits of using LIFO only exist when prices are rising.

The tax benefit of using LIFO when prices are rising was explained in Chapter 16. The LIFO cost flow assumption suggests that the newest, most recently purchased units are sold first. In times of rising prices, this means that the most expensive items are charged to cost of goods sold. The expense is maximized and, therefore, the net income figure is minimized. With the reduction in net income, income taxes will also be reduced.

B. The tax benefits of LIFO disappear, if the inventory is depleted.

Businesses that use LIFO for an extended period of time may be valuing ending inventory at very old prices. A firm that uses the assumption for twenty years could have some units of inventory valued at twenty-year-old prices. Such a firm can run into significant difficulty, if it does not replenish its inventory by year end. If units sold exceed units purchased, the firm dips into its LIFO base. Some of those units sold will be those valued at very old, very low unit cost. The units are sold at the current selling price. This may result in an immense net income and a substantially increased tax expense.

EXAMPLE 17-1: Stonom Corporation began 19x1 with 100 widgets. The widgets in the inventory were valued at $10 each. This beginning inventory includes a LIFO base that was established when the LIFO system was adopted fifteen years ago. In every year since adopting LIFO, the firm has purchased as many units as it has sold, so the LIFO base has been maintained. In 19x1, however, the firm had difficulty getting delivery of widgets from the supplier. As of the middle of December, the firm had only acquired 400 of the 500 widgets sold. Assume that

Widgets sold at $100 each during 19x1

Widgets purchased at $75 during 19x1

Other 19x1 expenses totaled $5,000

Income tax rate equals 40%

Based on these assumptions, Exhibit 17-1 shows what net income would be in 19x1 and 19x2 if the units purchased are equal to the units sold as compared to what it will be if the additional units are not purchased and the LIFO base is depleted.

EXHIBIT 17-1: Comparative Income Statement

	Units Purchased Equal Units Sold	Firm Depletes Stock of Widgets
Sales ($100 × 500)	$50,000	$50,000
Less Cost of Goods Sold:		
Beginning Inventory ($10)(100)	$ 1,000	$ 1,000
Purchases:		
($75 × 500)	37,500	
($75 × 400)		30,000
Cost of Goods Available for Sale	38,500	31,000
Less Ending Inventory:		
($10)(100)	1,000	0
Cost of Goods Sold	37,500	31,000
Gross Profit	12,500	19,000
Other Expenses	5,000	5,000
Net Income Before Taxes	7,500	14,000
Income Taxes (40%)	3,000	5,600
Net Income	$ 4,500	$ 8,400
Cost of Replenishing Inventory		
Early in 19x2 ($75 × 100)	0	7,500
Net Income Left After Replenishing		
Inventory Sold	$ 4,500	$ 900

If Stonom Corporation is unable to replenish its stock of widgets in 19x1, it dips into its old, low unit cost LIFO base. The cost of goods sold contains 100 units at an old cost of $10 each. Gross profit will be $6,500 greater as will net income before taxes. The firm's tax bill will be $5,600 rather than $3,000. The firm pays $2,600 more in taxes. If the stock is not replenished in late 19x1, it will have to be replenished in early 19x2. The firm will, however, have $2,600 less cash with which to buy inventory because it will have paid an extra $2,600 in taxes. The net income available to owners after the inventory has been replenished will be only $900.

Many firms constantly change what they carry in their inventory. Such firms are constantly building up an inventory of some items and depleting their stock of other items. Tax advantages accrue to the firm for items whose stock is increasing. Tax disadvantages are incurred by the firm for items whose stock is decreasing. The advantages and disadvantages may cancel out, giving no net benefit from the use of LIFO. Retail stores selling fashion merchandise find that they cannot gain tax benefits from the traditional LIFO system. Firms that stock basic, unchanging inventories such as steel girders, can derive significant tax benefits from traditional LIFO.

17-2. Dollar Value LIFO

Accountants have developed a different approach to LIFO called **Dollar Value LIFO**. The Dollar Value LIFO method collects various inventory items into a pool. A firm may have a single inventory pool comprised of the entire inventory or it may have several pools each composed of a set of similar items. When assigning a final value to the inventory, the firm counts the dollars invested in the inventory pool rather than counting the number of physical units of each separate item of inventory. The *dollar value* is equal to the number of dollars of base year purchasing power invested in the inventory pool. A LIFO layer is created by the base year investment. If the dollar value in the pool increases the next year, a LIFO layer is added to the inventory. LIFO layers are depleted, if the dollar value of the firm's investment in inventory decreases. The specific items in the pool may change. The firm may decrease the quantity of some things and increase the quantity of others without reducing the dollar value invested in the pool. Even a complete change in the composition of the inventory does not eliminate the tax benefits of the method so long as the dollar value invested in inventory increases each year.

A. There are six steps employed to compute the value of the ending inventory under the Dollar Value LIFO method.

The following steps must be carefully followed for each year, when computing the value of ending inventory using the Dollar Value LIFO method:

1. *Calculate the current cost of the inventory.* For each period being considered, multiply the number of units of each item in the inventory pool by the most recent unit purchase cost for that item. This will give you the ending inventory at current prices.

EXAMPLE 17-2: TYW Corporation uses the Dollar Value LIFO method of valuing ending inventory. The firm computed its inventory at the end of the base year (Year 0) and at the end of the next four years as follows:

	Base Year Year 0	Year 1	Year 2	Year 3	Year 4
(1) Ending Inv. Current Prices	$100,000	$150,000	$156,000	$154,000	$225,000

Ending inventory at current prices increased from $100,000 to $150,000 between Year 0 and Year 1. The inventory in Year 1 could have a larger value because there is more inventory and/or because prices increased. To find out if the size of the inventory increased we must eliminate the effect of price changes from the inventory valuation.

2. *Obtain a current year price index for the kind of goods included in the inventory pool.* A price index shows how the current year prices relate to the prices of the same type of item in the base year. The formula for computing a price index is as follows:

PRICE INDEX

$$\text{Current Year Price Index} = \frac{\text{Price in current year}}{\text{Price in base year}}$$

If the price index for the current year is 2.00, we know that goods which cost $1.00 in the base year now cost $2.00. Prices have doubled. We would have to pay twice as much today to obtain the same inventory as we had in the base year. If we have invested more than twice as many current dollars in the inventory than we did in the base year, the *dollar value* of the inventory has increased.

The U.S. Government and many industry groups calculate indices that can be used in dollar value LIFO calculations. Some firms compute their own specialized indices.

3. *Convert the current cost of the inventory to base year prices.* We can find out how much the ending inventory would have cost had it been purchased during the base year by dividing the ending inventory at current prices by the current year price index.

EXAMPLE 17-2 (cont.): TYW Corporation established index values for each year as shown in the example below. Ending inventory valued at base year prices (3) is computed by dividing the ending inventory at current prices (1) by the current year price index (2).

	Year 0	Year 1	Year 2	Year 3	Year 4
(1) Ending Inventory at Current Prices	$100,000	$150,000	$156,000	$154,000	$225,000
(2) Price Index	1.00	1.20	1.30	1.10	1.50
(3) Ending Inventory at Base Year Prices	C$100,000	C$125,000	C$120,000	C$140,000	C$150,000

(*Note:* The C$ symbol represents dollars of base year purchasing power. Such dollars are often called *constant dollars*. The use of the (C$) symbol indicates when the amounts are measured in constant as opposed to current dollars ($).)

At the end of Year 1, the inventory valued at current prices was $150,000. The price index for Year 1 was 1.20. This means that it cost $1.20 at the end of Year 1 to buy goods which cost only $1.00 at the end of the base year. If the Year 1 ending inventory had been purchased in the base year, it would have cost only $125,000 ($150,000/1.20). We now know that the size of the inventory measured in dollar value units increased between Year 0 and Year 1.

4. *Separate the ending inventory at base year prices into LIFO layers.* Each year's layer must be identified. The LIFO layer for the base year is equal to the ending inventory for that year. A LIFO layer is added in any year when the ending inventory at base year prices exceeds that of the preceeding year. Continuing Example 17-2 below we find that layers were added in Year 1, Year 3 and Year 4. When ending inventory at base year prices declines, the most recent LIFO layer is depleted. Notice that once a layer is depleted, it is never replenished. The Year 1 LIFO layer was reduced to C$20,000 in Year 2 and even though inventory was added in subsequent years, the size of the Year 1 layer was not restored to its original level. Layers are created only in years when ending inventory at base year prices increases. No LIFO layer was added in Year 2. There will never be a Year 2 LIFO layer.

Example 17-2 (continued):

	Year 0	Year 1	Year 2	Year 3	Year 4
(1) Ending Inventory at Current Prices	$100,000	$150,000	$156,000	$154,000	$225,000
(2) Price Index	1.00	1.20	1.30	1.10	1.50
(3) Ending Inventory at Base Year Prices	C$100,000	C$125,000	C$120,000	C$140,000	C$150,000
(4) LIFO Layers at Base Year Prices Year 0	C$100,000	C$100,000	C$100,000	C$100,000	C$100,000
Year 1		25,000	20,000	20,000	20,000
Year 2			0	0	0
Year 3				20,000	20,000
Year 4					10,000

5. *Convert the LIFO layers into the prices that existed at the time the layer was added.* Thus far we have calculated the base year or dollar value cost of each LIFO layer. We must now determine what each layer would have actually cost in the year it was added to the inventory. To find the value of the inventory in year of acquisition

prices, the base year value of each layer is multiplied by the price index for the year in which the layer was added to the inventory.

6. *Sum the year of acquisition values assigned to the layers in the ending inventory.* The ending inventory under the dollar value lifo method is found by summing the year of acquisition values assigned to the layers. The complete process followed by TYW Corporation is shown in the conclusion of Example 17-2 below.

Example 17-2 (concluded):

		Year 0	Year 1	Year 2	Year 3	Year 4
(1)	Ending Inventory at Current Prices	$100,000	$150,000	$156,000	$154,000	$225,000
(2)	Price Index	1.00	1.20	1.30	1.10	1.50
(3)	Ending Inventory at Base Year Prices	C$100,000	C$125,000	C$120,000	C$140,000	C$150,000
(4)	LIFO Layers at Base Year Prices					
	Year 0	C$100,000	C$100,000	C$100,000	C$100,000	C$100,000
	Year 1		25,000	20,000	20,000	20,000
	Year 2			0	0	0
	Year 3				20,000	20,000
	Year 4					10,000
(5)	LIFO Layers at Acquisition Prices					
	Year 0 × 1.00	$100,000	$100,000	$100,000	$100,000	$100,000
	Year 1 × 1.20		30,000	24,000	24,000	24,000
	Year 2 × 1.30			0	0	0
	Year 3 × 1.10				22,000	22,000
	Year 4 × 1.50					15,000
(6)	Ending Inventory at Dollar Value LIFO	$100,000	$130,000	$124,000	$146,000	$161,000

17-3. Lower of Cost or Market Valuation

Generally, assets are valued at what the company paid for them. Lower of cost or market valuation of inventory is a departure from the historical cost principle. APB 43 says that a departure from the cost principle is required when the "utility" of the inventory is less than its cost. Inventory has utility or usefulness because it can be sold. Inventory loses utility when its selling price diminishes because market conditions change, the goods deteriorate, or they become obsolete. As a general rule, a loss in the utility of an inventory item is signaled by a reduction in its replacement cost.

Application of lower of cost or market valuation requires that the firm value the ending inventory using one of the cost flow assumptions. The firm then ascertains a market (generally replacement cost) figure for each item. The final value of the inventory is the lower of the two amounts.

A. The term market usually refers to the replacement cost of the item.

As a general rule the selling price (utility) of an inventory item and the wholesale or replacement cost of the item will move in the same direction to about the same degree.

The decrease in the utility of the inventory can be approximated by the reduction in the replacement cost of the item. Replacement cost is the usual market value.

B. Occasionally replacement cost mismeasures the decline in utility of an inventory item.

The reduction in replacement cost does not accurately measure the loss in utility, if selling price and replacement cost do not move in the same direction to the same degree. Some other market measure is therefore required.

1. *The term market refers to net realizable value, if NRV is less than Replacement Cost.* If selling price declines at a faster rate than replacement cost, the loss in utility exceeds the reduction in replacement cost. Sometimes selling price will fall so precipitously that the item cannot be sold for as much as it would cost to replace it. When this happens, the highest logical market figure is net realizable value. Net realizable value equals selling price less any direct costs to complete and sell the product.

EXAMPLE 17-3: XYZ Company has an inventory of 50 Nifty computers. The computers cost $1,000 each. They can be replaced for $950. Competition from other brands has however, reduced their selling price from $1,250 to $800. In addition, the firm pays a 5% commission to the salesperson. Selling price has fallen faster than replacement cost. The net realizable value of each computer is only $760 [$800 − (.05 × $800)]. The maximum value that could be assigned to each computer is its NRV of $760.

2. *The term market refers to net realizable value less a normal gross profit if (NRV − Normal Gross Profit) is greater than Replacement Cost.* Sometimes the selling price or utility of the item declines less rapidly than the replacement cost. The decline in replacement cost overstates the loss in utility. The accountant will not write down the value to an amount less than NRV less a normal profit. If the accountant were to assign a lower amount, the firm would show unusually large profits in the accounting period when the item was sold.

EXAMPLE 17-4: Yummy Candy Company makes a delicious candy bar. The cost of the bars in the inventory is $30 per hundred. Chocolate prices have fallen so that the bars can now be produced for $20 per hundred. The selling price of the bars has also declined, but only from $40 to $35 per hundred. The firm usually earns a gross profit of $10 per hundred. This information can be summarized as follows:

Original Cost	$30
Replacement Cost	$20
NRV = Selling Price	$35
Normal Gross Profit	10
NRV − Normal Gross Profit	$25

The firm cannot value the inventory at less than $25 per hundred, the NRV less the normal gross profit. If the value were written down to the $20 replacement cost, the firm would show a gross profit of $15 ($35 − $20). when the candy bars were sold. This is $5 more than normal. The market figure to be used in this case is NRV − Normal Gross Profit.

C. The market figure used in LCM valuation will be the middle of three numbers: replacement cost, NRV, or NRV minus a normal gross profit.

Market is generally equal to replacement cost except that the market figure cannot exceed the net realizable value or be less than the net realizable value minus a normal gross profit. As a result, the market value will equal the replacement cost, the net realizable value, or the net realizable value minus a normal gross profit, whichever is the middle value.

WHEN:

```
                    (highest)
        NRV     ----------------┐
                                │
Replacement Cost  <----------┼----->   MARKET = Replacement Cost
                                │
NRV — Normal Profit  ----------┘
                    (lowest)
```

WHEN:

```
                        (highest)
Replacement Cost  ----------------┐
                                  │
        NRV     <-----------┼----->    MARKET = NRV
                                  │
NRV — Normal Profit  ------------┘
                        (lowest)
```

WHEN:

```
                    (highest)
        NRV     ----------------┐
                                │
NRV — Normal Profit  <-------┼----->   MARKET = NRV — Normal Profit
                                │
Replacement Cost  ------------┘
                    (lowest)
```

EXAMPLE 17-5: Gerhardt Corporation has five items in its inventory. The following information is available about these items:

Item	Cost	Replacement Cost	Estimated Sales Price	Selling Costs	Normal Profit
A	$5.00	$4.00	$ 6.50	$1.00	$2.50
B	9.00	9.50	10.50	2.00	.50
C	3.50	1.50	5.00	0	1.00
D	7.00	8.00	12.00	1.00	2.00
E	1.50	2.00	3.50	.50	1.00

The firm uses LCM valuation. The value assigned to each item will be

Item	Cost	Replacement Cost	Net Realizable Value	NRV — Normal Profit	Market	LCM
A	$5.00	$4.00	$6.50 — $1.00 = $5.50	$5.50 — $2.50 = $3.00	$4.00	$4.00
B	9.00	9.50	10.50 — 2.00 = 8.50	8.50 — .50 = 8.00	8.50	8.50
C	3.50	1.50	5.00 — 0.00 = 5.00	5.00 — 1.00 = 4.00	4.00	3.50
D	7.00	8.00	12.00 — 1.00 = 11.00	11.00 — 2.00 = 9.00	9.00	7.00
E	1.50	2.00	3.50 — .50 = 3.00	3.00 — 1.00 = 2.00	2.00	1.50

D. The lower of cost or market rule can be applied to inventory as a whole as well as on an item-by-item basis.

The process of valuing the inventory at lower of cost or market has been shown on an item-by-item basis up to this point. This is the most conservative approach because increases in the value of some items cannot offset decreases in the value of other items. However, the process may be applied to inventory as a whole. Here the *total* cost of inventory is compared to the *total* market value and the lower is chosen as the inventory value.

EXAMPLE 17-6: Gerhardt Corporation, Example 17-5, wants to compare the value of the inventory when LCM is applied on an item-by-item basis and as a whole. The computations are as follows:

LCM RULE APPLIED TO INVENTORY AS A WHOLE

Item	Quantity	Cost	Market	Total Cost (Qty × Cost)	Total Cost (Qty × Market)
A	200	$5.00	$4.00	200 × $5.00 = $1,000	200 × $4.00 = $ 800
B	100	9.00	8.50	100 × 9.00 = 900	100 × 8.50 = 850
C	300	3.50	4.00	300 × 3.50 = 1,050	300 × 4.00 = 1,200
D	400	7.00	9.00	400 × 7.00 = 2,800	400 × 9.00 = 3,600
E	100	1.50	2.00	100 × 1.50 = 150	100 × 2.00 = 200
Total				$5,900	$6,650

The inventory will be valued at $5,900.

LCM RULE APPLIED TO INVENTORY ITEM BY ITEM

Item	Quantity	Cost	Market	LCM	Total LCM (Qty × LCM)
A	200	$5.00	$4.00	$4.00	200 × $4.00 = $ 800
B	100	9.00	8.50	8.50	100 × 8.50 = 850
C	300	3.50	4.00	3.50	300 × 3.50 = 1,050
D	400	7.00	9.00	7.00	400 × 7.00 = 2,800
E	100	1.50	2.00	1.50	100 × 1.50 = 150
Total					$5,650

The inventory will be valued at $5,650.

E. The entry to record a writedown in inventory is made to an account such as Loss Due to Decline in Market Value of Inventory.

The entry to record the write down in inventory debits the expense account Loss Due to Decline in Market Value of Inventory. The Inventory account or an Allowance for Decline in Market Value of Inventory account is credited. The balance in the allowance account is subtracted from the inventory amount in valuing inventory on the balance sheet. The balance in the allowance account must be adjusted at the end of each accounting period to assure proper valuation of inventory.

17-4. Use of LCM for Tax Purposes

The tax laws will not allow taxpayers to use lower of cost or market valuation with a LIFO cost flow assumption. LCM can only be used when the cost of the inventory is determined using the weighted-average or FIFO cost flow assumption. Accounting theory does not forbid use of the LCM with a LIFO cost flow assumption. However, the tax laws require that the firm use the same inventory valuation method to report to stockholders as it uses to report to the government. This rule effectively limits the choices that firms have regarding inventory methods.

RAISE YOUR GRADES

Can you explain...?

☑ the conditions under which LIFO provides tax advantages
☑ how Dollar Value LIFO differs from traditional LIFO
☑ what is a price index
☑ the steps used to value inventory using the dollar value LIFO method
☑ how to compute ending inventory at base year prices when the dollar value LIFO method is used

☑ what is meant by the term lower of cost or market
☑ how to determine the market figure
☑ what are the two methods of applying LCM.
☑ what limitations surround the use of LCM for tax purposes

SUMMARY

1. In times of rising prices, LIFO yields the highest cost of goods sold, the lowest net income, and therefore yields the lowest tax liability.
2. The tax benefits of LIFO disappear if the inventory is depleted.
3. Dollar value LIFO counts dollars of base year purchasing power invested in a pool of inventory.
4. A Lifo layer is added under Dollar Value LIFO whenever ending inventory valued at base year prices increases.
5. The Dollar Value LIFO method maintains the LIFO base longer than the traditional LIFO method.
6. The price index is equal to the price in the current period divided by the price in the base period.
7. The LIFO layer valued at base year prices is calculated as the ending inventory valued at base year prices minus the sum of the base year values of the LIFO layers from preceding periods.
8. Lower of cost or market recognizes a decline in the utility of inventory.
9. Market value is the middle amount between the replacement cost, net realizable value, and the net realizable value minus normal gross profit.
10. The LCM rule can be applied to inventory as a whole or on an item-by-item basis.
11. Tax laws discourage the use of the LCM rule with the LIFO cost flow assumption by requiring the same method be used in reporting to stockholders as is used for reporting to the government.

RAPID REVIEW

1. LIFO minimizes taxes when there is (inflation/deflation) and the quantity of the inventory item is (increasing/decreasing).
2. The current cost of inventory is $50 per unit. The beginning inventory consisted of 1,000 units at $20 each. The firm uses a LIFO cost flow assumption. Sales during the year total 4,000 units. If the firm purchases 4,000 units of inventory during the year, the cost of goods sold will be _____.
3. If the firm described in Question #2 above buys only 3,000 units of inventory during the year, the cost of goods sold will be _____.
4. If the inventory in Questions #2 and #3 is NOT replenished during the accounting period, the net income before taxes of the firm will be _____ (higher/lower) than if the inventory is replenished during the accounting period.
5. If the income tax rate is 30%, taxes will be _____ (higher/lower) if the inventory in questions #2 and #3 is NOT replenished as compared to the taxes paid if the inventory level is maintained at 1,000 during the accounting period.

Use the information below to answer Questions 6 through 9.

The inventory of XYZ Company at the end of 19x0, the first year the Dollar Value LIFO system is used, totaled $50,000. The price index for the base year was 1.00. At the end of 19x1, the inventory valued at current prices totaled $63,250.

6. If the price index for 19x1 is 1.10, the end of 19x1 inventory valued at base year prices equals C$ _____.
7. The 19x1 inventory at base year prices must be separated into two layers. The base year layer at base year prices amounts to C$_____. The 19x1 layer at base year prices amounts to C$_____.

8. The base year layer at year of acquisition prices equals $ _____. The 19x1 layer at year of acquisition prices equals $ _____ .

9. Ending inventory at Dollar Value LIFO equals $ _____ .

10. If the price index for 19x0 equals 1.00 and the price index for 19x5 equals 2.50, goods which cost $5,000 in 19x0 would cost _____ in 19x5.

11. XYZ Company had $40,000 of inventory valued at end of 19x0 prices when the price index equaled 1.00. The firm had $56,000 of inventory at the end of 19x1 when the price index was 1.60. Measured in dollars of 19x0 purchasing power, the inventory at the end of 19x1 equals C$_____ .

12. The firm in Question 11 would (add a 19x1 LIFO layer/reduce the 19x0 LIFO layer).

13. XYZ Company carries inventory item X. The cost of the units in storage at the end of the year is $25. The replacement cost of the units is $26. These units can be sold for $35 after the firm spends $5 to complete them. The normal profit on the sale of these units is $10. The market valuation for purposes of LCM valuation will be _____ .

14. The value used for the item described in Question 13 will be $ _____ , if a LCM valuation system is used by the firm.

15. Market in LCM valuation usually equals _____ .

16. The highest amount that can be assigned as market value in a LCM system is _____ .

17. The lowest amount that can be assigned as market value is _____ .

18. LCM applied to the inventory on an item by item basis is (more/less) conservative than LCM applied to the inventory as a whole.

19. The cost of the ending inventory cannot be determined using LCM and the (weighted-average cost/FIFO/LIFO) cost flow assumption because the Government will not allow this combination for tax purposes.

Answers:

1. inflation; increasing [Section 17-1]
2. ($50)(4,000) = $200,000 [Section 17-1]
3. ($50)(3,000) + ($20)(1,000) = $170,000 [Section 17-1]
4. $200,000 − $170,000 = $30,000 higher [Section 17-1]
5. (.30)($30,000) = $9,000 higher [Section 17-1]
6. ($63,250)/1.10 = C$57,500 [Section 17-2]
7. C$50,000; C$7,500 [Section 17-2B]
8. (C$50,000)(1.00) = $50,000; (C$7,500)(1.10) = $8,250 [Section 17-2B]
9. $50,000 + $8,250 = $58,250 [Section 17-2]
10. ($5,000)(2.50) = $12,500 [Section 17-2]
11. ($56,000)/(1.60) = C$35,000 [Section 17-2]
12. reduce the 19x0 LIFO layer [Section 17-2]
13. RC = $26; NRV = $35 − $5 = $30;
    NRV − Normal Profit = $30 − $10 = $20; Middle Value = $26 [Section 17-3A]
14. Cost = $25 [Section 17-3A]
15. Replacement Cost [Section 17-3C]
16. Net Realizable Value [Section 17-3C]
17. NRV − Normal Profit [Section 17-3C]
18. more [Section 17-3D]
19. LIFO [Section 17-4]

SOLVED PROBLEMS

PROBLEM 17-1: Firms often select the LIFO cost flow assumption during periods of inflation because it results in a higher cost of goods sold figure thereby reducing taxable net income and income taxes owed. Explain why firms that use a LIFO cost flow assumption must be careful to replenish their stock of inventory by the end of the accounting period.

Answer: Firms that use LIFO for a long period of time will have LIFO layers valued at very old prices. The unit cost assigned to these layers may be very low relative to current replacement cost. If a firm is forced to dip into these low cost layers, the cost of goods sold will be low relative to current selling prices. Gross profit will be high, net income will be high and the income taxes owed will be greater than normal. The firm will pay more in taxes than it would have if the inventory had been replaced during the accounting period. The payment of additional taxes reduces the cash available to replenish the inventory stock in the next accounting period. **[Section 17-1B]**

PROBLEM 17-2: XYZ Corporation adopted the Dollar Value LIFO method in 19x5. In that year the price index was 1.00. Ending inventory was valued at $150,000. The price index rose in each suceeding year. Ending inventory valued at current year prices and the price index for each year are shown below.

Year	Ending Inventory	Price Index
19x6	$181,500	1.10
19x7	207,000	1.15
19x8	210,800	1.24
19x9	227,500	1.30

Prepare a schedule showing the value of the ending inventory for the years 19x5 through 19x9 using the Dollar Value LIFO method.

Answer:

	19x5	19x6	19x7	19x8	19x9
Ending Inventory at Current Prices	$150,000	$181,500	$207,000	$210,800	$227,500
Current Year Price Index	1.00	1.10	1.15	1.24	1.30
Ending Inventory at Base Year Prices*	$150,000	$165,000	$180,000	$170,000	$175,000
LIFO Layers at Base Year Prices:					
19x5	$150,000	$150,000	$150,000	$150,000	$150,000
19x6		15,000	15,000	15,000	15,000
19x7			15,000	5,000	5,000
19x8				0	0
19x9					5,000
LIFO Layers at Acquisition Prices:					
19x5 × 1.00	$150,000	$150,000	$150,000	$150,000	$150,000
19x6 × 1.10		16,500	16,500	16,500	16,500
19x7 × 1.15			17,250	5,750	5,750
19x8 × 1.24				0	0
19x9 × 1.30					6,500
Ending Inventory — Dollar Value LIFO	$150,000	$166,500	$183,750	$172,250	$178,750

* approximately

[Section 17-2B]

PROBLEM 17-3: Mighty Mo uses the Dollar Value LIFO method of valuing ending inventory. Inventory valued at end of year prices and the price index for each year are shown below. Prepare a schedule to compute the value of the ending inventory for each year using the Dollar Value LIFO method.

Year	Ending Inventory	Price Index
19x0	$ 75,000	1.00
19x1	$116,160	1.32
19x2	$109,500	1.50
19x3	$114,800	1.40

Answer:

	19x0	19x1	19x2	19x3
Ending Inventory at Current Prices	$75,000	$116,160	$109,500	$114,800
Current Year Price Index	1.00	1.32	1.50	1.40
Ending Inventory at Base Year Prices*	$75,000	$ 88,000	$ 73,000	$ 82,000
LIFO Layers at Base Year Prices				
19x0	$75,000	$ 75,000	$ 73,000	$ 73,000
19x1		13,000	0	0
19x2			0	0
19x3				9,000
LIFO Layers at Acquisition Prices				
19x0 × 1.00	$75,000	$ 75,000	$ 73,000	$ 73,000
19x1 × 1.32		17,160	0	0
19x2 × 1.50			0	0
19x3 × 1.40				12,600
Ending Inventory — Dollar LIFO Value	$75,000	$ 92,160	$ 73,000	$ 85,600

* approximately   **[Section 17-2B]**

PROBLEM 17-4: XYZ Corporation has five items in its ending inventory. Information about these items appears below.

Item	Cost	Replacement Cost	Sales Price	Selling Cost	Normal Profit
A	$50	$48	$60	$2	$12
B	$80	$75	$80	$8	$ 5
C	$30	$32	$33	$2	$ 1
D	$40	$35	$50	$5	$ 3
E	$20	$25	$29	$1	$ 5

Determine the market figure for each item. Compare the market figure to the cost figure and determine the LCM valuation.

Answer:

Item	Cost	Replacement Cost	NRV	NRV–Normal Profit	Market	LCM
A	$50	$48	$60 − $2 = $58	$58 − $12 = $46	$48	$48
B	80	75	80 − 8 = 72	72 − 5 = 67	72	72
C	30	32	33 − 2 = 31	31 − 1 = 30	31	30
D	40	35	50 − 5 = 45	45 − 3 = 42	42	40
E	20	25	29 − 1 = 28	28 − 5 = 23	25	20

[Section 17-3]

PROBLEM 17-5: XYZ Corporation described in Problem 17-4 has the following quantity of each of the five items in the inventory. Determine the value to be placed on the inventory if the LCM rule is applied to the inventory as a whole. Prepare any adjusting entry required.

Item	Quantity
A	500
B	300
C	700
D	400
E	100

Answer:

Item	Quantity	Cost	Market	Total Cost (Qty × Cost)	Total Market (Qty × Market)
A	500	$50	$48	500 × $50 = $25,000	500 × $48 = $24,000
B	300	80	72	300 × 80 = 24,000	300 × 72 = 21,600
C	700	30	31	700 × 30 = 21,000	700 × 31 = 21,700
D	400	40	42	400 × 40 = 16,000	400 × 42 = 16,800
E	100	20	25	100 × 20 = 2,000	100 × 25 = 2,500
Total				$88,000	$86,600

The inventory would be valued at $86,000.

The required adjusting entry is:

Loss Due to Decline in Market Value of Inventory (88,000 − 86,600)	1,400	
Inventory		1,400

[Section 17-3C]

PROBLEM 17-6: Use the information about the quantity of inventory presented in Problem 17-5 to determine the value of the ending inventory if the firm applies the LCM rule to the inventory on an item by item basis. Prepare any adjusting entry required.

Answer:

Item	Quantity	Cost	Market	LCM	Total LCM (Qty × LCM)
A	500	$50	$48	$48	500 × $48 = $24,000
B	300	80	72	72	300 × 72 = 21,600
C	700	30	31	30	700 × 30 = 21,000
D	400	40	42	40	400 × 40 = 16,000
E	100	20	25	20	100 × 20 = 2,000
Total					$84,600

The inventory would be valued at $84,600.

The required adjusting entry is:

Loss Due to Decline in Market Value of Inventory (88,000 − 84,600)	3,400	
Inventory		3,400

[Section 17-3C]

PROBLEM 17-7: FLC Corporation adopted the Dollar Value LIFO method in 19x5. In that year the price index was 1.00. Ending inventory was valued at $920,000. The price index rose in each suceeding year. Ending inventory valued at current year prices and the price index for each year are shown below.

Year	Ending Inventory	Price Index
19x6	$870,000	1.02
19x7	840,500	1.09
19x8	911,000	1.14
19x9	902,700	1.15

Prepare a schedule showing the value of the ending inventory for the years 19x5 through 19x9 using the Dollar Value LIFO method.

Answer:

	19x5	19x6	19x7	19x8	19x9
Ending Inventory at Current Prices	920,000	869,958	840,499	910,860	902,750
Current Year Price Index	1.00	1.02	1.09	1.14	1.15
Ending Inventory at Base Year Prices*	920,000	852,900	771,100	799,000	785,000
LIFO Layers at Base Year Prices:					
19x5	920,000	852,900	771,100	771,100	771,100
19x6		0	0	0	0
19x7			0	0	0
19x8				27,900	13,900
19x9					0
LIFO Layers at Acquisition Prices:					
19x5 × 1.00	920,000	852,900	771,100	771,100	771,100
19x6 × 1.02		0	0	0	0
19x7 × 1.09			0	0	0
19x8 × 1.14				31,806	15,846
19x9 ×					0
Ending Inventory — Dollar Value LIFO	$920,000	$852,900	$771,100	$802,906	$786,946

* approximately

[Section 17-2B]

PROBLEM 17-8: Jimmies' uses the Dollar Value LIFO method of valuing ending inventory. Inventory valued at end of year prices and the price index for each year are shown below. Prepare a schedule to compute the value of the ending inventory for each year using the Dollar Value LIFO method.

Year	Ending Inventory	Price Index
19x1	$60,000	1.00
19x2	$62,000	1.18
19x3	$71,000	1.25
19x4	$69,000	1.21

Answer:

	19x1	19x2	19x3	19x4
Ending Inventory at Current Prices	$60,000	$61,950	$71,000	$68,970
Current Year Price Index	1.00	1.18	1.25	1.21
Ending Inventory at Base Year Prices*	$60,000	$52,500	$56,800	$57,000
LIFO Layers at Base Year Prices				
19x1	60,000	52,500	52,500	52,500
19x2		0	0	0
19x3			4,300	4,300
19x4				200
LIFO Layers at Acquisition Prices				
19x1 × 1.00	60,000	52,500	52,500	52,500
19x2 × 1.18		0	0	0
19x3 × 1.25			5,375	5,375
19x4 × 1.21				242
Ending Inventory — Dollar LIFO Value	$60,000	$52,500	$57,875	$58,117

* approximately

[Section 17-2B]

PROBLEM 17-9: Toni Tot Company has five items in its ending inventory. Information about these items appears below.

Item	Cost	Replacement Cost	Sales Price	Selling Cost	Normal Profit
A	$600	$620	$ 700	$20	$35
B	$450	$419	$ 525	$20	$80
C	$920	$900	$1,000	$20	$50
D	$730	$745	$ 800	$20	$50

Determine the market figure for each item. Compare the market figure to the cost figure and determine the LCM valuation.

Answer:

Item	Cost	Replacement Cost	NRV	NRV–Normal Profit	Market	LCM
A	$600	$620	$ 700 − $20 = $680	$680 − $35 = $645	$645	$600
B	450	419	525 − 20 = 505	505 − 80 = 425	425	425
C	920	900	1,000 − 20 = 980	980 − 50 = 930	930	920
D	720	745	800 − 20 = 780	780 − 50 = 730	745	720

[Section 17-3]

PROBLEM 17-10: Toni Tot Company described in Problem 17-9 has the following quantity of each of the five items in the inventory. Determine the value to be placed on the inventory if the LCM rule is applied to the inventory as a whole. Prepare any adjusting entry required.

Item	Quantity
A	100
B	250
C	225
D	180

Answer:

Item	Quantity	Cost	Market	Total Cost (Qty × Cost)	Total Market (Qty × Market)
A	100	600	645	100 × $600 = $ 60,000	100 × $645 = $ 64,500
B	250	450	425	250 × 450 = 112,500	250 × 425 = 106,250
C	225	920	930	225 × 920 = 207,000	225 × 930 = 209,250
D	180	720	745	180 × 720 = 129,600	180 × 745 = 134,100
Total				$509,100	$514,100

The inventory would be valued at $509,100.
No adjusting entry is required, since the market value is higher than cost.

[Section 17-3B]

PROBLEM 17-11: Use the information about the quantity of inventory presented in Problem 17-10 to determine the value of the ending inventory if the firm applies the LCM rule to the inventory on an item by item basis. Prepare any adjusting entry required.

Answer:

Item	Quantity	Cost	Market	LCM	Total LCM (Qty × LCM)
A	100	600	645	600	100 × $600 = $ 60,000
B	250	450	425	425	250 × 425 = 106,250
C	225	920	930	920	225 × 920 = 207,000
D	180	720	745	720	180 × 720 = 129,600
Total					$502,850

The inventory would be valued at $502,850.
The required adjusting entry is:

Loss Due to Decline in Market Value of Inventory	6,250	
Inventory		6,250

[Section 17-3C]

PROBLEM 17-12: Gime Corporation adopted the Dollar Value LIFO method in 19x4. In that year the price index was 1.00. Ending inventory was valued at $180,000. Ending inventory valued at current year prices and the price index for each year are shown below.

Year	Ending Inventory	Price Index
19x5	$203,000	1.22
19x6	189,000	1.09
19x7	195,000	1.19
19x8	206,000	1.03

Prepare a schedule showing the value of the ending inventory for the years 19x4 through 19x8 using the Dollar Value LIFO method.

Answer:

	19x4	19x5	19x6	19x7	19x8
Ending Inventory at Current Prices	$180,000	$203,008	$189,006	$195,041	$206,000
Current Year Price Index	1.00	1.22	1.09	1.19	1.03
Ending Inventory at Base Year Prices*	$180,000	$166,400	$173,400	$163,900	$200,000
LIFO Layers at Base Year Prices:					
19x4	$180,000	$166,400	$166,400	$163,900	$163,900
19x5		0	0	0	0
19x6			7,000	0	0
19x7				0	0
19x8					36,100
LIFO Layers at Acquistion Prices:					
19x4 × 1.00	$180,000	$166,400	$166,400	$163,900	$163,900
19x5 × 1.22		0	0	0	0
19x6 × 1.09			7,630	0	0
19x7 × 1.19				0	0
19x8 × 1.03					37,183
Ending Inventory— Dollar Value LIFO	$180,000	$166,400	$174,030	$163,900	$201,083

* approximately

[Section 17-2B]

18 *INVENTORIES— ESTIMATION METHODS*

THIS CHAPTER IS ABOUT

- ☑ **The Reason for Estimation Methods**
- ☑ **Gross Profit Method**
- ☑ **Retail Inventory Method**
- ☑ **Markups and Markdowns**
- ☑ **Variations in the Retail Inventory Method**
- ☑ **Dollar Value LIFO Retail**

18-1. The Reason for Estimation Methods

Firms often wish to prepare financial statements at times when they do not wish to or cannot count the inventory.

- When using the periodic inventory system, records are only updated when physical inventories are taken. Statements may be required monthly but inventories may only be updated annually or semiannually. However, a value for ending inventory is required on the balance sheet and for computing cost of goods sold on the income statement. Therefore, the firm must estimate the amount of ending inventory in order to complete these statements.
- After a calamity, such as a fire, a firm may need to file some kind of statement with its insurance claim. A physical count, in this case, would be impossible. However, a reasonable estimate of the ending inventory and its value must be made before the claim can be processed and settled.

18-2. Gross Profit Method

The gross profit method relies on the historical relationship between sales and the cost of goods sold. For many firms, the cost of goods sold represents a reasonably stable percentage of the selling price. Consequently, gross profit (sales minus cost of goods sold) also represents a predictable percentage of sales. In a periodic inventory system, this information along with the firm's records of sales, beginning inventory, and purchases makes it possible to estimate the cost of ending inventory and the cost of goods sold.

EXAMPLE 18-1: On 3/18/x1, Misfortune Corporation's entire inventory was destroyed by a fire. The company's records indicated that the inventory on 1/1/x1 totaled $125,000. Merchandise worth $280,000 was purchased during the year. Sales totaled $425,000 through 3/17/x1, the last business day before the fire. Assuming that the firm's gross profits have been reasonably stable at 20% of sales, the gross profit method can be used to estimate the value of the inventory destroyed.

Sales.		$425,000
Less Cost of Goods Sold		
Beginning Inventory.	$125,000	
Purchases.	280,000	
Goods Available of Sale.	$405,000	
Less Ending Inventory	?	
Cost of Goods Sold		?
Gross Profit (.20)($425,000)		$ 85,000

The missing numbers are easily calculated.

$$\text{Cost of Goods Sold} = \$425{,}000 - \$85{,}000 = \$340{,}000$$

If gross profit represents 20% of sales, cost of goods sold must equal 80% of sales. Therefore cost of goods sold could also be computed as:

$$\text{Cost of Goods Sold} = (.80)(\$425{,}000) = \$340{,}000$$

The ending inventory equals the cost of goods available for sale that were not sold.

$$\text{Ending Inventory} = \$405{,}000 - \$340{,}000 = \$65{,}000$$

18-3. Retail Inventory Method

In the gross profit method, the firm uses the *historical* relationship between sales, cost of goods sold, and gross profit. In the retail inventory method, the firm uses *current* relationships. The retail method requires that the firm know its sales; the cost and selling price of its beginning inventory; and the cost and selling price of its purchases for the period. The *cost ratio* is then computed as follows:

COST RATIO $\quad$ **Cost Ratio = $\dfrac{\text{Cost of Goods Available for Sale}}{\text{Selling Price of Goods Available for Sale}}$**

The selling price of the ending inventory can then be multiplied by the cost ratio to find cost of the ending inventory. It is the cost, not the selling price, of the ending inventory that is needed to prepare the financial statements.

EXAMPLE 18-2: Donna Dayton Dresses began the year with an inventory which cost $15,000 and had a retail value of $25,000. During the year to date, the firm purchased new merchandise for $75,000 and assigned it a retail value of $125,000. Sales for the year to date totaled $110,000. The value of the ending inventory would be calculated as follows:

	Cost	Retail
Beginning Inventory	$15,000	$ 25,000
Purchases	75,000	125,000
Available for Sale	90,000	150,000
Less Sales		110,000
Ending Inventory at Retail		$ 40,000

For financial statement purposes, we need the value of the ending inventory at cost. We can convert the ending inventory at retail to the ending inventory at cost by determining the relationship between the cost of goods available for sale and the selling price of goods available for sale.

$$\text{Cost Ratio} = \text{CGAS/SPGAS} = \$90{,}000/\$150{,}000 = .60$$

The cost of the ending inventory is estimated to be equal to 60% of the selling price of the ending inventory. Therefore,

$$\text{Ending Inventory at Cost} = (\$40{,}000 \times .60) = \$24{,}000$$

18-4. Markups and Markdowns

An application of the basic retail inventory method is complicated by the fact that companies rarely mark all of their merchandise at a selling price that remains stable throughout the period. Firms constantly adjust selling prices to reflect the market conditions. The selling price of a single item may be *marked up* or *marked down* several times before it is finally sold. The retail industry uses a specialized set of terms to describe changes in selling price. Exhibit 18-1 illustrates and defines these terms.

EXHIBIT 18-1: Terms Used in Retail Inventory Method

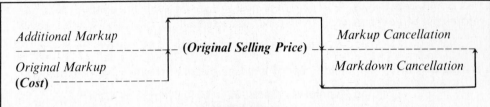

DEFINITIONS

1. *Original Markup*: Amount added to cost to obtain original selling price of item.

2. *Markup*: Additions beyond original selling price.

3. *Markup Cancellations*: Reductions which bring selling price down to the original level.

4. *Markdowns*: Reductions which bring selling price down below the original selling price.

5. *Markdown Cancellations*: Increases which bring selling price up to the original level.

6. *Net Markups*: Markups less markup cancellations.

7. *Net Markdown*: Markdowns less markdown cancellations.

EXAMPLE 18-3: CLR Corporation acquired three whizbangs (A, B, and C) at a cost of $100 each. The original markup was $20. Units B and C were marked up further by $5. Unit C's selling price was subsequently reduced by $12 and later increased by $4. The last selling price of each unit after all markups, markdowns, and cancellations is shown below. Assuming that Units A and B were sold, the ending inventory at retail will equal $117.

	Unit A	Unit B	Unit C	Total
Cost	$100	$100	$100	
Original Markup	20	20	20	
Original Selling Price	$120	$120	$120	$360
Markups		5	5	10
Markup Cancellations			(5)	(5)
Markdowns			(7)	(7)
Markdown Cancellations			4	4
Last Selling Price	$120	$125	$117	$362
Less Sales				245
Ending Inv. at Retail				$117

18-5. Variations in the Retail Inventory Method

The retail inventory method can be modified to approximate the lower of cost or market valuation. It can be modified to approximate weighted-average, LIFO, and FIFO cost flow assumptions. It can also be modified to approximate the Dollar Value LIFO method. The ending inventory at cost is always calculated by applying the cost ratio to the ending inventory's selling price (retail price). The approximations of the other valuations is accomplished by modifying the method used to compute the cost ratio.

A. The retail method can be used to approximate cost valuation under the weighted-average cost flow assumption (cost retail).

The retail method can approximate cost valuation under the weighted-average cost flow assumption by modifying the calculation of the cost ratio. The cost ratio would be based on a selling price that included both net markups and markdowns.

COST RATIO
(cost retail)

$$\text{Cost Ratio} = \frac{\text{Cost of Goods Available for Sale}}{\substack{\text{Selling Price of Goods Available for Sale}\\ \text{(including net markups and net markdowns)}}}$$

EXAMPLE 18-4: Discount Stores Corporation has the following inventory information for the year:

	Cost	Retail
Beginning Inventory	$ 1,200	$ 1,600
Purchases	44,000	57,300
	$45,200	$58,900
Markups		2,000
Markup Cancellations		(500)
Selling Price of Goods Available for Sale (including net markups only)	$45,200	$60,400
Markdowns		(7,400)
Markdown Cancellations		1,400
Selling Price of Goods Available for Sale (including net markups and net markdowns)	$45,200	$54,400
Sales		48,000
Selling Price of Ending Inventory		$ 6,400

The cost ratio under the cost retail method would be computed as follows:

$$\text{Cost Ratio} = \frac{\$45,200}{\$54,400} = .831$$

Cost of the ending inventory would equal

$$\$6,400 \times .831 = \$5,318$$

B. The retail method can be used to approximate cost valuation under the weighted-average cost flow assumption and lower of cost or market valuation (conventional retail).

The retail method can approximate the weighted-average cost flow assumption and lower of cost or market valuation by modifying the calculation of the cost ratio. The cost ratio would be based on a selling price that only includes net markups. By excluding the markdowns the selling price in the denominator of the cost ratio is higher, thus making a lower cost ratio. The lower cost ratio would reduce the cost value assigned to the ending inventory.

COST RATIO
(Conventional retail)

$$\text{Cost Ratio} = \frac{\text{Cost of Goods Available for Sale}}{\substack{\text{Selling Price of Goods Available for}\\ \text{Sale (including net markups only)}}}$$

EXAMPLE 18-5: The value placed on the ending inventory in Example 18-4 using the conventional retail method would be found by applying a cost ratio that excludes net markdowns.

$$\text{Cost Ratio Conventional Retail} = \$45,200/\$60,400 = .748$$
$$\text{Ending Inventory at Cost} = .748 \times 6,400 = \$4,787$$

Notice, the cost ratio is always applied to ending inventory at retail. Ending inventory at retail is always computed using all markups and markdowns.

C. The retail inventory method can approximate cost valuation with a LIFO cost flow assumption (LIFO Retail Method).

The retail inventory method can approximate a layering method with cost valuation by calculating the cost ratio including net markups and net markdowns for the purchased units only. A separate ratio is established for the beginning inventory and for the purchases. Layers are established. Each layer has its own cost ratio. When the LIFO cost flow assumption is desired, the ending inventory is assumed to contain the oldest layers.

EXAMPLE 18-6: The cost of the ending inventory in Example 18-4 can be computed at its value under the LIFO cost flow assumption. The LIFO method assumes that the last items into inventory (purchases) are the first sold. Therefore, the markups and markdowns related to purchases only. The calculations would therefore be as follows:

	Cost	Retail	Cost Ratio
Beginning Inventory	$ 1,200	$ 1,600	.75
Purchases	$44,000	$57,300	
Markups		2,000	
Markup Cancellations		(500)	
Markdowns		(7,400)	
Markdown Cancellations		1,400	
	$44,000	$52,800	.8333
Goods Available for Sale	$45,200	$54,400	
Less Sales		48,000	
Ending Inventory at Retail		$ 6,400	

The ending inventory at retail can be divided into LIFO layers

	Retail	Cost Ratio	Cost
Beginning Inventory	$1,600	.75	$1,200
Current Year Layer	4,800	.8333	4,000
Ending Inventory LIFO Retail	6,400		$5,200

D. The retail method can be used to approximate the LIFO cost flow assumption and lower of cost or market valuation.

The cost ratio is computed on purchases and uses a selling price that includes only net markups. Since the Government does not allow lower of cost or market valuation under the LIFO method, we will not explore this further.

E. The retail method can approximate the FIFO cost flow assumption and cost valuation.

If a FIFO cost flow assumption is desired, the ending inventory will consist of the newest layers. Cost valuation requires that the ratio include both net markups and markdowns. The markups and markdowns would apply only to the purchases. The retail inventory method is rarely used to approximate a FIFO cost flow assumption.

F. Variations of the retail inventory method can approximate cost or lower of cost or market valuation, and any of the cost flow assumptions.

The adjustment of the cost ratio and the use of layers makes the retail inventory method adaptable to both cost and lower of cost or market valuation and the average cost, LIFO, and FIFO cost flow assumptions. Exhibit 18-2 summarizes the variations that are possible with the retail inventory method.

EXHIBIT 18-2: Calculation of the Cost Ratio

Cost Flow Assumption	Valuation Methods	
	Cost	LCM
AVERAGE COST	Include net markups and net markdowns Include Purchases Include Beg. Inventory	Include net markups; Exclude net markdowns Include Purchases Include Beg. Inventory
FIFO	Include net markups and net markdowns Include Purchases Exclude Beg. Inventory Inv. Has Newest Layers	Include net markups; Exclude net markdowns Include Purchases Exclude Beg. Inventory Inv. Has Newest Layers
LIFO	Include net markups and net markdowns Include Purchases Exclude Beg. Inventory Inv. Has Oldest Layers	Include net markups; Exclude net markdowns Include Purchases Exclude Beg. Inventory Inv. Has Oldest Layers

Another way to summarize the variations in the retail inventory method appears in Exhibit 18-3.

EXHIBIT 18-3: Calculation of Cost Ratio

	Includes Net Markdowns	Excludes Net Markdowns
Includes Beg. Inv.	Cost Valuation Weighted-average Cost Flow	LCM Valuation Weighted-average Cost Flow
Excludes Beg. Inv.	Cost Valuation FIFO or LIFO	LCM Valuation FIFO or LIFO

EXAMPLE 18-7: XYZ Company begins the period with an inventory valued at $27,000 which would sell for $45,000. During the accounting period the firm purchases inventory costing $346,500 to sell for $480,000. Net markups during the period were $20,000 and net markdowns were $5,000. Sales totaled $484,000. The retail inventory method can be used to approximate cost or lower of cost market valuation and any cost flow assumption. The information from the example can be summarized as follows:

	Cost	Retail
Beginning Inventory	$ 27,000	$ 45,000
Purchases	346,500	480,000
Net Markups		20,000
Net Markdowns		(5,000)
Goods Available for Sale	$373,500	$540,000
Less Sales		484,000
Ending Inventory at Retail		$ 56,000

The cost ratio which approximates cost valuation with an average cost flow assumption (Cost Retail) includes beginning inventory and both net markups and net markdowns.

$$\text{Cost Ratio} = \$373,500/\$540,000 = .692$$
$$\text{Ending Inventory} = .692 \times \$56,000 = \$38,752$$

The cost ratio which approximates lower of cost or market valuation with an weighted-average cost flow assumption (conventional retail) includes beginning inventory but excludes net markdowns.

$$\text{Cost Ratio} = \$373,500/(\$540,000 + \$5,000)$$
$$= .685$$
$$\text{Ending Inventory} = .685 \times \$56,000 = \$38,360$$

LIFO with a cost valuation method requires that a cost ratio be determined excluding the beginning inventory and using both net markups and net markdowns. The ending inventory at retail is layered. The ending inventory consists of the oldest layers.

$$\text{Cost Ratio} = \$346,500/(\$480,000 + \$20,000 - \$5,000)$$
$$= .70$$

The ending inventory at retail can be divided into LIFO layers.

	Retail	Cost Ratio	Cost
Beginning Inventory	$45,000		$27,000
Current Year Layer	11,000	.70	7,700
Ending Inventory	$56,000		$34,700

Other combinations are possible. It is possible to approximate a FIFO-Cost valuation system, by changing the order in which the layers are developed. It is possible to approximate a layering method such as LIFO or FIFO with LCM valuation by computing the cost ratio on purchases only, while excluding net markdowns.

18-6. Dollar Value LIFO Retail

If price levels change over time the dollar value LIFO retail method is used in place of the LIFO retail method described earlier. The dollar value LIFO retail method adds steps which convert the ending inventory at retail to base year prices. The layers are established and converted to the retail prices that existed in the year the layer was added. The cost ratio for that year is then applied to each layer.

EXAMPLE 18-8: Assume that the retail price index in the current year is 1.12 in Example 18-7 above. The price index was 1.00 in the previous year when the beginning inventory was acquired. The value of the ending inventory calculated using the dollar value LIFO retail method is illustrated below.

	Cost	Retail	Cost Ratio
Beginning Inventory	$ 27,000	$ 45,000	.60
Purchases	$346,500	$480,000	
Net Markups		20,000	
Net Markdowns		(5,000)	
	$346,500	$495,000	.70
Goods Available for Sale	$373,500	$540,000	
Less Sales		484,000	
Ending Inventory at Retail		$ 56,000	
÷ Current Year Price Index		1.12	
Ending Inventory Base Year Retail		C$ 50,000	
LIFO Layers at Base Year Retail:			
Beginning Inventory		C$ 45,000	
Current Year Layer		5,000	
		C$ 50,000	
LIFO Layers at Year of Addition Retail:			
Beginning Inventory × 1.00		$ 45,000	
Current Year Layer × 1.12		5,600	
		$ 50,600	
LIFO Layers at Year of Addition Cost:			
Beginning Inventory × .60		$ 27,000	
Current Year Layer × .70		3,920	
Ending Inventory Dollar Value LIFO Retail		$ 30,920	

The steps followed in valuing the ending inventory using the dollar value LIFO retail method are as follows:

1. Determine the current period value of ending inventory at retail.
2. Compute the cost ratio for the current period using both markups and markdowns but excluding beginning inventory.
3. Determine current period ending inventory at base period retail prices by dividing the results of Step 1 by the current period price index.
4. Separate the current period ending inventory at base period retail prices into LIFO layers.
5. Convert the LIFO layers into the retail prices that existed when the layers were added. This is done by multiplying each layer by the price index for the period when the layer was added.
6. Convert the LIFO layers at year of addition retail prices to cost by multiplying the results of Step 5 by the cost ratio for the period when the layer was added.
7. Add the values found in Step 6 to compute the value of the ending inventory under the dollar value LIFO retail method.

Application of the cost ratio is the last step in computing cost in this method as is true for all of the retail inventory variations.

RAISE YOUR GRADES

Can you explain...?

☑ why estimation methods are needed

☑ how to compute the value of ending inventory using the gross profit method

☑ what information is required to use the retail inventory method

☑ what are the special terms used in the retail industry to describe changes made in the selling price

☑ the difference between the cost ratio when the retail inventory method approximates cost and LCM valuations

☑ the difference between the cost ratio when the retail inventory method approximates the weighted-average cost flow assumption and either the LIFO or FIFO cost flow assumption

☑ what cost flow assumption and valuation method is approximated by the conventional retail estimation method.

SUMMARY

1. Estimations of the cost of inventories are made when information is needed but a physical count cannot be made.

2. The gross profit method relies on the historical relationship between sales and the cost of goods sold.

3. The retail method relies on the current relationships between sales and cost of goods sold.

4. The cost ratio is equal to the cost of goods available for sale divided by the selling price of the goods available for sale.

5. The selling price of ending inventory is multiplied by the cost ratio to compute the cost of ending inventory, when retail inventory methods are used.

6. Original markup is the amount added to cost to obtain the original selling price of an item.

7. Markup is the amount added to the original selling price. Markup cancellation is a reduction down to the original selling price.

8. Net markup is equal to markups less markup cancellations.

9. Markdown is the amount subtracted from the original selling price. Markdown cancellation is an increase up to the original selling price.

10. Net markdown is equal to markdowns less markdown cancellations.

11. The retail inventory method can be modified to approximate weighted-average LIFO, FIFO, and dollar value LIFO cost flow assumptions. It can also approximate the cost or lower of cost or market valuation methods. This is accomplished by modifying the cost ratio.

12. The cost retail method approximates the inventory value under cost valuation and the weighted-average cost flow assumption. The selling price in its cost ratio computation includes net markups and net markdowns.

13. The conventional retail method approximates the lower of cost or market valuation of inventory with a weighted-average cost flow assumption. The cost ratio is computed based on a selling price which includes net markups but not net markdowns.

14. The LIFO retail method approximates the value of ending inventory under the LIFO cost flow assumption with cost valuation. The cost ratio is computed using purchases only and includes both markups and markdowns.

15. The retail inventory method can be used to approximate the lower of cost or market value of ending inventory under the LIFO cost flow assumption. However, this valuation is not allowed by Government for tax purposes.

16. When price levels are changing the LIFO retail method can be modified into a Dollar Value LIFO retail method by adjusting the ending inventory at current period retail prices into base period values.

RAPID REVIEW

1. If the gross profit ratio is .25 and sales are $150,000, the cost of goods sold must be $ _____.

2. If the beginning inventory was $10,000; purchases were $50,000; and the cost of goods sold is $35,000; the ending inventory must equal $_____.

3. If ending inventory at retail prices is $8,000 and the retail cost ratio is .85, the ending inventory at cost would be equal to $ _____.

Questions 4 through 10 refer to the information below.

	Cost	Retail
Beginning Inventory	$12,000	$ 15,000
Purchases	90,000	120,000
Net Markups		9,000
Net Markdowns		6,000
Sales		103,000

4. The ending inventory at retail equals $ _____.

5. The cost ratio if the cost retail inventory method is used is_____.

6. The ending inventory at cost if the cost retail inventory method is used is $ _____.

7. The cost ratio if the conventional retail inventory method is used is_____.

8. The ending inventory at cost if the conventional retail inventory method is used is $ _____.

9. The cost ratio if the LIFO retail inventory method is used is _____.

10. The ending inventory at cost if the LIFO retail inventory method is used is $ _____.

11. Lower of cost or market valuation uses a cost ratio that (includes/excludes) net markdowns.

12. Cost valuation uses a cost ratio that (includes/excludes) net markdowns.

13. Lower of cost or market valuation uses a cost ratio that (includes/excludes) net markups.

14. The weighted-average cost flow assumption uses a cost ratio that is computed (including/excluding) beginning inventory.

15. A FIFO cost flow assumption would use a cost ratio that is computed (including/excluding) beginning inventory.

16. The Dollar Value LIFO retail method uses a cost ratio which (includes/excludes) beginning inventory and (includes/excludes) net markups and (includes/excludes) net markdowns.

17. A cost ratio that includes net markups, excludes net markdowns, and includes beginning inventory approximates (cost/lower of cost or market) valuation with a (weighted-average cost/LIFO) cost flow assumption, and is called the _____ method.

Answers:

1. .75 × $150,000 = $112,500 [Section 18-2]
2. ($10,000 + $50,000) − $35,000 = $25,000 [Section 18-2]
3. .85 × $8,000 = $6,800 [Section 18-3]

4. $(15,000 + 120,000 + 9,000 - 6,000 - 103,000) = \$35,000$ [Section 18-4]
5. $(12,000 + 90,000)/(15,000 + 120,000 + 9,000 - 6,000) = .739$ [Section 18-5A]
6. $.739 \times \$35,000 = \$25,865$ [Section 18-5A]
7. $(12,000 + 90,000)/15,000 + 120,000 + 9,000) = .708$ [Section 18-5B]
8. $.708 \times \$35,000 = \$24,780$ [Section 18-5B]
9. $(90,000)/120,000 + 9,000 - 6,000) = .732$ [Section 18-5C]
10. $\$12,000 + (.732)(\$35,000 - \$15,000) = \$26,640$ [Section 18-5C]
11. excludes [Section 18-5D]
12. includes [Section 18-5A]
13. includes [Section 18-5D]
14. including [Section 18-5A]
15. excluding [Section 18-5E]
16. excludes; includes; includes [Section 18-6]
17. lower of cost or market; weighted-average cost; Conventional Retail Inventory [Section 18-5B]

SOLVED PROBLEMS

PROBLEM 18-1: On March 15, 19x1, a fire in Motley's warehouse destroyed all but $12,000 of the firm's inventory. Records that were not destroyed indicated that the beginning inventory totaled $123.000. The balance in the purchases account totaled $406,000 but this included $20,000 of merchandise in transit to the firm at the time of the fire, terms FOB shipping point. Sales through March 15 totaled $500,000. During the past three years, the firm's gross profit ratio has been quite steady at approximately .18. Compute the value of the inventory destroyed by the fire using the gross profit method.

Answer: The information from the problem can be summarized in the following format.

Beginning Inventory		$123,000
Purchases	$406,000	
Less Purchases in Transit	20,000	
Warehoused Purchases		386,000
Goods Available in Warehouse		$509,000
Less: Est. CGS (1-.18)($500,000)		410,000
Inventory in Warehouse at Time of Fire		$ 99,000
Inventory After Fire		12,000
Inventory Destroyed by Fire		$ 87,000

[Section 18-2]

Problems 18-2 through 18-5 refer to the information below.

DAD Corporation's inventory activity is summarized below.

	Cost	Retail
Beginning Inventory	$ 15,000	$ 25,000
Purchases	185,000	265,000
Net Markups		45,000
Net Markdowns		30,000
Sales		250,000

PROBLEM 18-2: Compute the value of the ending inventory at cost using the cost retail inventory method.

Answer: Ending inventory at cost using the cost retail inventory method is computed as follows:

	Cost	Retail	Cost Ratio
Beginning Inventory	$ 15,000	$ 25,000	
Purchases	185,000	265,000	
Net Markups		45,000	
Net Markdowns		(30,000)	
Goods Available for Sale	$200,000	$305,000	.656
Less Sales		250,000	
Ending Inventory at Retail		$ 55,000	

Ending Inventory (Cost Retail) = (.656)($55,000)

= 36,080

[Section 18-5A]

PROBLEM 18-3: Compute the value of the ending inventory using the conventional retail inventory method.

Answer: The ending inventory using the conventional retail inventory method is computed as follows:

	Cost	Retail	Cash Ratio
Beginning Inventory	$ 15,000	$ 25,000	
Purchases	185,000	265,000	
Net Markups		45,000	
	$200,000	$335,000	.597
Net Markdowns		(30,000)	
Goods Available for Sale		$305,000	
Less Sales		250,000	
Ending Inventory at Retail		$ 55,000	

Ending Inventory (Conventional Retail) = (.597)($55,000)

= $32,835

[Section 18-5B]

PROBLEM 18-4: Compute the value of the ending inventory at cost using the LIFO retail inventory method.

Answer: The ending inventory at cost using the LIFO retail inventory method is computed as follows:

	Cost	Retail	Cost Ratio
Beginning Inventory	$ 15,000	$ 25,000	.600
Purchases	$185,000	$265,000	
Net Markups		45,000	
Net Markdowns		(30,000)	
	$185,000	$280,000	.661
Goods Available for Sale		$305,000	
Less Sales		250,000	
Ending Inventory at Retail		$ 55,000	

	Retail	Cost Ratio	Cost
Beginning Inventory	$25,000	.600	$15,000
Current Year Layer	$30,000	.661	19,830
Ending Inventory (LIFO Retail)			$34,830

[Section 18-5C]

PROBLEM 18-5: Compute the value of the ending inventory using the dollar value LIFO retail method, if the price index for the year in which the beginning inventory was accumulated was 1.00 and the price index for the current year is 1.05.

Answer: The ending inventory using the dollar value LIFO retail inventory method is computed as follows:

	Cost	Retail	Cost Ratio
Beginning Inventory	$ 15,000	$ 25,000	.600
Purchases	$185,000	$265,000	
Net Markups		45,000	
Net Markdowns		(30,000)	
	$185,000	$280,000	.661
Goods Available for Sale		$305,000	
Less Sales		250,000	
Ending Inventory at Retail		$ 55,000	
÷ Price Index		1.05	
Ending Inventory at Base Year Retail		C$ 52,381	
LIFO Layers at Base Year Retail:			
Beginning Inventory		C$ 25,000	
Current Year Layer		27,381	
LIFO Layers at Yr of Addition Retail:			
Beginning Inventory × 1.00		$ 25,000	
Current Year Layer × 1.05		28,750	
LIFO Layers at Yr. of Addition Cost:			
Beginning Inventory × .600		$ 15,000	
Current Year Layer × .661		19,004	
Ending Inventory Dollar Value LIFO		$ 34,004	

[Section 18-6]

PROBLEM 18-6: DAD Corporation's ending inventory at retail was $50,000. Its ending inventory at cost using the cost retail method was $35,000. What would the value of the ending inventory be using the conventional retail inventory method, if net markdowns totaled $5,000 and the goods available for sale at retail totaled $180,000?

Answer: The information in the problem can be summarized as follows:

	Cost	Retail	Cost Ratio
Available for Sale before NMDwns	(c?)	(d?)	(e?)
Net Markdowns		(5,000)	
Goods Available for Sale	(c?)	$180,000	(a?)
Less Sales		(b?)	
Ending Inventory at Retail		$ 50,000	
Cost Retail Cost Ratio		(a?)	
Ending Inventory (Cost Retail)		$ 35,000	

The missing numbers can be filled in as follows:

(*a*) Cost Retail Cost Ratio = $35,000/$50,000 = .700
(*b*) Sales = $180,000 − $50,000 = $130,000
(*c*) Cost of Goods Available for Sale = .70 × $180,000 = $126,000
(*d*) Avail. for Sale Before NMDwns = $180,000 + $5,000 = $185,000
(*e*) Conventional Retail Cost Ratio = $126,000/$185,000 = .681

Ending Inventory Conventional Retail = .681 × $50,000 = $34,050

[Section 18-5]

PROBLEM 18-7: XYZ Corporation shows the following inventory activity for the year.

	Cost	Retail
Beginning Inventory	$ 14,000	$ 20,000
Purchases	$100,000	131,600
Net Markups		28,000
Net Markdowns		12,000

(*a*) Compute the cost ratio that would be used with the cost retail method. Does this ratio approximate cost or lower of cost or market valuation?

(*b*) Compute the cost ratio that would be used with the conventional retail method. Does this ratio approximate cost or lower of cost or market valuation?

(*c*) Compute the cost ratio that would be used with the LIFO retail method. Does this ratio approximate cost or lower of cost or market valuation?

(*d*) What modification of the ratio converts the retail inventory method from one which approximates cost valuation to one which approximates lower of cost or market valuation?

Answer:

(*a*) CR(cost retail) = (14,000 + 100,000)/(20,000 + 131,600 + 28,000 − 12,000)

     = .680

The cost retail cost ratio approximates cost valuation.

(*b*) CR(conventional retail) = (14,000 + 100,000)/(20,000 + 131,600 + 28,000)

     = .635

The conventional retail method approximates lower of cost or market valuation.

(*c*) CR(LIFO retail) = (100,000)/(131,600 + 28,000 − 12,000) = .678

LIFO retail approximates cost valuation.

(*d*) The cost valuation methods include net markdowns in the computation of the cost ratio. The lower of cost or market methods exclude net markdowns from the cost ratio.

[Section 18-5]

PROBLEM 18-8: TEA Company uses the Dollar Value LIFO retail method. Inventory activity is summarized below.

	Cost	Retail
Beginning Inventory	$ 40,000	$ 65,000
Purchases	230,000	385,000
Net Markups		30,000
Net Markdowns		35,000
Sales		360,000
Price Index Base Year		1.00
Price Index Current Year		1.20

Value the ending inventory using the Dollar Value LIFO method.

Answer:

	Cost	Retail	Cost Ratio
Beginning Inventory	$ 40,000	$ 65,000	.615
Purchases	230,000	385,000	
Net Markups		30,000	
Net Markdowns		(35,000)	
	$230,000	$380,000	.605
Goods Available for Sale		$445,000	
Less Sales		360,000	
Ending Inventory at Retail		$ 85,000	
÷ Price Index		1.20	
Ending Inventory at Base Year Retail		C$ 70,833	
LIFO Layers at Base Year Retail:			
Beginning Inventory		C$ 65,000	
Current Year Layer		5,833	
LIFO Layers at Year of Acquisition Retail:			
Beginning Inventory × 1.00		$ 65,000	
Current Year Layer × 1.20		7,000	
LIFO Layers at Year of Acquisition Cost:			
Beginning Inventory × .615		40,000	
Current Year Layer × .605		4,235	
Ending Inventory Dollar Value LIFO		$ 44,235	

Problems 18-9 through 18-12 refer to the following information.

Tryling Corporation's inventory activity is summarized below.

	Cost	Retail
Beginning Inventory	$ 36,000	$ 45,000
Purchases	200,000	280,000
Net Markups		87,000
Net Markdowns		30,000
Sales		205,000

PROBLEM 18-9: Compute the value of the ending inventory at cost using the cost retail inventory method.

Answer: Ending inventory at cost using the cost retail inventory method is computed as follows:

	Cost	Retail	Cost Ratio
Beginning Inventory	$ 36,000	$ 45,000	
Purchases	200,000	280,000	
Net Markups		87,000	
Net Markdowns		(30,000)	
Goods Available for Sale	$236,000	$382,000	.618
Less Sales		205,000	
Ending Inventory at Retail		$177,000	

Ending Inventory (Cost Retail) = $177,000 × .618
= $109,386

[Section 18-5A]

PROBLEM 18-10: Compute the value of the ending inventory using the conventional retail inventory method.

Answer: The ending inventory using the conventional retail inventory method is computed as follows:

	Cost	Retail	Cost Ratio
Beginning Inventory	$ 36,000	$ 45,000	
Purchases	200,000	280,000	
Net Markups		87,000	
	$236,000	$412,000	.573
Net Markdowns		(30,000)	
Goods Available for Sale		$382,000	
Less Sales		205,000	
Ending Inventory at Retail		$177,000	

Ending Inventory (Conventional Retail) = $177,000 × .573
= $101,421

[Section 18-5B]

PROBLEM 18-11: Compute the value of the ending inventory at cost using the LIFO retail inventory method.

Answer: The ending inventory at cost using the LIFO retail inventory method is computed as follows:

	Cost	Retail	Cost Ratio
Beginning Inventory	$ 36,000	$ 45,000	.800
Purchases	$200,000	$280,000	
Net Markups		87,000	
Net Markdowns		(30,000)	
	$200,000	$337,000	.593
Goods Available for Sale		$382,000	
Less Sales		205,000	
Ending Inventory at Retail		$177,000	

	Retail	Cost Ratio	Cost
Beginning Inventory	$ 45,000	.800	$ 36,000
Current Year Layer	132,000	.593	78,276
Ending Inventory (LIFO Retail)			$114,276

[Section 18-5C]

PROBLEM 18-12: Compute the value of the ending inventory using the dollar value LIFO retail method if the price index for the year in which the beginning inventory was accumulated was 1.00 and the price index for the current year is 1.03.

Answer: The ending inventory using the dollar value LIFO retail inventory method is computed as follows:

	Cost	Retail	Cost Ratio
Beginning Inventory	$ 36,000	$ 45,000	.800
Purchases	$200,000	$280,000	
Net Markups		87,000	
Net Markdowns		(30,000)	
	$200,000	$337,000	.593
Goods Available for Sale		$382,000	
Less Sales		205,000	
Ending Inventory at Retail		$177,000	
÷ Price Index		1.03	
Ending Inventory at Base Year Retail		C$171,845	
LIFO Layers at Base Year Retail:			
Beginning Inventory		C$ 45,000	
Current Year Layer		126,845	
LIFO Layers at Yr of Addition Retail:			
Beginning Inventory × 1.00		$ 45,000	
Current Year Layer × 1.03		130,650	
LIFO Layers at Yr. of Addition Cost:			
Beginning Inventory × .800		$ 36,000	
Current Year Layer × .593		77,475	
Ending Inventory Dollar Value LIFO		$113,475	

[Section 18-6]

19 MARKETABLE EQUITY SECURITIES

THIS CHAPTER IS ABOUT

☑ **The Definition of Marketable Equity Securities**
☑ **Classification of MES**
☑ **Methods of Accounting for MES**
☑ **Reclassifying MES**

19-1. The Definition of Marketable Equity Securities

Marketable equity securities (MES) are highly liquid investments that are actively traded on the national stock exchange or over-the-counter. MES include common stock, preferred stock, and other securities such as options and warrants that allow for the purchase of stock. Firms hold marketable securities either as a temporary investment of excess cash or as a long-term investment. The valuation of the MES depends upon the purpose of the investment and the degree to which the investor influences the investee.

19-2. Classification of MES

The balance sheet classification of MES depends upon the firm's purpose in holding the stock. If the company views the investment as a temporary use of cash, the MES are included in current assets. If the firm intends to make a long-term investment, the MES will be included in long-term assets.

19-3. Methods of Accounting for MES

The method used to account for MES will be determined by the situation. If the portfolio (the entire group of securities) is classified as a current asset, it will be valued at lower of cost or market on the balance sheet. If the portfolio is classified as a long-term investment and the firm does not exercise an influential interest over the investee, it will also be valued at lower of cost or market on the balance sheet and will be classified as a non current asset. When an influential interest is exercised, the portfolio is accounted for using an equity method and classified as a non current asset. A summary of the accounting methods is shown in Exhibit 19-1.

EXHIBIT 19-1: Accounting Methods for MES

Situation	Accounting Method
Temporary Investment	Valuation: Lower of Cost or Market Loss in market value shown on I/S

Long-term Investment No Influential Interest	Valuation: Lower of Cost or Market
	    Loss in market value not shown on
	    I/S—shown on B/S as negative equity
	      account

Long-term Investment With Influential Interest	Valuation: Equity Method

A. Short-term MES are valued at the lower of aggregate cost or market.

The firm will compare the *total* cost of the portfolio to its *total* market value. If the market value is less than the original cost, an unrealized loss on the valuation of the MES will be recognized. The loss will be recognized on the income statement by a debit to an "unrealized loss" which is an "other loss" account. The value of the portfolio will be reduced on the balance sheet by a credit to an allowance account which, in this case, is a contra asset (MES) account. Subsequent recovery of the market value is recognized by debiting the allowance account and crediting to a "recovery" account which is an "other income" account. Recovery means that unrealized losses are recovered. Therefore, gains above the original cost of MES are not recognized until the sale of the securities.

EXAMPLE 19-1: During 19x1, Investor Corporation acquired the following portfolio of stock. The market value of each security is also shown.

Marketable Equity Security	Cost	Market	Unrealized Gain (Loss)
Northwest Drilling	$300,000	$325,000	$ 25,000
Southeast Manufacturing	425,000	405,000	(20,000)
Midwest Engineering	180,000	130,000	(50,000)
Totals	$905,000	$860,000	$(45,000)

The entries to record the acquisition and year-end valuation of the portfolio will include the following:

MES (short-term)	905,000	
Cash		905,000
To record acquisition of the portfolio.		
Unrealized Loss on Valuation of MES	45,000	
Allowance for Decline in Market Value of MES		45,000
To record unrealized loss.		

After these entries are made, the value of the portfolio will equal its market value of $860,000 on the balance sheet.

EXAMPLE 19-2: During 19x2, the Investor Corporation in Example 19-1 sold its shares of Midwest Engineering for $150,000. The entry to record the sale of the stock would be as follows:

Cash	150,000	
Loss on Sale of MES.	30,000	
MES (short-term).		180,000
To record the sale of stock.		

The sale of stock is recorded without regard to the allowance account. We know that a portion of the balance in the allowance account related to the loss in market value of Midwest Engineering stock. The valuation process for MES is handled in the aggregate and the allowance account is not assigned to particular securities. A sale of a security will result in a realized gain, if the cash received exceeds the cost of the security. It results in a realized loss, if the cash received is less than the cost. The cost and market of the remaining shares in the portfolio appear below as of 12/31/x2.

Marketable Equity Security	Cost	Market	Unrealized Gain (Loss)
Northwest Drilling	$300,000	$305,000	$ 5,000
Southeast Manufacturing	425,000	410,000	(15,000)
Totals	$725,000	$715,000	$(10,000)

The balance in the allowance account must be adjusted from its current credit balance of $45,000 to its new credit balance of $10,000. This is done with the following entries:

Allowance for Decline in Market Value of MES . .	35,000	
Recovery of Unrealized Loss		35,000
To adjust balance in the allowance account.		

EXAMPLE 19-3: At the end of 19x3, the Investor Corporation in Example 19-2 still holds two securities. Their original cost and market value at the end of 19x3 is summarized below.

Marketable Equity Security	Cost	Market	Unrealized Gain (Loss)
Northwest Drilling	$300,000	$320,000	$20,000
Southeast Manufacturing	$425,000	$420,000	(5,000)
Totals	$725,000	$740,000	$15,000

The entry to adjust the valuation of MES at the end of 19x3 will be

Allowance for Decline in Market Value of MES . .	10,000	
Recovery on Unrealized Loss		10,000
To record recovery in market value.		

The firm has recovered all of the unrealized loss previously recognized. The market value of the portfolio now exceeds its cost. The recovery is, however, limited to the amount of previously recognized loss. The value of the portfolio on the balance sheet cannot exceed its original cost. The MES and allowance accounts would appear as follows after all the entries from Examples 19-1 through 19-3 have been posted:

Marketable Equity Securities

19x1 Purchase of Securities	905,000		
19x2 Balance	905,000		
		Sale of Securities	180,000
19x3 Balance	725,000		

Allowance for Decline in Market Value of MES

		19x1 12/31/x1 Adjusting	45,000
19x2 Adjusting	35,000	19x2 Balance	45,000
19x3 Adjusting	10,000	19x3 Balance	10,000
		19x4 Balance	0

B. Long-term MES held by a firm that does not exercise influential interest over the investee are valued at lower of cost or market.

A firm may acquire equity securities of another company with the intention of maintaining the investment for a considerable period of time. The MES will be classified as a long-term investment. It is generally assumed that the investor does not have an influential interest in the investee unless the investor owns 20% or more of the outstanding stock of the investee. Long-term MES where there is no influential interest are accounted for in nearly the same manner as short-term MES. The portfolio is valued at lower of cost or market. An allowance account is used to establish the proper valuation of the securities. The only difference between accounting for short and long-term MES is that unrealized losses on long-term MES are not reported as an other item on the income statement. The unrealized losses are debited to a negative owner's equity account called Net Unrealized Loss on Valuation of MES. The recovery of unrealized losses is credited to the same account. Neither the unrealized loss nor the recovery appear on the income statement. As with short-term MES, recovery is limited to previously recognized unrealized losses. (SFAC No. 5 includes the change in Net Unrealized Loss on Valuation of MES in the calculation of comprehensive net income. Adjustments of this account are not part of the earnings computation.)

EXAMPLE 19-4: During 19x1, XYZ Corporation purchases 100 shares of ABC Company stock for $10,000. XYZ Corporation considers this to be a long-term investment. XYZ Corporation owns 2% of ABC Corporation's outstanding stock. At the end of 19x1, the stock has a market value of $9,000. At the end of 19x2, the market value of the shares increased to $9,700. The entries made with regard to the investment will be

19x1	MES (long-term)	10,000	
	Cash.		10,000
	To record investment in ABC Co,		
	Net Unrealized Loss on Valuation of MES	1,000	
	Allowance for Decline in Market Value of MES		1,000
	To adjust balance in allowance account.		
19x2	Allowance for Decline in Market Value of MES	700	
	Net Unrealized Loss on Valuation of MES.		700
	To record recovery in market value.		

By the end of 19x1, the market value of the portfolio dropped by $1,000. The entry establishes the allowance account which is deducted from the balance in long-term MES so that the portfolio is valued on the balance sheet at $9,000 ($10,000 − $1,000), the market value of the portfolio. The account Net Unrealized Loss on Valuation of MES is deducted from the total of stockholders' equity on the balance sheet. No loss appears on the income statement.

During 19x2, the portfolio recovers $700 of the unrealized loss recognized in 19x1. The recovery is recorded by reversing the accounts that originally recorded the unrealized loss. The recovery does not appear on the income statement as other income.

C. Losses on long- and short-term MES which are deemed to be other than temporary are recorded as realized losses.

When a decline in the market value of an MES is deemed to be other than temporary, the loss is realized and the MES account is reduced. The cost of the stock is thenceforth considered to be the market value on the day the loss is recognized. Subsequent recovery above this new amount is not recognized until the stock is sold.

EXAMPLE 19-5: XYZ Company purchased 100 shares of Troubled Corporation for $50 per share. The shares are a part of the long-term portfolio. The market value of the stock has fallen to $20. The loss in market value is believed to be permanent. The entry to record a non-temporary loss in market value is

Realized Loss on MES	3,000	
MES (long-term)		3,000
To recognize a loss deemed other than temporary.		

No recovery of the realized loss is allowed for subsequent increases in market value. The entry would be essentially the same for a security in the short-term portfolio except that the credit would have been to short-term MES.

D. Entries to record income earned on short-term and non influential long-term investments generally do not change the value of the asset.

Firms which invest in MES will generally receive revenue in the form of dividends. Dividends received in cash are recorded as revenue equal to the amount of cash so long as the dividends do not exceed the retained earnings of the investee. Dividends in excess of retained earnings are called **liquidating dividends**. Such dividends reduce the value of the MES because the company the investments were made in is no longer worth as much as before assets were liquidated. Liquidating dividends are quite rare.

EXAMPLE 19-6: XYZ Corporation temporarily invested in shares of stock in two companies, Conserve Corporation and Payout Corporation. During 19x1, Conserve paid XYZ Corporation $10,000 in dividends. The dividends of Conserve Corporation represented 10% of the net income reported for the year. Payout Corporation has continued to pay dividends even though the firm has suffered several years of net losses. XYZ Corporation received $1,000 from Payout even though retained earnings were negative at both the beginning and end of the year. The entries to record the dividends received from each investee are

Cash	10,000	
Dividend Revenue.....................		10,000
To record receipt of dividend.		
Cash	1,000	
MES (short-term)......................		1,000
To record liquidating dividend.		

Dividends received in the form of stock do not represent income to the investor. The investor's cost basis for the stock is simply spread over more shares of stock making the cost of each share smaller.

EXAMPLE 19-7: XYZ Corporation purchased 100 shares of Multiply Corporation at a per share cost of $25 and a total cost of $2,500. Multiply declared a 10% stock dividend so XYZ Corporation was sent 10 additional shares of stock. No entry is made to record the stock dividend because no revenue is received by XYZ Corporation. XYZ Corporation now has 110 shares of Multiply Corporation. The cost of each share is now $22.73 each ($2,500/110). The stock dividend provides no revenue. The firm owns 110 shares at a cost of $22.73 each.

E. Long-term MES with an influential interest are valued using the equity method.

The equity method assumes a close economic relationship exists between the investor and investee when the investor has influential interest. The carrying value of the securities is increased by the investor's share of any increase in the stockholders' equity in the investee. The investment will ultimately be carried at an amount equal to the investor's share of the investee's equity or net assets. An influential interest is presumed when the investor controls 20% or more of the outstanding shares.

EXAMPLE 19-8: On 1/1/x1, Investor Corporation purchased 25% of Investee Corporation's stock for $100,000. The stockholders' equity of Investee on the day of the purchase totaled $400,000. During 19x1, Investee earned net income of $50,000 and paid dividends of $20,000. By year-end, Investee's stockholders' equity totaled $430,000 ($400,000 + $50,000 − $20,000). Investor Corporation will use the equity method to account for the investment in Investee Corporation's stock. The entries appear below.

Investment in Investee Corp.	100,000	
Cash		100,000
To record purchase of 25% of Investee Corporation stock		
Investment in Investee Corp.	12,500*	
Equity in Earnings of Investee Corp.		12,500
To record share of Investee Corporation's net income		
Cash	5,000**	
Investment in Investee Corporation		5,000
To record dividend received		

*$50,000 × 25% = $12,500
**$20,000 × 25% = $ 5,000

The investment is carried in an Investment in Investee account rather than in an account with the MES label. The investment account is debited with the original cost of the shares. The investment account is debited for Investor's share of Investee's net income and is credited for the dividends received from Investee. The investment account will appear as follows:

Investment in Investee Corporation

Purchase of Shares	100,000		
Share of Profits	12,500	Dividends Received	5,000
Balance	107,500		

The balance in the investment account corresponds to Investor's share of Investee's equity. Investee's equity at year end totals $430,000. Twenty-five percent of that amount equals $107,500 ($430,000)(.25). The entries made under the equity method value the investment at an amount equal to the investor's share of the investee's net assets.

The revenue from the investment is recorded in the account Equity in the Earnings of Investee. Dividends do not represent revenue. They are a reduction in the investment account.

F. Under the equity method, a differential between the amount paid for shares and the book value of net assets purchased is amortized over an appropriate period of time.

In Example 19-8, Investor Corporation purchased 25% of the shares of Investee Corporation for exactly 25% of the equity reported on the books of Investee Corporation. An exact correspondence between the cost per share and the net asset value per share would be highly unusual. There is virtually always some differential between the two amounts. The differential between the amount paid and the book value of net assets purchased is amortized over an appropriate period of time. Generally, the differential will be positive. Sometimes the investor will pay less than the book value of the net assets purchased. Then the differential would be negative.

EXAMPLE 19-9: On 1/1/x1, Investor Corporation purchased 25% of Investee Corporation's stock. Investor paid $120,000 for the 25% interest. Investee's stockholders' equity (net assets) at the time of the purchase totaled $400,000. Investor Corporation therefore paid $120,000 to acquire net assets valued on Investee's books at $100,000 (.25 × $400,000). The differential is attributed to the fact that some of Investee's property is worth more than its book value and Investee Corporation has created an excellent reputation for fast service (goodwill). The differential is explained as follows:

Explanation of Differential

Cost of Investment	$120,000
÷ Fraction of Investee Acquired	÷ .25
Implied Total Value of Net Assets	$480,000
Book Value of Net Assets	400,000
Implied Total Differential	$ 80,000
Accounted For	
Undervalued Fixed Assets	
(Remaining Useful Life 5 years)	$ 60,000
Goodwill	20,000
Total Differential Accounted For	$ 80,000

Investor's share of the differential is 25%. Its share of each component of the differential is also 25%. Investor's share of the differential is $20,000 ($80,000 × .25). Investor's share of the undervalued fixed assets is $15,000 (.25 × $60,000). Its share of the goodwill is $5,000 (.25 × $20,000). The differential paid will be amortized over an appropriate period by Investor. The appropriate period to amortize the $15,000 paid for undervalued assets is 5 years, their remaining useful life. Any differential paid for goodwill can be amortized over an arbitrary time period not to exceed 40 years. Investor will amortize its share of the differential as follows, assuming that goodwill is amortized over the maximum period:

Amortization of Differential Schedule

	Years x1–x5	Years x6–x40
Undervalued Assets:		
($15,000/5)	$3,000	$ 0
Goodwill ($5,000/40)	125	125
Annual Amortization	$3,125	$125

If the net income earned and dividends paid by Investee Corporation are the same as in Example 19-9, the entries would be as follows:

Investment in Investee Corporation	120,000	
Cash		120,000
To record purchase of 25% of Investee		
Corporation stock.		
Investment in Investee Corporation	12,500	
Equity in Earnings of Investee Corporation		12,500
To record 25% share of Investee		
Corporation's net income		
Cash	5,000	
Investment in Investee Corporation		5,000
To record dividend revenue.		
Equity in Earnings of Investee Corp.	3,125	
Investment in Investee Corporation		3,125
To record amortization of differential for		
Year 1.		

The investment account will appear as follows, after the posting of the journal entries:

Investment in Investee Corporation

Purchase of Stock	120,000		
25% of Profits	12,500		
		Dividends Received	5,000
		Amortization of Differential	3,125
Balance	124,375		

In forty years, the entire differential will be amortized. At that point the balance in the investment account will equal 25% of the net assets of Investee Corporation.

Under the equity method the revenue shown on the income statement as Equity in Earnings of Investee will equal

$$\text{Revenue From Equity Method Investment} = \left(\text{Investor's \% Ownership} \times \text{Investee's Profit} \right) \pm \text{Amortization of Differential}$$

19-4. Reclassifying MES

The classification of MES as short or long-term appears to be left to the discretion of the firm. What is to prevent a firm from continually reclassifying securities so that the firm obtains the best possible income statement results? A firm wishing to maximize reported profits would classify those securities that are losing market value as long-term to avoid recognizing the unrealized losses on the income statement. The firm would then classify securities that are recovering market value as short-term so that the recovery would appear as income on the income statement. The FASB requires that reclassified securities be transferred at lower of cost or market and that any unrealized loss on the transferred securities be recognized as a realized loss in the period of the transfer. The rule does not prevent firms from transferring long-term securities with market values above cost to the short-term account in order to reduce unrealized losses that would otherwise occur on short-term MES.

EXAMPLE 19-10: XYZ Corporation wishes to change the classification of two investments in MES from short to long-term. Information about the two securities on the date of reclassification appears on page 332.

Marketable Equity Securities	Cost	Market	Unrealized Gain (Loss)
Loser Company	$10,000	$ 8,000	$(2,000)
Winner Company	15,000	20,000	5,000
Total	$25,000	$28,000	$ 3,000

The firm will transfer each stock at its lower of cost or market value. Loser Company will be transferred to the long-term portfolio at $8,000. The $2,000 unrealized loss will be realized. Winner Company will be transferred at $15,000. No loss will be realized on the transfer. The entries to record the reclassification will be

```
MES (long-term). . . . . . . . . . . . . . . . . . . . . .   8,000
Realized Loss on MES . . . . . . . . . . . . . . . . .   2,000
    MES (short-term)                                              10,000
        To transfer Loser Company stock to the
        long-term portfolio.

MES (long-term). . . . . . . . . . . . . . . . . . . . . .  15,000
    MES (short-term). . . . . . . . . . . . . . . . . . . . .     15,000
        To transfer Winner Company stock to the
        long-term portfolio.
```

RAISE YOUR GRADES

Can you explain . . . ?

☑ what kinds of securities are classified as marketable equity securities
☑ what are the classifications of MES on the balance sheet
☑ how temporary declines in the market value of short-term MES are accounted for
☑ how temporary declines in the market value of long-term MES are accounted for when no influential interest exists.
☑ the general rule for determining whether there is an influential interest
☑ how temporary declines in the market value of long-term MES are accounted for when influential interest does exist
☑ how are MES reclassified
☑ how investment revenue is determined under the equity method
☑ what the value in the investment account tends to equal when the equity method is used

SUMMARY

1. Marketable securities are investments in stock that have high liquidity and are actively traded on the national stock exchange or over-the-counter.
2. The accounting for MES depends on the purpose of the investment and the degree to which the investor influences the investee.
3. MES held as a temporary use of cash are current assets. MES are otherwise classified as long-term assets.
4. MES classified as short-term investments (current assets) are valued at lower of cost or market.
5. If an investor holds more than 20% of an investee's stock, the investor is said to have an influential interest in the investee.

6. If the MES are classified as long-term and the firm does not exercise an influential interest over the investee, the MES are valued at lower of cost or market.

7. If the MES are classified as long-term and the firm does exercise an influential interest over the investee, the MES are valued under the equity method.

8. The valuation at lower of cost or market is based on total cost and total market of the portfolio not on individual stock valuations.

9. An unrealized loss on short-term MES due to a temporary decline in market value is recognized by a debit to an unrealized loss account and a credit to an allowance account.

10. Recovery of losses from Item #9 are recognized by a debit to the same allowance account and a credit to a recovery account.

11. Recovery of unrealized losses due to temporary market fluctuations can not exceed the amount of previously recognized loss.

12. An unrealized loss on long-term MES, with no influential interest, due to a temporary decline in market value is recognized by a debit to a contra equity account and a credit to an allowance account. The entries are reversed to recognize subsequent recoveries from this loss.

13. Losses that are deemed to be other than temporary are recognized as direct reductions in the value of the asset account. The loss is recognized on the income statement as realized. The reduced value of the MES now represents cost when computing future lower of cost or market valuations.

14. Cash dividends received on short- and long-term MES where no influential interest exists are recorded as dividend revenue.

15. Liquidating dividends are dividends paid in excess of retained earnings. They are recorded as a reduction in the MES value.

16. The equity method assumes a close economic relationship between the investor and investee. The equity method is used when influential interest exists.

17. Under the equity method investments are valued at an amount equal to the investor's share of the investee's equity.

18. The differential between the amount paid for shares and their book value is amortized as an adjustment to the income recognized on the investment.

19. The FASB requires that MES which are being reclassified be transferred at lower of cost or market.

RAPID REVIEW

1. Short-term MES are valued at _____ .

2. Long-term MES where no influential interest exists are valued at _____ .

3. Unrealized losses on short-term MES are reported on the (income statement only/balance sheet only/both the income statement and the balance sheet).

4. Unrealized losses on long-term MES are reported on the (income statement only/balance sheet only/both the income statement and the balance sheet).

Questions 5 through 10 relate to the following information about Investor Corporation's MES portfolio. All of the stock was purchased during the current year.

	Cost	Market
Company A	$5,000	$5,500
Company B	4,000	2,000
Company C	1,000	1,000

5. The aggregate cost of the portfolio was $ _____ .

6. The aggregate market value of the portfolio is $ _____ .

7. The balance in the allowance account should be a (debit/credit) balance of $ _____ .

8. If the portfolio listed above is classified as short-term, the entries to record the above information will
    (a) increase profits by $1,500.
    (b) decrease profits by $1,500.
    (c) increase profits by $8,500.
    (d) decrease profits by $8,500.
    (e) have no effect on profits.

9. If the portfolio listed above is classified as long-term, the entries to record the above information will
    (a) increase profits by $1,500.
    (b) decrease profits by $1,500.
    (c) increase profits by $8,500.
    (d) decrease profits by $8,500.
    (e) have no effect on profits.

10. If the portfolio had a market value of $12,000 at the end of the next year, the entry to record the change in value will (debit/credit) the allowance account for $ _____ .

11. An investor is assumed to have an influential interest in an investee if the investor owns _____ % or more of the outstanding stock of the investee.

12. Investments where the investor has an influential interest in the investee are accounted for by the _____ method.

Questions 13 through 19 relate to the information below.

Investor Company bought 30% of the outstanding stock of Investee Company for $30,000. The book value of the net assets of Investee Company totaled $100,000 at the time of the purchase. During the first full year of ownership, Investee earned net income of $25,000 and paid dividends of $12,000.

13. The amount debited into the investment account at the time of the purchase will be
    $ _____ .

14. Thirty percent of the book value of the net assets of Investee Company equal
    $ _____ .

15. The differential between the purchase price and the book value of the net assets purchased equals _____ .

16. The income reported from this investment on the income statement for the year will be
    $ _____ .

17. The account where the income from the investment is recorded is called _____ .

18. The balance in the investment account at the end of the year will be _____ .

19. Investee Company will show total equity of $_____ .

Answers:

1. lower of cost or market [Section 19-3A]
2. lower of cost or market [Section 19-3B]
3. both the income statement and the balance sheet [Sect   9-3A]
4. balance sheet only [Section 19-3B]
5. $5,000 + $4,000 + $1,000 = $10,000 [Section 19-3]
6. $5,500 + $2,000 + $1,000 = $8,500 [Section 19-3]
7. credit ($10,000 − $8,500) = $1,500 [Section 19-3A]
8. b [Section 19-3A]
9. e [Section 19-3B]
10. debit $1,500 [Section 19-3A]
11. 20% or more [Section 19-3B]
12. equity [Section 19-3E]
13. $30,000 [Section 19-3E]
14. (.30)($100,000) = $30,000 [Section 19-3E]

15. $0 [Section 19-3E]
16. (.30)($25,000) = $7,500 [Section 19-3E]
17. Equity in the Earnings of Investee Company [Section 19-3E]
18. $30,000 + $7,500 − (.30)($12,000) = $33,900 [Section 19-3E]
19. ($33,900)/(.30) = $113,000 = ($100,000 + $25,000 − $12,000) [Section 19-3E]

SOLVED PROBLEMS

PROBLEM 19-1: In accounting for short and long-term MES where there is no influential interest, recovery of unrealized losses is limited to the amount of losses previously recognized. Why does this limitation exist?

Answer: The limitation prevents valuation of the securities at more than their original cost. When an unrealized loss is recognized, the allowance account is credited. The credit balance in the allowance account is deducted from the debit balance in the MES account in valuing the securities on the balance sheet. Recovery is recorded with a debit into the allowance account. If there were no limit on the amount of recovery allowed, the allowance account could have a debit balance. The balance in the allowance account would then be added to the cost of securities recorded in the MES account giving a valuation in excess of original cost. **[Sections 19-3A and 19-3B]**

PROBLEM 19-2: On 1/1/x1, XYZ Corporation invested some of its excess cash in the stock of two other companies. Cost and market value at the end of 19x1 is given below along with information about the dividends paid by each investee company. The dividends were not liquidating dividends.

	Cost	Market	Dividends
Company A	$12,500	$11,200	$1,250
Company B	15,800	16,000	2,500

(a) Prepare all entries with regard to the investments in MES.
(b) How would your entries differ if the investment were viewed as long-term rather than short-term?
(c) Prepare the entry to sell one half of the shares of Company A stock early in 19x2 at a price of $7,100.
(d) Prepare the entry to adjust the value of the portfolio on 12/31/x2, if its market value was $23,000. (Don't forget that one half of the Company A stock was sold during 19x2.)

Answer:

(a)

MES (short-term)	28,300	
Cash		28,300
To record purchase of securities.		
Unrealized Loss on Valuation of MES	1,100	
Allowance for Decline in Market Value of MES		1,100
To reduce value of MES to market.		
Cash	3,750	
Dividend Revenue		3,750
To record dividend revenue.		

(b) If the securities had been placed in the long-term portfolio, the entries would have been the same except that the entry to reduce the value of the MES to market would have debited a negative owners' equity account rather than an other expense account. The debit would have been to Net Unrealized Loss on Valuation of MES.

(c) Cash   7,100

    MES (short-term) ($12,500 ÷ 2)   6,250

    Gain on Sale of MES   850

      To record sale of stock.

(d) Allowance for Decline in Market Value

    of MES   1,100

    Recovery of Unrealized Loss on MES   1,100

      To record recovery in market.

[Sections 19-3A and 19-3B]

PROBLEM 19-3: Explain how each of the following would affect net income.

(a) XYZ Company purchased 10% of the stock of Company A for $500,000 as a temporary investment of excess cash. Dividends received during the year totaled $20,000. At year end, the market value of the stock was $485,000.

(b) Refer to the information in Part A above. During the second year, $15,000 of dividends were received. One half of the stock was sold for $245,000. At year end, the market value of the remaining shares was $245,000.

(c) How would your answers to B and C be different, if the investment had been viewed as long-term?

Answer:

(a) Profits will include $20,000 of dividend revenue and an unrealized loss of $15,000 for a net positive effect of $5,000.

(b) Profits will include $15,000 of dividend revenue. They will also include a $5,000 realized loss on the sale of one half of the stock because stock costing $250,000 was sold for $245,000. The balance in the allowance account should be revised to equal the difference between the $250,000 cost of the remaining half of the stock and the $245,000 market value. The allowance balance should be $5,000 which means the firm has recovered $10,000 ($15,000 − $5,000) of the previously recognized unrealized loss. The recovery is other income to the firm on the income statement. The net effect on profits will be $20,000 ($15,000 − $5,000 + $10,000).

(c) Profits would not be affected by the unrealized loss in Part A or the recovery in Part B. In Part A, the net effect of profits would be a plus $20,000. In Part B, the effect would be a plus $10,000.   **[Section 19-3]**

PROBLEM 19-4: Why did the FASB institute the rule that securities must be reclassified (from short-term to long-term or vice versa) at lower of cost or market value and that any unrealized losses on the day of transfer be recognized as realized losses?

Answer: The rule was instituted to reduce manipulation of the financial statements. Firms would transfer stocks that were rising in value to the short-term account in order to reduce the unrealized losses on short-term MES reported on the income statement. Firms would transfer stock that was recovering in value to the short-term account in order to recognize the recovery on the income statement. Firms would transfer failing stocks to the long-term account to avoid recognizing unrealized losses on the income statement.

[Section 19-4]

PROBLEM 19-5: The portfolio of XYZ Company for the years 19x1 and 19x2 is listed below. The market value of each stock at the end of each year is also shown. You may assume that all of the shares listed as being owned in 19x1 were acquired during 19x1.

Prepare the entries implied by the information assuming the portfolio is a long-term investment and that the selling price of Firm A shares was $41.

| | | 19x1 | | | 19x2 | |
Company	No. of Shares	Cost per Share	Market Price	No. of Shares	Cost per Share	Market Price
Firm A	1,000	$40	$37	600	$40	$47
Firm B	2,000	10	8	2,000	10	9
Firm C	2,500	22	24	2,500	22	20
Firm D	0			1,000	5	4

Answer: The acquisition cost of the shares purchased during 19x1 was

	No. of Shares	Market Price	Total
Firm A	1,000	$40	$ 40,000
Firm B	2,000	10	20,000
Firm C	2,500	22	55,000
			$115,000

The entry to record the acquisition of the shares is

MES (long-term)........................	115,000	
Cash		115,000

The market value of the portfolio at the end of 19x1 is

	No. of Shares	Market Price	Total
Firm A	1,000	$37	$ 37,000
Firm B	2,000	8	16,000
Firm C	2,500	24	60,000
			$113,000

The entry to adjust the value of the portfolio to market is

Net Unrealized Loss on Long-term MES........	2,000	
Allowance for Decline in Market Value of MES		2,000

During 19x2, the entry to record the sale of 400 shares of Firm A stock would be

Cash ($41)(400)	16,400	
MES (long-term) ($40 × 400)		16,000
Gain on Sale of MES....................		400

The acquisition of stock in Firm D would be recorded as:

MES (long-term)($5 × 1,000)	5,000	
Cash		5,000

The cost and market value of the portfolio at the end of 19x2 are summarized below.

	Cost	Market
Firm A	$ 24,000	$ 28,200
Firm B	20,000	18,000
Firm C	55,000	50,000
Firm D	5,000	4,000
Total	$104,000	$100,200

The entry to adjust the valuation of MES must increase the allowance that was set up at the end of 19x1 because the portfolio now has a market value that is $3,800 less than cost. The entry must increase the balance in the allowance account from $2,000 to $3,800.

Net Realized Loss on MES (long-term).........	1,800	
Allowance for Decline in Market Value		
of MES		1,800

[Section 19-3B]

PROBLEM 19-6: XYZ Corporation purchased 40% of the stock of Acquired Corporation at a cost of $80,000. At the time of the purchase the book value of the net assets of Acquired Corporation was $200,000. During 19x1, Acquired earned a net income of $10,000 and paid dividends totaling $6,000. Prepare the entries to record these events on the books of XYZ Corporation. Compute the value that would be shown for XYZ Corporation's investment in Acquired Corporation's stock. How could you check to see if the balance in the Investment in Acquired Corporation account has the correct balance?

Answer:

Investment in Acquired Corp.	80,000	
Cash		80,000
To record purchase of 40% of company's stock.		
Investment in Acquired Corp.	4,000	
Equity in Income of Acquired Corp.		
($10,000 × .40)		4,000
To record share of Acquired Corp.'s net income.		
Cash ($6,000 × .40)	2,400	
Investment in Acquired Corp..............		2,400
To record receipt of dividend.		

The balance in the investment account will equal the cost of the stock plus XYZ Corporation's share of Acquired's net income less dividends received. The balance will equal $81,600 ($80,000 + $4,000 − $2,400).

The balance in the investment account should equal 40% of the net assets of Acquired Corporation. This is true because there was no differential to be amortized. Acquired Corporation will have equity equal to the beginning equity plus the net income minus the dividends. The net assets of Acquired Corporation equal $204,000 ($200,000 + $10,000 − $6,000). Forty percent of $204,000 is $81,600.   [Section 19-3E]

PROBLEM 19-7: Now assume the XYZ Corporation purchased 40% of the stock of Acquired Corporation for $100,000 and all other information is the same as it was in Problem 19-6. Prepare the entries to record the events described for the year. Any differential is due to undervalued property with a useful life of 10 years. Compute the balance in the investment account and explain the revenue that would appear on the income statement with regard to this investment.

Answer: In this problem the investor pays a positive differential for the 40% ownership purchased.

Explanation of Differential

Amount Paid for 40% Ownership	$100,000
÷ Percent of Firm Purchased	÷ .40
Implied Total Value of Equity	$250,000
Book Value of Net Assets	200,000
Implied Total Differential	$ 50,000

The total differential is explained by undervalued assets with a remaining useful life of 10 years. XYZ Corporation's share of the differential is $20,000, 40% of the total. This differential will be amortized over the next 10 years at a rate of $2,000 per year. The entries to record the events are shown below.

Investment in Acquired Corp.	100,000	
Cash		100,000
To record purchase of 40% of company's stock.		
Investment in Acquired Corp.	4,000	
Equity in Income of Acquired Corp.		4,000
To record share of Acquired Corp's net income.		
Cash	2,400	
Investment in Acquired Corp.		2,400
To record dividend revenue.		
Equity in Income of Acquired Corp.	2,000	
Investment in Acquired Corp.		2,000
To amortize differential.		

The revenue amount that appears on the income statement with regard to this investment will total $2,000 which equals XYZ Corporation's share of Acquired Corporation's net income minus one year's amortization of the differential. The investment account will contain a balance of $99,600 ($100,000 + $4,000 − $2,000 − $2,400).   **[Section 19-3E]**

PROBLEM 19-8: Contrast and compare balance sheet valuation of MES when the securities are held on a long-term basis and the firm has no influential interest to the balance sheet valuation of MES when the firm does have an influential interest.

Answer: MES held on a long-term basis when the investor does not have an influential interest are valued at lower of cost or market. At the end of each accounting period the aggregate cost of the portfolio is compared to its aggregate market value. If market value is less than cost, an allowance account is used to reduce the value reported on the balance sheet to the lower market figure. Net unrealized losses are accumulated and reported as a reduction in owners' equity.

MES held on a long-term basis where the investor has an influential interest are accounted for by the equity method. No effort is made to determine market value of the securities. The balance in the investment account will equal the investor's share of the book value of the investee's net assets plus any unamortized positive differential or minus any unamortized negative differential. The amortization of the differential assures that eventually the balance shown in the investment account will equal the investor's share of the book value of the net assets of the investee company.   **[Sections 19-3B and 19-3E]**

PROBLEM 19-9: Explain the difference between the way in which decreases in market value of MES are handled when the decreases are deemed to be temporary and when they are deemed to be other than temporary.

Answer: Temporary decreases in the market value of MES are recognized as unrealized losses. The unrealized loss will appear on the income statement, if the investment in MES is considered short-term. They will appear as a negative owner's equity item on the balance sheet if the investment in MES is considered long-term. Subsequent recovery of temporary decreases in market value can occur to the extent that unrealized losses were previously recognized.

Decreases in market value that are determined to be other than temporary are recognized as realized losses. The cost valuation of the specific security is written down. Recovery of this type of loss cannot occur until the stock is sold.   **[Section 19-3C]**

PROBLEM 19-10: The portfolio of Ziskin Company for the years 19x2 and 19x3 is listed below. The market value of each stock at the end of each year is also shown. You may assume that all of the shares listed as being owned in 19x2 were acquired during 19x2. Prepare the entries implied by the information assuming the portfolio is a long-term investment and that the selling price of Company A shares was $80.

		19x2			19x3	
Company	No. of Shares	Cost per Share	Market Price	No. of Shares	Cost per Share	Market Price
A	800	$77	$79	600	$77	$80
B	1,600	81	80	1,600	81	84
C	900	44	42	900	44	45

Answer: The acquisition cost of the shares purchased during 19x2 was

	No. of Shares	Cost	Total
A	800	$77	$ 61,600
B	1,600	81	129,600
C	900	44	39,600
			$230,800

The entry to record the acquisition of the shares is

MES (long-term).	230,800	
Cash		230,800

The market value of the portfolio at the end of 19x2 is

	No. of Shares	Market Price	Total
A	800	79	63,200
B	1,600	80	128,000
C	900	42	37,800
			229,000

The entry to adjust the value of the portfolio to market is

Net Unrealized Loss on Long-term MES	1,800	
Allowance for Decline in Market Value		
of MES		1,800

During 19x3, the entry to record the sale of 200 shares of Firm A stock would be:

Cash ($80)(200)	16,000	
MES (long-term) ($77 × 200)		15,400
Gain on Sale of MES		600

The cost and market value of the portfolio at the end of 19x3 are $215,400 and $222,900, respectively. The balance in the valuation account would be zero. The entry to record the recovery of previously recognized unrealized loss will be

Allowance for Decline in Market Value		
of MES		1,800
Net Unrealized Loss on Long-term MES	1,800	

[Section 19-3B]

PROBLEM 19-11: KAYLIN Corporation purchased 32% of the stock of Raffie Corporation at a cost of $9,600. At the time of the purchase the book value of the net assets of Raffie Corporation was $30,000. During 19x1, Raffie earned a net income of $12,000 and paid dividends totaling $3,000. Prepare the entries to record these events on the books of KAYLIN Corporation. Compute the value that would be shown for KAYLIN Corporation's investment in Raffie Corporation's stock.

Answer:

Investment in Raffie Corp.	9,600	
Cash		9,600
To record purchase of 32% of company's stock.		
Investment in Raffie Corp.	3,840	
Equity in Income of Raffie Corp.		
($12,000 × .32)		3,840
To record share of Raffie Corp.'s net income.		
Cash ($3,000 × .32)	960	
Investment in Raffie Corp.		960
To record receipt of dividend.		

The balance in the investment account will equal the cost of the stock plus KAYLIN Corporation's share of Raffie's net income less dividends received. The balance will equal $12,480 ($9,600 + $3,840 − $960).

   The balance in the investment account should equal 32% of the net assets of Raffie Corporation. This is true because there was no differential to be amortized. Raffie Corporation will have equity equal to the beginning equity plus the net income minus the dividends. The net assets of Raffie Corporation equal $39,000 ($30,000 + $12,000 − $3,000). Thirty-two percent of $39,000 is $12,480.   **[Section 19-3E]**

PROBLEM 19-12: Now assume the KAYLIN Corporation purchased 32% of the stock of Raffie Corporation for $10,000 and all other information is the same as it was in Problem 19-11. Prepare the entries to record the events described for the year. Any differential is due to undervalued property with a useful life of 10 years. Compute the balance in the investment account and explain the revenue that would appear on the income statement with regard to this investment.

Answer: In this problem, the investor pays a positive differential for the 32% ownership purchased.

Explanation of Differential

Amount Paid for 32% Ownership	$10,000
÷ Percent of Firm Purchased	÷.32
Implied Total Value of Equity	$31,250
Book Value of Net Assets	30,000
Implied Total Differential	$ 1,250

The total differential is explained by undervalued assets with a remaining useful life of 10 years. KAYLIN Corporation's share of the differential is $400, 32% of the total. This differential will be amortized over the next 10 years at a rate of $40 per year. The entries to record the events are shown below.

Investment in Raffie Corp.	10,000	
Cash		10,000
To record purchase of 32% of company's stock.		
Investment in Raffie Corp.	3,840	
Equity in Income of Raffie Corp.		3,840
To record share of Raffie Corp's net income.		

Cash	960	
Investment in Raffie Corp.		960
To record dividend received		
Equity in Income of Raffie Corp.	40	
Investment in Raffie Corp.		40
To amortize differential.		

The revenue amount that appears on the income statement with regard to this investment will total $3,800 which equals KAYLIN Corporation's share of Raffie Corporation's net income minus one year's amortization of the differential. The investment account will contain a balance of $12,840 ($10,000 + $3,840 − $960 − 40).   **[Section 19-3E]**

20 LONG-TERM NOTES RECEIVABLE

THIS CHAPTER IS ABOUT

☑ **The Definition of Notes Receivable**
☑ **Valuation of Long-term Notes Receivable**
☑ **Accounting for Interest Earned on Long-term Notes Receivable**

20-1. The Definition of Notes Receivable

A note receivable is a promise from a person or business to pay a specified sum of money on a specified future date. The amounts received during the life of the note generally contain interest revenue. The amounts received must be separated into interest and return of principal to be sure that the appropriate accounts are credited. If the maturity date of the note extends beyond one year or one operating cycle, whichever is longer, the note will be classified as a long-term asset.

20-2. Valuation of Long-term Notes Receivable

Recall from the discussion in Chapter 11 that a dollar to be received in the future is not as valuable as a dollar received today. Likewise, a note cannot be valued by simply adding the amounts of expected future cash flow. The expected future amounts must be discounted to their present value and totaled to arrive at the value of the long-term note. In computing the present value of these future amounts, careful attention must be given to

- understanding the terms of the note so that an accurate projection can be made of the amount and timing of the cash flows
- the discount rate used to compute the present value of the cash flows.

The problems which arise in valuing notes center on these two factors.

A. The initial value placed on a note will affect the amount of net income.

Often a note is accepted as payment for a sale. The amount of revenue recognized on the sale will depend upon the initial value placed on the note. The lender (seller) will also earn interest revenue on the long-term note. The amount of interest revenue earned over the life of the note will equal the difference between the initial value of the note and the cash received. The value assigned to the note therefore affects the amount of revenue and profit earned at the time of the sale and it affects the amount of interest revenue earned over the life of the note. The value assigned to a note is of such importance that the FASB has carefully set out rules for valuation of long-term notes. These rules are discussed in detail in the next three sections.

B. When a note is received solely in exchange for cash, the note will be valued at the amount of cash exchanged

It is assumed that when a lender makes a cash loan, the amount of the loan has been computed as the present value of all future cash flows. In such cases, the value of the note is equal to the amount of cash exchanged.

EXAMPLE 20-1: On 1/1/x1, Lender Corporation received a $10,000, ten-year, 8% note receivable from Borrower Corporation in exchange for $10,000 cash. The terms of the note indicated that Borrower would make regular semiannual interest payments until the note matured on 1/1/x11. This note would be valued at $10,000, the amount of the cash exchanged. This will be true even if 8% appears to be an unreasonably low or high interest rate at the time the note is received.

EXAMPLE 20-2: Lender Corporation received a ten-year note with a face value of $18,000 from Borrower Corporation in exchange for $10,000 cash on 1/1/x1. The terms of the note indicated that Borrower would make a single payment on 1/1/x11. This note would be valued at $10,000 on 1/1/x1, the amount of the cash exchanged. The present value of the $18,000 to be received at the end of the ten-year life of the note is presumed to be equal to the amount of the cash exchanged.

EXAMPLE 20-3: Lender Corporation received a ten-year note in which Borrower Corporation promised to pay $1,000 per year in interest plus $11,000 at the end of ten years. Lender Corporation gave the borrower $10,000 in exchange for this note. The note would be valued at $10,000, the amount of the cash exchanged. It is always assumed that the present value of the future cash flows from a note is equal to the amount of cash exchanged when a note is accepted solely in exchange for cash.

C. Notes received in exchange for property are valued at the fair market value (FMV) of the property, when the FMV can be reasonably estimated.

A note may be accepted in exchange for property. The value placed on the note will equal the FMV of the property exchanged if the FMV of the property can be reasonably estimated. The rule presumes that the present value of the cash flows is equal to the FMV of the property given up in exchange for the note.

EXAMPLE 20-4: Seller Corporation accepted a ten-year, $10,000, 8% note in exchange for merchandise which has a normal cash selling price of $10,000. The note provided that the buyer would make regular semiannual interest payments and would pay $10,000 upon maturity of the note. The note will be valued at an amount equal to the FMV of the property exchanged or $10,000. The present value of the future cash flows for interest and the payment upon the maturity of the note is presumed to equal the FMV of the property. The revenue earned on the sale will be $10,000.

EXAMPLE 20-5: Seller Corporation accepted a ten-year, $18,000 note in exchange for merchandise with a normal cash selling price of $10,000. The note requires the buyer to make a single payment of $18,000 upon maturity of the note. The note will be valued at $10,000 on the date of the sale and the revenue recorded on the sale will equal $10,000, the FMV of the property exchanged.

EXAMPLE 20-6: Seller Corporation accepted a ten-year, $9,000, 20% note in exchange for merchandise with a normal cash selling price of $10,000. The note requires that the buyer pay $9,000 in ten years and make regular semiannual interest payments at a 20% annual rate until the note matures. This note will be valued at $10,000 on the date of the sale. The value is determined by the FMV of the property exchanged.

D. Notes received in exchange for property where the FMV of the property cannot be reasonably estimated are valued at the present value of the promised cash flow.

The value assigned to a note should equal the present value of the future cash flows promised by the note. The value of a note exchanged for property where the FMV of the property cannot be reasonably estimated will equal the present value of the promised cash flows discounted at a reasonable interest rate. The imputed interest rate should equal the interest rate the borrower would have to pay, if the funds were obtained elsewhere. The interest rate the borrower would have to pay another lender is borrower's "incremental borrowing rate".

EXAMPLE 20-7: Seller Corporation sold property whose FMV could not be estimated to Buyer Corporation in exchange for a note in which the buyer agreed to make a single $18,000 payment at the end of ten years. Buyer Corporation would have to pay an annual interest rate of 10% to borrow money elsewhere. The note and amount of the sale would be valued at the present value of $18,000 to be received in ten years discounted at 10% per year. The value placed upon the note on the date it is accepted will be $6940 (.38554 × $18,000). The value is found by using the factor from the Present Value of $1 table in the row for 10 periods and under the 10% interest rate column.

EXAMPLE 20-8: Seller Corporation sold property whose FMV could not be estimated. The buyer signed a $10,000, 8%, ten-year note. The note required the buyer to pay $10,000 at the end of ten years and make regular semiannual interest payments. The borrower would have had to pay 12% to borrow money elsewhere. The note will be valued at the present value of the cash payments discounted at the borrower's incremental borrowing rate. The borrower would have to pay 12% annual interest or 6% each six months to borrow money elsewhere. The present value of the cash payments promised by the note will equal

Principal: Present Value of $10,000 to be discounted
for 20 six month periods; at 6% per period: $10,000 × .31180 = $3,118

Interest: Present Value of an ordinary annuity of
20 rents of $400 (.04 × $10,000);
discounted at 6% per period: $400 × 11.46992 = $\underline{4,588}$
Present Value of Note $\overline{\$7,706}$

The note and the sale will be valued at $7,706, the present value of the promised cash flows discounted at the buyer's incremental borrowing rate of 6% per six month period.

Present value calculations like those illustrated in Examples 20-7 and 20-8 are required only if two conditions exist. First the note must be accepted in return for property whose FMV cannot be reasonably estimated. Second, the interest rate on the note must be unreasonable given the buyer's cost of borrowing. If the FMV of the property is known, the note is valued at that amount. If the interest charged on the note is reasonable, then the present value of the note will equal its face value.

EXAMPLE 20-9: Seller Corporation sold property to Buyer Company. The fair market value of the property could not be reasonably estimated. The buyer signed a $10,000, 12%, ten-year note in which he agreed to pay $10,000 at the end of ten years and make regular semiannual interest payments up to the maturity of the note. Buyer Corporation would have to pay interest of 6% per six months to borrow money elsewhere. The present value of the 12% note discounted at the buyer's incremental borrowing rate of 6% per six months is shown below:

Principal: Present Value of $10,000 to be discounted
for 20 six month periods at 6% per period: $10,000(.31180) = $ 3,118

Interest: Present Value of an ordinary annuity of
20 rents of .06($10,000) discounted
at 6% per period: $600(11.46992) = $\underline{6,882}$
Present Value of Note $\overline{\$10,000}$

The note will be valued at its face value of $10,000. If the interest rate that appears on the face of the note is reasonable, the present value of the cash flows will equal the note's face value.

20-3. Accounting for Interest Earned on Long-term Notes

The accounting for interest earned on long-term notes receivable depends upon the relationship of the face value of the note to the present value of its cash flows.

A. When the face value of the note *equals* the present value of the cash flows, the interest rate specified on the note (nominal interest rate) defines the interest earned.

Accounting for interest earned on a long-term note is a straightforward process, if the face value of the note is equal to the present value of the cash flows promised in the note. The interest rate that appears on the face of the note (nominal interest rate) defines the amount of interest revenue earned in each interest payment period.

The face value of a note and its present value will be equal if any of the following are true:

- The note is accepted solely in exchange for cash equal to the face value of the note.
- The note is accepted in exchange for property that has a FMV equal to the face value of the note.
- The note is accepted in exchange for property whose FMV cannot be determined and the interest rate that appears on the face of the note equals the borrower's incremental borrowing rate.

EXAMPLE 20-10: XYZ Corporation lends $10,000 to Mr. Jones in exchange for a $10,000, 10%, three-year note. Mr. Jones agrees to make regular annual interest payments. The note will be valued at the amount of cash given which is equal to the face value of the note. The entry to record the acceptance of the note, the three annual interest payments, and the final repayment of principal upon maturity will be as follows:

Notes Receivable	10,000	
Cash		10,000
To record the acceptance of note in exchange for cash.		
Cash ($10,000 × .10)	1,000	
Interest Revenue.		1,000
To record receipt of first year's interest.		
Cash	1,000	
Interest Revenue.		1,000
To record 2d year's interest.		
Cash	1,000	
Interest Revenue.		1,000
To record 3d year's interest.		
Cash	10,000	
Notes Receivable		10,000
To record receipt of principal upon maturity.		

EXAMPLE 20-11: Virtually the same set of entries as shown in Example 20-10 would be made if the note had been accepted in exchange for property with a FMV equal to the face value of the note of $10,000. Only the first entry would be changed to reflect the fact that property rather than cash was given in exchange for the note. If the book value of the property exchanged equaled $8,000, the entry to record acceptance of the note would be

Notes Receivable	10,000	
Property		8,000
Gain on Sale of Property		2,000

EXAMPLE 20-12: The same set of entries as in Example 20-11 would be made if the note had been accepted in exchange for property whose FMV was not known and the incremental borrowing rate of the buyer equaled the 10% interest rate that appears on the face of the note. The present value of the note would equal its face value.

B. When the face value of a note is greater than the present value of the cash flows, the effective interest method is used to compute interest earned each period.

The face value of the note will exceed its present value when any of the following are true:

- The amount of cash given in exchange for a note is less than the face value of the note.
- The note is received in exchange for property whose estimated FMV value is less than the face value of the note.
- The note is received in exchange for property whose value cannot be estimated and the interest rate on the note is less than borrower's incremental borrowing rate.

1. *A Discount on Notes Receivable account will be credited when the face value of a note is greater than its present value.* The Discount on Notes Receivable account is a negative asset account. Its balance is deducted from the balance in Notes Receivable in valuing the notes on the balance sheet. The balance in the discount accounts represents interest that will be earned over the life of the note in addition to the interest specifically shown on the face of the note. This interest is included in the face value of the note. At any point in time, the value assigned to notes receivable will equal the face value of the note (debit balance in Notes Receivable) less interest included in the face of the note that has not yet been earned (credit balance in the discount account).

EXAMPLE 20-13: Seller Corporation accepts a three-year, $1331 note (no interest mentioned on the face of the note) in exchange for property with a book value of $800. The FMV of the property is estimated to be $1,000. The note will be valued at $1,000, the FMV of the property exchanged. The entry to record the acceptance of this note will be:

Notes Receivable	1,331	
Discount on Notes Receivable		331
Property		800
Gain on Sale of Property		200

The note will be valued on the balance sheet at $1,000 an amount equal to its face value of $1,331 less the $331 balance in the discount account. The discount account represents interest that is included in the face value that has not yet been earned by Seller Corporation. That interest will be earned over the three-year life of the note. (Note the importance of the valuation process to the profit reported on the sale of the property. The higher the value assigned to the note, the larger the profit made on the sale.)

2. *The effective interest rate on the loan is used to determine the interest revenue earned during each period the loan is outstanding.* The *effective* interest rate on the note will be greater than, not equal to, the *nominal* interest rate that appears on the face of the note. The balance in Discount on Notes Receivable will be amortized over the life of the note as additional interest revenue. The effective interest rate must be determined in order to record interest revenue. This can be a very difficult computation.

EXAMPLE 20-14: The *effective* interest rate on the note described in Example 20-13 is computed as follows. The *nominal* interest rate on this note is 0% because no interest is specifically mentioned on the face of the note. However, interest is being charged on this loan. The borrower receives property with a FMV of $1,000 and returns $1,331 at the end of three years. The three-year interest amount totals $331. The effective interest rate is computed using the present value tables.

Present Value = $1,000 = ($1,331) (Factor from PV of $1 Table)
Factor = $1,000/$1,331 = .75131

Using the Present Value of $1 table, looking across the row for 3 periods, we find that the present value of $1 to be received at the end of 3 periods discounted at 10% per period equals .75131. The effective rate of interest on this note is 10%.

3. *Interest revenue is calculated each period using the effective interest method.* Interest on long-term notes is required by the GAAP to be computed using the effective interest method unless the less cumbersome straight-line method described in Chapter 15 does not yield significantly different results. The effective interest rate method computes the period's interest revenue by applying the effective interest rate to the book value of the note. The difference between the interest revenue and the amount of cash interest received from the borrower reduces the balance in the discount account and increases the net value of notes receivable. It is generally wise to prepare an effective interest schedule when a long-term note is accepted.

EXAMPLE 20-15: An effective interest schedule for the note discussed in Examples 20-13 and 20-14 has been prepared and is shown below. The entries or interest revenue at the end of each of the three years of the note's life and for receipt of payment for the face value of the note are also shown below.

Year	(a) Note Rec. Balance	(b) Discount on Note Rec. Balance	(c) Book Value of Note Rec. (a − b)	(d) Effective Interest Rate	(e) Interest Revenue (c × d)	(f) Cash Interest Received	(g) Reduction in Discount (e − f)
1	$1,331	$331	$1,000	10%	$100	$0	$100
2	1,331	231	1,100	10%	110	0	110
3	1,331	121	1,210	10%	121	0	121

Notes Receivable		1,331	
Discount on Notes Receivable			331
Property			800
Gain on Sale of Property			200
To record acceptance of the note.			
Discount on Notes Receivable		100	
Interest Revenue			100
To record interest revenue for 1st year.			
Discount on Notes Receivable		110	
Interest Revenue			110
To record interest revenue for 2d year.			
Discount on Notes Receivable		121	
Interest Revenue			121
To record interest revenue for 3d year.			
Cash		1,331	
Notes Receivable			1,331
To record receipt of face value of note on maturity.			

Interest revenue for each period equals the effective interest rate times the book value of the note. During 19x1, the book value of the note was $1,000. This equals the value of the property given in exchange for the note. The book value of the note is found by subtracting the balance in the discount account from the balance of the note receivable. Interest earned during the first year was $100 ($1,000 × .10). The interest revenue collected was $0 because the borrower pays no cash until the note matures. The difference reduces the balance in the discount account. As of the end of year 1, only $221 of the discount represents interest included in the Notes Receivable account that has not yet been earned.

The book value of the note during the second year equals the $1,000 initially lent out plus the $100 interest due from the first year but which has not yet been collected. The book value can also be computed by subtracting the $231 balance in the discount account from the $1,331 balance in Notes Receivable. Interest revenue earned but not collected equals $110 ($1,100 × .10).

The book value of the note during the third year equals $1,210. This represents the $1,000 initially lent out plus the interest earned but not collected in the first and second years, $100 and $110, respectively. Interest revenue for the third year, therefore, equals $121 ($1,210 × .10).

By the end of the third year, the book value of the note equals its face value of $1,331. The balance in the discount account is zero because all of the interest included in the face of the note has been earned.

C. When the present value of the cash flow exceeds the face value of the note, the effective interest method is used to compute interest earned each period.

On some occasions the present value of the cash flows will exceed the face value of the note. This will occur under the following situations:

- The cash given for the note is greater than the face value of the note.
- The FMV of property given in exchange for the note is greater then the face value of the note.
- The note is received in exchange for property whose FMV cannot be estimated and the interest rate that appears on the face of the note is greater than the borrower's incremental borrowing rate.

1. *A Premium on Notes Receivable account is debited when the present value of the note exceeds its face value.* The Premium on Notes Receivable account increases the value of Notes Receivable on the balance sheet. Its balance is added to the balance in Notes Receivable on the balance sheet. The balance in the premium account represents cash to be received in the form of interest over the life of the note that is really a return of principal. At any point in time, the value assigned to Notes Receivable will equal the face value of the note (the debit balance in Notes Receivable) plus principal amounts that will be repaid as part of the interest payments that have not been collected as of the valuation date (the debit balance in the premium account).

EXAMPLE 20-16: Seller Corporation sells a piece of land with a book value of $7,000 and no estimated FMV to Buyer Company in exchange for the buyer's three year, $10,000, 16% note. The buyer agrees to make regular annual interest payments on the note. Seller estimates that Buyer Company's incremental borrowing rate is 12%. The note will be valued at the present value of the cash payments. The appropriate discount rate is 12% per annual interest period, the buyer's incremental borrowing rate. The present value of the note is computed as follows:

Principal: Present value of $10,000 to be discounted
for 3 annual periods at 12% per period: $10,000 × .71178 = $ 7,118

Interest: Present value of an ordinary annuity of
(.16)($10,000) = $1,600 for 3 periods
discounted at 12% per period: $1,600 × 2,40183 = $ 3,843
Present Value of Note $10,961

This note has a present value of $10,961. It has a face value of $10,000. The premium is $961, the difference between the present and face values of the note. The entry to record the acceptance of the note in exchange for the land is

Notes Receivable	10,000	
Premium on Notes Receivable	961	
Land		7,000
Gain on Sale of Land		3,961

The book value of the note, $10,961, is equal to the face value of $10,000 plus the $961 premium. The land was sold for $10,961 even though the face value of the note was only $10,000. Of the principal amount of the loan, $961 is being accounted for in the premium account. Note once again that the value assigned to the note determines the amount of the profit recognized on the sale. The valuation of the note receivable affects the reported profits of the firm.

2. *The effective interest rate is lower than the nominal interest rate when the present value of the cash flows is greater than the face value of the note.* The effective interest rate method will be used in computing the amount of interest revenue earned on the note for each period. The effective rate is lower than the nominal interest rate that appears on the face of the note when the present value of the note is greater than its face value.

EXAMPLE 20-17: The effective interest rate on the note described in Example 20-16 is 12% compounded annually. This is the interest rate used to establish the present value of the cash flows promised by the note.

Note the difference between the process to establish the present value of the note and the effective interest rate when the FMV of the property exchanged was known (Examples 20-13 and 20-14) and the process used when the FMV of the property was not known (Example 20-16 and 20-17). The present value of the note equaled the FMV of the property in Example 20-13 and the effective interest rate was computed in Example 20-14. The present value of the note was unknown and had to be computed in Example 20-16 but the effective interest rate was then known in the Example 20-17.

3. *Interest revenue is computed each period using the effective interest method.* The application of the effective interest method is essentially the same for a note accepted at a premium as for a note accepted at a discount. The interest for the period is computed by multiplying the book value of the note by the effective interest rate. The difference between the interest revenue and the cash interest received reduces the balance in the premium account. In the case of a premium, the cash interest received is greater than the interest revenue earned. Each cash interest payment is divided into an interest revenue portion and a return of principal portion. The return of principal portion reduces the balance in the premium account and reduces the book value of the note. At any point in time, the book value of the note equals its face value plus principal included in the premium account that has not been collected in cash.

EXAMPLE 20-18: An effective interest schedule for the note described in Examples 20-16 and 20-17 is shown below along with the entries that would be made to record the receipt of interest payments and the final settlement of the note upon maturity. The effective interest rate on the note is 12%. The nominal interest rate which established the amount of cash interest each year is 16%.

Effective Interest Schedule

Year	(a) Note Rec. Balance	(b) Premium on Note Rec. Balance	(c) Book Value of Note Rec. (a + b)	(d) Effective Interest Rate	(e) Interest Revenue (c × d)	(f) Cash Interest Received	(g) Reduction in Premium (f − e)
1	$10,000	$961	$10,961	12%	$1,315	$1,600	$285
2	10,000	676	10,676	12%	1,281	1,600	319
3	10,000	357	10,357	12%	1,243	1,600	357

The entries to record receipt of cash interest payments and the final payment of the face value of the note will be

Notes Receivable	10,000	
Premium on Notes Receivable.	961	
Land.		7,000
Gain on Sale of Land.		3,961
To record acceptance of the note.		
Cash	1,600	
Interest Revenue.		1,315
Premium on Notes Receivable		285
To record interest revenue for 1st year.		
Cash	1,600	
Interest Revenue.		1,281
Premium on Notes Receivable		319
To record interest revenue for 2d year.		
Cash	1,600	
Interest Revenue.		1,243
Premium on Notes Receivable		357
To record interest revenue for 3d year.		
Cash	10,000	
Notes Receivable		10,000
To record payment of face value on maturity.		

Interest revenue for each period equals the effective interest rate times the book value of the note. During 19x1, the book value of the note was $10,961. This equals the present value of the cash flows from the note discounted at the borrower's incremental borrowing rate. The book value of the note is also computed by adding the balance in the premium account to the balance in the Notes Receivable account. Interest earned during 19x1 was 12% of $10,961 or $1,315. The firm received $1,600 from the borrower so $285 ($1,600 − $1,315) must be a return of principal. This amount reduces the balance in the premium account.

The book value of the note during year 2 equals $10,676, the initial amount of the loan of $10,961 less the amount of principal that has been repaid of $285. The 19x2 book value can also be computed by adding the $10,000 balance in Notes Receivable to the $676 remaining balance in the premium account. Interest revenue in year 2 is 12% of $10,676 or $1,281; $1,600 is received from the borrower so $319 ($1,600 − $1,281) of the principal amount was repaid as a part of the cash interest payment.

The book value of the note during 19x3 equals $10,357. This represents the $10,961 originally lent out less $285 of the principal repaid in 19x1 and $319 repaid in 19x2. It also equals the $10,000 face value of the note plus the $357 remaining in the premium account. Interest revenue for year 3 equals 12% of $10,357 or $1,243. The $1,600 cash interest payment covers the interest revenue earned and includes $357 payment of the principal amount reducing the balance in the premium account to zero by the time the note matures.

RAISE YOUR GRADES

Can you explain...?

☑ how a long-term note is valued?
☑ why proper valuation of Notes Receivable is important
☑ how to value a note received in exchange for cash
☑ how to value a note received in exchange for property whose FMV is known
☑ how to value a note received in exchange for property whose FMV is not known

☑ what a Discount on Notes Receivable account represents
☑ how to calculate the book value of a note accepted at a discount
☑ how to calculate the book value of a note accepted at a premium
☑ how the effective and nominal interest rates are related to each other when a note is accepted at a premium
☑ what situations will lead to a note being accepted at a discount
☑ what the effective interest rate is
☑ what the nominal interest rate is
☑ how the effective and nominal interest rates are related to each other when a note is accepted at a discount
☑ how to compute interest revenue using the effective interest method
☑ what a Premium on Notes Receivable account represents

SUMMARY

1. Long-term notes are assigned a value equal to the present value of the cash flows promised by the note.
2. The present value of the cash flows of a note exchanged solely for cash equals the amount of cash exchanged.
3. The present value of the cash flows of a note exchanged for property whose FMV can be reasonably estimated equals the FMV of the property given in exchange for the note.
4. The present value of the cash flows of a note exchanged for property whose FMV cannot be reasonably estimated equals the present value of the cash flows discounted at the borrower's incremental borrowing rate.
5. The value placed upon a note affects the amount of profit recognized on a sale if the note is accepted in exchange for goods or property.
6. The value placed upon a note affects the amount of interest revenue recognized over the life of the note.
7. The nominal interest rate on a note is the interest rate mentioned on the face of the note.
8. The nominal interest rate on a non-interest bearing note is 0%.
9. The effective interest rate is the real rate of interest being charged on the loan.
10. If the face value of a note equals the present value of the cash flows, the nominal and effective interest rates are the same.
11. When the face value of a note exceeds the present value of the cash flows, the face value includes some amount of unearned interest.
12. A discount on notes receivable account is credited for the amount of unearned interest included in the face value of a note. The discount account is a negative asset account.
13. The effective interest rate is greater than the nominal interest rate when the face value of a note exceeds the present value of the cash flows.
14. The effective interest rate method computes each period's interest by multiplying the effective interest rate times the book value of the note.
15. The book value of a note accepted at a discount equals the balance in Notes Receivable less the balance in the discount account.
16. When a note is accepted at a discount, the full amount of the interest revenue is not collected each period. The uncollected interest revenue is added to the principal to be collected upon the maturity of the note.
17. When the present value of the cash flows from a note exceeds the face value of the note, the full principal amount of the loan is not included in the Notes Receivable account. The additional amount lent out is debited into a Premium on Notes Receivable account.
18. The effective interest rate is less than the nominal interest rate when the present value of the cash flows exceeds the face value of the note.

19. The book value of a note accepted at a premium equals the balance in Notes Receivable plus the balance in the premium account.
20. The effective interest rate is also used to compute interest revenue from a note issued at a premium.
21. When a note is accepted at a premium, the amount collected as interest each period exceeds the interest revenue earned on the note. A portion of each cash payment is a return of principal. The return of principal portion reduces the balance in the premium account and reduces the book value of the note.

RAPID REVIEW

1. Long-term notes are valued at _____.
   Value the notes accepted in Questions 2 through 4. Briefly explain the way in which the value was established.
2. A $6,000, 5 year, 6% note accepted in exchange for $4,000 cash. Borrower's incremental borrowing rate is 8%.
3. A $6,000, 5 year, 16% note accepted in exchange for property with a FMV of $6,300. Borrower's incremental borrowing rate is 14%.
4. A $6,000 non-interest bearing note to be paid in 3 years accepted in exchange for property. No reasonable estimate of FMV of property is available. Borrower's incremental borrowing rate is 12%.
5. Indicate whether each note in Questions 2 through 4 was accepted at a premium or a discount.
6. When the face value of a note exceeds the present value of the cash flows, the (discount/premium) on notes receivable account will be (debited/credited). The effective interest rate on the note will be (greater/less) than the nominal rate.
7. When the present value of the cash flows from a note exceeds the face value of the note, the (discount/premium) on notes receivable account will be (debited/credited). The effective interest rate on the note will be (greater/less) than the nominal rate.
8. When a note is accepted at a discount, the cash amount of interest received each period will be (greater/less) than the interest revenue earned each period. The balance in the discount account will (increase/decrease) and the book value of the note will (increase/decrease).
9. When a note is accepted at a premium, the cash amount of interest received each period will be (greater/less) than the interest revenue earned each period. The balance in the premium account will (increase/decrease) and the book value of the note will (increase/decrease).
10. XYZ Corporation accepted a long-term note with an effective interest rate of 9% per year and a nominal interest rate of 6%. The face value of the note was $10,000 and interest is paid annually.
    (a) The note was accepted at a (premium/discount).
    (b) The amount of cash collected on the note in the first year will equal _____.
    (c) If the balance in the premium or discount account was $600 at the beginning of the year, the amount of interest revenue recognized will be equal to _____.
    (d) The book value of the note at the end of the first year would then be _____.
11. XYZ Corporation accepted a note with an effective interest rate of 10% and a nominal interest rate of 12%. The face value of the note was $10,000 and interest is paid annually.
    (a) The note was accepted at a (discount/premium).
    (b) The amount of cash collected on the note in the first year equals _____.
    (c) If the balance in the premium or discount account was $800 at the beginning of the first year, the amount of interest revenue recognized would equal _____.
    (d) The book value of the note at the end of the first year would then be _____.

12. When a note is accepted at a discount, the amount of each periodic cash payment received will be (greater/less) than the amount of interest revenue recognized. The book value of the note (increases/decreases) each period.

13. When a note is accepted at a premium, the amount of each periodic cash payment received will be (greater/less) than the amount of interest revenue recognized. The book value of the note (increases/decreases) each period.

14. XYZ Corporation sells property for which a reasonable estimate of FMV cannot be made. The corporation accepts a note from the buyer. The profit on the sale will increase as the borrower's incremental borrowing rate (increases/decreases) because the present value of the cash flows promised by the note will be greater all other things being equal.

Answers:

1. the present value of promised cash flows. [Section 20-2]
2. $4,000; the amount of cash exchanged [Section 20-2B]
3. $6,300; the FMV of the property exchanged [Section 20-2C]
4. $6,000 × .71178 = $4,271; the present value of cash flows discounted at the borrower's incremental borrowing rate [Section 20-2D]
5. Question 2: discount
   Question 3: premium
   Question 4: discount [Section 20-3]
6. discount; credited; greater [Section 20-3B]
7. premium; debited; less [Section 20-3C]
8. less: decrease; increase [Section 20-3B]
9. greater; decrease; decrease [Section 20-3C]
10. (a) discount
    (b) .06 × $10,000 = $600
    (c) .09 × $9,400 = $846
    (d) $9,400 + ($846 − $600) = $9,646 [Section 20-3B]
11. (a) premium
    (b) .12 × $10,000 = $1,200
    (c) .10 × $10,800 = $1080
    (d) $10,800 − ($1,200 − $1,080) = $10,680 [Section 20-3C]
12. less; increases [Section 20-3B]
13. greater; decreases [Section 20-3C]
14. decreases [Section 20-2D]

SOLVED PROBLEMS

Problems 20-1 through 20-4 refer to the information below.

Extendaloan Corporation accepted a $20,000, non-interest bearing, 4 year note, from Moochalot Company. The note was accepted on 1/1/x1 and it matures on 12/31/x4.

PROBLEM 20-1: Prepare the entry to record the acceptance of the note on 1/1/x1 by Extendaloan Corporation. Extendaloan gives Moochalot Company $13,660 on the day the note was signed. Show the entry made on 1/1/x1, the day the note was accepted. Compute the effective interest rate on the loan. Prepare an effective interest amortization schedule and show the entries made each year to record interest revenue. Show the entry made on 12/31/x4 when the note is retired.

Answer: The present value of the cash flows from the note is presumed to be equal to the amount of cash exchanged when the note is issued solely in exchange for cash. The value assigned to this note on the day it is accepted will be $13,660. The entry to record the acceptance of the note will be

1/1/x1	Notes Receivable	20,000	
	Discount on Notes Receivable		6,340
	Cash.		13,660
	To record acceptance of the note.		

The effective interest rate on this loan can be calculated as follows:

$$PV = \$13,660 = (\$20,000) \text{ (Factor PV of \$1 Table)}$$
$$Factor = (\$13,660)/(\$20,000) = .683$$

The present value of $1 for 4 periods discounted at 10% per period equals .68301. Therefore, this loan carries an effective interest rate of 10%.

Effective Interest Schedule

Year	(a) Note Rec. Balance	(b) Discount on Note Rec. Balance	(c) Book Value of Note Rec. (a − b)	(d) Effective Interest Rate	(e) Interest Revenue (c × d)	(f) Cash Interest Received	(g) Reduction in Discount (e − f)
1	$20,000	$6,340	$13,660	10%	$1,366	$0	$1,366
2	20,000	4,974	15,026	10%	1,503	0	1,503
3	20,000	3,471	16,529	10%	1,653	0	1,653
4	20,000	1,818	18,182	10%	1,818	0	1,818

The entries to record interest earned and to account for the receipt of the face value of the note upon maturity appear below.

12/31/x1	Discount on Notes Receivable	1,366	
	Interest Revenue		1,366
	To record interest revenue for year 1.		
12/31/x2	Discount on Notes Receivable	1,503	
	Interest Revenue		1,503
	To record interest revenue for year 2.		
12/31/x3	Discount on Notes Receivable	1,653	
	Interest Revenue		1,653
	To record interest revenue for year 3.		
12/31/x4	Discount on Notes Receivable	1,818	
	Interest Revenue		1,818
	To record interest revenue for year 4.		
	Cash	20,000	
	Notes Receivable		20,000
	To record retirement of note.		

[Sections 20-2B and 20-3B]

PROBLEM 20-2: Now assume the note described above was accepted in return for property with a FMV of $14,701. The property had a book value of $10,000 at the time of the exchange. Prepare the entry to record the exchange. Determine the effective interest rate charged on the loan. Prepare an effective interest schedule for the loan. Show the entries to record interest earned on the loan each year and to account for the payment received upon maturity of the note.

Answer: The value assigned to the note will equal the FMV of the property given in exchange for the note.

1/1/x1	Notes Receivable	20,000	
	Discount on Notes Receivable		5,299
	Property		10,000
	Gain on Sale of Property		4,701
	To record acceptance of note in exchange for property.		

The effective interest rate on the loan is determined as follows:

$$PV = \$14,701 = \$20,000 \text{ (Factor from PV of \$1 Table)}$$
$$Factor = (\$14,701/\$20,000) = .73505$$

The Present Value of $1 Table indicates that the present value of $1 discounted for 4 periods at 8% equals .73503. The effective interest rate on this 4 year loan is 8%.

Effective Interest Schedule

Year	(a) Note Rec. Balance	(b) Discount on Note Rec. Balance	(c) Book Value of Note Rec. (a − b)	(d) Effective Interest Rate	(e) Interest Revenue (c × d)	(f) Cash Interest Received	(g) Reduction in Discount (e − f)
1	$20,000	$5,299	$14,701	8%	$1,176	$0	$1,176
2	20,000	4,123	15,877	8%	1,270	0	1,270
3	20,000	2,853	17,147	8%	1,372	0	1,372
4	20,000	1,481	18,519	8%	1,481	0	1,481

The entries to record interest and the payment received upon maturity will be

12/31/x1	Discount on Notes Receivable	1,176	
	Interest Revenue		1,176
	To record interest for year 1.		
12/31/x2	Discount on Notes Receivable	1,270	
	Interest Revenue		1,270
	To record interest for year 2.		
12/31/x3	Discount on Notes Receivable	1,372	
	Interest Revenue		1,372
	To record interest for year 3.		
12/31/x4	Discount on Notes Receivable	1,481	
	Interest Revenue		1,481
	To record interest for year 4.		
	Cash	20,000	
	Notes Receivable.		20,000
	To record payment upon maturity.		

[Sections 20-2C and 20-3B]

PROBLEM 20-3: Now suppose that the note described earlier is accepted in exchange for property whose FMV cannot be determined. The buyer's incremental borrowing rate is 16%. Determine the value to be assigned to the note on 1/1/x1 and prepare the journal entry to record the acceptance of the note, if the property had a book value at the time of the exchange of $10,000. Prepare an effective interest schedule and show the entries to record interest. Show the entry to record the receipt of payment upon the maturity of the note.

Answer: The value assigned to the note upon its acceptance will equal the present value of the cash flows discounted at the borrower's incremental borrowing rate. The cash flow from this note is a single payment of $20,000 to be received in 4 years.

The discount rate to be used is the borrower's incremental borrowing rate of 16% per year.

$$PV = (\$20,000)(\text{Factor from PV of \$1 Table})$$
$$= (\$20,000)(.55229) = \$11,046$$

The factor used is found in the 4 period row under 16% interest. The entry to record the acceptance of the note is

1/1/x1	Notes Receivable	20,000	
	Discount on Notes Receivable		8,954
	Property		10,000
	Gain on the Sale of Property		1,046
	To record acceptance of the note.		

The effective interest rate on the loan is 16%.

Effective Interest Schedule

Year	(a) Note Rec. Balance	(b) Discount on Note Rec. Balance	(c) Book Value of Note Rec. (a − b)	(d) Effective Interest Rate	(e) Interest Revenue (c × d)	(f) Cash Interest Received	(g) Reduction in Discount (e − f)
1	$20,000	$8,954	$11,046	16%	$1,767	$0	$1,767
2	20,000	7,187	12,813	16%	2,050	0	2,050
3	20,000	5,137	14,863	16%	2,378	0	2,378
4	20,000	2,759	17,241	16%	2,759	0	2,759

The entries to record interest and the payment at maturity are

12/31/x1	Discount on Notes Receivable	1,767	
	Interest Revenue		1,767
	To record interest for year 1.		
12/31/x2	Discount on Notes Receivable	2,050	
	Interest Revenue		2,050
	To record interest for year 2.		
12/31/x3	Discount on Notes Receivable	2,378	
	Interest Revenue		2,378
	To record interest for year 3.		
12/31/x4	Discount on Notes Receivable	2,759	
	Interest Revenue		2,759
	To record interest for year 4.		
	Cash	20,000	
	Notes Receivable.		20,000
	To record receipt of payment on maturity.		

[Sections 20-2D and 20-3B]

PROBLEM 20-4: Look at your answer to Problems 20-1 through 20-3 and answer the following questions:

(*a*) The nominal rate of interest on this note was _____ %.

(*b*) The note had the highest present value and the smallest discount when the effective interest rate was _____ %

(c) The note had the lowest present value the largest discount when the effective interest rate was _____ %

(d) The firm earned the least interest revenue in each year when the effective interest rate was _____ %

(e) The firm earned the most interest revenue in each year when the effective interest rate was _____ %

(f) For any given note, what is the relationship between the effective interest rate, the value initially assigned to the note, and the amount of interest revenue that is recognized over the life of the note?

Answer:

(a) 0%
(b) 8%
(c) 16%
(d) 8%
(e) 16%
(f) The higher the effective interest rate, the lower the value initially assigned to the note, and the larger the amount of interest revenue recognized over the life of the note.

[Sections 20-2 and 20-3]

Problems 20-5 through 20-8 refer to the note described below. XYZ Corporation accepts a four-year, 10%, $5,000 note on 1/1/x1. The note requires the borrower to make annual interest payments on 12/31 of each year and pay $5,000 on 12/31/x4.

PROBLEM 20-5: Assume that the note described above is accepted in exchange for $5,331 in cash lent to the borrower on 1/1/x1. Prepare the entry to record the acceptance of the note. The effective interest rate on this loan is 8%. Prepare an effective interest schedule for the loan. Show all entries to record receipt of interest. Prepare the entry to record the final settlement of the note.

Answer: The present value of a note accepted solely in exchange for cash is always equal to the amount of cash given up. The value assigned to this note will be $5,331. The entry to record the acceptance of the note will be

1/1/x1	Notes Receivable	5,000	
	Premium on Notes Receivable	331	
	Cash		5,331
	To record acceptance of note in exchange for cash.		

The borrower promises to pay back $5,000 at the end of four years and also promises to make regular annual interest payments of $500 (.10 × $5,000) at the end of each of the next four years. The present value of these promises is $5,331. This gives the lender an effective return of 8% compounded annually over the four year period that the loan is outstanding. It is possible to determine the effective interest rate on a loan of this type, but the computations are fairly complicated.

Effective Interest Schedule

Year	(a) Note Rec. Balance	(b) Premium on Note Rec. Balance	(c) Book Value of Note Rec. (a − b)	(d) Effective Interest Rate	(e) Interest Revenue (c × d)	(f) Cash Interest Received	(g) Reduction in Premium (f − e)
1	$5,000	$331	$5,331	8%	$426	$500	$74
2	5,000	257	5,257	8%	421	500	79
3	5,000	178	5,178	8%	414	500	86
4	5,000	92	5,092	8%	408	500	92

The entries will be

12/31/x1	Cash	500	
	Interest Revenue		426
	Premium on Notes Receivable ..		74
	To record interest revenue in year 1.		
12/31/x2	Cash	500	
	Interest Revenue		421
	Premium on Notes Receivable ..		79
	To record interest revenue in year 2.		
12/31/x3	Cash.....................	500	
	Interest Revenue		414
	Premium on Notes Receivable ..		86
	To record interest revenue in year 3.		
12/31/x4	Cash	500	
	Interest Revenue		408
	Premium on Notes Receivable ..		92
	To record interest revenue in year 4.		
	Cash	5,000	
	Notes Receivable		5,000
	To record receipt of payment upon maturity.		

[Sections 20-2B and 20-3C]

PROBLEM 20-6: How would the entries in Problem 20-5 be different if the note had been accepted in exchange for property with a book value of $4,500 and a FMV of $5,331?

Answer: The entry to record the acceptance of the note would recognize that property was given in exchange for the note rather than cash. The value assigned to the note would equal the FMV of the property which is $5,331. This is the same present value for the note as was assigned in Problem 20-5 when the note was accepted in exchange for cash. The entry to record the acceptance of the note would be

1/1/x1	Notes Receivable	5,000	
	Premium on Notes Receivable......	331	
	Property		4,500
	Gain on Sale of Property		831

All other entries would be the same because the effective interest rate used to calculate interest revenue is the same in both problems. **[Sections 20-2C and 20-3C]**

PROBLEM 20-7: Determine the value of the note and the effective interest rate if the note is accepted in exchange for property whose FMV is not known. The buyer's incremental borrowing rate is 6% per year. Prepare an effective interest schedule.

Answer: The value assigned to the note will equal the present value of the cash payments discounted at the borrower's incremental borrowing rate of 6% per period. The value assigned to the note will be:

Principal: Present value of $5,000 to be discounted
for 4 periods at 6% per period $= \$5,000 \times .79209 = \$3,960$

Interest: Present value of an ordinary annuity of
$500 for 4 periods discounted at 6% per   = $500 × 3.46511 = $\underline{1,733}$
period Present value of note $\overline{\$5,693}$

Effective Interest Schedule

Year	(a) Note Rec. Balance	(b) Premium on Note Rec. Balance	(c) Book Value of Note Rec. (a + b)	(d) Effective Interest Rate	(e) Interest Revenue (c × d)	(f) Cash Interest Received	(g) Reduction in Premium (f − e)
1	$5,000	$693	$5,693	6%	$342	$500	$158
2	5,000	535	5,535	6%	332	500	168
3	5,000	367	5,367	6%	322	500	178
4	5,000	189	5,189	6%	311	500	189

[Sections 20-2D and 20-3C]

PROBLEM 20-8: Now assume the note described above is accepted in exchange for property whose FMV is not determinable. The buyer's incremental borrowing rate is 12%. Determine the initial value to be assigned to the note. What amount of discount or premium will be recognized. Prepare an effective interest schedule for the note.

Answer: The note will be valued at the present value of the cash flows discounted at the borrower's incremental borrowing rate of 12%. The value assigned to the note will be:

Principal: Present value of $5,000 to be discounted
for 4 periods at 12% per period   = $5,000 × .63552 = $3,178

Interest: Present value of ordinary annuity
of $500 for 4 periods discounted
at 12% per period   = $500 × 3.03735 = $\underline{\$1,519}$
Present Value of Note $\overline{\$4,697}$

The note will be recorded with a DISCOUNT of $303 ($5,000 − $4697).

Effective Interest Schedule

Year	(a) Note Rec. Balance	(b) Discount on Note Rec. Balance	(c) Book Value of Note Rec. (a − b)	(d) Effective Interest Rate	(e) Interest Revenue (c × d)	(f) Cash Interest Received	(g) Reduction in Discount (e − f)
1	$5,000	$303	$4,697	12%	$564	$500	$64
2	5,000	239	4,761	12%	571	500	71
3	5,000	168	4,832	12%	580	500	80
4	5,000	88	4,912	12%	588	500	88

[Sections 20-2D and 20-3B]

PROBLEM 20-9: Fill in the missing numbers in the following effective interest schedule. The nominal interest rate is 8%.

Year	(a) Note Rec. Balance	(b) ____ on Note Rec. Balance	(c) Book Value of Note Rec. (a − b)	(d) Effective Interest Rate	(e) Interest Revenue (c × d)	(f) Cash Interest Received	(g) Reduction in Discount (e − f)
1	$10,000	?	?	?	$1,085	?	?
2	?	$676	?	?	?	?	?
3	?	?	?	?	?	?	?

Answer:

Year	(a) Note Rec. Balance	(b) Discount on Note Rec. Balance	(c) Book Value of Note Rec. (a − b)	(d) Effective Interest Rate	(e) Interest Revenue (c × d)	(f) Cash Interest Received	(g) Reduction in Discount (e − f)
1	$10,000	$961	$9,039	12%	$1,085	$800	$285
2	10,000	676	9,324	12%	1,119	800	319
3	10,000	357	9,643	12%	1,157	800	357

We know the note was accepted at a discount because interest revenue is greater than cash interest received.

First Line Computations: Cash interest received = $10,000 × .08 = $800
Reduction in discount = $1,085 − $800 = $285
Discount on Note Receivable = $285 + $676 = $961
Book value of Note Receivable = $10,000 − $961 = $9,039
Effective interest rate = $1,085 ÷ $9,039 = 12%

[Sections 20-3B and 20-3C]

PROBLEM 20-10: Reed Company accepted a $6,530, non-interest bearing, 4 year note, from Fischer Company. The note was accepted on 1/1/x2 and it matures on 12/31/x5. Prepare the entry to record the acceptance of the note on 1/1/x2 by Reed Company. Reed gives Fischer Company $4,800 on the day the note was signed. Show the entry made on 1/1/x2, the day the note was accepted. Compute the effective interest rate on the loan. Prepare an effective interest amortization schedule and show the entries made each year to record interest revenue. Show the entry made on 12/31/x5 when the note is retired.

Answer: The present value of the cash flows from the note is presumed to be equal to the amount of cash exchanged when the note is issued solely in exchange for cash. The value assigned to this note on the day it is accepted will be $4,800. The entry to record the acceptance of the note will be:

1/1/x2	Notes Receivable	6,530	
	Discount on Notes Receivable		1,730
	Cash.		4,800
	To record acceptance of the note.		

The effective interest rate on this loan can be calculated as follows:

PV = $4,800 = ($6,530)(Factor PV of $1 Table)
Factor = ($4,800)/($6,530) = .735

The present value of $1 for 4 periods discounted at 8% per period equals .73503. Therefore, this loan carries an effective interest rate of 8%.

Effective Interest Schedule

Year	(a) Note Rec. Balance	(b) Discount on Note Rec. Balance	(c) Book Value of Note Rec. (a − b)	(d) Effective Interest Rate	(e) Interest Revenue (c × d)	(f) Cash Interest Received	(g) Reduction in Discount (e − f)
1	6,530	1,730.00	4,800.00	8%	$384.00	$0	384.00
2	6,530	1,346.00	5,184.00	8%	414.72	0	414.72
3	6,530	931.28	5,598.72	8%	447.90	0	447.90
4	6,530	483.38	6,046.62	8%	483.38*	0	483.38

slight error due to rounding

The entries to record interest earned and to account for the receipt of the face value of the note upon maturity appear on page 362.

12/31/x2	Discount on Notes Receivable	384.00	
	Interest Revenue		384.00
	To record interest revenue		
	for year 1.		
12/31/x3	Discount on Notes Receivable	414.72	
	Interest Revenue		414.72
	To record interest revenue		
	for year 2.		
12/31/x4	Discount on Notes Receivable	447.90	
	Interest Revenue		447.90
	To record interest revenue		
	for year 3.		
12/31/x5	Discount on Notes Receivable	483.38	
	Interest Revenue		483.38
	To record interest revenue		
	for year 4.		
	Cash	6,530.00	
	Notes Receivable		6,530.00
	To record retirement of note.		

[Sections 20-2B and 20-3B]

PROBLEM 20-11: Now assume the note described above was accepted in return for property with a FMV of $5,172. The property had a book value of $4,000 at the time of the exchange. Prepare the entry to record the exchange. Determine the effective interest rate charged on the loan. Prepare an effective interest schedule for the loan. Show the entries to record interest earned on the loan each year and to account for the payment received upon maturity of the note.

Answer: The value assigned to the note will equal the FMV of the property given in exchange for the note.

1/1/x1	Notes Receivable	6,530	
	Discount on Notes Receivable		1,358
	Property		4,000
	Gain on Sale of Property		1,172
	To record acceptance of note in		
	exchange for property.		

The effective interest rate on the loan is determined as follows:

$$PV = \$5,172 = \$6,530 \text{ (Factor from PV of \$1 Table)}$$
$$\text{Factor} = (\$5,172/6,530) = .79203$$

The Present Value of $1 Table indicates that the present value of $1 discounted for 4 periods at 6% equals .79209. The effective interest rate on this 4 year loan is 6%.

Effective Interest Schedule

Year	(a) Note Rec. Balance	(b) Discount on Note Rec. Balance	(c) Book Value of Note Rec. (a − b)	(d) Effective Interest Rate	(e) Interest Revenue (c × d)	(f) Cash Interest Received	(g) Reduction in Discount (e − f)
1	$6,530	$1,358.00	$5,172.00	6%	$310.32	$0	$310.32
2	6,530	1,047.68	5,482.32	6%	328.94	0	328.94
3	6,530	718.74	5,811.26	6%	348.68	0	348.68
4	6,530	370.06	6,159.94	6%	370.06*	0	370.06

  * *slight error due to rounding*

The entries to record interest and the payment received upon maturity will be

12/31/x1	Discount on Notes Receivable	310.32	
	Interest Revenue		310.32
	To record interest for year 1.		
12/31/x2	Discount on Notes Receivable	328.94	
	Interest Revenue		328.94
	To record interest for year 2.		
12/31/x3	Discount on Notes Receivable	348.68	
	Interest Revenue		348.68
	To record interest for year 3.		
12/31/x4	Discount on Notes Receivable	370.06	
	Interest Revenue		370.06
	To record interest for year 4.		
	Cash	6,530.00	
	Notes Receivable.		6,530.00
	To record payment upon maturity.		

[Sections 20-2C and 20-3B]

PROBLEM 20-12: Now suppose that the note described earlier is accepted in exchange for property whose FMV cannot be determined. The buyer's incremental borrowing rate is 16%. Determine the value to be assigned to the note on 1/1/x1 and prepare the journal entry to record the acceptance of the note if the property had a book value at the time of the exchange of $4,000. Prepare an effective interest schedule and show the entries to record interest. Show the entry to record the receipt of payment upon the maturity of the note.

Answer: The value assigned to the note upon its acceptance will equal the present value of the cash flows discounted at the borrower's incremental borrowing rate. The cash flow from this note is a single payment of $6,530 to be received in 4 years. The discount rate to be used is the borrower's incremental borrowing rate of 16% per year.

$$PV = (\$6,530)(\text{Factor from PV of \$1 Table})$$
$$= (\$6,530)(.55229) = \$3,606.45$$

The factor used is found in the 4 period row under 16% interest. The entry to record the acceptance of the note is:

1/1/x1	Notes Receivable	6,530.00	
	Loss on the Sale of Property	393.55	
	Discount on Notes Receivable		2,923.55
	Property		4,000.00
	To record acceptance of the note.		

The effective interest rate on the loan is 16%.

Effective Interest Schedule

Year	(a) Note Rec. Balance	(b) Discount on Note Rec. Balance	(c) Book Value of Note Rec. (a − b)	(d) Effective Interest Rate	(e) Interest Revenue (c × d)	(f) Cash Interest Received	(g) Reduction in Discount (e − f)
1	6,530	2,923.55	3,606.45	16%	$577.03	$0	$577.03
2	6,530	2,346.52	4,183.48	16%	669.36	0	669.36
3	6,530	1,677.16	4,852.84	16%	776.45	0	776.45
4	6,530	900.71	5,629.29	16%	900.71*	0	900.71

* *slight error due to rounding*

The entries to record interest and the payment at maturity are:

12/31/x1	Discount on Notes Receivable	577.03	
	Interest Revenue		577.03
	To record interest for year 1.		
12/31/x2	Discount on Notes Receivable	669.36	
	Interest Revenue		699.36
	To record interest for year 2.		
12/31/x3	Discount on Notes Receivable	776.45	
	Interest Revenue		776.45
	To record interest for year 3.		
12/31/x4	Discount on Notes Receivable	900.71	
	Interest Revenue		900.71
	To record interest for year 4.		
	Cash	6,530.00	
	Notes Receivable		6,530.00
	To record receipt of payment on maturity.		

[Sections 20-2D and 20-3B]

EXAMINATION IV (Chapters 16–20)

1. Multiple Choice

1. A difference between the periodic and perpetual inventory systems is that
   (a) in a periodic system receipts of merchandise are not recorded, but receipts of merchandise are recorded under perpetual system
   (b) no inventory counts are made under the perpetual system but inventory counts are made under a periodic system
   (c) in a periodic system a cost of goods sold account is continuously updated as sales are made. No cost of goods sold account is updated in the perpetual system
   (d) a periodic system provides important information about when to reorder and about the amount of theft from inventory which is not available under a perpetual system
   (e) none of the above are true

2. XKZ Corporation's trial balance included the following account balances:

Purchases	$128,000
Purchase Discounts	7,500
Purchase Returns	9,000

   We know that this firm is using
   (a) the net method with a perpetual inventory system
   (b) the gross method with a perpetual inventory system
   (c) the net method with a periodic inventory system
   (d) the gross method with a periodic inventory system
   (e) we need more information to know what inventory methods are being used

3. Jones and Company counted the goods in its warehouse and valued them at $78,000. The accountant discovers that at the end of the period there were $8,500 of goods in transit to Jones and Company terms FOB shipping point, and $7,200 of goods in transit to Jones and Company terms FOB destination. Jones had sold $4,100 of goods to its customers that were being shipped FOB shipping point and $1,300 of goods being shipped FOB destination at the end of the year. Jones and Company had $500 of goods out on consignment and $700 of the goods in its warehouse that were accepted on consignment. The proper ending balance for Jones and Company's inventory is
   (a) $87,600
   (b) $88,300
   (c) $89,100
   (d) $90,400
   (e) none of the above

Questions 4 through 6 relate to the following information:

Soho Corporation began the year with 1,000 units each costing $6.50. During the year, the firm made the following inventory purchases:

	Units	Unit Cost
Purchase #1	2,000	8.00
Purchase #2	3,000	9.00
Purchase #3	1,000	10.00

At the end of the year, an inventory count revealed that 1,800 units remained in the inventory.

4. The value of the ending inventory using the average cost method would be
   (a) $15,300
   (b) $15,900
   (c) $16,200

(d) $18,000

(e) none of the above

5. The cost of goods sold using a LIFO cost flow assumption would be

(a) $17,200

(b) $41,800

(c) $42,300

(d) $47,700

(e) none of the above

6. The value of the ending inventory using a FIFO cost flow assumption would be

(a) $12,100

(b) $14,400

(c) $15,200

(d) $17,200

(e) none of the above

Questions 7 through 9 refer to the information below.

Value Corporation uses the dollar value LIFO method of valuing its ending inventory. Information for Years 1 through 3 is given below.

	Year 1	Year 2	Year 3
Ending Inventory at			
Current Prices	$1,000	$1,170	$1,650
Price Index	1.00	1.30	1.10

7. In valuing inventory at the end of Year 3, the Year 1 layer at acquisition prices would be

(a) $0

(b) $900

(c) $1,000

(d) $990

(e) none of the above

8. In valuing the inventory at the end of Year 3, the Year 2 layer at acquisition prices would be

(a) $0

(b) $221

(c) $900

(d) $1,300

(e) none of the above

9. The dollar value LIFO value of the inventory at the end of Year 3 would be

(a) $1,500

(b) $1,550

(c) $1,560

(d) $1,660

(e) none of the above

10. Mefirst Corporation has three items in its ending inventory. Information about these items is shown below.

Item	Unit Cost	Replacement Cost	Net Realizable Value	Normal Profit
A	$5	$4.50	$4.80	$.20
B	$7	$7.20	$7.50	$.60
C	$2	$1.80	$1.70	$.10

If Mefirst values its inventory at lower of cost or market, the unit prices used to value items A, B, and C respectively will be

(a) $4.50, $7.00, $1.70

(b) $4.50, $7.00, $1.80

(c) $4.60, $7.00, $1.70

(d) $4.60, $6.90, $1.60
(e) $4.80, $7.00, $1.70

11. On 3/1/x1, Firebug Corporation's warehouse was totally destroyed by fire. Company records indicated that the inventory on 1/1/x1 totaled $450,000. Merchandise worth $1,280,000 was purchased up to the time of the fire. The purchases figure included $41,000 of merchandise that arrived two days after the fire and had been purchased under shipping terms FOB shipping point. Sales through 2/28/x1 totaled $1,980,000. The firm has historically shown a gross profit equal to 20% of sales. What was the value of the inventory destroyed in the fire?
    (a) $105,000
    (b) $146,000
    (c) $187,000
    (d) $1,293,000
    (e) none of the above

12. The conventional retail inventory method approximates
    (a) a LIFO cost flow assumption with LCM valuation
    (b) average cost flow assumption with cost valuation
    (c) a FIFO cost flow assumption with cost valuation
    (d) average cost flow assumption with LCM valuation
    (e) a FIFO cost flow assumption with LCM valuation

13. In the retail inventory method, a cost ratio that excludes net markdowns will approximate
    (a) lower of cost or market valuation
    (b) average cost flow assumption
    (c) FIFO cost flow assumption
    (d) cost valuation
    (e) we cannot tell without additional information

Questions 14 and 15 relate to the following information:

XYZ Company begins the period with an inventory valued at $50,000 which would sell at retail prices for $75,000. During the accounting period, the firm purchased inventory costing $200,000 which was marked to sell for $335,000. Net markups for the period totaled $15,000 and net markdowns were $25,000. Sales totaled $300,000 and sales returns totaled $20,000. (Round cost ratio to three decimal places.)

14. Ending inventory valued using the cost retail method would be
    (a) $70,560
    (b) $75,000
    (c) $82,320
    (d) $85,260
    (e) $87,500

15. Ending inventory valued using the conventional retail method would be
    (a) $70,560
    (b) $75,000
    (c) $82,320
    (d) $85,260
    (e) $87,500

Questions 16 through 19 relate to the following information:

Lucky Corporation holds three stocks which were all purchased during 19x1. Information about these securities is summarized below.

Company	Total Cost	Total Market Value 12/31/x1	Total Market Value 12/31/x1
Dog Food Corporation	$10,000	$ 6,000	$12,000
Cat Food Corporation	30,000	32,000	29,000
Pig Food Corporation	12,000	11,000	12,500

16. If the stock is categorized as a short-term investment, the income statement for the year ending 12/31/x1 will show
    (a) an unrealized loss of $5,000
    (b) a realized loss of $5,000
    (c) an unrealized loss of $3,000
    (d) a realized loss of $3,000
    (e) nothing with regard to the stock

17. If the stock is categorized as a short-term investment, the income statement for the year ending 12/31/x2 will show
    (a) a recovery of $1,500
    (b) a recovery of $3,000
    (c) a recovery of $5,000
    (d) a recovery of $6,500
    (e) nothing with regard to the stock.

18. If the stock is categorized as a long-term investment, the income statement for the year ending 12/31/x1 will show
    (a) an unrealized loss of $5,000
    (b) a realized loss of $5,000
    (c) an unrealized loss of $3,000
    (d) a realized loss of $3,000
    (e) nothing with regard to the stock

19. If the stock is categorized as a long-term investment, the income statement for the year ending 12/31/x2 will show
    (a) an unrealized gain of $1,500
    (b) an unrealized gain of $3,000
    (c) an unrealized gain of $5,000
    (d) an unrealized gain of $6,500
    (e) nothing with regard to the stock

20. Investor Corporation purchased 40% of the stock of Deseree Corporation for $100,000. Deseree Corporation's books showed stockholders' equity of $250,000 at the time of the purchase. During 19x1, Deseree Corporation reported net income of $60,000 and paid dividends totaling $40,000. Investor Corporation would show revenue from this investment on its income statement of
    (a) $0
    (b) $24,000
    (c) $16,000
    (d) $8,000
    (e) $20,000

Questions 21 through 23 refer to the information below:

On 1/1/x1, Lender Corporation received a $10,000, 10% note from Inhock Corporation. The note required Inhock to pay the principal plus all of the interest at the end of two years. Inhock would normally pay 12% to borrow money. The present value of a dollar to be received in two periods discounted at 10% is .82645. The present value of a dollar to be received in two periods discounted at 12% is .79719.

21. If Lender Corporation accepted the note in exchange for some property with a fair market value of $9,000, the value assigned to the note upon its acceptance would be
    (a) $7,972
    (b) $8,265
    (c) $9,000
    (d) $9,917
    (e) $9,566

22. If Lender Corporation accepted the note in exchange for some property whose fair market value could not be determined, the value assigned to the note upon its

acceptance would be
  (a) $7,972
  (b) $8,265
  (c) $9,000
  (d) $9,917
  (e) $9,566

23. If Lender Corporation accepted the note in exchange for some property whose fair market value could not be determined, the amount of interest revenue that would be reported on the income statement for the year ended 12/31/x1 would be
  (a) $1,000
  (b) $1,200
  (c) $1,148
  (d) $1,190
  (e) $992

24. The Discount on Notes Receivable account will be credited when
  (a) the amount of cash given for a note is less than its face value
  (b) the note is received in exchange for property whose estimated FMV is less than the face value of the note
  (c) the note is received in exchange for property whose value cannot be estimated and the interest rate on the note is less than the borrower's incremental borrowing rate
  (d) all of the above
  (e) none of the above

25. Interest revenue is computed using the effective interest method by
  (a) multiplying the nominal interest rate by the face value on the note
  (b) multiplying the nominal interest rate by the book value of the note
  (c) multiplying the effective interest rate by the face value on the note
  (d) multiplying the effective interest rate by the book value on the note
  (e) multiplying the market interest rate by the market value of the note

II. Problems

1. Mr. Taxdodger has heard that LIFO can provide significant tax benefits, but he has also heard that the system can backfire and produce higher taxes in some years. Explain the tax benefits to be obtained by using traditional LIFO. Be sure to discuss the conditions that must exist for those benefits to be sustained.

2. On 1/1/x1, Stockbuyer Corporation purchased 10,000 shares of Stockseller Corporation at $5 per share. At the end of 19x1, the stock was selling for $3 on the market and, at the end of 19x2, it sold for $4.50. Stockseller earned net income in each of the two years of $1.00 per share and paid a dividend of $.25 per share.

  (a) Prepare the entries to record the information above assuming that Stockbuyer views its investment to be temporary.
  (b) Show any entries that would differ, if Stockbuyer views its investment to be long-term. Stockbuyer does not have influential interest over Stockseller.
  (c) Prepare the entries to record the information above assuming that Stockbuyer purchased 25% of the outstanding shares of Stockseller. Stockseller's equity at the time of the purchase totaled $200,000.

3. On 1/1/x1, XYZ Corporation accepted a five-year, 12% note with a face value of $100,000 in exchange for property whose value could not be established. The purchaser of the property agreed to pay interest on the face value of the note each December 31 and to repay the principal on 12/31/x5. The purchaser would have paid 10% interest to borrow money elsewhere.

  (a) What was the selling price of the land?
  (b) Prepare an effective interest schedule for this note.

ANSWERS TO EXAMINATION IV

Multiple Choice

1. e	**6.** d	**11.** a	**16.** c	**21.** c
2. d	**7.** b	**12.** d	**17.** b	**22.** e
3. a	**8.** a	**13.** a	**18.** e	**23.** c
4. a	**9.** c	**14.** b	**19.** e	**24.** d
5. e	**10.** c	**15.** a	**20.** b	**25.** d

Problems

Problem 1: Traditional LIFO provides tax benefits because it assumes that the newest units in the inventory have been sold. The cost of these units appears on the income statement as cost of goods sold expense. When prices are rising the most recently purchased units have the highest cost. The cost of goods sold will be highest using LIFO because the inventory with the highest unit cost is assumed to be sold. LIFO provides tax advantages by providing large CGS expense and therefore reduces taxable income. However, the benefits disappear if prices begin to fall. In a period of falling prices, LIFO assumes the newly purchased lower priced units have been sold giving a lower CGS figure than other methods.

Use of LIFO can create other tax problems. Inventory is valued at old, often very low prices when one assumes that the oldest units remain in the inventory for year after year. If the firm depletes its inventory stock it will be selling units with a very low book value. Cost of goods sold will reflect these old prices and the firm will report large profits. Traditional LIFO creates tax advantages when prices are rising and the size of the inventory stock is NOT depleted.

Problem 2

(*a*) The entries to record the events when the MES are considered to be a short-term investment are given below.

Year 1	MES — Short Term................	50,000	
	Cash		50,000
	To record the purchase of short-term MES.		
	Cash	2,500	
	Dividend Income...............		2,500
	To record receipt of dividends.		
	Unrealized Loss on Valuation of MES	20,000	
	Allowance for Decline in Market Value of MES		20,000
	To record unrealized loss on MES.		
Year 2	Cash	2,500	
	Dividend Income...............		2,500
	To record receipt of dividends.		
	Allowance for Decline in Market Value of MES.....................	15,000	
	Recovery of Unrealized Loss		15,000
	To record partial recovery of unrealized loss.		

(*b*) Only the entries to record reduction of MES to market and the recovery of market value would be different.

Year 1	Net Unrealized Loss on Valuation of MES	20,000	
	Allowance for Decline in Market Value of MES		20,000
Year 2	Allowance for Decline in Market Value of MES	15,000	
	Net Unrealized Loss on Valuation of MES		15,000

(c) The entries to record the events if the firm has an influential interest in the investee are as follows:

Year 1	Investment in Stockseller Corp.	50,000	
	Cash		50,000
	To record purchase of influential interest in Stockseller.		
	Cash	2,500	
	Investment in Stockseller Corp.		2,500
	To record receipt of dividend.		
	Investment in Stockseller Corp.	10,000	
	Equity in Earnings of Stockseller		10,000
	To record share of Stockseller's profits.		
Year 2	Cash	2,500	
	Investment in Stockseller Corp.		2,500
	To record receipt of dividend.		
	Investment in Stockseller Corp.	10,000	
	Equity in Earnings of Stockseller		10,000
	To record share of Stockseller's profit.		

Problem 3

(a) The selling price of the land is equal to the present value of the cash flows from the note.

Present Value of Cash Flows Discounted at 10%

PV of $100,000 to be received in 5 periods
$100,000(.62092) $ 62,092

PV of ordinary annuity of 5 rents of $12,000
$12,000(3.79079)   45,489

Present value of cash payments $107,581

(b)   **Effective Interest Schedule**

Year	Note Rec. Balance	Premium on Note Rec. Balance	Book Value	Effective Interest Rate	Interest Revenue	Cash Interest	Reduction of Premium
1	100,000	7,581	107,589	.10	10,759	12,000	1,241
2	100,000	6,340	106,340	.10	10,634	12,000	1,366
3	100,000	4,974	104,974	.10	10,497	12,000	1,503
4	100,000	3,471	103,471	.10	10,347	12,000	1,653
5	100,000	1,818	101,818	.10	10,182	12,000	1,818

GLOSSARY

A

Acid-Test Ratio Quick current assets ÷ current liabilities.

Account A form used to quickly sort and summarize changes or events concerning a particular item.

Account Form Format similar to that of a T account.

Account Receivable An amount owed to an entity by its customer.

Accounting The recording, classifying, summarizing, and interpreting of financial information.

Accounting Equation Assets = Liabilities + Owners' Equity.

Accounting Principles Board Body formerly responsible for setting accounting standards.

Accounting Research Bulletins (ARBs) Publications by the Committee on Accounting Principles to assist accountants in applying standards.

Accrual Accounting Method of accounting that measures the results of business activities in the period in which the activities take place.

Adjusted Trial Balance Proof of the equality of debits and credits in the adjusted ledger account balances.

Adjusting Entry Journal entry made to bring the ledger account up to date.

"All Financial Resources" Concept Requirement that the SCFP reveal information about all major financial transactions, even if they do not effect working capital or cash.

All Inclusive Net Income Measurement of net income which includes all revenue, expenses, gains, losses, the cumulative effect of accounting changes and prior period adjustments.

Allowance Method System in which an amount or share is allotted or granted in advance.

Amortize To systematically reduce in value.

Annual Occurring once a year.

Annuity A series of equal deposits or withdrawals (rents) made over equal time periods.

Annuity Due Rents made at the beginning of a period.

Annuity In Advance Rents made at the beginning of a period.

Annuity In Arrears Rents made at the end of a period.

APB Opinions (APBs) Publication by the Accounting Principles Board to assist accountants in applying standards.

APB Statement (see APB Opinions)

Asset A resource that an entity has control of, that may provide future benefit, and which was objectively valued by a transaction that has already taken place.

Average Unit Cost Cost of Goods Available for Sale ÷ Number of Units Available for Sale.

B

Bad Debt A receivable not expected to ever be collected.

Balance Sheet Financial statement that provides information on the assets, liabilities, and owners' equity of an entity.

Balance Sheet Method A system of estimating bad debt expense as a percentage of accounts receivable.

Bank Reconciliation Statement A formal report that explains the difference in the bank balance and the company book balance of the Cash in Bank account.

Base Year Year serving as the foundation for some calculation; year of reference.

Book of Original Entry A journal.

C

Cash Basis Method of accounting that measures the results of business activities only when cash is received or paid.

Close To make an account balance zero.

Closing Entry Journal entry made to prepare a temporary capital account for the next accounting period.

Combined Statement Statement that brings a closely related group of information together in one place for users' convenience.

Committee on Accounting Procedure Body formerly responsible for setting accounting standards.

Comparability Able to be examined for similarities and dissimilarities.

Compound Interest Interest computed on two or more periods of time. Interest computed on principal plus any unpaid interest from the previous period(s).

Compound Interest Formula $FV = PV(1 + r)^n$

Comprehensive Net Income Change in equity caused by all non-owner sources; is most extensive definition of net income.

Consignee Person receiving goods on consignment.

Consignment Act of transferring goods but not the title of the goods.

Consignor Person giving goods on consignment.

Consistency Tendency to continue without essential change.

Consistency Principle Rule that requires that firms use the same accounting methods from period to period.

Constant Dollars Dollars of base year purchasing power.

Contingent Dependent on something or someone else.

Continuity Assumption Assumption that accounting is done for a going concern.

Cost Ratio Cost of goods available for sale ÷ selling price of goods available for sale.

Credit An entry to the right side of an account.

Cumulative Effect of a Change in Accounting Procedure Section of the income statement that reflects the effects of a change in accounting principles on the current and past periods.

Current Operating Net Income Measurement of net income that includes only revenue, expenses, gains, and losses from major ongoing activities.

Current Ratio Current assets ÷ current liabilities.

Current Expected to be converted to cash or settled within one year or the operating cycle, whichever is longer.

Condensed Statements Statements that present only important figures and uses supplements and footnotes to show any other information.

D

Debit An entry to the left side of an account.

Debt Ratio Total assets ÷ total liabilities.

Default Failure to live up to an agreement.

Differential The amount paid for a share of stock less the book value of the investor's share in net assets.

Deferred Made due at a later date.

Deposit in Transit A deposit made but not recorded on the bank's records.

Depreciate To systematically reduce in value.

Direct Write-off Method of expensing bad debts in the period the account is determined to be uncollectible.

Discontinued Operations Section of the income statement that reports information about the termination of a major segment of a business.

Discount A reduction in price; fee charged by the buyer of a note.

Discounted With Recourse Selling a note with payment guaranteed.

Discounting A Note Selling a note receivable before its maturity date.

Disposal Date Date on which the assets are actually sold or abandoned.

Dollar Value LIFO Variation of LIFO which values inventory as a pool and counts dollars of base year purchasing power invested in inventory.

Dollar Value LIFO Retail Method of valuing inventory that combines the Dollar Value LIFO and retail inventory methods.

Double-entry Bookkeeping System that requires each transaction to be recorded in at least two accounts.

E

Earnings Measure of net income that includes revenue, expenses, gains, and losses and excludes items associated with prior periods.

Earnings Per Share (EPS) (Net income − preferred dividends) ÷ weighted average cost of shares outstanding.

Effective Interest Method System for computing the period's interest by applying the effective interest rate to the book value of the note.

Effective Interest Rate The actual rate of interest being charged.

Entry Any item recorded in a journal or ledger.

Equity The owners' interest in the firm.

Equity Method System that values an investment at an amount equal to the investors' share of the investee's equity or net assets.

Equity Ratio Total owner's equity divided by total assets.

Exception Principle Rule that allows the accountant to use some discretion in the application of other principles.

Expense A decrease in assets or increase in liabilities due to the using up of goods or services to produce revenue.

Extraordinary Material in amount, unusual in nature, and nonrecurring.

F

Financial Accounting Standards Board (FASB) The body currently responsible for setting accounting standards.

Finished Goods Goods held for resale.

First In-First Out (FIFO) Cost flow assumption that presumes the oldest units of inventory are sold first.

Freight On Board (FOB) Destination Title of good is transferred to the buyer when good reaches the warehouse.

Freight On Board (FOB) Shipping Point Title of good is transferred to the buyer as soon as the good is loaded on the carrier.

Full Disclosure Principle Rule that requires the accountant to include in the financial statements all information that may affect the users' understanding of company activities.

Funds Working capital or cash.

Future Value of a Single Sum $FV = PV(1 + r)^n$

Future Value of an Annuity Due The future value is equal to the future value of an ordinary annuity for "$n + 1$" periods less 1 rent.

Future Value of an Ordinary Annuity $FV = [(1 + i)^n - 1]/i$

G

Gain An increase in owners' equity due to transactions outside a firm's normal business activities.

Generally Accepted Accounting Principles (GAAP) Set of accounting standards that have substantial support and the general acceptance of the members of the accounting profession.

Gross Method System of valuing sales and accounts receivable at the undiscounted amount.

Gross Profit Method System of estimating cost of goods sold as a percentage of sales.

H

Historical Cost Principle Rule that dictates assets be valued at the amount originally paid for them.

I

Income Increase in assets and/or decrease in liabilities due to delivery of goods or rendering of service.

Income Statement Financial statement that provides information on the earnings of an entity over a period of time.

Income Statement Method System of estimating bad debt expense as a percentage of credit sales.

Inflation A continuous rise in prices.

Influential Interest Condition that is assumed to exist when an investor owns 20% of the outstanding stock of the investee.

Intangible Asset Asset with no physical substance.

Interest Fee charged for borrowing money.

Interest-bearing Note Note that carries the interest rate on its face.

Interest Rate Interest ÷ principal.

Inventory Record Form used to account for the amount and value of each inventory item in stock.

J

Journal A record in which the information about transactions is first recorded in chronological order.

L

Lower of Cost or Market (LCM) Method of valuing asset at the lesser of cost or market value.

Ledger A group of accounts.

Last In-First Out (LIFO) Cost flow assumption that presumes that the most recently purchased items in inventory are sold first.

LIFO Layer The difference between the amount of ending inventory for the current period and that of the preceeding period; equal to zero, if a deficit.

Liability A legal obligation to provide economic benefits to some other entity at a future time. It must result from a transaction that has already taken place so that it may be objectively valued.

Liquidating Dividends Dividends in excess of retained earnings.

Long-term Not expected to be turned into cash or settled within one year or the operating cycle.

Loss A decrease in equity due to transactions outside a firm's normal business operations.

M

Maker Entity borrowing through the use of a note payable.

Markdowns Reduction which brings the selling price down below its original level.

Markdown Cancellation Increase which brings the selling price up to the original level.

Market Value Generally refers to the replacement cost; the middle amount among replacement cost, net realizable value, and net realizable value less normal gross profit.

Marketable (equity) security A long- or short-term investment in stock, options, or warrants.

Markup Addition to selling price beyond the original selling price.

Markup Cancellation A reduction which brings the selling price down to its original level.

Matching Principle Rule that requires expenses to be recognized in the accounting period in which goods and services are used up to produce revenue.

Material Having real importance or able to cause a great difference.

Maturity Date The date on which a note becomes due.

Maturity Value The amount to be repaid on a note.

Measurement Date The date on which a firm commits itself to a formal plan to dispose of a major business segment.

Modified All-Inclusive Net Income Measurement of net income which includes all revenue, expenses, gains, losses, and the cumulative effect of accounting changes but excludes prior period adjustments.

Modifying Principle (See exception principle)

Multiple-step Format Format which separates operating revenue and expenses from financing activities.

N

Net Assets Total assets less total liabilities.

Net Income Revenue less expenses plus gains less losses.

Net Markdown Markdowns less markdown cancellations.

Net Markups Markups less markup cancellations.

Net Method System of valuing sales and accounts receivable at the selling price less discounts.

Net Realizable Value The amount of cash a firm expects to actually collect.

Nominal Interest Rate Interest rate that appears on the face of the note.

Non current (see long-term)

Non Interest-bearing Note A note which simply bears the maturity value on its face.

Note A formal IOU upon which a borrower agrees to pay a specified sum of money on a specified future date.

Note Receivable A formal account receivable.

O

Objectivity Principle Rule that requires accounting information to be based on fact rather than personal opinion.

Operating Cycle The average length of time required to convert raw materials into finished goods, sell the product, and receive payment.

Ordinary Annuity Rents made at the end of a period.

Outstanding Check Check written but not yet presented at the bank.

P

Payable An amount owed.

Periodic Inventory System System in which the balances in inventory and the cost of goods sold are adjusted at regular time intervals.

Periodicity Assumption Assumption that a firm's financial activities can be measured for certain periods of time.

Perpetual Inventory System System under which Inventory is updated each time goods are purchased or sold.

Pervasive Constraint The boundary between information whose benefits outweigh the cost of obtaining it.

Petty Cash Cash kept on hand to make small disbursements.

Petty Cash Voucher Prenumbered form documenting disbursements from petty cash.

Phase-out Period Time between the measurement date and the disposal date.

Physical Inventory Actual hands on count of inventory.

Posting Transferring information from a journal to the ledger.

Post-closing Trial Balance Proof of the equality of debits and credits in the ledger after the closing process.

Present Value of a Single Sum $PV = FV/(i + r)^n$

Present Value of an Annuity Due The present value is equal to the present value of an ordinary annuity for "$n - 1$" periods plus one rent.

Present Value of an Ordinary Annuity $1 - 1/(1 + i)^n/i$

Price Index Price in the current year ÷ the price in the base year.

Principal An amount borrowed.

Proceeds The amount received by the seller of a note.

Q

Quick Ratio Quick current assets ÷ current liabilities.

R

Raw Materials Goods to be used directly in production.

Receivable An amount due.

Relevant Timely, with predictive and feedback value.

Reliable Verifiable, neutral, and having representational faithfulness.

Rent (see annuity)

Report Form Simple vertical format.

Representational Faithfulness Presenting what is claimed to be presented.

Retail Inventory Method Method of estimating cost of goods sold based on a cost ratio derived from current information on the relationship of the cost of goods to the selling price.

Retained Earnings Portion of net income reinvested in an entity.

Revenue An increase in assets and/or a decrease in liabilities due to the delivery of goods or the rendering of services.

Revenue Recognition Principle Rule that dictates that revenue be recognized in the accounting period when goods are delivered or services are rendered.

Reversing Entry An entry made at the beginning of an accounting period to eliminate the effects of an adjusting entry from the previous period.

S

Semiannual Occurring twice a year.

Separate Entity Assumption Assumption that activities of one entity can clearly be separated from that of another.

Service Charge A fee that banks charge for services rendered.

Short-term (see current)

Simple Interest Interest computed for a specified single period of time; Principal × interest rate × time.

Single-step Format A format which does not separate operating revenue and expenses from financing activities.

Source document Proof that a transaction has taken place; contains information needed to make a journal entry.

Statement of Changes in Financial Position (SCFP) A financial statement that explains how a firm obtains and uses its funds.

Statement of Financial Accounting Standards (SFASs) Publications issued by the FASB to set accounting standards.

Statement of Financial Position Balance sheet.

Statement of Owners' Equity Report that explains the change in owners' equity over a period of time.

Statement of Retained Earnings Report that explains the change in retained earnings over a period of time.

Subsidiary Account An account containing supporting information for another account.

Subsidiary Ledger A ledger containing subsidiary or supporting accounts.

T

Terms Conditions under which an agreement is made.

Threshold of Recognition Boundary between information being material and immaterial.

Trial Balance A proof of the equality of debits and credits in the ledger.

U

Uncollectible account (see bad debt)

Units of Measure Assumption An assumption that the dollar is a reasonable and constant unit of measure.

W

Weighted Average Cost flow assumption that suggests that the average cost be assigned to the units sold and those left in the ending inventory.

Work Sheet A form used to sort and summarize information.

Working Capital Current assets minus current liabilities.

INDEX

A

Account format of balance sheet, *illus.*, 117
Accounting equation, 25-26
Accounting period
  and adjustment entry, 41-46
  and income statement, 83-84, 90-91
Accounting Principles Board, 1
  Opinion No. 30, 104-105
  Opinion No. 43, 295
Accounting procedure
  adjustment process
    consequences of omitting, 48-49
    purposes of, 41-48
    steps in, 41
  balancing and ruling accounts, *illus.*, 62-63
  basic steps, *illus.*, 23-24
  closing, 60-63
  daily transactions
    journalizing, 26-28
    posting, 28-30
    trial balance, 30-31
  equation, 25
  financial statements
    closing procedure, 60-63
    preparation of, 58-60
    reversing entries option, 63-65
Accounting Research Bulletins, 1
Accounting standards. *See*
  Generally accepted accounting principles (GAAP).
Accounting terms, defined, 11-14
Accounts
  and balances, 28-30
  closing procedure, 60-63
  defined, 24
  journal entry posted to, *illus.*, 28-30
  and missing information, 65-67
  subsidiary, 25
Accounts payable, as adjustments to net income, 167-169
Accounts receivable
  as adjustments to net income, 166-167
  and bad debts, 236-238
  as balance sheet asset, 119
  defined, 233
  and discounts, 233-234
  gross method of valuing, 234
  net method of valuing, 234-235
  in quick ratio, 125
Accrual basis accounting
  vs. cash basis, 2-3
  and revenue recognition principle, 16
Acid-test ratio, defined, 124-125
Adjusted trial balance, *illus.*, 59

Adjusting entries
  defined, 23
  illustrated, 41-57
  and reversing entries, 64-65
Advertising, as income statement expense, 85-86
"All financial resources" disclosure, in statement of changes in financial position, 145-146
All-inclusive income statement, *illus.*, 101
All-inclusive measurement of net income, 86-87
Allowance method, in accounting for bad debts, 236-238
Annuities
  defined, 202
  due, present/future value of, 203-210
  ordinary, present/future value of, 202-209
APB Opinions and *Statements*, 1
Assets
  in basic accounting equation, 25
  defined, 2, 11-12, 116
  and financing ratios, 123-125
  long-term, sale of, 143
  measuring value of, 4-5
  net, defined, 123
  non-current, 118-119
  and statement of changes in financial position, 137-150
Assumptions, underlying, in accounting, 14-15
Average unit cost of inventory, 274

B

Bad debts
  adjusting entries for, 46, 85
  methods of accounting for, 236-238
Balance
  temporary, 28-30
  trial, 23, 30-31
Balance sheet
  and accounting procedure, 24
  defined, 3, 58
  effect of inventory count on, 272-273
  equation for, 116
  and estimating bad debt expense, 238
  and explaining changes in working capital, 138-139
  and financing ratios, 123-125
  formats for, 116-118
  illus., 60, 117-188, 147, 171
  misconceptions about, 123
  paid-in capital section of, 122
  purpose of, 116

valuation of assets for, 116-121
valuation of liabilities for, 121-122
valuation of owner's equity for, 122
Bank reconciliation statement, 219-223
Basic accounting equation, 25-26
Benefits-exceed-cost, as pervasive constraint, 5
Book of original entry. *See* Journal.
Bookkeeping, double-entry, logic of, 26
Book value of note, 250, 343-351 *passim*
Borrowing, and working capital, 143-144
Buildings and equipment, as balance sheet asset, 120

C

Capital, working, and balance sheet, 122-123
Cash
  accounts, defined, 216
  as balance sheet asset, 119
  in bank, account for, 219-223
  as basis for statement of changes in financial position, 164-174
  internal control of, 216-218
  and net income, 165-169
  in quick ratio, 124-125
  sources of, 165-170
  T account worksheet for, 170-174
  uses of, 170
  and valuation of notes receivable, 343-344
Cash basis accounting vs. accrual basis, 2-3
Casualty, and income statement, 104-105
Changes in accounting principle
  cumulative effect of, 106
  as section of income statement, 88
Changes in financial position. *See* Statement of changes in financial position.
Closing entries, defined, 23
Closing procedure, 60-63
Collections, and bank statement reconciliation, 219-223 *passim*
Commission expense, and income statements, 85-86
Committee on Accounting Procedure, 1
Common stocks. *See* Marketable equity securities.
Comparability, as an accounting quality, 4, 5

379